For

EMERITUS PROFESSOR C. H. DOBINSON, C M G

Good European and good friend.

The Western European Idea in Education

by

VERNON MALLINSON, M.A.
Professor Emeritus of Comparative Education
at the University of Reading

PERGAMON PRESS

OXFORD · NEW YORK · TORONTO · SYDNEY · PARIS · FRANKFURT

U.K.	Pergamon Press Ltd., Headington Hill Hall, Oxford OX3 0BW, England
U.S.A.	Pergamon Press Inc., Maxwell House, Fairview Park, Elmsford, New York 10523, U.S.A.
CANADA	Pergamon of Canada, Suite 104, 150 Consumers Road, Willowdale, Ontario M2J 1P9, Canada
AUSTRALIA	Pergamon Press (Aust.) Pty. Ltd., P.O. Box 544, Potts Point, N.S.W. 2011, Australia
FRANCE	Pergamon Press SARL, 24 rue des Ecoles, 75240 Paris, Cedex 05, France
FEDERAL REPUBLIC OF GERMANY	Pergamon Press GmbH, 6242 Kronberg-Taunus, Pferdstrasse 1, Federal Republic of Germany

First edition 1980

British Library Cataloguing in Publication Data

Mallinson, Vernon
The Western European idea in education.
(International studies in education and
social change).
1. Education – Europe
2. Comparative education
I. Title II. Series
370.19'5'094   LA622   79-40852

ISBN 0-08-025208-7

Printed in Great Britain by Biddles Ltd, Guildford, Surrey

Contents

Preface

This book has grown from seminars and tutorials held over the last few years with students drawn from both the Graduate School of Contemporary European Studies and from the School of Education of the University of Reading. It starts from the premiss that, whilst the idea of Western European unity is in no sense new, it must in the context of the present world situation take on an entirely new dimension and so become of greater significance than ever before. In the author's view the study of education on a comparative basis must provide the only reliable guide to what different countries and different generations have meant at different times by that teasing and often misused word, *culture*. It is also the author's belief that only history can enable us properly to understand how educational ideals have been located and then transformed to be made to work to further the cultural aspirations of a given people. That, in brief, is the burden of the present exercise.

It is hoped that the book may make an appeal to the general public anxious to know where, culturally, Western Europe stands, and how in consequence it can be expected to react to challenge and change from both within and beyond its own confines. The book should also have something to offer to students in secondary and tertiary education who are beginning to include European Studies on their programmes. It seeks to enlighten (and thereby encourage) both students specifically training to become teachers and practising teachers and administrators by making them more acutely aware of the causes of present difficulties and discontent, as well as pointing the way ahead to securing viable solutions.

I am particularly indebted to my colleague, Professor Raymond Wilson, for his careful reading of the manuscript and for making several important suggestions for improvement; to a number of students who helped in devising most of the diagrams; to my former secretary, Yvonne Lowe, for her unfailing patience in meeting my sometimes near-impossible demands.

June 1979   Vernon Mallinson

CHAPTER 1

The Concept of Western European Unity

1

When we speak of Europe as a whole we are speaking of an area which is roughly the size of the USA, less than half the size of North America, and less than a quarter of the size of Asia. Similarly, though population figures can show great density in particular countries, the total population is no more than roughly 480 millions, or a quarter of that of Asia as a whole. When we exclude those territories over which the Soviet Union may be said to have control, then we are concerned with an assortment of separate nation-states — a kind of *societas societatum* — whose total population figures do not exceed some 300 million.

Yet this very Europe, if we consider it globally, is at the geometric centre of the modern world and at the natural crossroads of all main sea and air routes. Of all the continents it has the longest coastline, more ports, and the densest network of water communications. It is the only continent to be completely free from desert areas. It is deeply indented by the seas, traversed by mountains and rivers which are easily crossed, and almost naturally compartmentalised into areas which, being neither too large nor geographically cut off from one another, can freely communicate yet retain their own individuality — a society of societies, to translate my earlier phrase.

The climate is generally temperate if often unpredictable, and this, together with Western Europe's peculiar geographical features, has favoured from the very beginnings of Western European man a full exploitation of available natural resources. The relative ease with which this conquest of nature has been achieved, allied to the sharp lessons administered by un-intelligent or unplanned exploitation, has taught him that to be success-fully the measure of all things exacts a high degree of personal initiative and expertise. He has had to learn to respect the beneficence of nature and

1

in the process has developed a subtle awareness of the relationship which must always exist between the end result and the amount of effort and ingenuity expended to achieve that result. Hence his adaptability, his ceaseless questing curiosity and his inventiveness. And so the nations of Western Europe today have come to form a reservoir of capabilities unique in the world, and an economic power potential superior to that of the whole of the Soviet Union and very nearly equal to that of North America.

André Siegfried, in an interesting article entitled *The Spirit and Foundations of European Civilisation*, points out that Western European man has become *Homo economicus* above all else and draws a clear distinction between attitudes in other continents where "the expectation of nature is either too easy or too difficult", and where there is in consequence "a danger of falling into a state of excessive optimism or complete discouragement".[1] We can take his arguments still further by stressing how unique is Western European man in several other respects. Leaving aside for the time being the important fact that it was he who first developed the idea of the human race, of the dignity of man and of man's worth as an individual, it is important to stress that it was he who discovered the whole world, who exploited it, awakened it, spread the benefits (not always with happy results) of his form of civilisation, and then diplomatically withdrew to his own European fastness without once over the many centuries involved being threatened, circumscribed or ruled by a non-European power. A further peculiarity is that nowhere else in the world has a large number of nation-states been able to live in close geographical proximity and close association the one with the other without any single one of them losing its identity or the whole being swept into some imperial principle (e.g. the USA or the USSR).[2]

The most astonishing fact of all, however, is that the men who made Western Europe what it is today were of Eastern rather than of Western origin. And when Charlemagne attempted to weld together a Holy Roman Empire his peoples were already an extraordinary mixture of the oriental and the nordic, basing their religion and culture on values drawn from the

[1] *The Year Book of Education, 1957*, London, pp. 31-7.
[2] It is to be noted that the present idea of a European Community is simply that of a pooling of all possibilities and potentialities. There may be a European Parliament but Europe will essentially remain – in De Gaulle's historic phrase – a *Europe des États*.

Near East, community-minded even though individualistic, all with conflicting tendencies yet already conscious of the marked differences between their general way of life and that of their nearest eastern neighbours. By the eleventh century, if there was no political cohesion as such, there was at least a spiritual union based on the practice of Christianity. By the end of the twelfth century, under the pontificat of Innocent III (1198–1216), dubbed the "souzerain of Europe", mediaeval European civilisation could be said to have reached its peak. All that was now needed was for Islam to bar the way to the East to provoke a more practical sense of identity of purpose amongst the "Europeans" *qua* Europeans and so precipitate still greater dynamism in the direction of maritime adventure, exploration and scientific discovery.

2

It is thus fascinating and at the same time highly instructive to recall how centuries ago ideas for some form of European community were first tried out, lost to view, and then resurrected in the period between the two world wars, finally to come to fruition in the aftermath of the Second World War. If we consult a map of Western Europe we immediately note that it can be divided into four distinct regions with a fifth one shut in, as it were, by the other four. The four "enclosing" regions are those of France and the British Isles, of the German Hanseatic League, of the Danube basin, and of the Mediterranean. The fifth region is sometimes designated as that of the five rivers since it owes its identity and developing prosperity on the one hand to the Po–Saone–Rhone limiting boundary, and on the other to the important conjuncture of the Moselle, Rhine and Scheldt, the Scheldt estuary most opportunely directly facing that of the River Thames. This fifth (or middle) region came into political existence with the partitioning of Charlemagne's empire by the Treaty of Verdun of 843. It then comprised those parts of Europe known today as Northern Italy, Switzerland, Franche-Comté, Provence, Savoy, Burgundy, Lorraine, Alsace, Luxemburg, the Rhineland, Belgium and Holland. Over the centuries rival French, German and Italian forces disputed these territories amongst themselves so that finally only four clearly distinct national states were to emerge: Switzerland, Luxemburg, Belgium and Holland.

Between the fourteenth and sixteenth centuries, however, and particularly during what came to be known as the Burgundian period, this
"middle" region achieved a period of prosperity which led to the growth
of a powerful merchant bourgeoisie – all turning on the fact that the Low
Countries (today Belgium and Holland) now formed the nub of the main
European trade routes, as well as being at the crossroads of the Germanic
and Latin cultures. Even as early as A.D. 700 Flemish merchants had
regularly traded with Venice, Syria and Constantinople. By the tenth
century Liège already enjoyed cultural and commercial relations with
Poland. By the thirteenth century, as methods of commerce became more
sophisticated, Flanders and Brabant in particular became a highly urbanised
region, importing wool from England and exporting Flemish cloth in
quantity to Germany and Russia from whence came in return mainly
Russian wax and furs. The result was that long before the might of France
or that of the various German states could assert itself, strong independent
merchant cities had been established in Northern Italy, Switzerland, the
Moselle area, the Rhineland and the Low Countries. The commercial city
quickly became a focal point of political power. The new merchant bourgeoisie won charters of privilege from their supposed noble overlords for
their respective commercial centres. They established the principle of
communal autonomy. And as they recognised and skilfully exploited their
strength, so did they bring this "middle" region to live in a happy balance
between absolute sovereignty and representative government.

Such were the beginnings from which came the idea of European urban
civilisation which was progressively to replace the outmoded feudal system.
And the pattern so surely established itself that the "key" towns of Western
Europe were firmly fixed for some 500 years. Nor was there to be much
marked change over that period either in the machinery of government or
in the methods of agriculture and industry. Processes of law were now first
clearly delineated, courses of study in the universities determined, the
hierarchical structure of the church from the Pope downwards to parochial
level fixed (until Pope John XXIII summoned his Vatican Council in 1960).
From such beginnings also came the first glimmer of an idea for some kind
of concerted European (trade) policy. The Emperor Charles V (1500–58),
himself a native of Ghent, was quick to grasp the possibilities for the
whole of his empire of promoting and developing his "middle" region, and
in 1548 (by the Convention of Augsburg) he declared that the seventeen

provinces now comprising the area should be "one indivisible and inalienable block". He re-named them the Circle of Burgundy, gave them
the status of an independent sovereign state, and incorporated them into
the Holy Roman Empire.

Unfortunately for the rest of Western Europe, the union was to be
short-lived, firstly because of the abdication of Charles V in 1555, and
secondly because of the intransigence of his son Philip II (1527–98) who
had inherited the provinces along with the throne of Spain. Philip II
lacked both the vision to grasp the importance to the rest of Europe of the
Circle of Burgundy, and the intelligence to temper his religious zeal to
cope with the independent-minded merchant classes by now firmly established in their urban strongholds. From the bitter struggles which ensued,
merging into the Thirty Years' War (1618–48), that country which we
today call Holland (or the Netherlands) finally emerged as an independent
nation-state. The then so-called Spanish Lowlands (today Belgium) eventually passed out of the hands of Spain to the house of Austria which, along
with France, had by now carved up the remainder of the territory.

Yet dreams of a unified Europe still persisted. The German mathema-
tician and philosopher, Leibnitz (1646–1716), urged that a lasting peace
in Europe could be achieved if based on the formulation of an international
law, and was cheered in his last and neglected years by the publication of
the Abbé de Saint Pierre's *Projet pour rendre la paix perpétuelle en Europe*
(1713), a project which, in its basic essentials, was to be taken up some
200 years later by the creation of the League of Nations. Another Frenchman, Montesquieu (1689–1755), who spent lengthy periods of time
visiting other countries in Europe for the purpose of observing their customs and institutions, apart from extolling England as the model for the
ideal state (which by his definition should offer the maximum of freedom
with the maximum of security), also viewed the state as a moral entity. He
equally claimed that "the laws of education ought to be relative to the
principles of government", and his *Esprit des Lois* (1748) claimed that
laws, in their widest sense, are the necessary relationships which spring
from the nature of things. There was such a thing as a "Natural Law"
which had to be obeyed, and just as individuals in any one given state must
learn to bear with one another, respecting the opinions of others as being
as valid as their own, so must the various states seek amongst themselves
a necessary harmony. There must be a Society of Nations, larger than any

regional groups though not differing from them in kind, united together for their mutual advantage and carefully observing a single, uniform pact.

Montesquieu greatly influenced the thinking of the men of the Enlightenment (whom we shall discuss later) as he did that of those in particular who planned the revolutionary movement in France, and it is a great pity that neither they (in wishing to spread their revolutionary ideals throughout Europe) nor Napoleon (in seeking to extend his own empire throughout Europe) heeded either Voltaire's or Montesquieu's knowledgeable caution. Voltaire repeatedly warned that Europeans were forever restless. And Montesquieu, more to the point, observed throughout Europe "a spirit of freedom which makes each part of it very difficult to subjugate and to bring under a foreign power". We are back again with the idea of a *societas societatum* first mentioned at the beginning of this chapter.

As the greater powers of Europe assembled at Vienna in 1814, determined to set about the reconstruction of the moral order of Europe necessitated by the downfall of Napoleon, they had no real vision of a united Europe, but simply played the old balance-of-power game. Significantly perhaps, their real meddling concerned itself with what was left of that "middle region" which, by its very nature, still remained an important focal point. The sovereignty of Switzerland as a confederation of separate states had been recognised by the European powers at the Peace of Westphalia (1648). Napoleon had declared the country to be an independent republic in 1803. The Congress respected this decision and guaranteed the perpetual neutrality of the territory. The Grand Duchy of Luxemburg, a personal property of the House of Nassau, remained under the suzerainty of Holland until 1890 when, by common accord, it attained its independence. The former Spanish Netherlands, though still titularly dependent on Austria, almost cynically and with little regard for the wishes of either the Belgians or the Dutch, were declared to form one *bloc* with Holland and the so-called United Netherlands came into being. Thus was realised, under external pressure, a first "Benelux". Not surprisingly, however, the union failed and in 1830 the Spanish/Austrian Netherlands revolted to declare themselves an independent sovereign state (Belgium). The greater powers of Europe had to accept the situation, and manoeuvres to avoid upsetting the balance of power throughout Europe led to the acceptance by the Belgians of Leopold of the House of Coburg (widower of Princess Charlotte of England) as their first hereditary ruler. As in the case of Switzerland, the neutrality of Belgium was guaranteed in perpetuity.

3

Talk of a European federation or even of a United States of Europe went on throughout the nineteenth century, but even men of stature and importance like Victor Hugo or Mazzini were in effect dismissed as unpractical visionaries. The brutal facts were that Europe was now passing through a period of intense nationalism and imperial expansion and there was little hope of concerted European action in any sphere of human activity. It was not until after the First World War, and also after protracted negotiations with the French who had important industrial interests (mainly the railway network) in the Grand Duchy of Luxemburg, that a general European blessing was given to a loose economic union between Belgium and Luxemburg. A treaty to this effect was signed on 25 July 1921 to be binding for fifty years. The two countries grew closer together by a further agreement of 23 May 1935, and on the outbreak of the Second World War had become the greatest iron and steel exporters in the world, Luxemburg itself being designated the headquarters of the international steel cartel. This latest war turned the continent of Europe into one vast battleground, and over six long years of bitter fighting and dreary occupation men were driven for the first time for a century to some appraisal of the ideas they had lived by and which (indubitably) had led to the sorry state of affairs now engulfing them. It was impossible to escape the conclusion that the root causes of their troubles were to be found in the intense forms of nationalism which had been allowed to flourish to the point of obscuring the fact that, whilst there was (and always must be) inner diversity within the concert of Europe, Western Europe must remain fundamentally an entity if it was to have any chance of survival into the next century.

Not surprisingly, ·much of the thinking along these lines stemmed from the deliberations of patriotic resistance groups vowed to ceaseless clandestine warfare against the forces occupying their countries. Unfortunately, however, once peace came to bring some semblance of normality to European relationships (based inevitably on a *status quo ante*), the driving force of these groups had expended itself, with the sole exception of their Communist-inspired elements. These of course were immediately discredited because of the obvious threat the USSR now posed to the forward-looking intentions of all the Western world.[1] And so, significantly, it was left to Belgium, Holland and Luxemburg — the traditional hub of all European trade movements, and the first countries to suffer in consequence in times of war — to make the first practical move. On 5 September 1944 (two days after the liberation of Brussels from German occupation) the three countries came together at the London Convention to replace the former Belgo–Luxemburg Treaty by a new triple economic alliance which created Benelux.

Winston Churchill himself had by now become an ardent federalist,[2] but all major powers in Western Europe moved cautiously, Great Britain in particular finding itself committed both to the Commonwealth and to the Anglo-American special relationship fostered by Churchill and Roosevelt. In consequence almost four years elapsed from the creation of Benelux to the signing of the Brussels Treaty (17 March 1948) whereby Great Britain, France and the Benelux countries guaranteed one another mutual aid over a period of fifty years in matters military, economic, social and cultural. One month later (16 April 1948) action that had been jointly initiated by the British and French governments in July 1947 led to the signing in Paris of the Convention creating the Organisation for European Economic Co-operation (OEEC) — the first realistic step to be taken towards economic integration of the whole of Western Europe. The creation of the European Payments Union logically followed (19 September 1950) to ease the pressure on scarce monetary resources, to enable intra-European debts to be cancelled, and so remove grave hampering restrictions on the expansion of European trade generally.

Meantime the signing of the Brussels Treaty was immediately followed up by the calling of a conference at The Hague (May 1948) to discuss the possibilities of creating a genuine European movement. From these deliberations resulted the Council of Europe, with its permanent secretariat to be established at Strasbourg, and its aims and objectives clearly defined by the Treaty of London of 5 May 1949: "to achieve a greater unity between

---

[1] Paul Langevin's excellent project for the reform of French education, for example, was wrecked primarily because he and his immediate entourage were members of the French Communist Party. Ironically it was left to De Gaulle later to implement most of his proposals.

[2] See his speech delivered at the University of Zurich (September 1946) when he argued for the creation of a "United States of Europe".

Members for the purpose of safeguarding and realising the ideals and principles which are their common heritage and facilitating their economic and social progress". The number of participating nations increased from the original ten signatories to eighteen.[1] The work of the Council is conducted by a committee of ministers – in effect periodic meetings of the foreign ministers of the various member countries – and by a Consultative Assembly composed of parliamentary representatives of the member states. One of the first important decisions of the Council of Europe was to create a College of Europe for research and study into European affairs, and this college was founded in Bruges in May 1950. One important development since then has been the creation (1 January 1962) of a Council for Cultural Co-operation charged specifically with the administration of the Council of Europe's cultural and educational programmes. To this Council for Cultural Co-operation, Spain and the Holy See are adherents. As to OEEC, problems of administration soon swept it within the responsibility of the Council of Europe, and, as its first important task of administering Marshall Aid to the European Recovery Programme was completed, so it was transformed in December 1960 into the Organisation for Economic Co-operation and Development (OECD).[2] The United States and Canada, from being only associate members of OEEC, now became full members of the OECD which, whilst concerning itself with problems of economic development inside and outside Europe, was also intended to counteract any possible adverse economic effects of the split between the Common Market countries and EFTA (European Free Trade Association). With the entry of Japan into OECD in 1964 it could no longer be claimed that the organisation had any prime European purpose as had had OEEC. OEEC however had served a most useful purpose in that it had forcibly brought home to all the countries of Western Europe that their economic systems were interdependent and that they failed or prospered together.

[1] Greece withdrew on 31 December 1970. The remaining seventeen members are: Austria, Belgium, Cyprus, Denmark, France, the Federal Republic of Germany, Iceland, Ireland, Italy, Luxembourg, Malta, the Netherlands, Norway, Sweden, Switzerland, Turkey and the United Kingdom.
[2] The Marshall Plan got its name from a lecture delivered to the alumni of Harvard on 5 June 1947 by the then US Secretary of State (General George Marshall). Its aim was to grant urgent financial aid to a European recovery programme, one important condition being that recipients must agree to economic co-operation amongst themselves.

4

So far so good. But ardent federalists soon grasped that neither the working of OEEC nor the creation of the Council of Europe were of themselves going to provide sufficient impetus to bring closer their dream of a genuine United States of Europe. Indeed, these very organisations were being used by the faint-hearted as convenient buffers to any further immediate progress. And so, from the deliberations of two dynamic Frenchmen, Robert Schuman and Jean Monnet, the so-called Schuman Plan emerged. Its basic scheme was to integrate the economies of countries into one overall area of economic activity in the belief that not only would such a measure resolve the long-term problem of securing a balanced economic development programme for the whole of Western Europe, but also it would be a decisive step towards allaying traditional national suspicions centred on the problem of future political union. It was considered wise to make a start with the basic industries of coal and steel. The Council of Europe eagerly debated the proposal. Great Britain expressed misgivings, being reluctant to abrogate its own national rights to the control of what would amount to a supranational executive authority. In the event only six countries – Benelux, France, Italy and West Germany – were prepared to enter into serious negotiations, and the Schuman Plan finally came to fruition with the Treaty of Paris (18 April 1951) and the creation of the European Coal and Steel Community (ECSC). It was not until March 1962 that Britain saw real advantages for her coal industry in particular in joining the ECSC and made formal application for membership. French intransigence now prevented discussion passing beyond the preliminary negotiatory stages.

There had, of course, been a steady worsening of the international climate throughout all this period of negotiation for greater European unity. The *coup d'état* in Prague in 1948 brought Czechoslovakia firmly into the Russian camp. There had been the Russian blockade of Berlin. Mao Tse-Tung had launched his victorious offensive in China. All these events made it clear to the powers of the free world that some positive counter-defensive measures were needed. So at Washington on 4 April 1949 NATO came into existence and eclipsed the earlier Brussels Treaty of 1948. By 1950 America was urging some German military contribution, which could only mean the inclusion of Western German forces within NATO. This France firmly opposed on the grounds that the forces of

NATO were essentially national armies under one integrated command. Much discussion and abortive planning now resulted in an attempt to get round the dilemma of having to admit the military existence of Western Germany, and it was not until October 1954 that the Paris agreements extended the Treaty of Brussels to include Germany and Italy and led to the formation one year later of the Western European Union (WEU), designed in reality to permit German rearmament and so logically bring her within the much more comprehensive defence system afforded by NATO.

The next decisive step towards greater European unity was provoked by a series of apparently unrelated happenings. The East Berlin rebellion of 1953 was ruthlessly suppressed by Russian arms as was the Hungarian uprising of 1956. The Suez fiasco of 1956 was a rude reminder that no European could hope to play the same international role as heretofore, and that American influence could be alarmingly pervasive. One after the other, European colonial possessions in Africa began pressing for and securing their independence. By the late 1950s most Western Europeans were beginning to accept the fact that, in the long run, Europe would be much better off without its colonial commitments and to ponder how best to accommodate themselves to the inevitable death of colonialism. As for General de Gaulle, swept into power in 1958 by the collapse of the Fourth Republic (mainly over its inability to find a solution to the Algerian conflict), he was firm in his belief that there must be disengagement from American involvement in European affairs if both France's basic interests and those of Europe as a whole were to be preserved.

In the summer of 1955 the six foreign ministers of the ECSC met at Messina to discuss the possibility of establishing both a comprehensive customs union which would lead to a common market and the pooling of information concerning the uses to which atomic energy might be put. An inter-governmental committee was established under the presidency of Paul-Henri Spaak (Belgium) to produce a blueprint, and this was openly debated in the ECSC in March 1956. One year later (25 March 1957) the Treaties of Rome were ratified by the Six, and the EEC and the European Atomic Energy Community (Euratom) came into existence, Brussels (significantly) being eventually chosen as the headquarters for all Common Market activities. When in 1967 de Gaulle expelled SHAPE and NATO from France, Brussels immediately offered asylum and so now bids fair to become and remain the power house for ultimate political as well as economic union. The wheel has come full circle.

The rest of the story can be quickly told. Great Britain, whilst in theory approving of any moves to bring greater European unity, could not in practice approve of a drive towards integration which upset her own conceptions of the relationship in which she should stand with the rest of Europe. Nor was de Gaulle enthusiastic about British entry (plus American ties) constituting a probable threat to what he saw as France's dominant role in European community affairs. Great Britain contented herself with producing a counter-proposal for a comprehensive free trade area covering the whole of Western Europe, but *not* covering agriculture. She was, of course, protecting her Commonwealth interests. The Six appreciated this but also saw the serious implications for the newly-constituted EEC. They concluded that Great Britain was seeking to dilute all that had so far been achieved virtually to the point of destruction. Rebuffed, all Great Britain could now do was to create a rival European Free Trade Association (EFTA) which was joined by Austria, Denmark, Norway, Portugal, Sweden and Switzerland, the move being finally ratified at the Stockholm Convention of November 1959.

In 1961 the Macmillan Conservative government, faced with a worsening economic situation and deciding that in consequence the moment had arrived to break with Britain's isolationist policy, formally applied for membership of the EEC. Obviously this meant that several of the smaller countries within EFTA would follow her lead, and Benelux rejoiced in particular that her dream for a united Europe would thus be brought much closer. Benelux, however, reckoned without the lessened enthusiasm of the Germans, who were now economically riding high, and also failed to measure up to the intransigence of de Gaulle whose own grand design for a *Europe des Patries* now ran counter to the Benelux dream and threw power politics once again firmly into the arena. After two years of hard negotiation on terms for British entry, de Gaulle firmly vetoed the application and thereby placed his bid for European leadership. The fall of de Gaulle made it possible for the Heath Conservative government to re-open discussions. And on 22 January 1972 the Treaty of Accession to the EEC for Great Britain, Eire, Denmark and Norway was formally signed in Brussels. Eire, Denmark and Norway, however, had by their respective constitutions to seek approval for the move by means of a referendum amongst their people. The Norwegians vetoed the proposal, though a change of mind in the near future is not unlikely. Meantime, in January 1973, the "Six" now officially became the "Nine".

Of course, much still remains to be done. Nevertheless, what has already been achieved is a moving testimony to the far-sightedness and persistence of Frenchmen like Mollet and Schuman, to the doggedness of the Belgian, Paul-Henri Spaak, and to some fifty years of slow and laborious effort on the part of those modern heirs (Benelux) to the Burgundian aspirations made concrete by the Convention of Augsburg in 1548. That curious "middle region" at long last shows signs of coming into its own, already having the highest population density in the world, as well as being the world's fourth greatest economic power. Those countries forming Benelux need no longer individually fear any form of politico-military aggression from either France or Germany. But economically speaking, even collectively they can be at risk. Hence not only their persistence to widen the membership of the EEC, but also their unrelaxing efforts towards achieving a true federation of the countries of Western Europe, none of which can now claim that, acting alone, it will never be at such risk. Some form of federation is the only modern answer. And even before the first agreed enlargement of the community in January 1972, tentative discussions were already in progress envisaging the creation of an eventual common currency and Central Bank with its decision-making body in Brussels.

To sum up, the history of the vicissitudes of that important "middle" region in Western Europe reminds us that the history of Western Europe can never be taken as being the sum of the separate national histories placed in juxtaposition. For Western Europe as a meaningful entity was in existence long before the emergence of separate national states. Christian Europe had first to flourish to make possible the emergence of national politico-economic aspirations. By the same token, the nations themselves, taken as themselves, offer no valid explanation for the European idea. For that we must look beyond individual nations and examine in some detail their common cultural heritage of which the practice of Christianity has been one of the most important elements.

CHAPTER 2

The Cultural Heritage

[Europe is] a great republic divided between several states (Voltaire).

There is no longer a France, a Germany, a Spain, not even an English, there are only Europeans. All have the same tastes, the same passions, the same way of life (Rousseau).

1

Even today when the whole of Western Europe is in a ferment of educational reform, it is still possible in moving from country to country to be impressed not so much by the dissimilarities to be found between various educational practices as by the similarity between styles of education. In all countries there is evidence of a long tradition of a common culture and way of thinking unlike that of modern America or the USSR, and quite alien to what is to be found in the East. There is an underlying unity of thought which everywhere has led to the enunciation of certain basic principles which it is held must be followed as closely as possible in structuring any educational system. It is accepted as a starting-point that the chief aim of education must be, as Professor Jeffreys has so succinctly put it, "the nurture of personal growth", and that we must make of education "an instrument for conserving, transmitting and renewing culture".[1] From this it follows that the individual worth of persons must be constantly in view; that the home must be an important educative influence; that balance and harmony are essential to achieve proper moral, intellectual, emotional and spiritual satisfaction; that character development is important and must be seen as closely linked with the environment; that enlightened leaders are the mainstay of any form of democracy and that therefore the education of an élite is a most important consideration; that

[1] M. V. C. Jeffreys, *Glaucon*, (London, 1950).

leisure must be viewed in the Aristotelian sense as being purposeful activity; that a teaching body must be of the highest possible intellectual calibre. In a word, it is the Graeco-Roman-Judaic tradition which still remains dominant.

It was the Greeks who first stressed the individual worth of persons and caused the implications of the Delphic utterance "Know Thyself" to have the fullest significance. It was the Greeks who equated happiness with virtue and, by a prodigious metaphysical effort based on pure reasoning, in their search for virtue (and resultant happiness), arrived at the definition of "an unmoved mover" — a monotheistic, pre-Christian conception which prompted the story by Voltaire of Socrates being pointed to with scorn in the market-place as "that atheist who claims that there can be only one god". Socrates held that man's prime concern must be his own soul, which for him, of course, was not a supernatural entity but a natural faculty of the rational animal called man and the true source of man's distinctive excellence. The soul represented the normal consciousness, and the highest good to be sought was a positive human good sufficient to this life on earth alone. It was a good attainable by all men, through their own efforts and by the exercise of correct reasoning.

Following Socrates, Plato was chiefly concerned with the structure and organisation of the Ideal State, and the decadence he found about him in Athenian society he put down to faulty upbringing. These faults could be corrected if teachers would more closely identify their aims with the eternal and the absolute. Man must train his reasoning powers and so counter the influence of his senses and emotions. Understanding was the ultimate good. Rational contemplation of Forms — which alone could be the object of knowledge in the true sense — as opposed to phenomena (which were objects of opinion only) was the ideal. Such a system of education would, through intellectual training and exercise in argument and the handling of abstractions, produce the philosopher type so sorely needed. Thus Plato started the tradition of man using his reason to find out where his limitations lie, man as an individual (subject to no despotic rule) who can both think and control himself.

The pupil of Plato, Aristotle, was a biologist, whereas Plato had primarily interested himself in mathematics. Like Plato, however, Aristotle saw education and politics as being inextricably mixed, and he equally stressed the social importance of discussion and criticism. But he went further than Plato in insisting that there must be a purpose in things, a final cause, and a process of self-adaptation of evolving organisms towards some ultimate goal. He could not accept that Plato's Forms (or Universals) could have any separate existence and focussed attention thereby on the study of phenomena. He attempted a classification of the working of reason and so founded the science of formal logic. He asked what sort of a being man is and in what sort of societies he lives, arguing that the education received must be fitted to suit the way of life of a given society. Its aim is to produce the good man and the good citizen, and it is therefore too important to be left either to the whims of parents or in the hands of private individuals. Since the goal of human existence is happiness, and since we best enjoy happiness when at leisure, then we must make sure that leisure is purposeful activity — for we are only truly living when we are active. Finally, he stresses the importance of what has been termed the disinterested pursuit of knowledge, arguing that we should seek education "not as being useful or necessary, but because it is liberal and noble". Yet once again the emphasis is on the individual worth of persons.

It is, I think, no exaggeration to claim that Plato and Aristotle between them shaped the intellectual mould into which education was to be cast throughout Western Europe for well over 1000 years. Yet they themselves were creatures of their environment, even though they may be hailed as the philosopher–kings of it. The Greeks in their anonymity ventured far and wide beyond their native land on warring, trading or exploratory expeditions, learning much of the ways and customs of other peoples. They came in consequence both to understand and to appreciate the power of custom (particularly in its moral and religious aspects), and also to develop a sceptical attitude to authority in its many guises, including the use of magic and superstition. To them, with their democratic way of life, and the emphasis they placed on both mental and physical action as necessary tools for discovering the truth, the philosophy of the East with its stress on contemplation and its perpetual yearning for a kind of mystical inner experience could make no appeal.

Yet when it came to the point the Greeks could not rise above the idea of the city-state. It was left to Philip of Macedon and his son Alexander the Great (a pupil of Aristotle) to attempt to conquer the East and spread there the benefits of Greek culture. Had Alexander not died at the early age of 33 and his empire not collapsed, could Western Europe as we now know it have come about? A lasting empire would most certainly have prevented the expansion of Rome. If Hellenism had triumphed in the wake of Alexander's conquests it would surely have triumphed as part-Greek, part-Asiatic, and Mediterranean. But there would almost certainly have been no westwards move towards the Atlantic, and so no Western European civilisation such as we now enjoy. It is an intriguing thought.

2

If the guiding principle of the Greeks had been the worth of the individual, then that of the Romans was for unity, and they displayed a rare ability for organisation, for colonisation, and for the elaboration of a universal Roman Law — still finding some echoes in modern legal practice. Less brilliant and original than the Greeks, they were more stolid and practical. Their genius lay in their sound, common-sense approach to every problem they had to face. Thus, in colonising they used proved and able men of different races to govern, thereby underlying and illustrating the universality of Rome. They preserved for us the legacy of Greece by being content to borrow most of their culture from the Greeks, though giving it their own practical twist and making it more suitable for universal application. They adapted the philosophy of the Greeks to meet the needs of day-to-day government and so brought it within the reach of everyman as opposed to the "philosopher-king". They had not sought an empire consciously, as had Alexander the Great. By their defeat of Carthage they emerged as the greatest power in the Mediterranean, and everything then snowballed. They became cosmopolitan in the true sense of the word. Blessed with a more practical civic sense than the Greeks, they produced a majestic style in architecture, admirably combining form with function, laid out cities, planned sewerage systems, and produced central heating, public buildings, viaducts, aqueducts and highways to link their key towns and positions. The life of the well-to-do Roman anywhere in the Roman Empire could be as gracious, hygienic and comfortable as any twentieth-century European could desire. They eagerly packed off their studious young men to Greece to imbibe Platonic–Aristotelian philosophy. They schooled them well at home. And they succeeded in producing an urbane, polished and sensible man of the world such as Horace, Pliny the Younger, or Catullus. It is curious to reflect that in many respects the education of the English gentleman has more closely followed the Roman pattern than that of his counterpart anywhere else in Western Europe.

To try to give an answer to the inevitable question "How was all this achieved?" is not easy, though I am inclined to believe that the close attention paid to character training, right through the centuries from the earliest days of the Roman Republic, is an important key. The Roman historian Livy himself stressed how important had been the three cardinal virtues of *pietas, gravitas, simplicitas*, and to these I am tempted to add a fourth — *severitas*. *Pietas* implied deep-felt loyalty to the family, to the achievements of one's ancestors, and to the fatherland, and centred on the home (the focal point of both educational practice and religious activity) with the father (*paterfamilias*) very much in control. *Gravitas* I will interpret simply as being careful at all times to treat serious things seriously. *Simplicitas* is the refusal to complicate matters; is to accept one's limitations and willingly profit from another's experience; is constantly to adopt a practical and down-to-earth approach — probably the best example of this being the way in which the Romans endowed all their gods with very human qualities, and even had their own intimate household gods. *Severitas* I see simply as self-discipline of the kind which in the long span of Roman history produced models of courage, of dignity, and of a high sense of duty in all walks of life, and which gave the Roman Empire a notable number of emperors who were always careful to rule as conscientious and devoted servants. When Rome was at the peak of its achievements, moral training along these lines in the schools was strongly reinforced by example from the standards adhered to in adult life.

One signal achievement of Imperial Rome was that it brought peace to the Mediterranean for the unprecedented period of almost 200 years. And within the Empire, if one discounts the various uprisings of the intractable Hebrews, there were no rebellions. A second and more important achievement was both because of itself and in spite of itself. Saint Paul brought his version of the Christian message to Rome and perished as a martyr there. For 200 years the Christians were persecuted and yet flourished, thanks to the deep-seated tolerance of these "cultivated pagans". The Emperor Constantine (274–337) became a convert to Christianity in 306, and by the Edict of Milan (313) removed all the temporal disadvantages which had so far retarded the progress of the Christian faith. Shortly afterwards he declared Christianity the national religion of his empire and brought all the machinery of government both to propagate the faith and to stamp out heresy. His last important move was to recognise the superiority of the ecclesiastical orders in all matters spiritual, firmly retaining for himself all the temporal power.

Thus, it can with some justification be claimed that Christianity was the last great creation of ancient Greece and Rome, and thanks to the universality of Rome, to the *pax romana*, the Roman legal system, and the excellent system of communications both by sea and overland created by the Romans, the Christian religion, once officially launched, spread rapidly. Ordained bishops were strategically placed. Moreover, much of "paganism" – meaning Platonic–Aristotelian philosophy – was found to be relevant, or could be accommodated to be so. Saint Augustine himself, though a devout follower of the apostolic tradition and believing in a personal God with very positive characteristics, still viewed God (like a Neo-Platonist) as the source of all perfection and as the only true reality. As for the rank and file of converts to Christianity, they found it a transition both easy and natural to turn from their familiar and household gods to venerate those saints and martyrs, men and women like themselves, who had died for Christ crucified, as personifying God the Absolute.

The Sack of Rome in 409 by Alaric, king of the Visigoths, virtually marked the end of the Roman Empire, but it could be said that as the Empire finally disintegrated in 476 so did the Christian church firmly establish itself. It organised itself along Roman models. It became the most important force in civilising the conquering Germanic tribes. It transmitted its inherited imperial traditions, together with its Christian teaching, in a form that was at once Roman, Greek and universal. In seeking to rebuild some semblance of social order it sought its ideal in one law, one language (Latin), and one moral and philosophical code. Its moral standards were derived from the Jewish prophets and the Greek and Roman Stoics. The Roman church grew, as it were, into a kind of *Imperium Romanum* and imposed its ideals on the whole of Western Europe to hold it together as a recognisable entity. Or, as Bertrand Russell puts it: "The unity of the Church echoed the unity of the Roman Empire; its liturgy was Latin and its dominant men were mostly Italian, Spanish or Southern French. Their education, when education revived, was classical. The Church represented at once continuity with the past and what was most civilised in the present".[1]

---

[1] Bertrand Russell, *History of Western Philosophy*, London, 1946, p. 17.

3

As Europe stumbled through the Dark Ages which followed the collapse of Rome, whatever education was available was exclusively in the hands of the church. Equally the church was the primary inspiration for all forms of art and the accepted basis of all philosophical, scientific, political and economic thinking. All educated men spoke Latin. There were neither fixed boundaries nor armed frontiers, and merchants, artisans, priests, pedlars, troubadours and students wandered freely everywhere. The relative simplicity of the mediaeval mind has in retrospect a certain charm, as has the way in which life was lived with colour, abandon and gusto, but there is another side to the picture. These "new" Europeans were very conscious of their inheritance, stood in some awe of it, and did not know how properly to cope. Their exuberance and ingenuousness led them to extremes in matters both sacred and profane and, as the practice of the Christian religion became more and more an integral part of everyday life, so was it cheapened. Priests and laymen alike found it difficult to reconcile the divide between the fleshly and the spiritual, difficult to distinguish Saint Augustine's infamous Earthly City from the supposedly highly preferable City of God, were impatient at the restrictive and pessimistic doctrine of the Saint, and forgot how to identify religious practice with morality as the earlier Hebraic apostles had so successfully taught.

As for the theologians proper, they betrayed little short of a Neo-Platonic arrogance in the assumption that they were in the possession of pure, intangible and untranslatable truths. It was left to Peter Abelard (1079–1142) to declare that the Church Fathers were not infallible guides and to bring reason to help elucidate revealed Truth. Saint Thomas Aquinas (1226–74) took up where the persecuted Abelard left off, turned from Plato to Aristotle, claimed that "everything that is in the intellect has been in the senses" and, holding that Aristotle's philosophy contained the essential truth about the natural world, attempted to reconcile it with Christianity.[1] He opposed Saint Augustine's teaching that knowledge of the natural world is unimportant, or that the Scriptures

[1] Helen Waddell's *Peter Abelard*, Canon Roger Lloyd's *Peter Abelard: the Orthodox Rebel*, and Régine Pernoud's *Héloïse et Abelard* are easy reading and throw considerable light on this period.

tell us all we need to know about it, and concluded that false ideas about God's handiwork must lead to false conclusions about God himself. He embodied his great learning in his *Summa Theologica* which to this day remains an inspirational source for the teachings of the Catholic church.

The mediaeval church, however, having achieved temporary power of considerable importance with the introduction, early in the thirteenth century, of the principle that any sovereign only held his crown on condition that he extirpate heresy, and thus in effect also introducing the principle of rule by divine right, did not match up to the high expectations held for it.[1] In its attempts to play a full political role as representing a "kingdom not of this world" it got itself inextricably caught up in the toils of this world and became an immense worldly kingdom with a highly sophisticated and elaborate organisation which could be matched by no king or emperor. The immediate consequences of all this were roundly denounced by Voltaire when he labelled the Middle Ages as the chief source of all the superstition, prejudice and tyranny that had stood for so long in the way of human progress.

4

The period today referred to as that of the Renaissance and Reformation was the one in which the mind of man was first enabled to break away from the teachings of mediaeval orthodoxy and make a fresh and critical examination of all political, ethical, scientific and human problems. Both movements were in essence reform movements, but neither sought a complete break with the past. On the contrary, the Humanists (or Renaissance men) sought to correct the faults of the immediate past by a return to a study of the ancient literature of Greece and Rome, to a reappraisal of what had been the glory of Greece and the grandeur of Rome; and the reformers turned back to the Gospels for inspiration to sweep away the corruption of the church. Humanists like Erasmus (1466–1536) thought to purge the church through the dissemination of the literature of both classical and Christian antiquity, seeking the same sort of synthesis as had Saint Thomas Aquinas. A humanist such as Montaigne (1533–92) allowed

[1] The idea started as early as 751 when Pépin I had himself crowned *and anointed* at Soissons.

the sages of antiquity to mould and possess his mind, marvelled at the infinite variety in human nature revealed thereby, was led to lay a new stress on the dignity and worth of man in terms of the contemporary scene, yet sceptically wondered what truths man's puny intellect could grasp. Inescapably he came to the conclusion that in the domain of theology the human intellect is incapable; that there can be no bridge between man's reasoning and the practice of his religion; and that therefore religion must be humbly and simply accepted and placed outside reason's reach. The reformers prepared the way for both religious and political freedom, stressed man's individual responsibilities and rights, and in the meantime plunged Europe into the religious wars.

This rebirth of interest in the study of classical authors and in the reading of the Gospels in the original Greek texts was furthered by the invention of printing. Similarly, the discovery of new parts of the world, and new customs and practices, brought man to review more discerningly his own condition. There was the urge to travel, and with a definite set purpose. The Englishman, Colet, had studied in Italy and on his return to Oxford astounded everybody by announcing a series of lectures on the Epistles of Saint Paul as from the Greek. Erasmus, already convinced that the only way to bring about desirable reforms was through education, and that just as education must be his most important instrument so was the printing press his most important tool, crossed to England in 1499, listened to Colet, became the familiar of both Colet and such men as Thomas More, William Latimer, Thomas Linacre and William Grocyn, and returned to Europe fired with renewed zeal for his project and determined to master himself the Greek tongue. Colet became Dean of Saint Paul's, founded his own school in the shadow of the cathedral, and insisted on the teaching of Greek, and of pure Ciceronian Latin to replace the "mish-mash" that mediaeval Latin as a *lingua franca* had become. So did he create the prototype of the reformed English grammar school.

Erasmus, who returned frequently to England, became now   e firmly dedicated to the dissemination of the classical Christian heritage and centred his educational ideal on the two concepts of *humanitas* and *pietas*. The latter implied commitment to the Christian religion which would enrich by its gentle and compassionate nature the love of mankind (*humanitas*) which stressed the dignity of man, alone endowed with speech and reason. These ideals were to be inculcated through a study of the best of classical authors (with insistence on the purity of Ciceronian Latin and Cicero's concept of *humanitas*) and of the Scriptures. Thus, the Classics and the Bible should be the basis of education for all men in all walks of life. It is interesting to note that the way in which the Reformation took hold in England allowed this synthesis, whereas on the continent of Europe the reaffirmation of the hold of the Catholic church through the Counter-Reformation brought the spiritual heirs of the Renaissance movement to live "in a world of art, letters and science seldom touched by religion, in effect abandoning ecclesiastical affairs to the unaided efforts of the monks and clergy".[1]

In other words, Erasmus did not fully prevail in Europe despite his international reputation and his undoubted zeal and sincerity. What did prevail in the rest of Europe was the sceptical approach typified by Montaigne, also a man of moderation who like Erasmus saw clearly through the ambiguities in human nature. "Man is the fool of the farce", claimed Montaigne and then enjoined man to master the script and follow the stage directions if he would enjoy himself and heed the claim of Rabelais that "laughter is man's birthright". Compared with leaders of the Reformation such as Luther and Calvin, humanists such as Erasmus and Montaigne were, however, in the long run, more important. The Reformation movement throughout Europe was then as hostile to enlightenment as to liberty, and with Luther in particular any scientific development which seemed to contradict the Bible stood as little chance of approval as with the Pope. The Reformation plunged Europe into a series of disastrous religious wars which spread the slow poison of nationalistic aspirations to weaken those intellectual ties which had so far bound the Christian world together. Yet even at the height of the Reformation movement, when countries were torn in conflict, Europe still possessed a greater intellectual unity (based on classical learning) than it has ever since enjoyed. Montaigne's untiring efforts at moderating between Catholic and Huguenot factions in his own country afford perhaps one of the best examples of a sincere attempt by one of the most progressive of humanists to maintain that unity, and create a true intellectual atmosphere in which the emancipation of reason could be profitably used to extend man's knowledge both of himself and of the world about him. And it is significant that the

[1] G. M. Trevelyan, *History of England*, London, 1926, p. 290.

next important step forward came only when Descartes (1596–1650), a fervent if not uncritical student of Montaigne, attempted the formulation of a firm philosophy based on these early humanistic (and sceptical) fumblings.

The immediate importance of the Humanists, of course, is the emphasis they placed on education of the right kind. They broke firmly with the mental gymnastics and empty verbal juggling of the scholastics. In purifying the use of the Latin tongue they introduced exercises of a kind which still dominate the teaching of the Classics: textual criticism, unseen translation, prose composition, versification, Latin speeches and dissertations on a variety of subjects. It was felt that a sound classical education must be basic. They upheld the Aristotelian claim that true education resided in the disinterested pursuit of knowledge, spurning any utilitarian approach though according the study of other subjects a worthy if subordinate place. Man's capacity for reasoning must be developed to the full, as also his ability to form correct judgements. And this again would come through classical studies, bolstered by mathematics and history, for man's puny reasoning powers could not be directed to debating Revealed Truth. The theologians proper would deal with all that. Many would claim that the natural heirs to this humanistic system of education (which, as Montaigne clearly saw, could easily descend to mere pedantry) have been the Jesuits, and it is their enlightened teaching, paradoxically enough, which throughout subsequent centuries has produced some of the acutest minds in Europe vowed to attack the impregnable position the Catholic church has sought to maintain. Voltaire remains the outstanding example, for the so-called Age of Reason (or Enlightenment) is the century of Voltaire.

5

To the Age of Enlightenment there were, of course, important forerunners. Descartes, as I have already indicated, moved from the sceptical position maintained by Montaigne to sweep away the vestiges of Platonic mystical symbolism and formulate a philosophy epitomised in the phrase *"Cogito ergo sum"* (I think, therefore I am). His most fundamental assumption was that truths about the existent world can be discovered by reasoning only. Reason, he argued, is the same in all men and we need only to develop and arouse it for all problems to solve themselves. He outlined a mathematical interpretation of nature and saw the world as governed by natural, mechanical laws. At the same time, whilst agreeing with Galileo (1564–1642) that matter is in constant motion, and that such should be the true field of study, he carefully distinguished between matter and mind. Contrary to what Locke (a former disciple) would later teach, Descartes claimed that the mind was not a blank which passively received messages from without, but was internally supplied with a number of fixed (innate) ideas. With the help of these ideas human reason could arrive, by reflection, at the truth. The mind, however, has two clear and separate functions: understanding and willing. To reach the truth we need to apprehend and then give assent to what we have apprehended. Since the will is infinite, and there is nothing to which we cannot give our assent if we so choose, then error will creep in if we give assent to something of which we have not attained clear understanding. Descartes tried to have the best of both worlds by this attempted reconciliation of a rational spirit of inquiry with Revealed Truth of the Catholic church (innate ideas), claiming that God must be the continuous support of a world in a state of flux and perpetual change. His educational importance is that his particular form of rational intellectualism has much influenced educational method at both primary and secondary level throughout Western Europe (excluding the British Isles) and particularly in France where even today his *Discours de la Méthode* can still be required reading for intending teachers.

It was Newton (1642–1727) who, by formulating his four rules for scientific reasoning, laid the foundations which made possible the whole of subsequent scientific achievement. He took up where Galileo had had to leave off, and with him the experimental–mathematical method came into its own. John Locke (1632–1704) was a personal friend of Newton, and as such came to oppose Descartes by affirming that our knowledge of nature is restricted to ideas which come from outside through the senses. Knowledge for him, therefore, is simply ordered experience, and he found no difficulty in reconciling his stand with membership of the Anglican church. He holds that we know self by intuition, God by demonstration, and everything else through sensation. Most men, he argues, are good or bad, useful or useless to society, according to the education they have received, Advocating an empirical approach and a free spirit of inquiry if we are ever properly to understand the universe we live in, and to understand how we come to understand, he most naturally proposed a system of education along these basic empirical lines which, allied to his views on toleration and on the form democracy should take, was to be a liberalising force making practical suggestions for a better social order. John Locke's influence has, of course, permeated thinking on education throughout the Anglo-Saxon world (including the USA). And he became in effect the acknowledged head of that school of empirical psychologists amongst whom were to be numbered the Scots philosopher Hume (1711–76), the Frenchman, Condillac (1715–80), and the German, Herbart (1776–1841).

It was during a period of enforced exile in England (1726–28/9) that Voltaire (1694–1778) became familiar with English philosophical thought, and he was indeed counselled by Bolingbroke to give Locke's *Essay Concerning Human Understanding* preference to Descartes. Whether Voltaire learned to think in England (as he claimed) is a moot point, but he certainly never forgot what he learned there in the field of politics and government, and his scepticism, together with his already strong sense of justice and toleration, was most certainly strengthened and confirmed by his experiences there. His famous *Letters Concerning the English Nation* were first published in England in English in 1733, and, whilst devoting most space to the Quakers, he spoke most persuasively in favour of the philosophical–scientific movement represented by Francis Bacon, Isaac Newton and John Locke. His various notebooks reveal that he was also familiar with the writings of Hobbes and Hume (whose *History of England* he was later to review), and he set himself the task of popularising Newton's ideas by publishing (in French) his *Elements of the Philosophy of Newton to be Understood by Everybody* (Amsterdam, 1738). Soon all fashionable Paris was discussing Newtonian ideas as expounded in Voltaire's "little catechism of gravitation", and Voltaire in turn was honoured and rewarded by election as a Fellow of both the Royal Society and the Royal Society of Edinburgh. In short, Voltaire was chiefly responsible for introducing into the mainstream of French and European thought new and challenging ideas from across the Channel which could not be ignored, and helped to launch the so-called Age of Reason (or Enlightenment).

6

As Immanuel Kant (1724–1804) was later to explain in his *Was ist Aufklärung?* (1784), the Age of Enlightenment became really a growing-up stage in the development of European man in that he had now dared to begin to think for himself. What the philosophers were really challenging were the military and Christian virtues extolled by the *ancien régime*, and the use of the Scriptures and the Classics as undisputed sources of authority, both implying that civilisation had somehow degenerated from a Golden Age in which Rome itself stood for those highly desirable attributes of timelessness, rationality and universality. Descartes had evolved a mechanistic interpretation of the universe. Newton had stressed the impossibility of man ever attaining understanding of final causes and was a Deist (such as Voltaire himself could claim to be) in that he felt that proof of the existence of God was linked with the stability of the world. As Newton brought to eighteenth-century man illumination on the nature of the material universe, so did Locke bring enlightenment on the working of the human mind, and the result was that men now came gradually to believe that the universe did not revolve entirely around man. It became increasingly necessary to move the emphasis from knowledge and intelligence (though of course necessary) to insight and understanding, and to be always accessible to new ideas. Humanity as a whole was seen as at long last freeing itself from prejudice and superstition, and in the process came a boundless faith in the power of reason. Reason could answer all questions and solve all problems, for reason stemmed (as Newton had so dazzlingly demonstrated) from Nature and from the Natural Law.

The consequences of all this ferment of ideas were both immediate and far-reaching. Since Nature was now an open book man could find there his "natural rights" (Rousseau) as well as a "natural religion" stripped of all mystery, God being still in his Heaven as the Author of Nature. Christians, poets and philosophers could ceaselessly admire the extraordinary fitness of the cosmic order of things. All were persuaded that happiness on earth was the ultimate (and natural) good, and that it was the duty of governments to use reason to promote it. All equally felt it was their own duty to take in the whole of human knowledge, though acknowledging that the main problem was not so much the acquisition of knowledge as that of distinguishing truth from plausible error. It was felt necessary to create the right attitude of mind to the problems posed, and to this end came the publication of the seventeen volumes of the *Encyclopédie* (1751–65). These were used as much as a propaganda exercise as for disseminating knowledge and avowedly had a two-fold objective: firstly, to familiarise

the layman with the new discoveries in science and the new forms of
rational thinking which sprang from these discoveries; secondly, to inculcate a critical approach to all human relationships. The publication of the
Encyclopédie (directed by d'Alembert and Diderot and enthusiastically
supported by both Voltaire and Rousseau) marked the beginning of a new
epoch in European thinking and served to destroy the foundations of belief
on which rested the doctrines of absolutism and of a privileged society.

By the second half of the eighteenth century a rapid spread in the
dissemination of periodical literature had also been achieved. The *Spec-
tator* in England was regularly publishing between 20,000 and 30,000
copies of each issue. From 1770 onwards the French provincial press
firmly established itself. Germany, if only because of the political frag-
mentation of the country, had a bewildering multiplicity of local news-
sheets. The 1770s mark the beginnings of the publications of periodical
literature in Austria and in the Netherlands. And even in Spain, despite
strong clerical opposition, some headway was made. Literacy, in fact, was
now beginning to extend itself to a considerable proportion of the population of Western Europe, and though the masses of the people remained
illiterate, by the end of the century skilled workers in the most advanced
countries could and did read all they might come by.

Of course, the ideas of the Enlightenment were both supported and
furthered by the existence of a strong, literate middle class which must
have numbered some several millions throughout Western Europe. These
men and women eagerly formed discussion groups of suitable size (the
coffee house; the French *salon*; Freemasons' Lodges), pursued some
worthy cause such as the abolition of the slave trade (based on a belief
in the natural rights of man rather than out of any real sense of compassion
or pity), betrayed some interest in anthropological studies by debating
some favourite civilisation of the past which could be held up as an example,
and were firmly convinced (this a keystone of Masonic belief) that there
existed a beneficent Providence which regulated not only the course of
Nature but also the promptings of the heart. It was an attitude of mind
that was created, and an attitude which came to accept sentiment as an
important source of a kind of knowledge to which intelligence alone could
not aspire, and which in effect was the mainspring and arbiter for most of
man's actions. The men of the Enlightenment might affect to despise the
men of the Middle Ages but they had, in reality, many affinities with

them: they had equally their own gospel of salvation – a clear vision of a Heavenly City on earth which should be revealed through Science rather than through the Scriptures or the church's interpretations of the Scriptures, and an attitude towards religion (particularly in Germany) which held that God could be revealed to us only through the senses; that all instincts, even the sexual instinct, were evidence of God's beneficence.

7

This peculiar German viewpoint is important if only for the fact that in the long run it came to differentiate the main trends in German educational practice from those in England and France. Frederick the Great of Prussia had given the lead by reviving the Royal Academy of Science and Letters in Berlin in 1743; by making elementary education compulsory between the ages of 5 and 13/14, giving it a firm religious basis, and inculcating a strong sense of moral and civic duty (1763); by bidding Voltaire and other like-minded philosophers of the Enlightenment to his court; by creating a new order in Freemasonry with its own peculiar mystical–religious outlook, strongly Christian and making a ready emotional appeal.

Thus, when Kant came to inquire *Was ist Aufklärung?* he could distinguish three clear trends: the English, whilst they might be philosophers to a point, were too much in love with their ease and comforts to wish to delve deeply into ideas; the French philosophised with their wit, and though brilliant were careless and superficial; the Germans were the level-headed ones, not to be carried away by flights of fancy, and by nature endowed with a taste for scholarship. The Germans would play their part in the movement throughout Europe towards a philosophy of enlightenment but would take care not to be swallowed up in it, adopting a position which both frowned upon the easy if brilliant scepticism of the *Encyclopédistes* as being an aberration of the mind and which also sought to curb the enthusiasms of so many over-heated imaginations. For them the empirical was as significant as the rationalistic and they would in consequence attach less importance to deductive reasoning and more to instinct, sentiment and sensual impressions. Experience could in one sense lay claim to being the only truth, and man should therefore live his life not primarily according to any dogma or precept but mainly in reliance on his own feelings – an attitude to life defined by Herder as "sensuous certainty".

All this hotch-potch of contradictions, primarily the fruit of the extravagance of ideas of the *Sturm und Drang* movement (typified by the young Goethe, Herder, Lenz, Merck and Klinger), needed some key to bring shape and coherence to it. Immanuel Kant met the need, started a tradition of philosophy for the Germans, and to this day remains the most important theoretical philosopher Germany has produced. Like Rousseau (whom he much admired) Kant was careful to dissociate judgement from perception, was much preoccupied with the sanctity of the individual conscience, and held that responsibility for moral action was solely due to the mind's intuitive awareness of itself and its obligations. "Reason", he argued, "and not the experience of impressions and objects is the source of moral obligation", and he held the individual person to be a morally autonomous unit whose obligations must be self-imposed and in consequence owe nothing either to external authority, or to religious beliefs, or to the deterministic pressures of the material environment. Reason makes what it wills of all our sense impressions, for "pure" Reason is independent of all sense experiences and represents knowledge belonging to us by the inherent nature and structure of the mind. Reason in the pure and practical sense must aim at the perfect good (the *summum bonum*), and thus postulates both the immortality of the soul and the existence of God as the necessary condition for attainment of the *summum bonum*.[1] Man can only hope to approach the perfect good by careful training of the will to accord with the moral law, it being remembered that only an action performed out of a sense of duty (as opposed to fear or inclination) can have true moral worth. For the only unqualified good to be found in this world is a good will – a will to follow the moral law regardless of profit or loss to ourselves. Man should not simply seek to be happy, but should, by absolute obedience to the moral law, seek to become worthy of that happiness which only God can bestow.

Obviously, then, education's prime concern must be the inculcation of the will to act rightly, and, in his notes for the course of lectures on education he was obliged to deliver at the University of Koenigsberg, Kant seeks to have put into practice the main tenets of his philosophical system. Since

[1] A close affinity is here to be noted with basic Masonic ritual.

evil is only the result of nature not being brought properly under control — for Kant held with Rousseau that in man there can only be germs of good — it is necessary for the child to experience restraint the better to develop his natural gifts and ensure that he fulfils his true destiny. The aim of education must be the development of character, the total acceptance of the moral law (for it is morality alone which gives meaning to man), and a conception of duty as "stern Daughter of the Voice of God". Only when the child has been so conditioned can he in adolescence be allowed to exercise his free will, in terms of the moral law, and so be initiated to a system of values which make him constantly strive to reach a still higher stage of culture. "A teacher should make of his hearer first an *intelligent*, then a *reasonable*, and finally a *learned* man". The most valuable thing we can give a pupil is not knowledge but through self-discipline a salutary way of acquiring knowledge and an independent way of action.

8

Kant, or course, was speaking of man in general. It was left to two of his own students, Herder (1744–1803) and Fichte (1762–1814), to Hegel (1771–1831), himself a pupil of Fichte, to Schopenhauer (1788–1860), and to Neitzsche (1844–1900), progressively to elaborate on Kant and give his idealistic philosophy a peculiarly Germanic twist. The cantankerous Herder and the young Goethe together despised the domination of polite society by French culture, Goethe resolving forthwith to abandon French as his second language and devote himself solely to his mother tongue, Herder unwittingly contributing a new and important dimension to the study of history by insisting that the German language be freed from all imitation of foreign models and restored to its pristine purity. This led him to a close study of the native folk-lore and poetry of the *Volk*, of popular ballads and proverbs, of institutions, and to declare that language was the most significant of all cultural phenomena. "Each nation speaks in the manner it thinks," he declared, "and thinks in the manner it speaks." The *Stürmer* heartily agreed with Herder when he declared that truth could only be found in "the total, unfragmented, deep feeling of things". Historians, philologists and scholars of all kinds eagerly followed the lead given by Herder and set about collecting and preserving all they could of former or moribund national traditions. And Herder went on to argue that each nation, through its language, became a dynamic force, a cultural totality, a law unto itself with a truth uniquely its own which was compounded of blood, environment and experience. Men do not create nations for their own convenience. A nation brings forth men, the whole being more real than the parts. Thus, in developing his theory of the Folk Soul with its roots in the chain of national tradition from primitive times onwards, Herder led his fellow Germans to an idealisation of the national past and prepared the way for nascent German nationalism to characterise itself by a quest for meaning, by a musing about the nature of the national soul and its mission. Resenting more and more Germany's dependence on the West, the *Stürmer* and succeeding intellectuals looked to their own heritage as a basis for national revival.

And it was Napoleon's attempt to impose a universal pattern throughout Europe which provoked each conquered or threatened nation to identify its independence with the preservation of its historic way of life and to assert its own national personality. Napoleon's ultimate defeat could not have been possible without an upward surge of *Folk-feeling* which led to the replacement of mercenary troops by enthusiastic volunteers imbued with a new and (to the peacemakers at the Congress of Vienna) frightening spirit of patriotism. Germany was particularly vulnerable in that its aristocracy had fawned on the conqueror. With the disastrous defeat of the Prussians at Jena (1806), a defeat which highlighted the characterlessness of the ruling aristocracy, the middle-classes were more than ready to heed the message Fichte broadcast to them from his Chair in the University of Berlin − significantly entitled "Addresses to the German Nation" (1807-8) − and Fichte's earlier publicised philosophical ideas now took on a special significance.

Following Kant, Fichte had claimed that the only reality was the mind, objects existing only as perceptions of the mind. Thus, man could only be important as mind, the individual mind being part of a universal mind from which it derived any significance it had. In the development of humanity Fichte saw five distinct periods: that of the Normal People, to whom reason and rational conduct were natural and therefore effortless; that of the Fall, when these fortunate ones were driven out to mix with a totally barbarous mixture of peoples; a period during which "hero" figures emerged from among the Normal People to impose their civilising will on the barbarians − Alexander the Great is quoted by Fichte as a good example of such a "hero" figure;[1] a period (that through which Germany was then passing) marked by the struggle of reason against the domination of self-interest and love of material gain;[2] a final period which would lead back to Sweetness and Light through the determined efforts of individuals to subordinate their separate wills to the collective will of the community (echoes of Rousseau). Man, Fichte argued, is only Man as he has his definite part to play in the world; and he plays his part, not through passively observing what is going on, but by actively intervening. All our thought is founded on our impulses; as a man's affections are, so is his knowledge. Will, reason and emotion have together an equal right, together form a unity, together enable us to triumph.

Fichte's *Addresses to the German Nation*, published at real personal risk since French troops were still garrisoned in Berlin, were a stirring call to Germans everywhere to abandon their supine subservience to what he termed the Enlightenment Militant of the French and to dare to lay claim to their birthright. He now insisted that, in the historical process, a special role had been reserved for Germany, and to be a true German meant being true to one's destiny. Was it not the Germanic people who had broken through the defences of the Roman Empire to conquer and colonise almost the whole of Europe? Were not the present Germanic people the *Urvolk*, the original race among European peoples and the only great nation in Europe to have retained their original language (*Ursprache*)? Had they not forged for themselves the valid approach to the Christian message (Martin Luther) which was now adopted elsewhere in Europe? Were they not a mature nation of real spiritual depth, the original creative force in Europe who would seem to be "the elect of the universal divine plan"? The English, French, Spaniards and Italians were imitators entirely lacking in originality, speaking languages which were a hotch-potch of other languages, devoting themselves to a scramble for wealth and power, subjugating other nations and ruthlessly exploiting conquered and primitive

---

[1] Significantly, Fichte goes on to say: "the civilised must rule and the uncivilised must obey, if Right is to be the Law of the World. . . . Tell me not of the thousands who fell around his [Alexander's] path; speak not of his own early ensuing death – after the realisation of his idea, what was there greater for him to do than die?"

[2] There is one place in the world [Germany] where this egotistical being has perished as he reached maturity; he has destroyed both his personality and his independence; he who would be no other than himself has seen himself imposed upon by a foreign power [France] and directed towards goals totally alien to his nature."

tribes. There was but one way, he concluded, to rejuvenate the lagging spirit of the German people: through education, whereby the intellectual and moral grandeur, and consequently, the material grandeur, of Germany might be restored.

Here, Fichte stressed (as had Kant) the virtues of duty, sacrifice and self-abnegation, arguing also that to exclude from man everything that is not reason is to rob the soul of its greatest impulses. Every noble nature, he insisted, would value life not for its own sake, but for the work which it can accomplish; and the perpetuity of that work can be assured only by the survival of the nation which values and protects it. There must be a new, national education to "fashion the German people to a unity throbbing through all its limbs". As Germany had perished owing to the selfishness of its members, so now it could be restored only by a new ideal, the self-surrender of the individual for the good of the community: "We must form men so that they can only will what we wish them to will." In the same way as it takes children from the family to turn them into soldiers, so must the state take children and turn them into good citizens, away from the self-seeking influences of family life. The education given must be based on public service, on healthy exercise, on social conformity, and (since we are dealing with the *Urvolk*) a patriotic form of religious observance which took note of their apparent position as "the elect of the universal divine plan". Ironically enough, Fichte was proposing for the *whole* of German youth a programme which (*mutatis mutandis*) was to be the pattern for the *select few* in the English public school system of the nineteenth century.

Fichte's pupil, Hegel, in his popular lectures on the philosophy of history (posthumously published in 1832), argued history to be a logical and inevitable process which man could recognise but not change. The great men of history — the hero figures of Fichte — were mere agents of impersonal forces, the World Spirit operating through a succession of emergent nations and outstanding individuals by the dialectical process of having every situation in the world, every idea, lead irresistably to its opposite and then unite with it to form a higher and more complex whole. This process meant that the function of man's mind was to discover the unity which is potential in diversity, and that man as mind could have significance only as part of the national community by which his whole existence was determined. Thus Hegel led the German people to conclude that man makes history and that the ideal must be what is made factually real. He equally insisted that mind is the all-embracing reality, being identical with behaviour and experience. And since all experiences have their source and become unified in the individual, then the main purpose of education must be that of producing well-rounded and harmoniously developed personalities, actively seeking perfection, actively striving towards the perfect German state. For the World Spirit, working its own turbulent way through three great periods in history (the Oriental, the Classical and the Germanic), has shown that everything − even pain − has its rationale, and that life is not made for happiness but for achievement. "The history of the world is not the theatre of happiness; periods of happiness are blank passages in it, for they are periods of harmony"; therefore man must always seek, not to live his own life, but to place himself at the service of the World Spirit. This meant that the Germans, in Hegel's view, had their own peculiar historic role to play, for the German state had arrived at a point of synthesis in the dialectical process when, given real commitment on the part of its people, the rule of reason would triumph over the opposing ideas of Force and Freedom, the state representing true freedom in freedom organised. Here, quite starkly, was justification for a politics of absolute obedience. We know how Karl Marx, adopting the Hegelian dialectic, proposed mass movements and economic forces as the basic causes of fundamental change rather than accept the omnipotence of the World Spirit.

The pessimistic Schopenhauer accepted the Kantian position that the external world is known to us only through our sensations and ideas, but went on to assert that the only essential reality in the world is the will, and that all visible and tangible phenomena are merely subjective representations of that will which is the only "thing-in-itself" which actually exists. Character lies in the will, and not in the intellect, for character (like the will) is continuity of purpose and attitude. So, if we are to live happily and fruitfully, the will, which always represents man's self-interests and desires, must be correctly disciplined. Cultivation of the intellect alone is no good, for the intellect tires, the will never. Increase of knowledge is no solution either, because since life is evil the greater the knowledge the greater the suffering. We "purify" the will through the introspective powers of philosophy, philosophy being understood as experience and thought, not reading or passive study. Life, then, before books − the intelligent contemplation of life and familiarity with the achievements of the great of all times in all spheres of creative activity — is the only possible answer. For genius is the highest form of will-less knowledge, genius in the arts in particular forcing us to forget the individual self and its material interests and elevating our minds to the will-less contemplation of the truth. This, averred Schopenhauer, is particularly true of music. The importance of Schopenhauer is that he gave the death-blow to the conception of man as, above all, a thinking animal. He demonstrated that behind all thought is desire, and behind the intellect, instinct. He gave new leads to the psychologists, but above all (apart from furthering the hero-worship cult of Fichte) he sought to demonstrate that the ultimate good is beauty, and that the only true joy in man must lie in the creation or appreciation of the beautiful.

Nietzsche, a sensitive man whose fastidious nature was appalled by all the ugliness and cant he saw about him in the rising and thriving German bourgeoisie, in one sense followed closely in the wake of Darwin. The Encyclopaedists had removed the theological basis for moral behaviour, whilst leaving morality itself inviolate. Darwin's evolutionary theories had given the lie to the comfortable moral principle of the equality of all souls before God. All intelligent men, argued Nietzsche, must now accept the basic truth that to win the battle of life we need not goodness but strength; not humility but pride; not justice but power; not altruism but intelligence of the finest order. Ideas of equality and democracy are incompatible with the principle of selection and survival, for the goal of evolution must be seen, not as the triumph of the masses but as the emergence of the genius or the superman. And, significantly, Nietzsche was writing at a time when Bismarck, denying any altruism among nations, was most successfully pursuing his blood and iron policy, humbling France and fusing the various German states into one formidable empire. In his one important educational piece of writing, *The Future of our Educational Institutions* (1872), Nietzsche argues that we need neither cultural philistines nor a superficial culture of the masses. True education can never be utilitarian. Knowledge can never be a substitute for culture. True culture is only possible through the fullest development of the personality, and this development involves a process in which "every conquest, every step forward in knowledge, is the outcome of courage, of hardness, of cleanliness towards oneself". The weak in spirit must and will be annihilated. The few must dominate, and it is on the few we must concentrate our attentions so that the superman may emerge.

9

Thus, as Europe moved out of the traumatic experience of the French Revolution and Napoleonic Wars to cope with nineteenth-century problems of industrialisation which tended to be resolved on a basis of the assertion of a national identity (first fostered by the Napoleonic Wars), so did three main trends in European thought emerge on lines which the Aufklärer had first glimpsed. The Anglo-Saxons, essentially empirical in their thinking, have also remained closest to that form of humanism typified by Erasmus. To the Lockeian doctrine that the liberty of the individual, his happiness and dignity must be the basic elements of all national life, and that the government of a nation is a moral trust dependent on the free consent of the governed, they have subscribed the belief that, in matters concerning truth, taste and the difference between right and wrong, every man must judge for himself; that the so-called religious virtues are nothing more than natural human virtues; that society must be so constituted that it serves and satisfies all human needs;[1] and that to be fired with a desire to seek out the source and criterion of all that is to be considered good, just and beautiful among the human gifts is a most laudible aim. In England the nation-state became a protective shell for the free interplay of individual forces, and individual privacy was meticulously respected.

In France, on the other hand, though she was originally inspired by the English model of constitutional liberty, her authoritarian traditions had not prepared the people for self-government and the limitation of the powers of the sovereign. Therefore, the absolute sovereignty of the king was replaced by the absolute sovereignty of the people, French nationalism stressing that the duty of the citizen lay in political activity, whilst his fulfilment must be found in accord with the nation-state. Thus society owes education to the child more for his own sake (as a future French citizen) than for the advantages he will reap from that education, the two most important tasks of the school system being those of (a) integration and (b) the making of citizens – "integration" meaning the maintenance of the moral and intellectual homogeneity of the whole nation. The ideal type sought is a Cartesian rationalist with all the civic and civilised virtues of Ancient Rome. The Ancients are studied in detail in order to arrive at a

---

[1] This idea was first put forward by Sir Thomas More in his *Utopia*, 1515–16.

concept of excellence. The study of mathematics yields the *esprit de géométrie*, a Pascalian quality of logical thinking. The whole is based on the desire to give to each and every child a *culture générale* which links in closely with the idea of *l'honnête homme* or *l'homme cultivé* which certainly goes as far back as Montaigne. And it is this centuries-old belief in the superiority of his own culture, the Frenchman regarding himself as the true heir to all that was best in Roman and Greek cultures, which can make him at times appear to others so irritatingly chauvinistic.

We have already shown how German intellectuals became increasingly irritated by the way in which the French way of life and culture dominated within the separate states of Germany. Growing resentment against Germany's intellectual subservience led the Germans earnestly to seek their own identity through a study of their heritage and the development of the theory of the folk soul, and German nationalism thus came to be characterised by a quest for meaning and a musing about the national soul and its mission. An intensive educational programme was used to develop a strong national spirit, and, as the Germans rejected French culture, so they found themselves more in sympathy with Anglo-Saxon attitudes, English Romanticism in particular making its appeal. Yet the fervour and intensity of the search for national identity by the intellectuals, allied to the Teutonic predilection for general ideas, led them into formulating their theories in academic isolation and growing dangerously politically ignorant. The Englishman has become (in a sense) a political animal. The Frenchman has been schooled to strive at all levels *ad maiorem Francorum gloriam* (for the greater glory of the French). The German has become introspective, self-absorbed, fervent in his allegiance to his *Land*.

Generally speaking, the Scandinavian countries can be said to have felt mostly the impact of Lutheranism and the implications of the doctrine *cuius regio eius religio*. Nineteenth-century possibilities for the rise of a kind of "Scandinavianism" to match the German movement were shattered when, in 1864, prudent Sweden refrained from going to the assistance of Denmark against Bismarck (resulting in the loss of Schleswig-Holstein by Denmark), and the "off-shore" position of the whole of Scandinavia has since been marked, particularly in the case of Sweden. As we have seen in Chapter 1, Holland, Belgium, the Grand Duchy of Luxemburg and Switzerland, by the happy chance of geographical situation, developed along their own idiosyncratic ways. They were, however, wide open to be influenced in their thinking by the greater powers, but realistic and sufficiently self-assured to take what suited them and shrug off the rest, even under domination by a greater power.

Italy, of course, with Florence as an important centre of the learning of the Renaissance, with Rome as the important focal point of Christendom for all Catholics, and with Rome equally the main inspiration behind a classical education, remained in close contact with all developments throughout Western Europe. Increasingly, however, she found herself searching for that identity so far denied her by the domination of her lands by the greater powers. Steeped in a form of humanism dating back to the prosperity of the various city states, she has thrown up sound and courageous thinkers who, throughout the centuries, have preached the important message of enlightened liberal principles, of toleration, of real democracy within a framework of conscious national endeavour. The first stirrings of the Risorgimento movement in the eighteenth century coincided with the first ferment caused by the *Aufklärer*, and, though the absolute mind of the Germans was quite alien to her realistic and mercurial temperament, she could show herself as idealistic as any German. Once the unification of Italy had become an accomplished fact in 1871, a peculiar Italian interpretation of the Hegelian ideal, perhaps best illustrated in the writings of Benedetto Croce (1866–1952), was soon manifest. Whilst retaining the Hegelian view that mind is fundamental to the universe, Croce has concentrated above all on the immediacy of changing individual experience. Life for him is a persistent moral struggle, an endless effort to create good out of evil and passion. Reality is to be found only in the progressive revelation of history, and history must be thought of not as just past, but here and now and endlessly becoming. Since 1871, a constant effort has been made to awaken the Italian to a full consciousness of his important heritage, and liberal idealists have never ceased in their attempts to shape the whole pattern of instruction in the schools towards that end.

Spain and Portugal, though they dropped back in the march of ideas from the eighteenth century onwards and could only revert to the somewhat sterile traditions of their past greatness, still kept the classical spirit alive. Spain in particular came under the influence of French culture, and, in common with the Germans, the Italians and the Portuguese, Spaniards were indebted to the French for first introducing them to English literature and styles of thought. Yet national pride and a deep-rooted sense of national honour stopped foreign influences from ever holding too great sway. Spain might create an Academy (1714) and start work on a national dictionary (1726), but in the long run she was determined to remain herself and shrug off what she deemed to be the passing whims and fancies of the times.

10

Other than on its traditional base of Graeco-Roman-Judaic influences, where, then, can the oneness of Western Europe be said today to reside? Has not the diversity of aims and interests which have evolved throughout the centuries eroded the feeling for unity originally there? Have not national upsurges of feeling worked their own insidious poison through the whole? Was Voltaire too naïve and too simplist in his view of Europe as one great family: "a kind of great republic comprising several states, some monarchical, some mixed; some aristocratic, some democratic, but all in relationship with one another, all having the same fundamental religious basis even though sectarianly divided, all having the same principles of public law and the same political ideals, all unknown in other parts of the world"?[1]

It is perhaps as a family — a large, quarrelsome yet closely-knit family — that we can best view Western Europe and so get things into proper perspective. Her real strength is that, though belonging to the same civilisation, she has seen each separate nation-state develop its own cultural values. Her originality, indeed, depends on her diversity, and this diversity of interests has made modern Europe of much greater worth than the ancient world as it has given her (certainly down to the nineteenth century) intellectual superiority over the whole world. Even as early as Montaigne (1533–1592), though the various nationals of Europe might dress differently and have different languages and customs, they travelled widely throughout their "estate", Montaigne himself taking an eager interest in frequenting as many as possible of the fellow members of this one great "family", noting with approval what could be usefully cherished, and disapproving of what he considered to be non-civilised and therefore unworthy. By the eighteenth century European travel had become almost

[1] Flammarion, *Siècle de Louis XIV*, Volume One, p. 10.

a habit for the well-to-do European, an apprenticeship to living (as Locke considered it), the finishing touch to education, and the various divergent customs and institutions were now readily accepted as part of the *European* way of life, thereby implying their intrinsic worth and superiority to whatever was to be encountered elsewhere in the "outer" world. This "outer" world, of course, had become a place for adventure, for the seeking of glory and profit. There was no intention of seeking closer cultural ties with the people who inhabited it. On the contrary, the blessings of European civilisation were to be extended to those "beyond the pale" – thrust upon them where necessary or commercially expedient – the European contenting himself with shrewdly borrowing from these peoples ideas or inventions (printing, gunpowder, the compass) which he could most purposefully put to good use on his own account. So did the missionary zeal of Europe acquire its impetus. And so have we now recently been witnessing the back-lash effect.

If, however, we seek to pinpoint the two outstanding characteristics of European man, then these must be noted as his unquenchable passion for arriving at the truth and the tremendous importance he attaches to man's worth, man's dignity, man's place in the universe. From these all else stems. Through the method of deductive reasoning originating among the Greeks, *Homo sapiens* separated himself from *Homo faber* – and in the process came to view all forms of manual dexterity as but second best, mechanical contrivances (though useful) as merely evidence of man's ability to conquer the universe. European man has refused to accept that what is must be so of necessity. Or, as Lessing put it: "What constitutes man's worth is not the truth he possesses, or thinks he possesses. It is the sincerity of the effort he makes to approach the truth." Similarly the Christian message, allied to the philosophies of ancient Greece and of the Hebrews, has ensured that all philosophers throughout the centuries, and down to modern times to include the Catholic Gabriel Marcel or the atheistic existentialist Jean-Paul Sartre, have had *man* as the central and focal point of their thinking. European man divorces himself from the rest of nature and will allow her no share in the moral struggle he must constantly wage. His approach is theocentric and anthropocentric with the importance of the individual held constantly in view. In similar terms the Chinese could be called "cosmocentric" since they neither separate the individual from society as a whole, nor isolate society from nature, stressing at all times the perfect harmony which should reign between the social and the universal order. Various forms of Indian culture would seem to view man's personality as the outstanding obstacle to be overcome if man is ever to attain perfect union with the Absolute. It is tempting (and perhaps rash) to push this kind of classification further and suggest that, whilst the Russians and their satellites have tended to merge the individual with the state to have their aspirations identical, the Americans have made of him a kind of cipher for the great American dream.

European man, by virtue of the intellectual tools he has fashioned for himself, has come to attach the greatest importance to knowledge, which he sees as a system of intelligible truths which can be rationally demonstrated. His prime concern has always been with the nature of man, the nature of society, and the nature of knowledge itself. Unlike the Moslem, he cannot accept that knowledge may not be altered or changed, and, though he can accept with the Moslem that we are moving towards the world-to-be, there is no room in his philosophy for the Moslem's fatalism or lack of concern for his future. His is the empirical way to truth and insistence on reasoned and logical explanation. His quest is the *natural law*, for he holds that nature, both human and physical, expresses her purpose in her structure; that she follows consistent and permanent laws; that she speaks to us in detail, and that it is only through a complete understanding of the detail that we can build up a pattern which can at least give us glimpses of the grand design. Descartes argued that experience is not in itself a method. Method arises in the interpretation of experiences, and we must move from the particular to the general to the universal in a rigorously determined order. Newtonian physics did the rest, and European scientific method, becoming a combination of the empirical and the rational, the experimental and the logical, has (at least until recently) put European man intellectually far ahead of all other peoples in all fields of human endeavour.

Finally, what has been unique in all this has been man's concern for man, and the way in which this concern has (even in the darkest moments of history) never been wholly lost to view. The Holy Inquisition had its own peculiar logic to sustain it. Colonisation might have manifested at times an almost cynical disregard for the peoples who were being exploited, but the colonising peoples of Europe saw themselves as conferring the blessing of a superior civilisation and way of life on the exploited.

Europeans could again take a firm stand on principles of individual liberty and liberty of conscience, and (like Sir Thomas More and so many others) pay the exacted penalty rather than degrade themselves and (to themselves as well as to others) betray the unique nature of man. For, holding himself aloof from the rest of nature the better to understand and control it, European man had of necessity to make himself of prime concern. Similarly, in grappling with the meaning of the universe he was creating tensions (important to his intellectual development) between the real and the ideal, between the meaning of this world and the next. The structure of the world in proportion as he mastered it led him increasingly to seek the good life here on earth, not as the Moslem solely for immediate profit but as a necessary step forwards in understanding and perfectibility. This again focussed attention on individual man and led to the creation of a kind of prototype of essential man towards which all would aspire. The writings of Erasmus and Montaigne alone clearly reveal that by the sixteenth century there was emphasis on the full and all-round development of the human personality; a belief that each individual must be prized for himself and for the contribution he can make; that freedom is precious and must often be dearly bought; that all men have a claim to liberty and justice; that the state in consequence cannot impose arbitrary laws but must seek them in the nature of human relations. From all of this has resulted that precarious balance between power and dissent, between conservatism and innovation, between freedom and constraint (well exemplified in the school systems), which has been made to work and which in consequence has become traditional to the European way of life.

CHAPTER 3

The Traditional Elements in European Education

1

Today, then, the various nation-states of Western Europe, conscious of the differences in cultural attitudes amongst themselves as they are equally conscious of belonging to a greater whole, can be said to have certain marked characteristics as nation-states.[1] Firstly, they are conscious of their numerical size, as also of the relative strengths, weaknesses and influence of sub-groups, and try to effect as harmonious a balance as possible between constantly conflicting interests. The smaller the nation-state, and we must remember such states as Lichtenstein, Luxemburg, Andorra and Monaco, the more proudly does it assert its uniqueness and find greater harmony amongst its inhabitants whilst for all practical purposes conforming to social and economic pressures about it. Secondly, all nation-states, large and small, have today a geographical identity and are conscious of themselves as clearly defined human groups who through various accidents of history have acquired a certain territory on which they have been proud to leave their own indelible cultural imprint. Thirdly, they each constitute a clearly defined political entity in that, both to safeguard their common interests and also to co-ordinate the conflicting interests within the group, they have submitted themselves to the direction of one central and *representative* authority, in various ways carefully limiting its overall powers. They are fourthly each an economic unit, bound together by common economic interests, vowed to safeguard basic national industries and economic interests, and latterly having to face up to the fact that for individual

---

[1] This is not to argue, of course, that such characteristics are peculiar to the nation-states of Western Europe.

survival in competition with the greater powers in the world, they must in some measure pool economic resources and work towards economic and financial stability for the whole of Western Europe. They are fifthly clearly marked out as separate social units with their own customs, habits and ways of life which together carefully regulate most forms of social intercourse, social intermingling, schooling, and certain aspects of domestic life. Lastly, each nation-state may be said to constitute a separate moral unit with common traditions, memories and aspirations, and this moral climate of opinion is such that it transcends all problems of race, language and religion. Belgium, for example, accepts three national languages (French, Dutch and German). Switzerland accepts four (French, German, Italian and Romansche). And Holland has organised its school system largely on a basis of the religious persuasions of parents. True, most Western European countries have witnessed struggles (often extravagent and acrimonious) between church and state for the control of education, but these would seem to have been in some measure resolved in the aftermath of the Second World War.

Yet all these separate manifestations of individuality are, as we have seen earlier, co-related in various ways to the extent that they combine to form the greater whole of Western European culture. There has been a constant cross-fertilisation of ideas from one nation-state to another, constant borrowing and adaptation, and above all tremendous insistence on acquiring knowledge of the right kind in what was thought to be the right way – through processes of deductive reasoning. Hence the importance attached to analysis, to getting to the simple through the complex, and to ideas behind things. Knowledge has come to be defined as a system of intelligible truths which can be rationally demonstrated, and it is constantly stressed that all evidence put forward must not only be intelligible but also made intelligible to all. Educational institutions have, in consequence, been slowly developed to serve these ends, the school coming to be regarded primarily as a place for the acquisition of culture and not as a kind of professional factory, and the intellectual acquiring his own special place in the social hierarchy.[1] Economic factors (as we

[1] Compare, for example, the awe in which a German professor can still be held. Consider also the social cleavage (based on so-called intellectual superiority) which still tends to persist between the elementary school *teacher* and the (academic) secondary school *master* or *professeur*.

have again seen earlier) have contributed to the rise of an urban civilisation, and on this basis school systems everywhere have been used both as agents of urbanisation, adapting their pupils to life in cities rather than in the countryside, and also as enabling institutions for children of proved and outstanding ability to rise in the social hierarchy.

2

By the beginning of the nineteenth century two distinct but parallel types of schooling had begun to emerge. For the many there was the "short" elementary school designed to train literate, patriotic and morally sound workers. For the few there was an academic type of education geared to producing an élite of scholars, leaders and gentlemen. Industrialisation both forged and highlighted new divisions of the people into two main social classes — an urban middle class and an industrial working class — and the strivings of these two groups to establish their separate identities generated political energy which, in both cases, came to insist on an extension of educational provision by direct state intervention. And so, as the twentieth century ushered in problems that are still with us and becoming increasingly complicated, so could education now be seen in its broadest aspects as having become four-dimensional in nature.

First and most important was the class dimension which assumed that each social class must of necessity have its own peculiar form of education, and which also cut right across all forms of religious belief — this perhaps being most marked in predominantly Catholic countries. Thus, in France, the (Catholic) aristocracy would send their sons away to be educated in prestigious Jesuit schools, their daughters to convent schools. If they were to be educated at home, then the choice would be a famous *lycée* or Catholic *collège*. The urban middle classes favoured the state *lycée*, the child entering the preparatory department for his primary instruction and progressing upwards to sit eventually the coveted *baccalauréat*. The industrial working class and the peasantry had the state elementary system which awarded a leaving certificate, theoretically taken at age 14 but which could be taken earlier by a bright child (when, of course, he could leave school), and also the higher elementary school which awarded its further leaving certificate to guarantee either possible acceptance in a teacher-training college to train as an *elementary* school teacher or immediate employment in a host of minor civil service jobs. Nor must we forget that the efforts of the Jesuits to provide Catholic academic secondary education for those who could afford to pay for it were matched principally by the creation of the Christian schools by La Salle in 1684. In forming his order of the Brethren of the Christian Schools, La Salle made the first systematic effort to organise popular education on behalf of the Catholic church. The schools were free and he would have made education obligatory for all. He stressed the importance of a properly trained cadre of teachers. And with rare foresight he began the organisation of technical instruction for the poor by opening near Rouen a school to prepare its pupils fittingly to occupy various commercial, industrial, and administrative positions.

What we may term the family dimension can be seen as the next in importance. By this we mean the pressures exerted by the family for education to be acquired in a certain way and over a certain period of time, either in a church or state institution according to tradition or beliefs. A peasant family would seek the absolute minimum of education in order to get extra hands at work as soon as possible in the fields, on the farms and in the vineyards.[1] Working-class families would rarely go beyond the minimum necessary to acquire basic skills, and would certainly never aspire to any form of higher academic education for their children.[2] The urban middle class, growing steadily more prosperous and more self-assured, and throughout the nineteenth century increasingly coming to regard themselves as the "new" aristocracy, sought the best education available – and in their view this was given, for example, either in the public schools of England (until then largely a traditional aristocratic preserve), or in the Jesuit colleges of France, and certainly in the Napoleonic French *lycée*. That the teaching in such institutions was remote from real-life situations, conferring no immediately realisable benefits,

---

[1] The distinguished French Catholic philosopher, Gustave Thibon, is such an example. He passed his primary school leaving examination at the age of 12 and immediately went to work in his father's vineyards in the Dordogne. From then onwards he slowly and painstakingly educated himself.

[2] This is still true. Available statistics show the universities to be mainly peopled by students of middle-class origins, and the working class loth to avail themselves of present opportunities for their promising children to profit from an academic secondary education.

merely served to enhance its value: it was the well-disciplined mind which counted, in theory at least then able to tackle and solve any problem as it presented itself. Thus, at the family level, and first of all only as far as the prosperous bourgeoisie were concerned, attention came to be increasingly focussed on education as a means to social advancement. Because this education was, however, "unreal" in the eyes of the mass of the people, they felt more or less content with what was on offer at the elementary and higher elementary levels, their one clear path to any kind of social advancement (or increased respectability in the eyes of their neighbours) consisting of having a son become a priest or a son or daughter enter the teaching profession – at the elementary levels, of course.[1]

I think we may safely call the third dimension an intellectual one, and it relates most closely to what has just been said. The grammar schools of England, the *collèges* and *lyceés* of France, Italy and Belgium, the *Gymnasien* of Austria, Germany and Scandinavia became firmly wedded to a kind of humanistic education based largely on close study of the classical languages, and this had been (in general terms) outlined for them as early as the sixteenth century by Erasmus and given its first practical application in the refounding of St. Paul's School in London by Dean Colet in 1509. True, writers of the Enlightenment made their mark from the eighteenth century onwards when they were first able to see schools established specifically for the training of those who would be employed in a widening range of skills and professions – this following closely on the ideas of La Salle – but such schools as were established were, paradoxically, held distinct from the truly academic school whilst closely imitating its general approach in an attempt to make these more mundane studies more academically respectable. In Germany, for example, the *Realschule* (the title is significant) came into existence as early as the seventeenth century, and was closely modelled on the ideas put forward by Comenius (1592–1671) who sought a general education which would teach *all* men *all*

---

[1] There is much literature available of a fictional or semi-autobiographical nature to illustrate many of the points made throughout the whole of this section. For Italy read Bassani's *Behind the Door* and *Letter to a Teacher* by pupils from the school at Barbiana; for France consult Vaillant-Couturier's *Enfance*, Saint Pierre's *Les Nouveaux Aristocrates* and Crémieux's *Le Premier de la Classe*; for Austria, Musil's *Young Törless*; for Germany, Thomas Mann's *Buddenbrooks* and *Tonio Kröger*. These are but a few suggestions. Consult also my article in *Comparative Education, IV* (3) June 1968.

subjects of human concern. Throughout the next two centuries the *Realschule* acted as an effective counterbalance to extreme attitudes in the German *Gymnasium* and began to give the kind of education most needed by those who would be entering trade or commerce. It was not empowered, however, to present its students for the *Abitur* (and so for entry to university) until well into the twentieth century. Today, whilst the entire structure of German secondary education is being radically revised, the classical *Gymnasium* holds only third place in popularity to first of all the *Realgymnasium* which emphasises the teaching of Latin and one foreign language (usually English) together with more instruction in mathematics and the natural sciences, and the *Oberrealschule* which has no Latin but two modern languages and again emphasises science and mathematics.

In point of fact, the pressures resulting from industrialisation led throughout Western Europe generally to the creation of various kinds of "real" schools, but if not closely modelled on the traditional classical school (and some came increasingly to be so) these schools were at pains to prove that the treatment of more modern subjects could be as academically exacting as that of the classical tongues. So it was that when the teaching of a modern language became imperative it was often felt that it should be taught along the well-tried (and dessicated) approach used to impart a knowledge of Latin or Greek. The Belgian creation of the *école moyenne* in 1850 and the story of its development down to modern times is as good an illustration as any of the way most such schools fared. The *école moyenne* was originally intended to be a school for the children of the lower middle classes and of ambitious working-class parents, the supposition being that the brighter and more ambitious pupils would (after a three-year course between the ages of 12 and 15) automatically transfer to the upper forms of the classical-type secondary school. By the school law of 1881, admission to the *école moyenne* was put on par with that to the secondary school proper; it was allowed in its own right to give its own form of secondary education; and the first two years of instruction were made identical with that in the prestige establishment. A fourth year was added to the course in 1897 to give increased and better opportunities to those who would not go on to the academic school. In 1924, work in the three basic classes of the *école moyenne* was made identical with that in the three lowest forms of the academic secondary schools; certain *écoles moyennes* were empowered to introduce Latin and Greek sections; others (in areas ill-served by the traditional secondary school) were allowed to attach to themselves the three upper forms of the traditional school and to function entirely as such a school without the name. In the long run, the *école moyenne* became nothing more than a faithful imitation of the prestige establishment, differing only in that it specialised in the teaching of "modern" subjects the more easily to fit its pupils for entry into the fields of industry and commerce.[1]

Nor did the intellectual dimension leave the primary school untouched. Significantly, the Germans have named it the *Grundschule* and demanded of it thorough instruction in the basic essentials of a sound, general education. And these essentials are variously listed as: confident oral and written use of the mother tongue; assurance with figures; familiarity with the objects and workings of nature; appreciation of poetry (and the arts in general); a knowledge of history closely geared to the study of the workings of a democratic society. The French have not dissimilar aims, stress the importance of a sound grasp of national history and geography if only to reinforce France's belief in the value of its traditional history and culture, and seek in the process to form conscientious and loyal citizens who will perpetuate the glory that is France. To try to make things too easy for the pupil – to try to sugarcoat the pill to the extent that it is all sugar and no pill – is to do the pupil a great disservice. "The teacher who seeks to please is but a confidence trickster", says Alain, the distinguished French philosopher and practising schoolmaster. "I find it preposterous that the choice can be left to children or to their families to learn this rather than that. Preposterous also to charge the state with wishing to impose this or that".[2] To sum up, the aim everywhere throughout Western Europe, even in the primary systems, has been to impart what the French call *une culture générale* with each individual entitled to receive the sum of knowledge common to all, more for his own sake as a future citizen of his

[1] See *Compare* (Journal of the British Section of the Comparative Education Society in Europe), *IV* (1). January 1974, for an account of how even the modern *scuola media unica* in Italy is still aridly intellectual.

[2] Alain, *Propos sur l'Éducation*, Presses Universitaires de France, 1948, pp. 33 and 35.

country than for the practical advantages he can reap from that education.[1]

The historical dimension subsumes all the above, deals with the forces of tradition, and relates to the cautious balance all countries have sought to maintain between traditional attitudes and innovatory ideas. A country is often loth to reject or even seriously modify an approach that has safely withstood the test of time even when the situation can be seen to have become most critical. And it is in this context that the French proverb, *plus ça change plus c'est la même chose*, must be used sympathetically and not cynically when applied to the countless attempts made at reforming the French educational system since 1945. When the experimental *classes nouvelles* were first started immediately after the last war, it was the parents who insisted that their children would not take part unless Latin remained firmly on the curriculum there. Parental attitudes, indeed, have had to be heeded everywhere whenever reform in education has been mooted. Nor can the entrenched interests, status and professional expertise of the teaching cadre be neglected. Parents and teachers have been vociferous in England and Wales over the closure of well-tried grammar schools in favour of larger (and in their view anonymous) comprehensive units. Despite the growing cost of maintaining a complicated system of "free" schools belonging to private trusts, towns, communes, or religious bodies throughout Holland, the Dutch still insist on the parents' rights to their own convictions in the bringing up of their own children.

In matters religious, indeed, it can be fairly claimed that it is only in Great Britain that the old controversy between church and state as to who shall be responsible for education has been finally settled – though (incidentally) Great Britain is probably the one country in which parents have least say (unless they happen to be rich enough to afford private education) in the choice of school their child shall attend! Elsewhere in Western Europe the aftermath of the last war saw a determined effort to arrive at some acceptable compromise between the two contenders. The

---

[1] Many Frenchmen with whom I have discussed the matter would agree with me that the one Western country coming nearest to achieving the French ideal of *une culture générale* is, paradoxically perhaps, America – though, of course, the intellectual rigour so dear to the French is conspicuously lacking. But is that necessarily a condemnation?

Schools' Pact of 1959 in Belgium and the later decrees of De Gaulle in France in effect made substantial grants from the public purse to the maintenance of Catholic schools and sought to guarantee parity of esteem for all properly qualified teachers in such schools with those serving under the state systems. Nevertheless, it is important to remember that in Belgium, even today, slightly more than half of the school population is educated in Catholic schools, and that a recent opinion poll conducted in France revealed that almost 40 per cent of parents of children of school age would (given the opportunity) prefer to have their children educated in Catholic schools. Nor should we forget that an Italian government was recently defeated by the Catholic party over its intention to establish a much-needed state system of nursery school education.

Generally speaking, the Catholic church, whilst nowadays accepting the right of the state to create and maintain its own schools, willing even to allow Catholic parents to opt to send their children to a state school rather than to a Catholic one, still maintains its traditional vigilance in all matters educational. It is in the Catholic tradition that boys and girls must be educated separately in separate schools once the nursery stage is over, boys then having male teachers. It is equally traditional that secondary education, particularly of the purely academic kind (and also technical education), shall be mainly a masculine preserve. True, the most recent reforms in education in all Catholic countries have considerably eased the position, but in actual practice it is lip-service paid to the principles of co-education rather than co-education in the sense in which it is understood in American schools, and the percentage of girls in academic secondary education still remains everywhere low.

It is, in conclusion, when we come to consider reform movements in education that we realise how strong have been the forces of tradition almost everywhere. The classical languages still retain their prestige even where they may no longer be the backbone of the secondary school curriculum. Greek may go, in favour (usually) of a second modern foreign language, but Latin remains, and the foreign language teaching, at the top levels of the school at least, is made to be as exacting as possible.[1]

---

[1] The author was recently privileged to take part in an English oral examination required of pupils submitting themselves for the *Abitur* in Land Hesse (Germany). Each pupil read aloud a passage he had been given about twenty minutes to prepare.

Again, in marked contrast either with American practice, which "graduates" pupils from High School on a range of subjects of their own choosing, or British practice which demands study in depth of only three closely related subjects before applying for university entrance, Western Europe generally insists upon still turning out the educated man in the humanist sense: six or even seven subjects can be required, all studied to the same level and made to counterbalance one another, so that future scientists must have modern languages and future arts graduates at least mathematics – that great stimulator of logical thought processes and careful deductive reasoning. Present reforms in education have not seriously affected this basic structure to such examinations as the *Abitur* or the *baccalauréat*. On the contrary, what I will term this humanist approach has been strengthened first of all by the invention of the *European Baccalauréat* on offer to children attending the various European schools created to serve the needs of parents working administratively or commercially within the framework of the EEC, and secondly by the launching of an *International Baccalauréat* so persuasively championed in Great Britain by Alec Peterson, former Director of the Oxford University Department of Educational Studies. All this has in turn prompted rumblings for reform of current British practice along similar lines.

Historical precedent, however, can be seen most firmly entrenched in the ways in which all countries at first reacted to pressures for change as they built up after the last war. The first attempted solution was to create entirely new institutions and leave the basic pattern unimpaired. Only when this was proved inadequate were more radical solutions attempted. It had to be demonstrated all over again that, despite reform, the links between short- and long-term (academic) education were still too few and far too tenuous. If it was finally grasped that selection processes for some form of "long" education at the age of about 12 were not properly fulfilling the alleged purpose of making for equality of opportunity, even on a basis of free and universal education, it was only after much heart-searching that selection was abandoned in favour – usually not of a common school for all between the ages of 12 and 15 so that decisions as to the child's future could be postponed as long as possible and so help the

He was then closely questioned (in English) not only to ensure that he had understood the passage but also to stimulate a quite searching discussion on literary style, philosophical content and implications, and relative importance to present-day issues.

"late-developer" – but of a so-called "common-core" curriculum between 12 and 15 to be given in the various existing establishments. Of course, economic factors were speciously quoted as being the main reason for this. Financial stringency would not permit a lavish supply of new, purpose-built institutions. The result was, not surprisingly, that if a child happened to attend an academic secondary school to work through the "common-core" part of his studies he had advantages (if only accruing from the quality of the teaching staff) denied his peers elsewhere and so stood a very good chance of remaining where he had started.[1]

Meantime Sweden, over years of careful thought and experimentation (backed by lavish financial grants-in-aid) had evolved for itself its own peculiar form of comprehensive school based on the philosophy of *suum cuique* and not *idem cuique* (not "the same for everybody" but "to each his own"). Perhaps originally inspired by the American High School, it carefully fitted itself to European academic commitments. The rest of Europe had to take notice. And so, gradually over the last several years, other European countries have worked out for themselves individual types of comprehensive education which in each case closely align themselves with national and cultural aspirations. For the student of comparative education it becomes a fascinating exercise to note variations from country to country, to account for these, and to attempt a prediction on a basis of the causes of variations of possible outcomes and future problems. All this, however, must be left to a later chapter. We now need to look more specifically at traditional European attitudes as a whole.

3

We have, I think, already said enough to make clear that educational systems are determined by a nation's convictions about what it, as a nation, both needs and seeks. And when we come to look more closely at the Western European approach as a whole we see the general aim as not to achieve manpower but rather manhood. Education is interested

---

[1] Diagrams printed in Appendix 2 show how different reforms have been implemented at different times by various countries, France proving a most interesting study. All, however, merit close attention.

primarily in the development of human beings through the development of their minds, concerned with enabling man to develop to the full his potential, rather than with fitting him into a preconceived system. It is accepted without question that education and culture must have the same aims; that educational systems must be determined by the prevailing culture patterns; and it follows that any move towards educational reform is more likely to be the result rather than the cause of alteration in social perspectives. The one important role education is called upon to play is that of constantly making moral and value judgements, training pupils in the process to be constructively critical, and so gradually leading to a healthy shift in emphasis on various values – transforming them, even – in accord with changing social requirements.

Concomitant with all this, however, runs the almost unquestioning acceptance of a highly stratified society, the necessity for such stratification, and the organisation of education to meet the requirements of such a society. It has to be acknowledged that the sheet anchor for Western European continuity has been throughout the centuries the existence of sovereign national states, based on a firmly established social order consisting of a prosperous property-owning and merchant middle class which has not scorned constantly to expand itself by the absorption of increasingly larger segments of the working class. How this has worked itself out in practice is perhaps best illustrated and highlighted by the example of Belgium, so recently a sovereign national state. Belgian merchants, becoming increasingly more prosperous and self-sufficient, owing nothing to anybody and everything to their own individual efforts, rose to real importance and power from the end of the eighteenth century, as the older and aristocratic bourgeoisie found itself unable to adapt itself to changing economic conditions in which individualism and free competition were given full scope. It was this new bourgeoisie which found a revolution on its hands in 1830, restored law and order and created a separate sovereign state and educational system vowed to the preservation of its own firmly held principles of what democracy is all about. In the field of education this has meant that it must be the responsibility of the state to provide a sound education for everybody and yet at the same time sort out most carefully the élite, capable of inspiring others by their example to greater effort, and showing that anyone of proven ability can join that élite. It is firmly held that every healthy society needs its élite, and that false conceptions over equality of opportunity can dangerously lower standards both of intellectual attainment and also of national vitality. There is no reason, however, why this élite should be chosen from only one class. Demonstrably, this new bourgeoisie has brought Belgium safely through crisis after crisis and in consequence has constantly recruited to its ranks anybody from any walk of life possessed of industry, ability and promise. The structural pattern of education has been deliberately evolved to this end. That it has accepted a clear differentiation between the functions of primary and post-primary education and led to the children of the middle and upper classes receiving the best schooling matters little provided adequate steps are taken constantly to rejuvenate these classes from below. We have already noted how, with the creation of the *école moyenne* as early as 1850, Belgium was among the first of Western European countries to provide the necessary "bridge" to try to resolve the problem.

When we come to look at the schools themselves we find the approach almost diametrically opposed to that of the Dewey-inspired American school. For Dewey, the school is not a preparation for life but life itself. The European would have his school a kind of protective oasis in which the child is given a training *not* to prepare him for the outside world but rather to protect him against the corruptive influences of society – a school in which the child imbibes a culture which can be shown to transcend the constantly changing requirements of politics and the economic situation. Only when this has been done, it is argued, can we turn to the task of preparing the child to fill a specific role in society. The French sociologist, Emile Durkheim, puts this approach in more practical terms when he argues that education's aim is to develop in the child "a certain number of physical, intellectual and moral qualities which are expected of him both by political society collectively and by the particular environment in which he is destined to live as an individual". Alain in turn argues that the school is a very necessary disciplinary antidote to the cocooning nature of the family which does not allow the child to develop his potential to the full. "In his family, the child is not himself since he borrows and imitates attitudes not proper to his age . . . the school is the natural milieu for the child" isolating him from the turbulence of human affairs. "The school is a society apart, distinct from the family, distinct from the society of men" and where serious study of things that matter forms the best apprenticeship to living. In reality, and in his own idiosyncratic way, Alain, is highlighting that peculiarity of the European approach which (Great Britain apart) seeks to separate *instruction* from *education*. *Education* — by which is meant formal training in the social graces, religious observances, traditional (family) attitudes, etc. — is more properly the task of the home. The school's task is austerely to provide *instruction* and stretch the child's intellectual capacities to their fullest potential. Naturally (and Alain would be the first to admit this), where *instruction* is properly given much of it will be inescapably *educative*, but this must be seen as an important by-product and not as the main aim.

And the *instruction*? Firstly it derives from the humanistic belief that the most important knowledge for mankind is knowledge of man, and it is to be gained primarily from the study of literature, of history, and of moral philosophy. But withdrawal from the present is necessary to get everything in proper focus. Because the child is looking to the future, "it is not the last achievements of man we must have him study but the first" (Alain). Our civilisation is based on that of Greece and Rome, and there we must return. Classical literature contains all the indispensable insights, is the repository of that essential wisdom needed to maintain the values of civilised existence. All this must be supplemented by the teaching of mathematics and science, but with geometry and physics especially singled out as subjects of a more formal and logical nature to be enjoyed for their own sake and for the disciplinary value they have on the mind. Latin and geometry, says Alain unequivocally, teach the child to think, and that is their justification. In other words, in all this range of subjects to be taught, the aim is not the application of general ideas to specific problems out of school, but of appreciation, enjoyment, insight, and skill in handling words and symbols.

The abstract nature of all this kind of teaching is not questioned, if only because of the emphasis placed on analytical exposition, on formal argumentation, and on the acquisition of verbal skills. Man must be in a position to communicate with man in the fullest possible ways. And, if the manual skills are neglected, as well as any kind of learning or inquiry involving physical manipulation of the environment, this is because the abstract and the general are more accessible to the understanding of the child than natural objects which one cannot explain but which one can only dissect or observe. Alain's own defence in this respect is that geometry is the "key" study since the theoretician, the geometrician, is the one who best understands the "real"; he alone properly understands an eclipse.

If education, then, is an affair of thought, with the teacher thinking aloud in the pupils' presence with the object of stimulating in them further thoughts of their own, the correct mastery of language is most important. From the primary school upwards emphasis will be placed on the ability to speak, read and write the mother tongue, not only elegantly but with precision and incisiveness. All the literary skills must be mastered, and here again we must return to classical authors who provide the best examples to emulate. One must read incessantly, and, in spurring the child on to read, recourse in the schools must be made to passages which illustrate moral lessons which have transcendent validity, this being particularly true in the teaching of history.

Obviously, the role of the teacher is a key one and one which makes serious intellectual demands on him, even in the primary school. This also is taken care of. The professional status of the teacher is held to be of paramount importance – that is why in most European countries they are civil servants – but this professional status demands of him that he be sent to work where he is most needed and where his expertise can best be used. Again, since education is seen as being mainly concerned with thought processes, it is important to ensure as rigorous a training at his level for the embryonic teacher (whether primary, secondary or technical) as he in turn is expected to exact from his pupils. Hence the insistence on selecting only the very best of potential recruits available, and again only the best at the passing-out examinations, often on a highly competitive (and civil service) basis.

France offers the classical example with the award of its much coveted *agrégation*, it being no uncommon thing for a candidate to present himself years running and grow increasingly desperate as he sees himself approaching the fixed upper age limit of 30. Of course, changing post-war circumstances have led to the creation of a lower (less intellectually stringent) qualification for permanent appointment, the CAPES (*certificat d'aptitude au professorat de l'enseignement public du second degré*), but it is held and considered as a second-rate qualification for work in the secondary school sector. Similarly, work in the *école normale* (an institution formerly training teachers for the primary sector only) has been stepped up, with the aim of having each primary teacher obtain a university qualification the better to be able to work at the lowest end of secondary education in some consort with the more highly specialised university graduate who has opted solely for the secondary sphere. Yet emphasis, be it noted, tends everywhere to be placed on intellectual attainment rather than on teaching techniques, the unspoken theory behind this appearing to be that someone passionately interested in his subject will inescapably communicate his enthusiasm to his pupils. All this is again related to parental attitudes, conditioned over the years, which expect a teacher to "deliver the (intellectual) goods". So it can even today be said in France that a child will listen to a dull teacher, rag an incompetent one, and complain if the goods are not delivered. That great French essayist, Montaigne, best sums up the whole position when he claims: "I speak as one who questions because he does not know. I do not teach. I relate."

4

Naturally, reform movements everywhere are increasingly challenging this total traditional and peculiarly Western European approach, and our next concern must be to consider the impact and influence such movements have had. Meantime, we can best round off this chapter by reminding readers once again that the French, German and English traditions have proved most influential in shaping Western European attitudes to education and determining what form that education shall take. It is held that the mind can be trained to think abstractly, and correctly, to arrive at the truth; that certain subjects are of paramount importance (if correctly taught) in this training process; that character can be trained and personality developed through application to such studies, in depth, and that example (the role of the teacher) will be an important motivating force.

The Frenchman's standpoint is, of course, still very much Cartesian. All education depends on communication which must operate through that faculty common to all men: reason. Only that is true which can be comprehended, and that truth must be sought through the most rigorous application of reason. In this sense education is moral, truth and goodness of necessity being closely related, the very process of thinking one's way through to the truth becoming a moral decision. Individual responsibility at arriving at the correct decisions is stressed, and in consequence each individual is entitled to receive the sum of knowledge common to all, with no special consideration being shown for any particular individual as such. German education is primarily concerned with the moral personality and the inner freedom of the individual, and (apart from being used as a unifying force to weld the peoples of the various *Länder* into *one* nation, *one* culture, *one* state) has as its chief aim that of the transformation of man into a worthy being whose life is determined by the desire for values. Hence the prevalence of the ideal of a "general education" (*Allegemeine Bildung*) to be concerned with the whole of Nature and the whole of Man. The aim of education in Great Britain has been that of permitting the individual to achieve personal significance, and to participate fully in the social and political life of his country. It draws on a lengthy tradition of self-discipline and voluntary co-operation. Formal instruction in the school has never been prized as highly as in France or Germany, the discipline of experience being preferred to the discipline of school, the Englishman seeking his philosophy through action instead of determining his actions by principles of philosophy. Study is a means to an end and is not allowed to become an end in itself, the aim being above all to foster the development of personality through the training of moral character.

Put still another way we can say that France educates for individual responsibility within the centralising framework of the state; Germany educates for the strongly unified state; Great Britain educates for individual responsibility that makes the state. Or, as the late Sir Michael Salder once wittily put it' "The German is apt to ask about a young man, 'What does he know?' The American to ask, 'What can he do?' The Frenchman to ask, 'What examinations has he passed?' The Englishman's usual question is, 'What sort of a fellow is he?'"[1] The remaining democracies of Western Europe stress in varying degrees the importance of there being "no better baggage on a journey than much of knowledge". Scandinavia and Holland fall much under the spell of German intellectualism, Belgium less so if only because it tends to perpetuate the Jesuit cult of scholarship for its own sake and for the intellectual discipline thereby afforded. Italy rather more diffusely follows a path parallel to that of the French, but coming under the double influence of the Catholic church and the idealistic (Hegelian-inspired) philosophy of Benedetto Croce.

---

[1] Quoted by J. H. Higginson, An English scholar's studies of Education in Europe, *International Review of Education, I*, (2) 197-8.

CHAPTER 4

The Critical Moment

The land of humanism has become the Europe of today, the land of
inhumanity (Albert Camus).

1

That all would be well in Western Europe as she lumbered comfortably
out of the nineteenth and into the twentieth century was much more than
a pious hope. She commanded all the important world markets. She had
pioneered technological change on all fronts and was reaping the consequent financial rewards. Advances in medicine and hygiene had led to
an abrupt decline in the death rate (virtually static between 1840 and
1870) so that in the more advanced countries population soared: a mere
30 million increase between 1850 and 1870 had risen to 100 million in
the subsequent thirty years.[1] Concomitant with all this had come the rise
of a modern urban civilisation and a highly industrialised society so that,
whereas in 1900 Western Europe could boast only four towns with a
population of more than 1 million, by 1960 she had no fewer than five
with more than 2 million inhabitants and fourteen with between 1 and 2
million.[2] Inevitably, education became a much-debated issue, firstly by
industrial leaders as a means of securing more efficient manpower, secondly
by the working classes who saw it as a means of social advancement, and

[1] This figure includes some 40 per cent who were hived off by emigration.

[2] In 1900 North America had only three cities with a population of more than
1 million; South America had two such cities and Asia had three. By 1960 North
America had four cities of over 2 million and three over 1 million; South America
had four and four, respectively; Asia had eleven and fifteen. Russia is excluded.
For 1960, her figures are two and one respectively.

61

thirdly by humanitarians who looked upon it (provided it was of the right kind) as a much-needed panacea. The result was that throughout the nineteenth century education gradually became a government and public responsibility. It was then that teacher-training institutions were first established. By the end of the century interest in providing some form of equality of opportunity for the brightest of the educationally underprivileged was manifest; grants (however meagre) began to be made to promising youngsters, and opportunities for some form of post-primary education were widened.

In the period between the two World Wars more and more "bridging" schools were established to make for easier transition from primary to secondary education, more "modern" schools were opened, secondary technical schools began to appear, and the idea of a "common" school for all was first given serious consideration by the establishment in 1924 of a *Commission de l'École Unique*. Three years earlier (1921), the international nature of all the problems centred on modernisation of education was realised by the creation of the New Education Fellowship which, through regular national meetings geared to frequent international conferences, gathered together some of the most influential and persuasive of educationists and so made possible many of the reforms which are now taken for granted.[1] None the less, this period remained very much a doldrum period. Whilst education became generally free and in theory open to all, access to secondary education was still *selective* rather than *elective* − a principle which even today would seem to have been fully applied only within the Swedish comprehensive school system, and even there running into some difficulties. It had to be recognised that to achieve Condorcet's aim and ideal as expounded to the French revolutionaries in 1792 cost money, and that that money was just not being made available.[2]

What finally needed to be realised was that as education in the pre-scientific and pre-technical age had been humanist and thus well-suited to

---

[1] Consult Boyd and Rawson, *The Story of the New Education*, London, 1965.

[2] "The degree of equality in education we can reasonably hope to obtain", wrote Condorcet (1743−94), "is that which excludes all dependence, either forced or voluntary . . . . We shall prove that, by a suitable choice of syllabus and methods of education, we can teach the citizen . . . to be able to manage his household, administer his affairs and employ his labours and his faculties in freedom; to know his rights and to be able to exercise them."

an essentially unchanging and settled way of life, education must now begin to be seen in terms of the rapid shifts, changes and vicissitudes of modern existence. The demands of a technological age cannot be ignored, but at the same time the value of the individual needs stressing perhaps as never before as we move into an increasingly mechanistic and depersonalised age. To use the Latin tag, we need *Homo faber et sapiens*, which can roughly be paraphrased as technological man who is above all conscious of the individual's worth – humanistic in a strictly modern sense. We are in effect now witnessing a disintegration of the bourgeois synthesis (on which I have already dwelt lengthily) based on that humanistic tradition which has dominated Western Europe since the Renaissance. In short, as historians repeatedly tell us, there come times when humanity swings out of old paths and abandons a well-marked route to turn in entirely new directions. The period of the Renaissance and Reformation is the most recent example of this. The first half of the twentieth century can now clearly be seen as heralding a similar period of revolutionary change and crisis. The new synthesis which Western Europe seeks could well be acclaimed by future historians as a kind of second Renaissance.

2

Meantime, Western European man finds himself in what I can best describe as a kind of Hegelian dilemma. In attempting to do what he would *will* to do he is so often led into doing that which he did not originally intend. Conflict ensues. The unintention has somehow to be resolved. Accommodation is the outcome with which nobody is really satisfied. Never before in his history has Western European man been beset by so many problems and so many uncertainties at one and the same time. The main traditions on which a stable society was normally based have been undermined. The progress of science from determinism to indeterminacy has affected every field of human thought, including that of religious experience. The authority of the family has declined to the extent that its traditional role of giving advice and providing moral training has increasingly to be supplemented by other agencies. Everything is being organised into larger and larger units – the technical mass-order, as Karl Jaspers puts it – with the effect of robbing the individual life of meaning, significance and quality. We have made the illiterate masses literate (or tried to do so) but literate for what? More often than not they become the demagogue's tool and show themselves incapable of any meaningful constructive criticism.

Not unnaturally, amid all this uncertainty and perplexity, increasing attention has been paid to school systems and they have been looked to, probably as never before, at one and the same time to be both guardians of the cultural heritage of a nation and also innovatory forces. Their task has proved well-nigh impossible for two main reasons: firstly, because it has not yet been fully grasped that schools cannot make a stable world out of an unstable one since they can but reflect prevailing cultural attitudes; secondly, because the schools themselves have been overwhelmed by the consequences of what I have elsewhere termed the triple "explosion" – of knowledge, of population, and of aspirations. In the first fifty years of this century probably more scientific discoveries of far-reaching importance were made than in the preceding 500 years. Apart from the problem of how best to impart this knowledge and how best to slot it into the already overcrowded traditional and humanistic school curriculum came the consequences of the practical application of such discoveries which, as I have already instanced, led to an unprecedented rise in population figures everywhere, to the development of sprawling conurbations, and to the taxing of school resources and accommodation beyond all reasonable limits. At the same time material prosperity which generally resulted from the technical application of the new knowledge led to the working classes everywhere seeking a longer and more relevant kind of education for their children than had previously been provided in the terminal elementary school or even in various post-elementary forms of education so far provided. School systems were again ill-equipped to match up to such aspirations.

However, there were still further far-reaching consequences of the explosion of knowledge, the most striking being a gradual but progressive transformation in the role and function of the worker. More and more have poured into industrial occupations and fewer have stayed in agriculture. At the same time, because of sophisticated new techniques in both industry and agriculture, there has been a significant increase in the number of workers in the service industries.[1] The same new techniques,

[1] Consult Poignant, *L'Enseignement dans les Pays du Marché Commun*, Paris, 1965, p. 34.

leading to automation and increased mechanisation, have rendered numbers of unskilled workers redundant. This in turn has focussed attention on inadequacies in traditional educational provision. The "mix" has proved hopelessly wrong to cope. The obsolescence and irrelevance of much of the educational content and methods in use have been highlighted, and it has had to be recognised (often belatedly) that nowadays no educational system can afford to ignore prospective manpower needs and job opportunities. In proportion as this is recognised, so have other important conclusions to follow. Firstly, that we can no longer afford the luxury of having education seen as merely a preparation for life but must make it an integral part of life — even "an instrument of man's evolution" as Julian Huxley once put it. This means redressing the imbalance between formal and informal education, and, indeed, ensuring that education becomes a lifelong process. Secondly such is the complexity of the situation that education can no longer be left as the chief concern of private bodies or local authorities, for only the state is in a position to assure overall responsibility for overall educational policies. Thirdly, and because there must be increasing state control of education, it is important for planners to think in terms of people, of individuals, and not primarily of the abstract needs of society. Work must not only be financially but also psychologically rewarding. Fourthly, the gaps between a general education and a vocational education, as between humanistic and technical thinking, must be bridged. Nor must it be forgotten that increases at both a personal and a national income level have not necessarily been the result of either more or better formal educational facilities.

Of course, the obvious disparity between available educational facilities and the needs created by new social and industrial conditions has arisen primarily because of the sharp increase in popular aspirations for education allied to an acute scarcity of resources in the immediate post-war period. It has, however, also been caused by the inherent inertia of educational systems themselves and the reluctance of society as a whole to overcome its own inertia. For, whilst society might justifiably claim that the rapidity of population growth and aspirations has not given us time properly to readjust our thinking, it must also admit that it has not as yet properly faced up to the problems raised by universally extended schooling. It has not yet fully grasped the idea that in this modern age to be fully educated is not to have arrived at a predetermined destination but to be constantly travelling and preparing oneself adequately to meet every new eventuality that may arise. We need again, as the American Admiral Rickover once put it, to accept the diversity of man and every man's right to be himself. We need, in short, to recognise the inescapable historical fact that the intellectual development of any given society only expands to that point to which society requires it to expand. A kind of mental plateau is then reached when, because man can now supply his basic needs of livelihood and also earn prestige, there is no incentive either to add further to his skills or knowledge or to move from his comfortable "plateau". The sheer necessity in survival terms for making a move precipitates a crisis, throws society into disarray, and (if it is not to fall a victim to the historical processes of cyclic change) demands that by conscious acts of will it renovate itself.

3

Thus, reform movements in education have gradually gathered momentum throughout Western Europe since the stock-taking days of the immediate post-war period. All countries without exception find themselves faced with the same problems. And these problems all turn on the simple fact that the number of children seeking some form of post-primary education has grown out of all proportion to the birth rate bulge of post-war years, now showing signs of receding. It has followed from this that the main target for reform has been that of post-primary education, but at the same time primary education in all its aspects has had to be considered if only for the fact that children have also started to go to school earlier. Education has been prolonged to at least 15 or 16 years of age, mostly on a voluntary basis, so that the legal raising of the school-leaving age to beyond 14 has often proved necessary if only to regularise a trend. With an increasing demand for more and more opportunities in some form of post-primary education there has also resulted, firstly, a broadening of basic work achieved in the primary school proper and, secondly, a merging of the work now done in the upper classes of the primary school with that done in the lowest groupings in post-primary education. A. N. Whitehead's idea that education must be seen as a seamless robe is beginning to be realised. *Primary* education is now seen as basic for all classes of society, its very name indicating that it is only initial training, and the new primary school has everywhere replaced the former *elementary* school which was considered as providing sufficient terminal education for the masses of workers and was therefore frequented mainly by the children of the working classes.

It is again recognised that today's worker needs much more than basic training in manual skills or routine office work. He must be taught to think, to concentrate, to persevere, to become adaptable – for already technological developments indicate that the average worker must expect to have to change his approach and even re-learn his skills at least two if not three times during his working career. The schools, therefore, must prepare not only for employment but also for further study. They must create the right climate for securing adaptability. They must equally make for higher social mobility if only to ensure that the right people are employed on the right jobs, thus contributing both to their own self-fulfilment and to the economic well-being of the nation as a whole. But, as adaptability becomes more and more important, so does the need for a good general secondary education. As the need for greater social mobility is recognised, so is it grasped that there must be undifferentiated secondary education to as late an age as possible, with an integrated curriculum to replace the former crazy patchwork of differentiation. And, because the increasing complexity of modern living demands a corresponding increase in the numbers of men and women of high competence and ability to cope, so must the intellectual force of each individual be strengthened to the utmost. Once more we have the kind of Hegelian dilemma I spoke of earlier: there must be identity of opportunity for all, and yet a variety of new kinds of élites must emerge which must bring in their train new class differences.

Broadly stated, then, the main overall aim throughout Western Europe is the generalisation of secondary education in the belief that there are large reservoirs of ability still untapped. Equally, emphasis must be placed on increasing the educational chances of all those of proven ability. In practice this has so far led to ensuring that all should follow a basic general secondary education up to the age of at least 15 or 16 with specialisation then to follow. It has meant that the former "middle" school, socially and academically inferior to the traditional lower forms of the academic secondary school, has been made (as far as possible) academically "respectable" both by the upgrading of its offerings and also by its being ensured that the same offerings are available in both institutions. In other words, some kind of comprehensive secondary education for all has been secured up to the age of 15–16, even though offered in distinctly different institutions which can, with some justification, be labelled still as socially divisive. Thus, we find that between 1950 and 1965 enrolments in some form of secondary education trebled in France and Portugal; more than doubled in Spain and Italy; doubled in Eire, Holland and Norway; increased by about 75 per cent in Belgium, Denmark, England and Wales, Luxemburg and Sweden; and increased by less than half in Austria and Western Germany.[1]

More and more educational planning has become necessary if only to cope with the increased financial burdens involved. The central governments have had to assert themselves in areas where a decentralisation of authority had formerly been the rule, whereas the highly centralised control of education (as in France) has had to be relaxed to deal with specialised regional problems. The main problems, however, apart from finance, have centred on securing a sufficiently large and properly trained cadre of teachers to deal with ever-changing demands; on modernising a curriculum which is hopelessly out of date; on coping with the intractable problem of growing urbanisation as more and more people have left the land and flocked to service industries; on coping also with large influxes of immigrants, also to urban areas, where they have been glad to take on jobs despised by the bulk of the indigenous population.[2]

Indeed, in all highly urbanised countries real tension has been created between habitual and traditional forms of education and the challenges thrown up by an altered life style (complicated further by immigration problems) which insists on plurality development and full exploitation of every new possibility. It has had to be recognised also that the larger or more complex the urban area or conurbation the more intractable of solution become problems of poverty, of race, and of what I will call cultural sufficiency – by which I mean a certain stability and self-assuredness in family life which both make the child himself feel secure and also

[1] Consult OECD, *Development of Secondary Education*, Paris, 1969. In a later chapter we shall consider in some detail varying approaches to the problem of securing a comprehensive type of education for all between the ages of 12 and 16.

[2] About one-third of France's dramatic increase in population is due to immigration.

provide the impetus for him to take fullest advantage of all educational opportunities offered him. Despite every strategem so far adopted throughout Western Europe, the wastage rate in secondary education (by which is meant the proportion of those who leave school as soon as it becomes legally possible to do so) is still high. The immediate and pat answer to why this should be so turns on the tension we have just noted: both educational institutions and teachers, equally wedded to tradition, are conspicuously failing (a) administratively to change to allow for more pupil involvement, and (b) technically to make their courses more relevant and challenging to match the greater sophistication of today's student population.[1]

Whilst all this is true, it is only part of the answer. The really bedevilling factor is that it has to be admitted that the various systems of financing education bear little or no relationship to present needs and problems. They have been designed to further and perpetuate the Erasmian idea of what a civilised man should be and have tacitly accepted the premise that in any given social group there can not be at any time anything other than a small civilised nucleus. The bigger the nucleus, of course, the better for civilisation as a whole, and school systems have existed to encourage enlargement whilst also tacitly acquiescing in the assumption that there must always be a body of helots who will willingly serve the whims and wishes of a particular kind of "civilised" élite. It has been accepted as almost axiomatic that large numbers of children would wish to leave school as soon as they reached the statutory leaving age, and school building programmes have in consequence proved totally inadequate to cope with present demands. There are too few schools, too many in the wrong places, too few capable of being adapted to more sophisticated techniques and approaches nowadays required. It has been assumed that the brighter children need to have more spent on them in the provision of scholastic materials and amenities of all kinds than the less able, just as it has become almost traditional to claim that the brightest need the very

---

[1] The events of 1968 in France, when students from eight Parisian *lycées* joined a strike in support of workers' claims, dramatically illustrates feelings of frustration in (admittedly) a highly sensitive area. The students were originally 500 in number. By May, when the barricades went up, there were some 3000 *lycée* students involved with about 50,000 other young people from varying social backgrounds. When a general strike was declared, 10,000 *lycée* students became directly involved demanding the right to political action and administrative reforms in schools.

best of teachers to spur them on to a maximum peak of efficiency. Educational investment everywhere has favoured the education of boys rather than that of girls. And, for all the reasons just given, prosperous rather than poor areas have constantly been advantaged.

Only recently, indeed, has it been recognised that to come anywhere near achieving the laudable aim of equality of educational opportunity demands a drastic revision of attitudes right across the board, a firm commitment on the part of governments everywhere to do their best to overcome so many apparently insuperable factors. Firstly, there is the problem of what I will term geographical "isolation". The actual place of residence of a child's parents is far too decisive in determining not only where a child will begin his school career but also in affording him opportunities for further development according to his developing potential. The disadvantages a child will suffer when living in a remote rural area, where even today means of transport are not all that easy, in comparison with the advantages a child has living in a large thriving metropolis, are obvious. Not so immediately obvious, however, are the disadvantages facing a child within that metropolis should he be condemned to live in the poorer, run-down areas where violence is too often rife and teacher supply of the right kind difficult both to recruit and to keep. Nor are the school buildings and general facilities in such an area other than "run-down" themselves.[1]

Secondly, and stemming from all that has gone before, is the educational factor, turning not only on the actual structure of the school system, but on the curriculum offered in any given school, the capacity of the teaching staff to cope (academically) with the particular curriculum on offer, the state of preparedness of the staff to be innovatory and progressive in a realistic way – it being remembered that nowadays a child is being educated to take his place *not* in a stable world with

[1] Within the last five years the author visited a high school in North Dakota and one in Cleveland, Ohio. The school in Cleveland (sited in a well-to-do area on the periphery of the town) could easily match up to any academic secondary school in Western Europe and boasted a teaching staff of tremendous intellectual force and dedication. The school in North Dakota was a wooden construction of few classrooms and little or no laboratory facilities, visual aids, etc. The teaching staff were apathetic, apparently resigned to their lot, and without exception well passed middle age.

which he is familiar but in one he will have largely to create for himself. Important also is the head of the school whose vision and determination, provided administratively he is not hampered, can inspire confidence and trust and lead both teachers and taught to overcome what at times must appear (at least in disadvantaged areas) almost insuperable obstacles which, if not overcome, bring in their train lethargy, inertia, and finally despair.

The third and fourth factors militating against the achievement of equality of opportunity lie outside the schools systems proper, but for that very reason demand from governments the most close and immediate attention, particularly as it is at last seen that the only way to find a permanent solution is likely to be through speedy implementation of programmes of recurrent (or continuous) education. They turn, of course, on the home – on home influences and immediate environmental pressures. For some time it has been recognised that the level of parental education is a strong motivating force (or otherwise) to a child's scholastic achievements and ambitions, though it is only recently that it has been accepted that to attempt to "divorce" the pupil from his family background is bound to create tensions and in consequence be non-productive. The pupil must gradually be weaned from his background, and parents (and relatives) educated to give unqualified support to the weaning process. Hence, for example, the growing importance attached to guidance and counselling services everywhere, those offered in Belgium being perhaps of particular note because the Belgians were amongst the first to implement such services and have over the years elaborated and perfected them to cope with increasingly complicated demands.

Amongst these demands, common to the whole of Western Europe, must now be listed those concerned with language, with religion, and with race. In a multi-lingual society it is important to ensure that linguistic minorities are in no way disadvantaged, and the ways in which this is achieved in Belgium (where three languages hold parity of esteem) and Switzerland (where there are four languages) again merit attention. We have already touched briefly on the religious question as a "Catholic versus state" or Catholic–Protestant controversy, and here we should note not only how Belgium and France have sought acceptable solutions but also how Holland manages adequately to cater for a variety of beliefs, this being of particular importance when a country has to deal with relatively large influxes of immigrants from beyond Western Europe, whose religious customs and practices are at variance with Christian practice if not with the Christian ethic. Problems of racial discrimination obviously turn mainly on immigrants, it being an unhappy but inescapable fact that the lower the level of education of the native to a particular country, the more intolerant, suspicious and prejudiced he becomes in his dealings with immigrants. Here, heed might most usefully be taken of conditions prevailing in the two Pestalozzi Children's Villages at Trogen in Switzerland and at Sedlescombe in Sussex – and, at a higher educational level, of the organisation of Atlantic College in Wales and its sister international institutions throughout the world. The only possible long-term solution, of course, lies in carefully devised programmes of continuous education.

Finally, amongst environmental pressures we have to note the important parts played by the parent's occupation, his income level, the kind of housing he enjoys and where the house is situated, the general health and consequent vitality of the family as a whole. An unskilled (an uneducated) worker earning a large weekly wage which he can be said to squander in what is to him luxury living – on the principle of enjoying the benefits to the full so long as they last – will be only too ready to allow his off-spring to leave school early and embark on similar lucrative and dead-end jobs. And the ambitious working-class child, even with the tacit backing of his parents, can come under pressures, both from inadequacy of home conditions for study and from his peers (having already left school to earn good money), to give up the struggle. We must not, however, fall into the error of thinking that the dice are loaded solely against the children of poor, feckless or uneducated parents, even though they are a majority and must in consequence be our main concern. It should also be remembered that deprivation, in the sense in which we have just been arguing, can affect all members of the community, rich or poor. Deprivation can be psychological and emotional as well as economic. The un-wanted child in any family can be emotionally deprived. The spoiled only child can be psychologically deprived, as can the child whose parents are far too busily engaged in their private (and often selfish) pursuits to create a proper family atmosphere.

4

Obviously, the vast increase in enrolments everywhere into some form of post-primary education has had its repercussions in what we will now call the tertiary phase of education if only to stress the fact that nowadays university education must be considered as only one of the several offerings available at this level. Nevertheless, it has to be remembered that the university continues to be the prestige institution, and it is therefore not surprising to find that as more and more students at the academic secondary levels obtain the coveted passport (*Abitur, baccalauréat*, a necessary combination of subjects successfully studied at an advanced level) for university entrance, so do they demand university places as a right. And, generally speaking, it can be said that over the fifteen years between 1950 and 1965 enrolements at university level had almost everywhere (with the exception of Spain and Portugal) more than doubled. How to cope with this increase, not only in terms of sheer student numbers but also in terms of an increasing number of new demands made on the teaching staff, has been the major headache of the universities, and has led in extreme cases of frustration on the part of the student body to insurrection of the kind dramatically highlighted by the events of May 1968 in Paris.

It has to be remembered that European universities, unlike most of their American counterparts, assume that the general education of the student is complete before entry, and therefore plunge him immediately into highly specialised studies. They have for centuries considered themselves as existing to train a professional élite and equally as being havens of pure research and centres of advanced learning for the select few. It has been argued that the only proper function of a university as a place of learning is to stimulate and satisfy the mental curiosity of those who have shown they can benefit from the rigorous academic disciplines involved in studying in depth one or more subjects traditionally held to be important because they are exacting in their demands. And the student is considered highly fortunate to be in a position of relative carefree independence for a number of years to exercise, stretch and develop to the full his mind via his own chosen specialist subject(s). The university, it is further maintained, is not a weather-vane responsive to every variation of popular whim or fashion. It must give society what it needs, but what society needs may be quite different from what it is asking for. In this sense, the university may be said to have moral obligations (as opposed to professional obligations) to society, and its moral force is derived from the intensity and seriousness of its intellectual life.

This "ivory tower" syndrome is now for the first time seriously challenged, the challenge arising directly from the concomitance of the three "explosions", of knowledge, of population, and of aspirations. As more and more students have demanded a university education as a right – and have, indeed, been encouraged by successive governments to do so, in the belief that a university education is a good investment and that students are "economically" important – so have the universities, swamped by the deluge, been obliged to multiply themselves, to sub-divide themselves, and (often reluctantly) to recognise that a number of other higher educational institutions (mainly technical) were already doing work comparable with university work yet were not empowered to award the *cachet* of a university degree.[1] Equally, they had had to face the unpalatable fact that such institutions were, in the long run, much more economically productive for the country as a whole. Many such institutions have had to be upgraded to university level, since they already had the prestige, and by the same token the universities have had to admit as "respectable" academic disciplines subjects they had previously scorned themselves to teach.[2]

Since 1945, indeed, attention focussed on various aspects of tertiary education has revealed inadequacies in the three main kinds of provision generally offered, and reforms have had to be made at all levels. The most striking changes have perhaps come in what we may call short-term tertiary education – that offered for about two years as a follow-on from training in a secondary establishment and designed primarily to train specialists as middle men on the industrial and commercial scene. Growing demands of the economy allied to the continued development of more and more sophisticated techniques have highlighted the inadequacies of what has in the past been mainly an extended technical training and shown that today's middle-grade executive needs a fuller and more complete general education.

[1] The *Université du Travail* at Charleroi, Belgium, is one outstanding example still not recognised as a degree-awarding body.

[2] Note, for example, the relatively recent creation of the B.Ed. degree in England and Wales.

This has led to these establishments of short-term tertiary education increasingly developing as institutions in their own right in one of two ways – either as distinctly separate from any other form of secondary or post-secondary education, or as a university institute of technology. The recent creation of the IUT in France, for example, is a good illustration of the advantages and disadvantages accruing from the establishment of such a university liaison: status is acquired, but it can so easily be forgotten that these special short courses must be concerned with performance rather than with research, and the more able students too often aspire to join an approved university faculty, provision indeed being made in France to facilitate this bridging. Of the separate establishments which prefer to go it alone we can name the "district high schools" of Norway, the "engineers" schools of Germany, higher *periti* schools in Italy and Spain, and (in a special sense) the middle levels of the *Université du Travail* at Charleroi in Belgium.

Long-term tertiary education is provided, of course, in the traditional university setting, and in various types of *grandes écoles*, or institutes of advanced technology, which act quite independently of the universities, can have even higher prestige, and train senior civil servants and leaders in the industrial and commercial fields. Immediate problems facing all these institutions are many and can briefly be referred to here as: firstly, how to gear themselves to cope with an influx of highly capable women students who now demand as a right to enter fields which have traditionally been a male preserve; secondly, how to make courses on offer more relevant to the needs of the times – which implies the introduction of courses not formerly taught, as well as the acceptance of candidates with secondary school-leaving qualifications not formerly recognised;[1] thirdly, how drastically to reduce the high failure rate of candidates both at qualifying and at final degree levels;[2] fourthly, how best to re-structure

[1] The 1964 Belgian regulation which allowed students with secondary technical school leaving certificates to enter university almost doubled the overall intake, thus further exacerbating the population problem.

[2] Figures for failure rates are difficult to come by, and only England and Wales offer a tentative figure of 14 per cent. Recently in Belgium some 35 per cent arts students and some 36 per cent science students failed the two-year qualifying examination. Of those going forward to sit the final degree examinations the failure rate in science was only 5 per cent, and in arts 12 per cent. It must be remembered, however, that England and Wales are more rigorous than most other countries in selecting their students for university education.

the examination system at one and the same time to meet modern demands, bring down the failure rate, and yet maintain standards of academic excellence; fifthly, how to overcome the inescapable fact that, despite all modern reforms at the lower levels of education to give even the poorest boy or girl a chance of a university education, the university still remains "bourgeois orientated" and is failing (proportionately) to attract more promising students from the working class, ratios remaining more or less constant over the years.

Other important problems which will have to be solved before members of the European Economic Community can fully realise the ideal of having students move freely from university to university throughout Western Europe – much as they did in the Middle Ages – turn on important variations in course structure and on the time needed to qualify for the first degree. England and Wales are generally considered to be the most economical over the time factor, requiring often only three years to qualify and never more than four (if medicine and dentistry are excluded). Belgium requires a minimum of four years, Denmark six, and in Holland, Germany and the rest of Scandinavia it can run from five to eight years. Course structure is concerned with the debate on how best to secure the "educated mind" for the leap forward into the twenty-first century, and more immediately with somewhat tardy recognition of the fact that the intellectual capital of a first degree is nowadays all too soon exhausted.

As we observe in detail changes taking place in individual countries two main objectives generally stand out. The first is to stem the present waste of ability, the second to recruit more widely than from the traditional academic schools – this involving the acceptance of "mature" students who, for a variety of reasons, have been unable or unwilling to follow one or other of the traditional paths to the university. Following on from this comes closer liaison with other tertiary establishments, or the gradual transformation of such establishments under careful regulation into degree-awarding bodies in their own right. The Federal Republic of Germany has perhaps so far gone furthest in this direction by the recent creation of eight new "comprehensive" universities which combine, sometimes on the same campus, existing institutions of higher education with teacher-training establishments and technical colleges. And, as doctors, teachers, engineers, philologists, pure scientists etc. all train together, so is it being urged that, in an age when any professional man may have to change his job two or three times, it can no longer be realistic to train solely along one line of specialism. There must in future be built-in possibilities for cross-training, one important suggestion put forward from Heidelberg being that only 50 per cent of a student's time be devoted to his main subject. The time thus saved should be equally divided between studies related to the main subject and others totally divorced from it.

Immediate goals everywhere, however, are concerned with assuring that teaching and learning both cease to be a kind of prolongation of the sort of work done in the top forms of the traditional academic secondary school; that the student is treated as a participating adult, is brought into much closer co-operation and relationships with his tutors, and that his studies have meaning for *him*, being initially based on his own concrete interests rather than on a professor's predilections or research interests; that the student sees himself as not in the university passively to imbibe knowledge to be spewed forth at appropriate examination intervals, but as being there to penetrate and get to know – to know in particular what decisive part in shaping the world of the future the expertise he acquires will be required to play; that the university itself is revitalised and geared to its changing role by responsible student participation in government at all appropriate levels. It is finally held that the task of the modern university must be for all concerned to work together as contributory members of different generations to secure an understanding of the wholeness of knowledge and its application to satisfy the needs of modern society.

5

All envisaged reforms, however, at all levels of education, depend for their successful implementation on an adequately trained body of teachers whose commitments must be much more varied and in a sense more responsible than in the past. The traditional authoritarian role of the teacher, who dispenses to relatively docile (and non-participatory) classes of youngsters the accumulated wisdom it is agreed they must somehow imbibe, is now for the first time everywhere seriously challenged. It is challenged mainly because of the pressures now brought to bear, not only to extend education, but also to democratise and to modernise it. Extension of education demands that, in addition to speeding the bright pupil to the top, the teacher should be equally concerned with widening the horizon of the ordinary student; that the educative process adapt itself to the needs of every kind of student; that in consequence instruction be individualised. Democratisation of education, which also thinks of education as a constant on-going process to include recurrent education, calls not only for specialists in agreed disciplines (as heretofore) but also for a teacher with a broad background of general cultural training, it being argued (quite rightly) that only the teacher who has himself enjoyed a broad liberal education can hope to avoid the pitfalls of routine pedestrianism and show resourcefulness and enterprise in his work. Modernisation exacts (along with democratisation) the breakdown of artificial divisions between teachers doing primary, secondary and technical work, stresses the necessity to train *all* teachers along the same broad and agreed lines, involves teachers in curriculum planning as never before, and destroys the splendid isolation of the teacher – particularly the specialist. Now, such is the complexity of the learning processes that no single teacher, however highly specialised, can hope to function adequately without constant reference to what his colleagues are doing – in fact, without becoming involved in some form of team-teaching enterprise at however simplified a level. Similarly, he must form closer links with his pupils, and through them with parents, the better to give increasingly necessary guidance and counselling.

The four outstanding problems in teacher supply are firstly concerned with the quantitative aspect (recruiting sufficient extra staff not only to cope with increased entries but also with the necessity to keep class numbers as low as possible); secondly with the qualitative aspect (recruiting men and women of sufficiently high calibre to meet the challenge of present-day complexities); thirdly with a very necessary total reform of teacher training; and lastly with the "generation gap", it having to be remembered when implementing any reform in teacher training that up to 75 per cent of the teaching staff of any institution will be past the age of 30, already "set" in their ways, and in consequence often sceptical of, if not directly hostile to newer approaches persuasively advocated by their junior colleagues. It can now be argued that quantitatively speaking the general shortage of teachers has been overcome, except perhaps in certain subjects such as mathematics and science (and, in certain countries, modern languages). On the other hand, the quality of the recruitment gives cause for concern everywhere. Formerly, to become a teacher was the one sure and certain way for the bright ambitious child from a working-class background to achieve higher social status, and everything possible was done to help him realise his goal. Nowadays, the democratisation of education, allied to technological and scientific advance, has made available many more exciting and promising careers open to both boys and girls of ability, whatever their background. The result has been that, apart from a continuous steady flow of men and women who are really dedicated to teaching and whom nothing will deviate from their purpose, the bulk of those joining the profession come to it in consequence as a kind of "second best". And this is perfectly understandable. Teaching as a career has lost its former charismatic appeal and, as I have heard argued persuasively in several countries, takes on the complexion of a dead-end job compared with that, say, of starting as an errand boy in a store to move slowly up the hierarchy to chief salesman and, with luck, to branch manager.

Thus, the teaching profession must be given back its own charisma, not merely by making it much more financially attractive but more importantly by making it as challenging a job as any to be found elsewhere. Most countries have now realised the importance of this, and reforms in teacher training are everywhere in some measure directed towards this end. One needs firmly individualistic teachers to best serve our present mass-minded generations. One needs men and women capable of asserting their authority, not to discipline along old-fashioned lines, but to break the stranglehold of the *present* on the mind; capable of demonstrating to their pupils in this machine-minded age that life is *not* just a series of things that happen, but that there should be a discernible pattern evolved to give back to life both meaning and significance; able to reconcile the sense of pattern and direction deriving from heritage with the sense of experiment and innovation deriving from modern scientific advance. And, as it is now increasingly seen that the grave mistake over the last few decades has been to use democratic methods rather than train for democracy, so must teachers organise themselves together to teach their youngsters to think effectively and without prejudice; how to communicate thought – it being constantly borne in mind that the imagination is at all times an indispensable element in effective thinking; how to make relevant judgements; and how to discriminate among values.

The first important move made by various countries has been to upgrade the quality of those recruited to the profession by insisting that all intending teachers must initially have satisfactorily completed a full secondary school course up to at least the age of 18. True, they may still leave their secondary school at about 15 to enter a training college, but nowadays they are required to complete in the training college their secondary education proper before embarking on teacher-training programmes. A second step that logically follows on this decision is to allow the most able students (particularly in Belgium and Norway) to transfer directly to university degree courses. All countries are seeking closer links between training colleges and universities, whilst in England and Wales the universities have gone so far as to create a special B.Ed. (Bachelor of Education) degree, first introduced between 1968 and 1970, which is now sat for annually by almost 10 per cent of college students, tutored mainly in the colleges themselves though it is not unknown for a university deliberately to mix such students in certain classes with its own undergraduates. The aim of such university involvement as exists in various countries is, of course, to get rid of the traditional isolation of the college-trained teacher from, not only his counterpart who trains as a specialist in the universities, but also from other students of the same age level who will be studying other disciplines and with whom the university-trained teacher has always been associated. It would be wrong, however, to infer from all these closer links now being established that most European countries are ceasing to regard primary and secondary teachers as constituting two separate and distinct classes. Teachers are still classified according to the functions they perform, trained to perform one specific function, and are accordingly treated quite differently as regards training, pay, conditions of work, and social esteem. And this situation seems likely to persist for some time to come, somewhat ameliorated, perhaps, by the fact that lines of demarcation between primary and secondary education are becoming increasingly blurred, as by the fact that in the lowest forms of secondary education (becoming increasingly comprehensive in style) teachers from both "camps" are required to work together and to interrelate their teaching.

Reforms in teacher-training programmes are obviously based on the higher age levels exacted for entry as also on the greater intellectual maturity of the students resultant therefrom. As the universities have always prepared specialists in certain groupings of subjects, so now are training colleges moving in the same direction: more and more specialists (of the right kind) are required as newer techniques of teaching (including team-teaching) are employed. It is interesting to note that the lead to make for more rigorous academic training in training colleges came from Belgium as early as 1852 when programmes were first devised to take the most promising students and turn them into *régents* who would then teach, not at the primary level but in a newly created *école moyenne* which functioned on a par with the lowest forms of the traditional academic secondary school. It is equally interesting to observe that in England and Wales, with the creation of the B.Ed. degree, which combines specialist academic training with professional training, the necessary logical step has now been taken beyond the earlier concept of training for the *régent* to make for the award of a university degree proper.[1] In England and Wales, however (unlike the rest of Europe) graduate teachers increasingly function over the whole spectrum of the educational process from the nursery school upwards.

Professional training of teachers is equally coming under close scrutiny, and this is closely allied to the necessity for turning out a number of specialists in various fields. It is generally agreed, however, that one of the main functions of the middle (or lower secondary) school must increasingly become one of orientation and guidance, and teachers (not only at this level) must be fully trained to cope. All teachers must equally undergo thorough training along psycho-sociological lines the better to participate in team-teaching and also to function increasingly not as a "master" but as one whose important task is to give a positive lead in integrating the school more closely with the community. Similarly, they must be actively involved in the design and preparation of various kinds of teaching aids, brought to reflect on their own aims and methods – and in consequence made to participate, even during their preliminary training, in various (obviously small-scale) research projects. They must from the beginning be trained in experimental attitudes which will keep them for ever questioning the validity of their approach, never satisfied with things as they are, and on the *qui-vive* for implementing desirable change *whenever it is clearly and irrefutably demonstrated that change is imperative.*

[1] Scotland has always demanded graduate training for all teachers.

It is, of course, totally impossible to attempt to carry out such programmes within the short space of time devoted to the actual preparation of a beginner teacher, and it is now stressed that teacher preparation must be a continuous, on-going process. Programmes of in-service training are therefore imperative, and as the teacher begins to find his feet in his job and matures, so must he repeatedly be brought back for further training commensurate with his own feelings of inadequacy. It is also held that such in-service courses, as tailor-made as possible to suit individual requirements, are indispensable in attempting to surmount the "generation gap" amongst teachers in any given institution of which we spoke earlier. How best to administer the complex of arrangements necessary is still much a matter for debate, except for a general feeling that the whole should be under the umbrella of the university re-defined along lines which we have already mentioned. We can perhaps best conclude this section by noting that from England and Wales comes the first practical suggestion that every teacher be required to spend one-fifth of his first year's service and a term at least once every seven years in full-time study.

6

It is now time to turn our attention to detailed consideration of moves in various countries at various levels to deal with problems which are increasingly seen as common to all the nations of Western Europe. If we list these in broad, general terms we see them as hinging on the need to make much more efficient use of all educational resources; to modernise educational management particularly to include participation of all involved in the educative processes. drastically to reconsider curricula and method; and finally to create a modern teaching force imaginatively competent to break the stranglehold, not particularly of the past but more importantly of the present, on the minds of men. The more these problems are considered the more it is realised that co-operation between countries and co-ordination of effort are essential if only because education is now everywhere in demand as a human right to satisfy social and political needs and to cope with economic strains and stresses to which Western Europe as a whole is constantly subjected and which it must overcome as a whole if it is to survive in competition with other world powers.

Put bluntly, what is needed is a radical transformation of the role, functions and nature of education and a break with palliative in favour of long-term objectives. It can no longer be assumed that the main role of education must remain that of imparting the knowledge and traditions of society to each succeeding generation; increasingly it is becoming an instrument of social policy, increasingly a part of overall national policy, and this is reflected in the fact that in all countries education has now become the second biggest single item of expenditure – defence usually holding first place. It is no longer possible to treat the various stages of education in isolation (pre-school, primary, secondary, technical and vocational, higher education), for change in any one area is bound to have its repercussions elsewhere.[1] Nor can any one country afford to ignore reforms initiated elsewhere in Western Europe. In a word, harmonisation of educational planning and practice (which we shall discuss in detail in our last chapter) is perhaps the most important mainspring of all reforms now taking place throughout Western Europe.

Thus, in the second part of this book we shall have to consider educational patterns in separate countries, not on the somewhat traditional lines of outdated division into primary, secondary, etc., but in terms of the main currents of change common (in most respects) to all countries. We shall note shifting and different emphases, try to explain these, and hope to show that where differences in interpretation of the meaning in practical terms of (often emotive) expressions such as "comprehensive education", "education of an élite", and even of "basic education" occur, these differences can be seen to be rooted in still strongly held feelings of national identity – and pride.

---

[1] One simple example of this is the experiment of attempting to introduce the teaching of French in the primary school in England and Wales. There was no liaison with the secondary schools who remained often at a loss as to how best cope with such pupils as they received among others who had not yet started to learn the language.

CHAPTER 5

Basic Schooling

1

The expression "basic schooling" is deliberately used for two main reasons. In the first place it has to be remembered that, as education becomes universal and is seen more clearly as pertaining to the life-span of any individual, so does it become less formalised and less school-based, the total educational opportunities available stemming from an extremely short (though important) period of formalised instruction in traditionally accepted school systems. Secondly, since we wish to consider in this chapter the total period of instruction which precedes what is commonly called the "secondary level", the term "basic" seems to be the most appropriate. Thus, "basic schooling" can be defined as school-based instruction available to all over a period of up to ten years from about the age of 2 or 3. It encompasses both pre-school education, itself already a blanket term to cover all forms of organised groupings of children under the starting age of compulsory schooling, and what has now come to be called primary education which, according to whatever dictionary definition is favoured, can mean first, original, preparatory, or highest in rank or importance. Difficulties of definition, of course, relate to the earlier historical role of the *elementary* school (which prepared the majority to become wage earners in some form whilst sorting out the brightest to be recruited into some form of secondary education, usually academic), and it has perhaps been left to the Germans to furnish the clearest of definitions – *Grundschule* – which, strictly speaking, is applicable only at the primary levels of instruction.

Further difficulties arise from the fact that no two countries are exactly in agreement as to the actual duration of this period of basic schooling, nor even in agreement as to the *functional* role of the institutions involved. Changing attitudes have again caused confusion, and the main influences at work have been the raising of the school-leaving age, the abandonment of some form of selection for entry to post-primary education (eleven-plus and the like), the consequent natural flow of all pupils into the lower secondary stages of post-primary work, the remarkable increase everywhere in nursery (or pre-primary) education, and the all-embracing nature of such comprehensive patterns (as in Sweden) which run a nine-year unitary school system straight through from the age of 7 to 16. Thus, there is no longer any clear-cut division of schooling into clearly recognisable sections to enable us to define with exactitude what is meant by primary education.

In England and Wales, for example, the kind of division now finding favour is: ages 5–9 years, compulsory basic schooling; 9–13 years, middle school; 13–18 years, upper school. Holland and Belgium would consider compulsory basic schooling as extending between the ages of 6 and 12. France and Italy opt for an age range of 6 to 11, but Italy does make a break at the age of 8. West Germany has at present an age range of 6 to 10, but hopes to start compulsory schooling at the age of 5 by 1980 and so complete basic training by the age of 9. The Scandinavian countries all think in terms of a common people's school extending unbrokenly between the ages of 7 and 16, though in practice Denmark allows some differentiation to take place between the ages of 12 and 14. Norway holds that pre-secondary education should be completed after the first six grades (at age 13), and Sweden divides the nine-year school into three – lower, middle and upper.

All we can really say is that primary education is now held to be that period of education which, leading naturally on from pre-school education, enables a child to master the three Rs in terms of communi-cating, of socialising, and of imagining in order to give training in the development of conceptual thought processes. It is definitely not a child-minding centre, for serious work is constantly done there. The curriculum must be basic and not determinative. It must also be exploratory, con-stantly to awaken the curiosity of the child, *but* in a disciplined way. And, since all pressures on the school have been relaxed with the dis-appearance of an examination hurdle before post-primary education can begin, it can now seek out its own objectives in its own way by its own methods. In France, for example, a move has already been made away from the former rigorous division of the weekly timetable into so many half-hours devoted to reading, writing, arithmetic, history, geography, by dividing the whole week into three main divisions: six hours for stimulating activities, six hours for physical education and games, and (for the fundamental disciplines) ten hours devoted to language work and five hours to mathematics. England and Wales speak of the integrated day which can have no rigidly structured timetable.[1] Sweden groups different subjects into various fields of activity. Belgium tends to follow the Decroly pattern of basing all teaching on centres of interest.

Detailed examination of curricula in the various countries indicates that, whilst important emphasis is still placed on teaching the mother tongue, there is a move away from basing the teaching on spelling lessons and rigid grammatical drills (parsing and analysing) and equally from slavish imitation of supposedly good models of style and expression. As the Decroly system in Belgium has been advocating for decades, an attempt is now made to start from the child's own interests and his own command of and competence in the other tongue. Spontaneity and vividness are encouraged in both oral and written work, and group work particularly at the oral level (still a strong feature in most Western European countries) is encouraged through dramatic activities of various kinds, including puppet plays. Television and the radio have again helped in the trend towards more imaginative teaching, and attention is paid to both the good and the possibly harmful effects on the child of the mass media, especially in home surroundings.

A somewhat controversial decision taken by the Committee of Ministers of the Council of Europe to recommend the teaching of at least one widely spoken foreign language in the primary school course has been tentatively experimented with in some countries, envisaged in the reform plans of others (West Germany), implemented already in Sweden (1972), and carefully planned in Holland where English is the language specifically chosen, it being argued that it is "a universal language with great practical value . . . and the same foreign language taught in Holland's neighbouring countries". Italy on the other hand has voiced doubts, arguing that to teach a child imperfectly to use another language when he cannot yet perfectly use the mother tongue (and overcome dialectal differences)

---

[1] Here, the importance of having highly competent teachers in charge cannot be over-emphasised. The Belgians, having originally abolished all time-tabling at this level, have now felt it necessary to impose guide-lines to ensure that *all* children satisfactorily complete the minimum requirements in a given year of study.

can do more harm than good. And Italian strictures would now seem to be supported by the recently published (1974) findings of a research team from the National Foundation for Educational Research (England and Wales) on the effects of the experimental introduction of the teaching of French into a number of English and Welsh schools.[1] Wherever a modern foreign language is taught, however, English would appear to be the popular choice, and in Belgium – a country deeply divided on the linguistic question to the point where some form of federalism would seem to be the only solution – some are already advocating the choice of English as a lingua franca and as the only means at a national level of overcoming the deepening distrust of the Dutch-speaking Flemings and the French-speaking Walloons of each other's intentions.

New approaches to the teaching of mathematics are also much in evidence, old ideas on the teaching of techniques passively to solve problems (however closely related to daily life) yielding to a desire to bring the child to a real understanding of the mathematical concepts underlying such techniques. It is argued that the young child is capable of grasping intellectual and abstract concepts much more readily than had previously been supposed – particularly if these are presented in a cyclical way (cf. the Decroly method) which leads to constant re-introduction and re-affirmation – and that in any case technological advance has already rendered obsolete the mastery of many simple arithmetical techniques. Nor must it be forgotten that today's child is embarking on a process of lifelong education; that in consequence the basic concepts must be mastered as fully as possible as early as possible; and that (as Professor Bloom of the University of Chicago has demonstrated) the most important years for a child's intellectual development lie between the ages of 0 and 8, all which comes after being dependent in large measure on the foundations then laid. Science teaching at this level is conditioned by the same kind of thinking, it being considered necessary so to structure experiences for the child that he is led to "discover" for himself important fundamental concepts. History and geography now tend to be subsumed under the general title of social studies, the aim being not so much to stress the importance of national heroes and national endeavour as to show how national potential has been (and can be) used for co-operative effort on an international basis.

[1] *Primary French in the Balance.*

To sum up, the chief characteristics of this basic school are firstly to provide a basic training from which every child may draw confidence to embark on some form of secondary education – in other words to ensure that a common basic education is provided which can later lead to differentiation in terms of *suum cuique* (to each his own) rather than of *idem cuique* (the same for all).[1] For, despite what may be said in some quarters, this period of schooling still remains a "diagnostic" period, it now being accepted that a child's intelligence is largely shaped by the time he reaches the age of 6-plus. This latter fact highlights the importance of a good home environment, stresses the need for adequate provision of pre-school education for all who seek it, and leads to the need for much more careful parental involvement in all aspects of school life, the idea being to lead parents to abandon their former passive role to become genuinely participatory and critical – involved to the extent of actively helping to integrate the school with life via their own attitudes and example and their own use of the media. It is here interesting to note that early leads as to the right direction to take have been furnished by the Catholic church in various countries. In Belgium a group of Jesuit priests were originally active in promoting the publication of a children's comic weekly (*Tintin*) which would be aesthetically sound, educational (both in the moral and general senses), and yet tremendously funny and exciting. *Tintin* has now achieved a vast circulation in French-speaking countries, has been translated into English for publication in book form, and has had its imitators in various guises with relatively equal success. The church in Belgium and elsewhere has also promoted film sessions for both parents *and* children to enjoy and criticise constructively together, "pop" group performances, and various other manifestations of lesiure-seeking activities. Quite recently also, a group of Italian priests has started experimenting with TV at a regional level actively to involve all classes to take a pride in their own customs, traditions and creative potential.

The second main characteristic of the basic school, following as a corollary from the first, is to give each child such feelings of security as to enable him to cope adequately with each situation as it arises, and so gain the necessary confidence and zest to pursue his studies and prolong them. It is here felt that continuity of association with the same teacher

[1] It is interesting to note that America has now taken up a not dissimilar attitude.

is essential for as long a period as proves feasible. This teacher will get to know each pupil well and will give him all the individual attention possible, and the pupil will be allowed to progress at his own speed in so far as he is not impossibly dropping behind to endanger his chances of satisfactorily completing a given year's assignment of work. Remedial classes for children who are having difficulties in some branch of their studies are becoming increasingly important, again with the object of ensuring that a child is not "kept down" at the end of the school year to repeat everything again and so feel stigmatised among his peers. And, more usually in Catholic countries on the Continent but also more generally practised than in England and Wales, it is held that once the pre-school period of education is over there should be men teachers for boys as a matter of principle wherever co-education is not in force.

The basic school is finally seen as the important first element in securing that proper gestation on which success in providing permanent education of the right kind must depend – permanent education being defined as a flow of continuous educational opportunities throughout life. No school can now be an end in itself as was the case with the old-fashioned elementary (primary) school. The traditional academic importance of this school is gradually being diminished in proportion as permanent education is being stressed. Indeed, to end on a somewhat paradoxical note, we can argue that European educators in general have heeded what Illich has had to say on de-schooling and are now aiming, not at de-schooling in Illich's negative sense, but at de-schooling in a positive sense of renewal. There are already infinite and exciting opportunities ahead for today's teaching force.

2

We have already noted how the various countries of Western Europe differ among themselves as to which is the best age at which to start compulsory schooling, and this is one important factor (among several others) accounting for the growing popularity of pre-school education over the last few decades. Most countries now recognise that the child must spend longer in school than ever before if he is properly to learn to cope with the complexities of modern living. Most of them have to face problems of dealing with the children of immigrants, as with children from socially deprived backgrounds. Most of them are harassed by the ever-growing complexities of urbanisation, again leading to perhaps more subtle forms of child-deprivation (lack of adequate and safe play facilities, lack of contact with other children of the same age range, lack of necessary enriching play experience *outside* the home and family), as also with the increasingly familiar pattern of both parents being out at work, not necessarily for basic economic reasons but often to enhance their own *adult* life-style. And all countries are agreed that the sooner individual handicaps are diagnosed among children, and dealt with, the more confidently will they tackle the later stages of their school career to make the fullest use (commensurate with their ability) of the opportunities afforded. Finally, as parents are brought more and more to realise that modern conditions of home life are not always the best for children beyond a certain age, so do they become involved along with their children in the pre-school situation and are fully encouraged to do so – the whole process becoming a happy partnership with the school that it is hoped will lay the firm foundations for future close parent–teacher–pupil collaboration over increasingly important decisions which will have to be taken as the pupil's future is mapped out. The "educative family" is the ideal sought from the very beginning as a necessary prerequisite to making permanent (recurrent) education a reality.

It is when we come to examine available figures for attendance of children in the pre-school situation that we fully realise how widespread already is the move to consider extending the benefits of some kind of formal education within the context of organised schooling to children well below the compulsory starting age. France and the Benelux countries can claim virtually 100 per cent attendance between the ages of 5 and 6, and certainly up to 80 per cent between 3 and 5. In Western Germany there is an attendance of about one-third of the age range 3 to 6 at present, but as it is hoped by 1980 to lower the starting age for compulsory education to 5, so it is expected by then to have a voluntary attendance of some 75 per cent of 3- to 4-year-olds, and by 1990 total attendance of the age group. Italy (where statistics are not so readily available) must have an attendance rate between the ages of 3 and 6 of about 50 per cent, the proportion being much higher among 5-year-olds and much lower at the age of 3.

The Scandinavian countries, where it is traditional to expect the most formative period of a child's life to be spent at the mother's knee, and where compulsory schooling does not begin until the age of 7, have an enrolment in pre-school classes of under 15 per cent. On the other hand it has to be remembered that Norway and Sweden in particular are sparsely populated, that with the development of industry there has been a marked movement of population from rural areas to towns (over 70 per cent of Swedes are now town dwellers), and that it is in the towns where there is most need of pre-school education. In any case, exceptions are constantly being made in approved circumstances for children to enter the compulsory schooling phase earlier than the age of 7, and strenuous efforts are presently being made to increase the provision of pre-school places where most needed.

If the current figure for pre-school attendance between the ages of 3 and 5 in England and Wales is still as low as 12 per cent, it has first of all to be remembered that these are the only countries (excepting the Republic of Ireland which surprisingly – and particularly so for a predominantly rural community – has a pre-school attendance of about 55 per cent) which start compulsory education as early as 5 years of age. Thus, practice in the Benelux countries and in France is (on a non-compulsory basis) in effect on a par with that in England and Wales. True, the situation for children between the ages of 3 and 5 is the least satisfactory throughout Western Europe, but policy in England and Wales remains firm in not sacrificing quality for quantity at this important level of education. The teaching staff is highly trained and class numbers are kept small to ensure that correct individual attention may be given. As in the case of Scandinavia, ways and means of increasing provision are constantly under review, but (given the present reorganisation of basic schooling as a whole) not everyone is convinced of the necessity to attempt to match up to achievements elsewhere in Western Europe. It is frequently argued that to provide more places at the pre-school level than are genuinely needed is to do family life a disservice at the very time when we should be trying to strengthen family bonds. It is a point of view to be taken seriously.

3

Pre-school education in its various phases (crèche, nursery school and kindergarten) has already a long and distinguished history and everywhere betrays the common influence of a number of key educators. If Rousseau was the first to emphasise the need for child study and for education via concrete objects and experiences, with great reliance being placed on nature and natural development, Jean Oberlin (1740–1826) was the first to open a school (1771) in his native Alsace for children up to the age of 6, in which instruction would be combined with amusement and much activity. As his influence spread in particular through France, Switzerland and Germany, Pestalozzi (1746–1827) founded his own school in Switzerland in 1805, and though he was not particularly concerned with the education of very young children, his ideas greatly influenced Froebel (1782–1852) whose first *Kindergarten* was opened in Germany in 1837. Taking many of Pestalozzi's ideas, he developed them further and laid his main stress on the need for self-activity among children and on the value of play. He agreed with Pestalozzi that children need to deal with concrete objects and experiences before they can properly manipulate the related vocabulary and ideas, but he changed Pestalozzi's somewhat passive ideas on learning for his own on learning by doing, emphasising constantly both motor and physical activity.[1]

Froebel's influence spread rapidly. A Froebel *Kindergarten* was first opened in Great Britain in 1851 and the Froebel Society was founded there twenty years later. When Froebel schools were closed in Germany in 1851 by order of the Prussian government, many emigrants went to America and continued his work there, though it was the theoretical side which came to arouse the greatest interest. John Dewey (1859–1952) in fact accepted most of Froebel's ideas and practices on active learning (though disagreeing with some of his philosophy, including the idea of nature mysticism inherited from Rousseau), and expanded and developed them to work them out in the context of early twentieth-century America. Believing that all education should be rooted in the activities of children, he decried artificial motivation. Less formal in his ideas than Froebel, he stressed that education was a continuing and changing process with little place for fixed goals. And, like his distinguished contemporaries, Madame Montessori (1870–1952) and Ovide Decroly (1871–1932), he urged the need for more psychological research into the way young people develop and learn.

[1] I have deliberately omitted Comenius (1592–1671) since he argued that up to the age of 6 the child should be educated at home by the mother.

Maria Montessori was an Italian doctor who came to specialise in the education of the under-privileged and backward child and later extended her ideas to the education of normal children. She held that freedom for the child is essentially biological, his chief requisite during growth being the absence of interference. The only worthwhile education for her is what she calls "auto-education" and she lays particular emphasis on sense and muscle training. Special didactic materials are devised for use in the Montessori school, and the child selects the activity which interests him, working at it without interference. There are definite periods, claimed Madame Montessori, in the development of each child, and her didactic material was arranged in a systematic sequence to suit these periods. Should a child fail to achieve the desired result with any piece of material that was a sure sign he was not yet ready to take the next step forward. Gymnastic training is used to make for harmonious development of the whole of the motor mechanisms, and one of the few disciplines imposed on the child is turned into a kind of game: this is a silence period during which the child learns to control his movements by remaining quiet and with closed eyes.

Though her work had much influence during her lifetime, this has lessened over the last few decades, her method being attacked both for its rigid and somewhat artificial method of approach and also for her tendency to neglect the importance of play, of creative activities, and of emotional development generally. French pre-primary education, however, is still strongly influenced by her work, and her approach to the education of under-privileged children with difficult or poor homes has been of relevance in other countries (Great Britain and America for instance) in tackling the problems of slum dwellers. In America in particular the 1964 "Operation Headstart" saw the opening of more than 100 Montessori schools for children from poor backgrounds.

Ovide Decroly was a Belgian doctor who, like Madame Montessori, began by specialising in the education of backward and difficult children and later extended his ideas to normal children. His influence has in many ways been much greater than hers if only because it has embraced the whole education of the child through to university entrance, and because his basic principles (particularly for learning to read and to write) have been largely adopted throughout the whole of the primary school system of Belgium, have influenced to a great degree the post-war outlook on basic education in France, and have been borrowed by educationaists in several other countries. His method is not one of dogmatic teaching, but one which adapts itself to the psychology of the child and his ever-changing environment. Psychological observation of the child is therefore of paramount importance, and on a basis of such close psychological observation Decroly finally elaborated five guiding principles for the satisfactory running of a Decroly school:

(1) The child is a living organism which must be prepared for social living. Hence, education must be for life by living. *L'école pour la vie par la vie*.

(2) The child is a living, growing whole. Every moment marks growth, and at every age the child is different.

(3) Children of the same age differ considerably from one another.

(4) Certain interests are peculiar to each age, and these govern the child's mental activities.

(5) The child's most important activity is motor. Motor activities properly encouraged and controlled by the intellect are necessarily associated with all other activities.

Decroly again concluded that it was indispensable in the educative process to tie together the following activities:

(a) *Observation*, which puts the child in contact with the material world. Thus, in a Decroly school there are many domestic pets, animals and birds, and from the earliest days there are simple biological studies, observation of the weather, seasons, growth, and the passage of time.

(b) *Association in time and space*, which links knowledge acquired through observation with more abstract ideas and helps the understanding of history and geography.

(c) *Expression work* to translate these ideas into action, words and forms.

To maintain the necessary functional unity of all the various mechanisms of mind Decroly adopted as a teaching technique the principle of centres of interest, but – because the most important things to be known concern the child himself – the centres of interest must always be based on the child's needs: the need for food, the need for protection against the elements, the need for defence against enemies (including illnesses), the need for play, work, rest.

The method of teaching to read and to write which Decroly advocated is based on the theory that, whilst the child will normally seek to move from the simple to the more complex, the contrary is true of these branches of learning. Thus in a Decroly school the child is presented with simple sentences related to an action he is performing or an observation he has made. He reiterates these simple sentences, sees them written up on the board (with simple illustration), copies this into his own work book, and thus gradually builds up a kind of classroom reader. Only when he has "globally" understood does he feel the need to break down a sentence into its separate words, and later the words into letters. The children are further encouraged in this method by the use of hand printing sets for them to set up their own readers on a basis of their own original compositions. In effect the children work both individually and in groups, the work of course being fully discussed in advance and carefully planned in collaboration with the teacher. For children to learn to live together they must both respect an individual's privacy and also experience participatory membership of a group.

Last of the important educationists whose work has had considerable influence on the systems of pre-school education in Western Europe generally and to some extent in America is the Swiss-born Jean Piaget (1896). His researches into how children learn, and the stages of learning through which they pass to a full grasp of a concept, are well known to educationists everywhere. He has also attempted to show that in the correct social environment the child will spontaneously feel the need to move towards the right kind of self-discipline that is required by man in his social setting. The more a child's individuality is respected — and the more, therefore, the techniques of the educative process respect his individuality — the more fully will the child be fitted to become an active contributory member of modern society.

It is to be noted that all these educationists, except for Madame Montessori and Froebel, are interested in the total development of the child well beyond the period of infancy, and their influence has in consequence had a two-fold effect. Firstly, they have shown that not only are the earliest years of a child's life the most formative but also that internal "conflicts" caused either in the home or in school by mistaken methods or failure to understand the child on the part of adults can seriously affect his later development. Or, as W. D. Wall once put it: "Satisfactory human development depends upon the success with which the fundamental emotional needs of each individual are met within the framework of the demands of the society in which he grows up.'[1] The more countries have learned to appreciate the truth and importance of these statements, the greater has become the tendency everywhere to consider pre-school education as an essential part of a total educational experience to be enjoyed by as many young children as possible.

These same writers (and practitioners) have also demonstrated the rightness of A. N. Whitehead's contention that education must be considered as a seamless robe. There can be no abrupt break between pre-school and primary classes, nor indeed between primary and secondary work. The flow must be continuous, this leading in practice to close integration of the pre-school period with the primary school, each influencing the other to the mutual advantage of both, and both equally seeking full parental co-operation and participation. It is for these reasons that in a number of countries pre-school classes are made deliberately part of the primary school complex, and that the primary school inspectorate is often also responsible for the oversight of work in both areas. In like manner, efforts are also being made everywhere to upgrade the training of pre-school teachers to that level required of the primary teacher, so that (at least in theory) the same teacher might be called upon to serve anywhere within the basic school system and receive the same pay as the primary teacher.

Of recent years also, particularly in view of the experience of "Headstart" programmes in America and of research carried out in Western Germany, the importance of a more "intellectual" approach at the preschool level has been stressed.[2] This is not meant to run counter to the by now almost traditionally accepted informal and unstructured approach

---

[1] W. D. Wall, *Education and Mental Health*, for UNESCO, London, 1955.

[2] Operation Headstart resulted from the Economic Opportunity Act (1964) which launched the so-called "War on Poverty". Children between the ages of 3 and 4 were recruited into pre-school classes to overcome cultural deprivation due to home circumstances. It was soon discovered that such children (because of their poor cultural background) could not benefit from the kind of totally unstructured programmes catering for middle-class children (some of whom could also fail to profit) but needed to be set definite goals for achievement.

to learning at this level through play, but rather to bolster the Froebelian ideal by laying the emphasis on verbal development and simple calculation through task-oriented programmes geared to observation, and carefully devised by a warm, supportive and stimulating teacher. The best actual examples of how this can work out in practice are to be found in the Decroly pre-school sectors where, for example, children observe and plot the weather day by day, compare and measure growth of themselves, plants and animals, and enter into the simplest of time calculations. Ultimately, the aim is to secure the all-round social, physical and emotional development of each individual child, his individuality being carefully respected. It is to encourage independence for each child in association with sympathetic adults (other than parents) and with his peers (other than brothers and sisters). It is to encourage self-control and self-discipline through teaching a child to function as the need arises as a member of a group and so make from the earliest years for correct social adjustment. In all of this the teacher has an important and sensitive role to play, the aim being to provide indirect guidance and inspiration rather than any kind of formal instruction.

4

And now, in considering individual countries in some detail we should perhaps first begin with France and the Benelux countries. Here compulsory education starts for all four at the age of 6, and France is the only one of the countries under consideration to transfer children from the basic school system to post-primary education at the age of 11; the others insist on a full six years of primary instruction. In all these countries, however, there is virtually universal schooling on a non-compulsory basis between the ages of 5 and 6, and they can all lay claim to having the highest attendance figures throughout Western Europe for the age range 2 to 5. In France, schools are administered either by the state or by the Catholic church; in Belgium by either the state, the Catholic church, provinces or townships; in Holland by the state and various religious denominations; in the Grand Duchy of Luxemburg solely by the state, any private body receiving no subsidies of any kind. In effect, therefore, basic education is everywhere free, except that in Holland, at the pre-school level, all but necessitous parents are required to pay a small weekly contribution to running costs. All the countries have rapidly expanded pre-school provision since the last war, carefully building on past achievement and traditions extending over a long period of time; and all, having constantly sought to involve parents at the pre-school level, have now found it relatively easy to extend this involvement up into the primary levels of instruction. Parents everywhere have equally the right, particularly at the pre-school level, to demand the establishment of a school wherever it can be shown that no adequate provision exists to meet their needs, religious or otherwise.

Pre-school education generally, of course, dates from the nineteenth century when it became imperative on social and humanitarian grounds to make some sort of provision to care for the children of working-class parents, particularly in highly industrialised areas, where crèches were set up in which a working mother might deposit her child on her way to the factory or mine to reclaim it as she returned home in the evening. Such crèches still exist in the industrial areas, but nowadays they tend to be managed either by private charitable bodies or by factories, for the benefit of their workpeople, when a small charge can often be made for services rendered. The day of the hopelessly indigent is now, happily, almost a thing of the past. Whereas the crèches regularly take children from as early as 6 months of age, the following schools (kindergarten and nursery) have usually admitted from the age of 3; and though they were originally catering for the children of working-class parents they now tend to draw children from every social group, becoming (in the best sense of the word) democratising institutions. It is increasingly grasped that only by freely mixing with their peers away from the boredom and often inescapable petty restrictions of home life for a number of hours each day in the kind of calm and relaxed atmosphere that the trained kindergarten/nursery school teacher engenders can children at pre-primary ages find proper self-fulfilment in relation to themselves, to others, and to the exciting world about them. Only by such a pre-apprenticeship is the child fully prepared to benefit from his primary school education by being given a wider cultural background than even the best of homes can normally provide. At the same time the schools (mostly indirectly) are educating parents at *all* social levels in proper child care, and stimulating parental interest in the total education of the child at a time when growth in material wealth is leading to a lessening of family ties and substituting a variety of interests that money can afford and which are no longer primarily centred on home life.

Belgium and the Grand Duchy of Luxemburg

The position in Belgium is easily the most complicated in that the country is deeply divided linguistically, the division also affecting political affilia- tions and to some extent religious attitudes, and the whole influencing educational provision to an extent not experienced in any other country. A line drawn roughly west to east just south of the capital city, Brussels, marks this linguistic division. North of the line live the Flemings who speak the Dutch tongue (with local variants); south of the line are the French-speaking Walloons; and the capital city (though in Flemish-speaking territory) is nominally bilingual, though French-speakers easily predomi- nate. For centuries the Flemings have been the "poor relation", and as such have had both their cultural way of life (by no means unimpressive) and their tongue despised by the Walloons who both gloried in the high esteem in which the French language was held throughout Europe from the eighteenth century onwards and profited from the rapid industrialisa- tion of large parts of their territory. It was not until 1898 that, after a long struggle, the Flemings managed to get Dutch recognised as an official language alongside French. The struggle to obtain parity of esteem in the educational sector was equally drawn-out and arduous, and until 1930, for example, all teaching was in French at university level. Only in that year did the Flemings realise their aim of having *their* university in Ghent become a pure Dutch-medium institution.[1]

The tide began to turn in favour of the Flemings when in 1947 a language census was taken which revealed that of the total population of Belgium 51 per cent were Dutch-speaking, 33 per cent French, 15 per cent bilingual (but predominantly French-speaking and in the Brussels area), and 1 per cent German-speaking, in the *Cantons de l'Est* east of Spa and Eupen. Meantime, industrially, the Walloon provinces were clearly on the decline with their industrial apparatus outmoded, their coalfields

---

[1] Readers interested in a detailed discussion of the Fleming–Walloon struggles should consult my two books: *Power and Politics in Belgian Education*, London, 1963; and *Belgium*, London, 1969.

exhausting themselves, their communications inadequate to cope with any modernisation attempted. Meantime also Brussels' bureaucrats seemed to the frustrated Walloons deliberately to be favouring the Flemings by now establishing new technological projects in their area and attracting foreign capital for that purpose. It was useless to point out that the swing of modern industrial plant to Flemish territory was inevitable given the rapid technological changes, and that nowadays it was imperative to have new plants as near as possible to the great international port of Antwerp. Intransigent positions have been taken up on both sides and both sides have come to attack "bureaucratic" Brussels, reminding its inhabitants tartly that Brussels (with a population of 1 million) has for too long had too much to say in what should and should not be done with the remaining 8 million inhabitants of Belgium. Some sort of federal structure for the country would seem inevitable for the not too distant future. For the present, parity of esteem for the two contending factions is obtained by carefully duplicating all the various important administrative functions of government – giving, for example, two ministers for education (one Flemish, one Walloon) and parallel committees at all levels.

The impact of all this on the educational scene can be assessed from the passing of two successive linguistic laws in 1962 and 1963. The medium of instruction in schools must be Dutch in the Flemish provinces and French in Wallonia. In the Brussels agglomeration a pupil must attend either a Dutch-speaking or a French-speaking school according to the language spoken in the home, whilst in the eastern (Germanic) area, German must be used. A fair number of schools which formerly ran parallel streams in one building for Dutch and French speakers have now been abolished, and the universities of Brussels and Louvain (which formerly ran parallel courses) have fallen into line by themselves splitting into two separate entities. As far as the teaching of foreign languages is concerned, a former ruling whereby the first foreign language taught in a Dutch-speaking school must be French, and vice versa, has now been abolished except for the Brussels area. Outside Brussels the first foreign language may be either of the two national languages not used in the school as a medium of instruction, or English. The second foreign language may be any of the above or Italian, Spanish or Russian.

But it does not all end there. Since the creation of the kingdom of Belgium in 1830 there has been waged a constant and often bitter struggle between the Catholic church and the state for the control of the education of the young, and this struggle has been further complicated by the fact that the Flemings are the main supporters of and adherents to Catholicism. Various compromises have been arrived at over the years, but the simple fact that by 1959 more than half the school population was being educated in Catholic as opposed to lay schools made further legislation imperative.[1] The present situation is that schools are provided either by the state, or by a province, or at communal level (when they are all lay schools) or by the church, and parents by law must have free and ready access to the school of their choice. An Education Pact of 1959 approved by all three main political parties abolished all school fees everywhere (except for boarding), reiterated freedom of choice for parents, and made the state responsible for paying the salaries of *all* teachers in full (as well as guaranteeing sick pay and pension rights). In addition the state, whilst naturally fully responsible for its own schools, agreed to pay up to 60 per cent of the cost of building projects for provincial and town schools, but nothing to the "free" Catholic sector where many teachers are members of religious orders and in consequence do not handle their salary which is ploughed back into the funds of the respective religious orders. However, in January 1973 government support for the "free" sector was broadened to pay the salaries of non-teaching staff and to provide urgently needed physical training facilities. Economy measures to offset to some extent the enormous cost involved in all these measures have been mooted but not yet implemented, largely due to a marked lack of enthusiasm from the "free" sector. The proposal, which would also solve many problems by helping to abolish the excessive degree of distinction between Catholic and state education, is to create a number of experimental "community" schools which would combine in one building the Catholic and non-Catholic sectors whilst still rigorously safeguarding parental choice.

It must be admitted that the Belgian educational system as it exists today is an extremely elaborate and complicated one, and made more complicated by the sincere desire to have justice seen to be done to all. In a spirit of true democracy it is held that it must be the responsibility of the state to ensure the provision of a sound education for everybody. At the same time, and in the same democratic way, it is also held that

---

[1] For further details refer again to the two books mentioned above.

the powers of the state must be most clearly defined. In seeing that all may benefit it must dispense its benefits impartially and justly, and it may in no sense dictate what shall be done. "The state itself takes no initiative; it encourages initiative, and then controls and harmonises as necessary."[1] Its job is primarily to organise *for* education, to intervene only when the interests of the whole state are in peril, and therefore in general to ensure that there is real respect for human personality, a genuine spirit of tolerance, a developing sense of civic pride, and a clear notion in men's minds of their duties towards their neighbours and towards the whole of humanity. Just as it is conceded that the number of groups a person can belong to is bound to restrict his personal liberty in a variety of directions, so it is held that to belong to *one* group only can lead to enslavement to that group. Thus, the state's function is to see to it that people are not subject to the domination of one particular social group, and to make for as much diversity as possible within the general framework of government at both local and national levels.

As might be expected, the situation within the Grand Duchy of Luxemburg is less complicated. The country is, however, unique in being more or less trilingual, not in the sense of Switzerland where different languages are spoken in different areas, but in that everybody speaks Letzeburgish (a form of German dialect akin to Dutch or Flemish) in the home, German as the language of common culture, and French as a "first" foreign language. Again, since Roman Catholicism is the official state religion, there is no felt need for specifically Catholic schools, and instruction in the Catholic religion is everywhere compulsory though on a conscience clause parents may have their children excused such lessons. All public education is free and under the direct control of a Minister for Education who makes local authorities responsible for the education of pre-school and primary school children and for the appointment of the teachers. The staff of all other branches of education, however, are appointed by the Grand Duke.

Whereas Luxemburg admits children to pre-school education normally only between the ages of 4 and 6, Belgium has recently decided to lower the age of admission to its schools from 3 to 1½, thus making pre-school provision in Belgium far wider than in any other Western European country.

---

[1] Lameere and De Coster, *Espirit d'une politique générale de l'éducation*, Brussels, 1946, p. 23.

Latest available figures already show some 10 per cent of 2-year-olds admitted, 90 per cent of 3-year-olds (compared with France's 75 per cent and the UK's 3 per cent), 95 per cent of 4-year-olds (94 per cent in France and 30 per cent in the UK), and 100 per cent of 5-year-olds. Altogether Belgium has almost half a million children in some 5000 kindergartens with an obviously high pupil–teacher ratio of 30:1, this mainly to keep down costs – a decision which is giving rise to some concern that quality is being sacrificed to quantity. Of these children 171,000 are French-speaking, 281,000 Duthc-speaking, and 2000 German-speaking. Again in round figures, we find 280,000 in mainly "free" Catholic institutions (numbering 3000), 125,000 in communal schools (numbering 2000), 49,000 in state schools (numbering 494), and 308 pupils only in five provincially controlled schools.

Neither in Belgium nor in Luxemburg is any formal instruction permitted at the pre-school level, and the classes are usually attached to a primary school under the overall supervision of the primary school head teacher and the primary school inspectorate. Transition to primary school education proper is thus made as natural as possible, and particularly so when it is remembered that general Decroly principles are in force at both the pre-school and primary school levels. These it will be remembered, stress the necessity to base all teaching on the child's own activities and interests, and these needs are used to develop in the child a sense of discipline, a sense of taste, and powers of observation and manual dexterity. Simple elocution lessons, mostly involving the memorising of poems, etc. and their recitation singly and in groups, are used to correct and improve the child's speech. Physical education comes through games and exercises, as does social education; moral education through talks and practice; and the development of an aesthetic sense and of physical dexterity are encouraged by simple handicrafts such as paper cutting, bead, raffia and wool work, clay modelling, dancing, singing, story telling, and rhythmic exercises of all kinds. Parents are constantly involved and invited to the schools, and one simple method of having the parent keep in touch is to send the child home each week with a report book which has to be countersigned and in which the parent may make any observation she (it is usually the mother) thinks fit. In both countries no language other than the mother tongue is taught.

Primary education in both Belgium and Luxembourg is confined to the first six years of compulsory schooling (children aged 6–12). At the primary level in Belgium some 414,000 children speak French, 569,000 Dutch, and 6000 German. There are 521,000 children in "free" Catholic schools (to the number of 4000), 324,000 children in 4000 communal schools, 142,000 children in 606 state schools, and 2000 children in twelve provincial schools. Two periods per week are by law set aside for religious instruction which may be given by a Catholic (layman or priest), by a Protestant or by a Jewish Rabbi. Parents may opt out of this in which case their children must follow a course of lay moral instruction, also of two periods per week. In Luxemburg, Catholicism being the official religion, non-conforming parents may withdraw their children from this instruction if they so desire. Few do.

In Luxemburg there is a constant progression through the six grades of primary instruction, whereas in Belgium, mainly due to the influence of Decroly, the six years are divided into three two-year cycles. The teacher moves up with his children for each cycle, the child being required to show that he has fully mastered the work of his present cycle with his present teacher before advancing further, though remedial teaching takes place to obviate as far as possible having to hold a child back. Because the school-leaving age is still 14 in Belgium there also exists a fourth cycle for those boys and girls who do not wish to prolong their studies beyond the age of 14. This fourth cycle (or *quatrième degré*) is now fast disappearing, however, as more and more children and parents come to value some kind of secondary education, and the pleasing situation is now being achieved where most boys and girls are voluntarily prolonging their education usually up to 16 years of age and often beyond. Luxemburg insists on nine years of compulsory schooling to the age of 15.

In Belgium the language of instruction is Dutch in Flanders, French in Wallonia, German in the *Cantons de l'Est*, and the language of the child's home in Brussels. In the Brussels area (as in communities along the linguistic frontiers) the teaching of the second national language is compulsory from the third year (age 8–9) for a minimum of three hours and a maximum of six hours per week. In other areas the second national language may optionally be taught from the fifth year (age 10–11). In Luxemburg the mother tongue, German and French are taught, German from the beginning of the first year, French from the beginning of the second year.

One of the first tasks of the primary school is to enable children to express themselves easily and clearly in the mother tongue, to read and to understand what is read, to write correctly, and to do arithmetical calculations quickly and accurately. Considerable emphasis is also placed on the value of systematic exercises, especially with regard to spelling and multiplication tables — it being baldly stated in the Bovesse Plan for Belgium (1936) that "only when computation has become a subconscious technique can the mind be more free to reason". Apart from the mother tongue and arithmetic, religious (or moral) instruction and the elements of a second (or in Luxemburg a third) language, the curriculum will include some basic notions of the natural sciences, national history and geography, drawing, hygiene, singing, physical training. For girls there is also needlework and for boys in rural areas, gardening. In accord with Decroly's idea that the curriculum should not be split up, but "should gravitate around a theme or centre of interest", certain subjects are not originally studied for themselves but are incorporated in other school activities — for example, geography, history and the natural sciences can be fused to form a study of the environment based on exercises in observation. It is the principle of globalisation, or wholeness — the principle used in teaching the child to read and write.

Nevertheless, and despite the considerable influence of Decroly's ideas on primary education, criticism of the formal nature of instruction at the primary level — particularly in the last two years when studies become more subject-centred and are gradually expanded and organised in a more systematic way — has been on the increase. In theory, in Belgium there is an unstructured time-table, but as far back as 1958 it was felt necessary to restrict the teacher's freedom to some extent by laying down firm guide-lines to make for greater uniformity in pupil preparation. This, it is felt, has led to the education given to be not sufficiently child-centred; to placing too much emphasis on the acquisition of facts and too little on the development of the child as a person. Thus, in the school year beginning September 1971 an experiment was launched in Belgium involving twenty-six state schools and fifty-seven communal schools. In these schools, normal class teaching takes place only in the morning with the emphasis on changing the approach to the teaching of the two most important subjects, the mother tongue and arithmetic. The afternoons are then devoted to team work, cultural activities, games, etc. The idea is to create a climate which will favour self-expression and creativity, encourage discovery techniques, emphasise the importance of oral communication (which already plays such a large part in pre-school education) and produce situations in which each and every child can expect to succeed, and measure for himself his success. There is a constant exchange of views amongst teachers themselves, the inspectorate and the local authorities involved, and on a basis of these discussions it is hoped gradually to modify and extend the experiment further afield. In the meantime, of course, and in keeping with the traditional approach, no decision at a governmental level will be taken.

Holland

As in Belgium there is no state monopoly for education, nor is the Ministry of Education looked upon as a kind of "schoolmaster-in-chief" as in France. There is, in consequence, a high degree of decentralisation which stems from a wish to give as much freedom as possible to all sections of the community. Unity out of diversity is the ideal, it being maintained that a healthy democracy must be based on recognition of and respect for a variety of attitudes and opinions. This reduces the function of the state to ensuring uniformity of standards throughout the school systems, of making for identity of opportunity (as opposed to equality of opportunity), of seeing that all who legally seek to run their own schools may do so, and of footing the bill. In actual practice this means that the state pays all salaries to all teachers on the same uniform scale, and that the municipality meets all the running expenses of all its schools whether publicly or privately maintained. The state, however, safeguards itself by giving subventions at the pre-school and primary levels on an approved teacher–pupil ratio, and at secondary levels there is a reassessment every three years to ensure the schools are generally conforming to numerical and other standards of competence laid down by the state. Should a subvention be withdrawn, the municipality must bear the whole cost.

The Dutch love of freedom and independence, which probably found its greatest expression for all time in the eighty years' struggle to secure freedom from the Spanish yoke, finds its modern expression in this present system which harmoniously combines the benefits of both a centralised and a decentralised system of educational administration.

What are sometimes referred to as the three main pillars of Dutch society are the Catholic church (accounting for some 40 per cent of the population and residing mainly in the south), the Dutch Reformed church (comprising the state church, which is Lutheran, and the more extreme Calvinist Protestant church), and the Neutrals. Neutrals usually refuse on principle to have anything to do with either of the two main religious bodies (the division between which is deep-rooted and intense), and are equally averse to submitting to state direction, arguing that every parent must be free to choose exactly how his child shall be educated. Catholics hold the church to be the only proper educator. Protestants (and particularly the Calvinists with their extremely democratic organisation) argue that parents must be the main if not the sole educators of their children. Thus, there are four types of school, three private and one state-controlled. Most recent figures indicate that some 44 per cent of children are in Catholic schools, some 27 per cent in Protestant schools, about 25 per cent in the *openbaar* (state-controlled) schools, and about 3 per cent in private (usually prestigious) neutral establishments. It should also be noted that this religious divisiveness extends itself not only to newspapers, broadcasting and trade unions, but also to the provision of social amenities and welfare generally — it being even today not unknown for some towns still to run three separate public libraries.

Because of the in-built divisiveness in educational provision, the state inspectorate plays an important part in co-ordination, administration, the production of various material aids, the approval of basic textbooks, and the maintenance of uniform standards throughout the country. Pre-primary education, for example, is controlled by two chief inspectors and an assistant, the whole country being divided into twenty-eight districts, each under a chief inspector and with a total of sixty-nine inspectors divided amongst the four regions. General secondary education has seventeen inspectors, pre-university secondary education is divided among six teams, each with four inspectors, and there are inspectors for every branch of technical, vocational and special education. Directors of education in the municipalities play a role which is mainly financial, the powers of a local education authority being much more limited than, say, in England or America.

The Pre-Primary Education Act of 1955 both encourages and assists the establishment of pre-primary schools for children between the ages of 4 and 7, the higher age level being concerned (as in West Germany) with the slow developer. Only about 20 per cent of these schools are state controlled, and all but the very poor are required in all schools to pay a weekly contribution that varies according to circumstances but is usually not more than about 50 pence per week, the main burden being shared by the state and the municipal councils. Latest figures indicate that 80 per cent of the 4-plus age group and 90 per cent of the 5-plus group are in attendance. To qualify for a grant, schools must be open on Mondays, Tuesdays, Thursdays and Fridays from 8.30 to 11.30, and from 2.30 to 4.30, and on Wednesdays from 8.30 to 11.30 only. It has been common practice to run these schools as separate establishments (and, as we have seen, with their separate inspectorate), but the government is already beginning to integrate pre-primary and primary schools and hopes to make education compulsory and free certainly from 5-plus and possibly later from 4-plus when a nursery section will be introduced from 3-plus. Most pre-primary schools have only two or three teachers, except in the most densely populated areas, but classes rarely exceed thirty in number and are often smaller. A parents' committee is attached to each school, and in towns possessing several schools a joint parents' committee is usually set up for general oversight and co-ordination of policy throughout the town's school system. Teachers at the pre-primary level have usually been recruited at the age of 15–16 on successful completion of a four-year general secondary school course, or after three years in a pre-university school. After three years' training they can qualify for their teacher's certificate, and a further successful year will give them a head teacher's certificate which also qualifies them for ordinary primary school teaching. Now, in line with projected new reforms, it is hoped to eliminate the lower standard of entry to pre-primary teaching, to combine the training of both pre-primary and primary teachers, and to pay both the same salary scales. Latest available statistics (1973) show that 7108 pre-primary schools are staffed by 17,465 teachers and cater for about 506,000 pupils.

The majority of the schools employ the Froebel system as opposed to that of Madame Montessori, though more modern influences (including that of Decroly supporters) are to be found everywhere. It is held that the main functions of the pre-primary school are to be directed towards the elimination of social disadvantage, to help minimise the effects of urbanisation, to make for correct social behaviour, and to make a start with diagnostic testing and remedial teaching (as necessary) in order to make for confidence and success in the later stages of schooling. No attempt is made to prepare children for work they will later do in the primary school, however, and at present there is no co-ordination of effort between the two schools. There is no structured day. Work and play alternate. And the timetable (universally applied) includes physical activities, modelling, drawing and painting, music, story telling, and the learning by heart of simple poems and nursery rhymes – the whole involving creative and dramatic activities. In short, the schools are more akin to the infant departments to be found in any British primary school than to a typical British nursery school. No school meals are provided, the children being expected to go home for the two-hour lunch break.

Since 1954 the period of compulsory education has been free, and it is now held to extend from the age of 6-plus for nine full years or until the end of the school year in which a pupil reaches the age of 16. Education beyond 16 can be assisted as necessary either by scholarships or interest-free loans. When the period of compulsory education became free, all schools began to be equally subsidised by the state, but the private schools have still continued the traditional practice of seeking financial support from other sources (e.g. church funds, or simply by charging fees). Thus the "neutral" schools in particular – usually prestige schools – charge the highest fees, attract better staff (because of higher rates of pay) and tend to have much better equipment. A move to counter the disadvantages a child in the *openbaar* school thus runs is sometimes made by the larger municipalities to divide their *openbaar* schools into categories A and B, to channel more money into the favoured A-type school, and to have it pursue an extended curriculum more in keeping with work done in the private sector. Socialist governmental pressures since 1973 are seeking to do away with all these discrepancies by abolishing school fees at both primary and secondary levels, by making education a joint community responsibility to be wholly financed by taxes, to have all types of secondary education under one roof, and (as we have noted already) to fuse pre-primary and primary education. Success must ultimately depend on amicable compromise arrangements among the three aforementioned pillars of Dutch society.

The normal age range in the primary school is between 6 and 12, and the practice of having to repeat a year has now almost been eliminated.

All but Catholic schools are co-educational, and all schools are usually well furnished and equipped. Record cards are kept and the pupils are continuously assessed. Whilst the scattered population leads to more than half the primary schools having only three or four teachers, the larger towns can have schools of up to 400 pupils, though (except in a few areas of expanding population) classes do not generally exceed thirty in number. And, whilst the pre-primary sector is entirely staffed by women, men preponderate at the primary level, few teachers being over the age of 40 since women leave to marry and rear families and men seek promotion into the lower secondary sector.

The timetable is again universally applied and covers the three Rs, the Dutch language and literature (and Frisian in appropriate areas), history, geography, speech training, natural science (including hygiene), music, art, handicrafts and physical education (including swimming). All pupils receive instruction in traffic regulations and road safety – a very necessary precaution in the land of the bicycle! Since the end of the last war a distinguished modern linguist and secondary school headmaster (a personal friend of the author by the name of van Willigen) has campaigned for the abolition of an almost traditional practice of having French taught in the upper forms of the school – out of hours and on a fee-paying basis – to pupils whose parents have been ambitious for their later success at an academic secondary level. His main objections have been aimed at the inadequate nature of the instruction offered, failure to adjust the teaching to the nature of the child and to integrate it into the primary school course proper, and the selection of pupils (only some 9 per cent from the two top streams) on grounds not relevant to language learning but to a parent's social and financial status.

Following on the 1970 amendments to the 1920 Primary Education Act, van Willigen's campaigning can be seen to have had its effect, though not necessarily exactly as he intended. *English* has now been made a compulsory subject throughout all primary schools as from the autumn of 1975 from the age of 10, though schools who so wish may start from the moment the child begins compulsory education. The aim is to make all Dutch citizens capable of communicating in English which is "a universal language of great practical value . . . easily the most international language, which will be taught to our young children by tapes and other audio-visual aids. . . . We hope to produce a totally bilingual generation of

14-year-olds by 1985."[1] To this end courses in English are already under way for the 50,000 teachers in Holland's 8000 primary schools, and colleges of education are being required to have trained at least 16,000 specialist English teachers for primary schools by 1980.

Other changes implemented by the 1970 ruling include obliging teachers to abandon narrow subject teaching in favour of treating their subjects as coming within the broader range of the three Rs, and the elimination of divisions into classes by years. Nevertheless, outside observers still remark on the traditional and teacher-centred approach in most schools. Dutch educationists are acutely aware of .this criticism, and experimentation is going on in certain municipalities directed in the main to the elimination of poor performance, to coping with special problems of educating children in deprived areas, and to having children work "packages" at their own pace. They will still reply, however, that in a true democracy the freedom of parents to choose an education for their children in accordance with their beliefs and principles must be safeguarded. The role of the educationist must be to advise and guide but never to dictate. Parents still consider the main function of the school to be that of instilling knowledge and the ability to think, as well as to prepare boys and girls for their future careers. If the primary school is now a basic school frequented by all children, it still carefully prepares each and every child for the appropriate kind of post-primary education for which he seems to be best suited. Social differences, it is claimed, are allowed to be neither a handicap nor an advantage.

France

As we have already instanced, educational practice in France has been shaped by Humanists such as Montaigne, Descartes and Pascal, later by others of the eighteenth-century Enlightenment, and finally by Napoleon's determination to bring the whole of the system under the control of the Imperial University. From all this have resulted those characteristics which have made for France's greatest strength and also its weakness when faced with the intractable problems of coming to terms with modern technological

[1] Dr. Jacques Carpay of the Psycho-Linguistics Department of the University of Utrecht who has carried out a pilot scheme with 350 10-year-olds.

development and the democratisation of education which has become an inescapable concomitant. From Humanism stems the concept of *culture générale*, a kind of schooling based primarily on a study of literature and of the humanities, geared to enable the recipient to attain that wisdom considered to be an essential part of civilised life. And from this there equally stems an emphasis on training in the art of rational objective thinking and expression. Such an education, however, can only be for a minority — whether of birth or proven ability — and the constant problem dogging educational reform throughout the nineteenth and twentieth centuries has been how to reconcile the training of such an intellectual élite with the principles of equality in education (as in other matters) first enunciated by the French Revolutionaries. Since 1945 a bewildering and rapid succession of reforms have grappled with this question; it is now openly admitted that the traditional system can no longer serve the needs of modern industrial society; and the latest of these reforms (implemented as from September 1976) baldly declares its aim as being that of achieving a system of *éducation permanente* by which is meant a system designed to meet both the educational and cultural needs of every person throughout his life in accordance with his abilities.

A further problem (as in Belgium) has been the struggle between church and state for the control of education, somewhat intensified since the last war by a reformist neo-Catholic movement, led for the most part by laymen and supported by the younger clergy. It has to be remembered that nominally about 80 per cent of the population of France are Catholic, with the church still a potent force in areas such as Brittany and Alsace. Roughly 43 per cent of Frenchmen (according to *Le Monde*) affirmed in June 1959 that they would prefer to send their children to Catholic schools could they afford to do so. And recent statistics (1971–72) reveal some 16 per cent of the total school population to be in the private sector. In January 1960, De Gaulle bowed to Catholic pressure and passed a bill to give that financial aid already overdue to Catholic schools if they were to remain in a position to continue to offer facilities comparable with those in the state-controlled sector. Put very simply, the bill has allowed all accredited Catholic schools (i.e. those with qualified teaching personnel) to enter into contracts with the government whereby all such teachers' salaries are paid by the state, whilst day-to-day running expenses of the schools become a charge on the local authorities. In return, no fees may be charged in any school at any level except for religious instruction and incidentals (such as music) and even then permission must first be sought from the Ministry of Education. Boarding fees, of course, lie outside this jurisdiction. It must also be remembered that, since all examinations throughout France are state-controlled, the curriculum throughout the private sector must resemble that in comparable state schools.

This principle of the centralisation of education was first enunciated by La Chalotais in 1763, upheld by the writers of the French Revolution, and cast in its final practical mould by Napoleon in 1808, to be later modified and modernised as circumstances dictated. The latest reorganisation dates from May 1973. All authority is exercised by the Minister of Education, under the control of Parliament, and by his delegates in each of the 26 *Académies* into which the country is now administratively divided. At the head of each academy is the *recteur* who is nominated by the President of the Republic and directly responsible to the Minister. Usually he is chosen from among the university professors and needs to be a man of high academic and administrative standing. Within his academy he has almost absolute (though not very precisely defined) powers; he directs the whole system of education from the nursery schools upwards and is responsible for the general supervision of all private schools. He is assisted, of course, by a permanent administration, an inspectorate, and various regional advisory councils. Again since 1973, a policy of "deconcentration and decentralisation" has been followed with the stated aim of making the implementation of reforms more effective, particularly at a regional level to suit regional conditions. This has thrown more responsibility on the office of *recteur* who is seen as increasingly becoming more of a decision-maker and less an interpreter of orders from central authority, particularly as regards the organisation of education and the administration of the teaching force dependent upon him. Nevertheless, the Minister of Education still remains as "schoolmaster-in-chief", and there is firm central control of all aspects of educational policy and planning which assures uniformity of standards throughout the country whether in the public or private sectors of education, and at any level.

Education is now compulsory from 6 to 16, the school-leaving age having been raised from 14 (since 1936) to 16 in 1967, although this did not actually become fully effective until 1972. Pre-primary schooling usually begins at 3, but sometimes at 2 or at 4. The proportion of the age group undergoing such voluntary education is higher in France than in any other European country except for Belgium. Latest figures (1973) indicate 100 per cent attendance between the ages of 5 and 6, 92 per cent of 4-year-olds, 72 per cent of 3-year-olds, and 33 per cent of 2-year-olds. True, these high attendance figures are achieved only at the expense of crowding many more children into classes than is desirable on every count − and this is particularly true of Paris − but the Ministry is well aware of the situation and is actively planning to provide enough places with a lower pupil−teacher ratio for all 2- to 5-year-olds. Further, the most recently promulgated reform for the whole of education envisages provision of the same instruction for all children between the ages of 2 and 16, allows for considerable flexibility regarding the age at which individual children may pass from one level to the next, and stipulates that there must be pre-primary schools to cater for all who want them between the ages of 2 and 6. This new type of pre-primary school would be divided into two age groups: for ages 2-4 it would be nursery-type education; between the ages of 4 and 6 the work done would be more like that done in an English infant school, though the three Rs would be taught there − the aim being to allow the brightest to leave at 5 to attend the primary school proper and to keep those with learning difficulties (if necessary) up to the age of 7.

The French are justifiably proud of the part played by pre-primary classes (the *école maternelle* reaching as far back as 1837) as an important social force in caring for the children of working-class parents in particular. And because of the unique nature of this task (intensified by the continued flight from the land of the poverty-stricken peasantry to more lucrative industrial pursuits)[1] the schools have been highly successful in extending their influence from giving simple child care to becoming a positive help to all young children (and of instruction to their parents) in the highly formative years before compulsory education starts. As a result, the schools have been allowed to experiment freely and have acquired to themselves their own specialised inspectorate which, though still answerable to the Ministry of Education, actively encourages innova-

---

[1] In 1800, agricultural work occupied 85 per cent of the total population; this figure had declined to 27 per cent by 1954, representing some 5 million agricultural workers; by 1965 a further million workers had left agriculture, and the drain continues.

tion. Thus, over the last decade or so, experiments have been going on with the teaching of a modern language (English or German) on a purely oral method and by utilising the services of student-teachers in training from the appropriate countries who will at least familiarise the youngsters with "the music of language". Again, where the pre-primary classes are attached to a primary school (they are usually separate) the pre-primary teacher with the 5- to 6-year-olds has been allowed to move up into the primary school proper with her charges and so gradually initiate them into the more rigorous procedures involved at that level. The teachers, incidentally, receive the same two-year training and have the same salary scale as primary teachers, being recruited since 1972 by competitive examination after having taken the *baccalauréat*.[1] Following traditional practice, good all-round intellectual achievement is exacted in every branch of the teaching profession!

Any *commune* which so wishes may open a pre-primary school, but if it does so it pledges itself to operate it for thirty years. In return, the state will pay all teachers' salaries and up to 85 per cent of the cost of the school, the *commune* thereafter being responsible for general maintenance. *Communes* with more than 2000 inhabitants are required by law to provide such a school. The sharp decline from 72 per cent attendance for the 3–4 age group to only 33 per cent at the lowest age level can be attributed to the fact that, still basically Catholic in temper, France looks to the church and to the family as the most important influences in the early life of the child. Nor can the working-class origins of the pre-primary school make an easy early appeal to the still class-conscious bourgeoisie with its conception of an intellectual élite which only the best schools can properly train. Unlike Belgian schools, therefore, which really supply the needs of all social groups, the French pre-primary school recruits to it, up to the age of 4, mainly the children of the working class, and beyond that age children of the lower middle class — teachers, tradesmen, minor civil servants who are anxious to miss no opportunity of giving their children every possible advantage in the gruelling scholastic courses that lie ahead. It is such parents who have stolidly resisted any reforming tendencies to reduce an emphasis on teaching the three Rs in the 5–6 age range.

---

[1] In practice, however, mainly due to lack of places in training colleges, and to meet an urgent demand, many are still trained on the job by the local inspector.

Organisation is into three sections: the first, for 2- to 4-year-olds, is called *la classe petite*; the second section (for 4- to 5-year-olds) is called *la classe moyenne*; the last section, *la grande classe*. The schools are open for six hours a day, three in the morning and three in the afternoon, and since the schools are voluntary there is no specified arrival time. In industrial areas the school can remain open twelve hours a day to cater for children whilst their mothers are out at work, and in such cases it is not the teacher but a specially trained force of women (*gardiennes*) who look after the child outside the class-room. All children receive regular medical examination, and there is specific training in hygiene both for mothers and children, the former being encouraged in every possible way (as in Belgium) to take an active interest in the work of the school and to relate what is done in school (including feeding and dieting) with attitudes in the home.

Whilst educationists are usually quick to point out that the French pre-primary school does not follow any one educational method but leaves teachers free to experiment to find the best approach suited to their charges, the influence of such personalities as Madame Montessori, Decroly, Piaget, Claparède and Ferrière is much in evidence. Generally speaking, however, we can say that the overall influence has been that of the distinguished late nineteenth-century inspectress, Mme Kergomard, who, in the 1880s, turned what had been so far mainly child-minding centres into the prototypes for today's pre-school classes. The aim is to develop the body, mind and heart of the child in an atmosphere of calm and order. The programme laid down includes physical exercises (breathing, games, movement, songs); manual work and drawing; language exercises and recitation; observation exercises built around carefully chosen centres of interest; exercises designed to give basic moral instruction; and, for those in the top group, elements of reading, writing and arithmetic. The week is divided up roughly as follows:

Recreation and "cleanliness" (hygiene)	5	hours
Rhythmic exercises	2½	"
Singing and music	2½	"
Stories	2	"
Sensorial and observation exercises	2	"
Modelling and drawing	2	"
Handicrafts	2	"
Top group only French (elocution, reading, writing)	10	"
Arithmetic	2	"

The guiding principles are carefully listed by the Ministry of Education as: a respect for the child's personality; use of active methods; education of the senses through creative activities; wide use of all means of expression; moral and social education through activity and life in a community; physical education through play; intellectual education through free though controlled observation; an atmosphere of freedom as a prerequisite for developing self-discipline. In 1973 there were some 2 million children in the pre-primary state sector as opposed to about 340,000 in Catholic schools — giving a figure of 17 per cent outside the state system.

The primary school is still looked upon as playing an important role in helping to form conscientious and loyal citizens and also in providing the pupil with those elements of practical knowledge necessary for him to perform his daily task as a worker. It is recognised that the majority of pupils passing through the primary schools (even when the latest reforms are taken into consideration) will move on to some form of manual or agricultural work. Latest estimates, for example, indicate that even though all children will be kept in a common school at least up to the age of 15 only some 35 per cent will then opt for an academic course; some form of technical or commercial instruction will be followed by 45 per cent; and the remaining 20 per cent will form an unskilled labour force. The main aim in the primary school, therefore, is to pick up where pre-primary education ends and to teach not a great deal but teach it well. In practice this resolves itself into giving a thorough grounding in the three Rs, with insistence on ability to handle the French tongue expertly and elegantly, the teaching of geography and history centred almost exclusively on France, and some elementary science crammed in where possible. Old, well-tried and proven methods of instruction are not abandoned but may be seen today continued alongside more modern activity approaches. There is still much learning by heart, but also group work and group discussions, studies of local interest, creative writing, and the delivery of lecturettes by individual pupils designed to encourage the development of particular interests. And, though the practice of setting homework was abandoned in 1956 along with the 11-plus examination for transfer to some form of post-primary education, children (on parental request) may still have up to five hours of private supervised study each week on school premises.

Whilst pre-primary classes are mixed, children are usually segregated in the primary school which has to work to a curriculum in general terms common to the whole of France, and which is divided into three sections: *cours préparatoire* for the first year's intake (aged 6–7), *cours élémentaire* for the next two years (aged 7–9), and *cours moyen* for the last two years (aged 9–11). Pupils who fail to make a grade will be kept back to repeat the year, and recent estimates (on which present proposed reforms are based) show that only some 25 per cent of primary pupils manage to complete the whole course without repeating at least one grade. Thus, a young child who (for whatever reason) is deprived of a good start at a very early (and crucial) age is straightway handicapped for the rest of his school career. He passes on to post-primary education on the strength of his primary school performance, and the poor performer will almost automatically be drafted into the third ability stream there with little or no chance of ever moving out of it.

All educationists, of course, have long been aware of the fact that this system works to the disadvantage of children from the lower income groups or of those who receive inadequate home support, and have over the last several years been carefully implementing changes, all based on successful pilot schemes first started in the 1950s. In 1969 it was decided to reduce the working week in the primary school from thirty to twenty-seven hours and to make Wednesday and Saturday afternoons free. The timetable was at the same time re-structured to give fifteen hours to basic studies (French and mathematics), six hours to *activités d'éveil* (to stimulate the child's cultural and personal interests) to be shared by history, geography, moral education, observation projects, handwork, modelling and music, and six hours to physical education and sport – this including (as appropriate) classes "in the snow" or by the sea during term time. In 1973 the division of the school year into two long semesters was replaced by a three-term year separated by fixed holidays at Christmas, in the spring and in the summer (July and August).

And now, finally, comes the overall proposed reform of education which it was originally hoped to implement as from September 1976 and which takes particular note of the vital need to cater for the interests of *every* child at this early age, implying that not only shall the disadvantaged child be given all help possible but that the bright child shall equally be spurred on. The new primary school would be divided into three two-year cycles (as in Belgium). Entry to the primary school (as we have seen) would be between the ages of 5 and 7 according to the child's readiness. There would in future be no repeating of a year, for just as the child could enter the primary school early, so might he leave it at any age between 10 and 13 to proceed to secondary education proper. In effect, what is exacted is six full years in the primary school for every child except the most precocious, the ultimate success of the scheme turning on having every child in the pre-primary school from at least the age of 4. Given the present pre-primary figures for attendance and the intense drive to improve still further facilities in these schools, and their efficiency, this should not present any real problem.

In 1973 there were some 4 million children attending state primary schools and roughly 700,000 in the private (mainly Catholic) sector, again giving a figure of 17 per cent outside the state system.

5

The Scandinavian countries have both geographically and historically been kept somewhat apart from the main stream of Western European life, and it is only recently that economic and technological factors have drawn them closer. It is therefore not surprising to find that, whilst they have many characteristics in common among themselves, they diverge considerably from the general Western European pattern in particular over the organisation of education. They are the only countries which insist that compulsory education shall not begin until the age of 7. They are the only countries not to be pushed towards providing near universal pre-primary education, still maintaining that, all things being equal, the proper place for the young child is at the mother's knee. They are even more significantly the only countries which have, over the years since the last war, evolved a system of truly comprehensive education for every child between the ages of 7 and 16. The most important single influence on education has been that of the Lutheran church which, with its emphasis on individual salvation and equality in the face of God, resulted not only in the need for universal compulsory education but also in the conviction that this should equally be available to both boys and girls. True, the Lutheran church today does not have the same hold on the people as in the past, but it has remained the state church and in consequence there has never been anything but harmony between church and state over the control and conduct of education. All schools are in consequence state schools (a very few private institutions are tolerated), or rather the people's schools carefully controlled at a local level but under overall state supervision, and run on the most democratic lines which today result in often effective (if sometimes somewhat disconcerting) pupil participation.

It was from amongst a group of various scattered kingdoms comprising what we today call Scandinavia that there gradually emerged the three distinct kingdoms of Denmark, Norway and Sweden. Intermarriages eventually led to a union of the three countries in 1397 with Denmark soon asserting its authority and command over its two partners. Repeatedly Norway and Sweden attempted to break away. Sweden succeeded as early as 1523, but Norway was to remain more or less a Danish province (though still retaining its hereditary monarchs and Diet) until 1814 when it was attached to Sweden. Throughout the nineteenth century Norwegians chafed against this unwarranted and undesired subservience to Sweden, and finally, on the results of a national plebiscite held in 1905, they at last achieved their independence. By a happy arrangement Prince Charles of Denmark, who had married Maud, the youngest daughter of King Edward VII of England, was proposed as the first constitutional monarch and was popularly elected and acclaimed.

Thus, all three countries are now constitutional monarchies in which the functions of the Crown are analagous to those of the Crown in Great Britain. The controlling power of government is invested in the people who elect their parliamentary bodies on a principal of universal suffrage. The dissemination of culture is wide, and all classes of people play an active part in community and social life – the system of decentralisation being imposed on the people by the Lutheran church which held that Christian salvation came only through enlightenment of the people and that the only way to work at the people's level was through the small parish community. Characteristic also of these countries is that private capitalism and social collectivism are co-extensive. In Sweden, for example, all public utility services are the concern of either the state or the local government – yet most industrial workers are privately employed. Throughout Scandinavia generally the whole of the arable land is privately owned and worked – yet the farmers form themselves into co-operative societies to market their produce. Finally, it should be noted that the "welfare state" has long been the concern of these countries as a means of achieving real economic and social stability. Throughout the centuries, education has been deliberately used to bring about a high degree of voluntary collectivism, and public education as part of the urge towards popular enlightenment which came with the Reformation has been a national concern since the sixteenth century.

Denmark

Responsibility for education is shared between the central and local authorities with the Ministry of Education having overall responsibility and control. The Ministry issues guidelines and instructions regulating school timetables, public examinations, and (in order to achieve uniformity of standards throughout the school system) the subject matter to be taught. It appoints all senior staff in schools and in the administration, controls higher education directly, and controls most of the *gymnasier* and about two-thirds of teacher-training colleges. Local authorities have administrative and financial control of primary and lower secondary schooling, and some responsibility for the *gymnasier*. They are equally held responsible for feeding back to the Ministry statistical information on the distribution of schools in their area, on staffing, on health and welfare facilities, and on general progress being made. The capital city, Copenhagen, has enjoyed independent status since 1658, and this it still jealously preserves, running its own School Directorate which reports directly to the Ministry.

Parental involvement in the running of schools is traditional, and this is obtained by having a system of school boards, one for each school and each with from two to four representatives of the parents according to size. In addition, two members of the local education authority must be elected from among members of the school boards. Nor are the teachers forgotten. There are teachers' councils in all but the smallest schools, and joint teachers' councils are elected to represent the total teaching force at local authority level. They are strongly represented on school boards and attend meetings of the local education authority without voting rights.

The principle of education in the home has become so deeply rooted in the traditions of Denmark that even today no parent is obliged to send his child to school provided he is willing and able to secure the necessary instruction for his child in other ways — this being a legacy from early

Lutheran stress on the primacy of the family in education. This obviously is an important reason for the lack of any substantial pre-school provision for children before the compulsory starting age of 7. Other conditioning factors, however, are the rather harsh climate (almost the whole of Denmark lies as far north as the northern half of Labrador), and the scattered nature of its population of some 5 million people: one-quarter of the total population lives in Copenhagen, another quarter in small townships, and fully 50 per cent are scattered over the countryside (or on small islands). Not surprisingly, pre-school education is confined to the larger towns, and (as in most other countries) there has been a sharp rise in attendance figures from a mere 3739 in 1960 to 20,874 in 1965, and to 38,000 for 1972.

Nowadays, Denmark finds it necessary to run crèches for the children of working mothers up to the age of 3, and pre-primary classes proper for children between the ages of 3 and 7. These classes are provided either by the municipal authorities or on private initiative and fall under the general supervision of the Ministry of Social Security. Private institutions may in certain circumstances be subsidised by the state, and fees are charged (commensurate with ability to pay) in all the schools. Teaching methods are along approved Montessori, Froebel and Decroly lines. A rough calculation would indicate that about 25 per cent of the age range 3 to 7 are at present in pre-school attendance, whilst the crèches work out at one place per thousand inhabitants. It is, however, hoped to double this pre-school attendance figure by 1980.

The Danes are rightly proud of the fact that King Frederick VI was well in advance of most other countries when in 1814 he made basic schooling compulsory for three days a week between the ages of 7 and 14 and insisted that every township must have its elementary school. In 1849, compulsory schooling was extended to cover a full six-day week. Attempts to co-ordinate the work of the primary and secondary schools was begun as early as 1903, and secondary education for all became a reality in 1937. The Education Act of 1958, whilst insisting on a comprehensive form of education for all up to the age of 14 (as opposed to hiving off the supposedly academically-minded at age 11), made no effort to raise the school leaving age beyond 14. This, in effect, was a sop to the farming communities who have always looked to the folk high school to provide any further education in farming pursuits, and a tribute to the good work being done in the numerous village schools in educating their children to wish voluntarily to pursue their studies further. In 1972, with well over 90 per cent of all pupils voluntarily staying beyond the age of 14, the Danish parliament raised the school leaving age to 15. In 1974 the leaving age was raised to 16, though pupils may still leave at 14 provided they propose proceeding to some form of regular vocational education. And for the not too distant future a full twelve-year school (ages 7 to 19) is envisaged with built-in vocational training and no selection of any kind to be made of pupils before they reach the age of 14. In a word, Denmark has now brought herself into line with Norway and Sweden by establishing one single *folkeskole* (people's school) and has followed a general Western European trend in permitting differentiation only after the age of about 14. In the meantime, local authorities may at their discretion extend schooling to the age of 17.

Danish schools function between 8 a.m. and 2 p.m., the day being divided into six periods of fifty minutes each. Pupils in the first two years work only four hours; for years three and four they work five hours; the full six hours are worked only from about the age of 11. Promotion from one class to the next is automatic and no examinations are held before the age of 15-plus, though parents receive regular reports on their children's progress. A child who leaves at 14-plus will get a certificate stating his proficiency in the subjects taught, together with comments on his interests and aptitudes. A child staying for nine or ten years may sit a state examination which will give him a certificate giving more precise information in terms of performance.

The first five years of schooling give the common basic groundwork: the three Rs, history, geography, biology, physical education, music, the creative arts and religion. In the sixth year in all schools science, woodwork for boys and housecraft for girls, and one foreign language (usually English) are introduced. It is about this time that what is sometimes called "tentative differentiation" starts. The seventh year is concerned with rounding off the education of children (in the predominantly rural areas) who will be leaving school; with organising the curriculum in terms of local opportunities for employment and in accordance with the child's aptitudes, ability, and desire for some form of further education; with beginning the teaching of a second foreign language (usually German) and the addition of more mathematics for those wishing to pass on to some form of academic secondary education. It is at this point that so far there has been a clear division of pupils into academic and non-academic streams, but the most recent directive issued by the Ministry of Education required that from August 1975 such streaming be modified. It is suggested that there should be mixed-ability teaching in Danish and the humanities with setting possible for English, German, mathematics and science. There should be more attention paid to the teaching of Danish and consideration given to introducing the teaching of English one year earlier. No form of leaving examination should in future be taken.

Further suggestions turn on the permissive nature of life in Denmark where, it will be remembered, the *Little Red Schoolbook*, radically questioning all forms of authority, first appeared in 1969. It is proposed rigorously to exclude any kind of political and religious indoctrination in the schools — a move certainly to be interpreted by many as a conservative attack against Marxist teachers! It is also tacitly acknowledged that teaching to date has been in all respects too traditionalist and too formal, the timetable too rigidly structured. More flexibility is urged, together with an implicit promise of greater freedom at local level for experimentation. How much of all this will finally become law remains to be seen. What is certain is that, as in the past, the legislators will go cautiously and be as conciliatory as possible.

To sum up, Denmark has gradually worked her way to achieving a nine-year school common to all and capped by an optional tenth year. The first five years are considered as basic; the remaining four years will inescapably show some differentiation though this will be reduced to a minimum. And it should still be possible to leave at 14, provided education is to be continued in some other establishment.

It is perhaps worthwhile finally to note recent innovations in child minding generally which the Danes are beginning to feel can be held to some extent at least to account for the noted low level of juvenile delinquency everywhere. The aim is to place the young child in a community not only of his peers but of others both older and younger than himself. The state-run Kennedy Garden in Copenhagen, for example, houses under one roof crèches, a day nursery, a nursery school, a leisure-time club, youth clubs, and facilities for the old. As a child enters a nursery school at 3-plus he joins the lowest of four groups and moves up year by year. From the age of 6, however, to combat possible boredom, the child is then automatically enrolled in a leisure-time club run by a specially two-year trained child care officer. The club meets after school hours, caters for children between the ages of 6 and 12 only, runs its own monthly newspaper (managed by the children), and specialises in music and music-making, theatricals and puppet shows. In addition, there are also mini-clubs within the club proper for the older children between the ages of 10 and 12 who, as they feel the need for quiet relaxation and privacy, can retire to their own special quarters — an old disused bus, for example — to read suitable magazines and books. All such activities now come under the responsibility of a recently created Ministry for Family Affairs.

Norway

Though Norway covers an area of some 125,000 square miles it has a population of only 4½ million, most of whom live in isolated communities in the north and west, and with greater concentration in the lowlands of the south and east. The average population density, indeed, is only 30 per square mile, thus making Norway the most thinly populated political unit in Europe. Today, however, 52 per cent live in urban areas, the capital, Oslo, housing close on half a million people, and the two next largest towns (Bergen and Trondheim) sheltering 100,000 each. Some 20 per cent of the total population is engaged in agriculture, forestry and fishing; industry and mining account for 25 per cent; commerce claims 13 per cent, and the professions generally 20 per cent. Almost three-quarters of the country is made up of mountain ranges, barren rocks and waste land, 24 per cent is covered by forests, and a meagre 4 per cent only is suited to arable farming. The climate is a rigorous one, and geographical configurations make communications and transport difficult, industry often having to go to the countryside to the people — the converse of what happened in England at the time of the Industrial Revolution. Towards the end of the nineteenth century sheer poverty led to massive migration to the United States, and this led to far-reaching state interference in society in the form of social welfare programmes and attempts to create economic outlets in the remoter regions — the aim being to ensure that none should have too much, none too little, and that human resources were used to the best possible advantage of all. Individual and co-operative efforts were stressed, social welfare coming to be seen as a supplement to individual effort, whilst educationists aimed at ensuring as far as possible that the children should be brought up in an atmosphere of economic and industrial stability and of democratic co-operation between government and people, whether as workers, families, or employers.

Thus, because families have been driven by circumstances to be self-supporting, there is a high degree of craft culture and a respect for it. The home becomes the focal point of activity and the family unit is all-important — though nowadays (as in all Western societies) generation conflicts are manifest, notably in the urban areas. Because they have to help one another, neighbourliness, friendliness and tolerance abound. Because of the rigours of the climate it is considered impossible to send children to school before the age of 7, and because of the closeness of family ties it is equally unthinkable to have boarding schools for children — except for the few who come from the most inaccessible places. The schools are looked upon as the people's schools, and they are required to give conscious expression of the people's needs and aspirations. They are happy, friendly places, and no matter what part of the country the visitor is in he cannot fail to be impressed by the warmth of fellow-feeling they engender. The education system, indeed, grew naturally out of peasant life, and its aim is not to produce a type (as in France or even in Belgium) but to meet the needs of the child, the family and the community.

As a result of geographical and social circumstances and in order that equality of opportunity be available for all children regardless of where they live, the central government controls directly all forms of higher and technical education and at other levels imposes its wishes on all local authorities in matters concerning curricula, examinations, choice of textbooks, hours of work, class numbers, building standards, and salaries paid to teachers. It also meets 55 per cent of total educational expenditure, requiring the remainder to be met by local funds. Thus, the schools are very much "local" schools, being democratically controlled by local and municipal boards and by parents' and teachers' councils, the teacher ranking high in the community as fulfilling an important role in the community's interests and often playing an important part in local or national government. Each elected local council sets up its own school board, to which is attached a local school inspector (a municipal employee), and these boards are held responsible for daily administration and control, being also charged to ensure that "children receive a good and sound education and that methods of teaching are up-to-date". Again, because the boards can be challenged and forced to discuss any matter openly with both parents and teachers, this means that parents, as electors, are involved in the educative process in a very real and democratic way.

The fact that at the Reformation the vast majority of the population adhered to Lutheranism has meant that a division between church and state in education has never arisen, and the central ministry is today still known as the Ministry of Church and Education, the church still playing a vital role in all affairs. It was indeed the so-called Pietist movement (whose influence rapidly spread throughout the country in the eighteenth century) which first introduced compulsory education and fixed the starting age for schooling at 7. The movement insisted that confirmation as members of the Lutheran church should be compulsory, required a school system to carry out the necessary preliminary instruction, and laid down that no child might leave school until adequately prepared for confirmation. After dissolution of the union with Denmark in 1814, the ecclesiastic authorities quickly sought a legal basis for compulsory schooling, and the first Primary School Act was passed in 1827 making elementary education compulsory for three years. In 1869 an academic school was built onto the three-year school. Twenty years later a compulsory seven-year basic school was introduced, and in 1896 secondary provision was made for all who wanted it after five years of elementary schooling.

The twentieth century heralded industrialisation as a major preoccupation, and the aftermath of two World Wars led to a rejection of Germanic élitism in favour of newer ideas in education from Great Britain and the USA. Between 1935 and 1946 no fewer than five education acts attempted to grapple with problems centred on remote or disadvantaged areas, and in 1954 the Experiment in Education Act proposed as a solution a nine-year comprehensive school. Five years later the Law on Compulsory Education (Primary Schools Act) called on all communes to extend their "people's" school to a full nine years. By 1963/4, 105 communes out of a total of 525 had introduced the new type of school, and by 1971, with the passing of the Law on Compulsory Education, the change-over for the whole country was virtually completed, though in the more sparsely populated areas the principle of simply adding a further two years to the original seven-year school is followed.

If there is no state versus church controversy, there are, however, certain linguistic complications rooted in the past history of the Norwegians. There are in effect two distinct and rival norms: *riksmal* or *bokmal* (the national language or language of literary expression) and *nynorsk* (a common nationwide language), together with various urban and rural dialectal forms. Although both *riksmal* and *nynorsk* are legally equal, both being taught in the schools, 75 per cent of all children use *riksmal* as their main language. *Nynorsk* finds its greatest support in the west and is in reality an artificial development which has grown up in the last century in an attempt to create a truly "Norwegian" language independent of all Danish influence. Repeated efforts to blend the two languages into one common language, *samnorsk*, have constantly failed — even though it is admitted that outstanding literary figures (such as Ibsen) have always used the Danish "tainted" *riksmal*.

Pre-primary education is entirely voluntary and a variety of such schools for children between the ages of 3-plus and 6-plus can be found throughout the country but especially in urban areas, and particularly in Oslo where in 1971 almost 22 per cent of the age range were enrolled as opposed to barely 2 per cent in rural areas. At a rough calculation the figure for the country overall cannot be more than about 15 per cent with virtually nil returns for the under-3s. So far pre-primary education has remained in the hands of private or parental organisations, with approved schools being subsidised up to 85 per cent of running costs by the Ministry of Family and Consumer Affairs under whose supervision they fall. Local authorities have also been encouraged to establish their own pre-primary schools, and a State Commission set up in 1969 reported in 1972 that there should be a substantial expansion in pre-primary education to provide enough places for 125,000 children (as opposed to the present figure of roughly 15,000) by 1981; that the local authorities should become responsible for all pre-primary education, the cost being shared equally by the state (after an 85 per cent capital cost grant), the local authorities and the parents; that there should be close links and continuity between pre-primary and primary education; and that special accommodation should be provided for handicapped children. At the time of writing (1976), these recommendations have not been implemented. Nothing need here be said about the general approach to pre-primary education since teaching methods run along traditional modern lines, as in Denmark.

The normal pattern for compulsory education is the *grunnskolen* (basic school) which itself consists of a six-year primary school followed by three years in a comprehensive lower secondary school. As we have already instanced, however, in the remoter districts the original seven-year school is allowed to add to itself a two-year continuation school (*framhald-skole*) and make do with that. In any case, Norwegians today speak in both cases of the nine-year school or the extended primary school. All schools are co-educational. The school year runs from August to June, covers thirty-eight weeks with thirty forty-five-minute periods per week, and (as in Denmark) functions six days a week in the mornings only. The aims of this basic school are clearly laid down in the 1969 Education Act as being those of making pupils good members of the community; helping to give pupils a Christian and moral upbringing; developing their mental and physical abilities; and giving them a good general knowledge "so that they may become useful and self-reliant human beings both at home and in the community".

The curriculum for the first six years stresses the teaching of Norwegian, arithmetic, religious studies, and arts and crafts. For the first three years there are home environmental studies superseded for the last three years by history, civics and geography. For the last three years everybody studies science, and from the fourth year onwards English is a compulsory language taught for four periods a week. The seventh grade continues with this general teaching plan, but in Grades 8 and 9 (in accordance with pupil and parental wishes, guided by the teachers) pupils find themselves separating into broadly-based theoretical and practical sides of instruction, the choice of electives being both complex and highly varied. In the eighth grade a second foreign language (German) is allotted five periods a week for the more academically minded, others taking more vocational electives. Further modifications follow in Grade 9 dependent on whether science, English or German is to be the main subject, the more academically-minded opting usually for the stiffer two-language course, and perhaps extra science. Up to twenty periods a week can now be used for electives, with three clearly differentiated levels of instruction emerging, whilst those pupils wishing to proceed to the academic *gymnasium* must take two foreign languages and the stiffer courses in the other basic subjects. Ultimately, six different lines of preparation emerge: general theoretical, commercial, agricultural, industrial, fishing and seafaring, and (for girls) domestic subjects. At the end of Grade 9 all pupils have the option of staying on for a further year either to improve their marks or to mature further before starting work or moving forward to some form of higher education.

"There is no better baggage on a journey than much of knowledge" runs a well-known Scandinavian proverb, and work in this nine-year people's school is indeed in keeping with this generally held view. The school's purpose is to instruct, and, whilst the atmosphere is friendly, real hard work goes on at all stages. There is no time for sport, for the team spirit or for extra-mural activities as in an English or an American school. Similarly, the whole conception of comprehensive education shows radical differences, particularly in comparison with its English counterpart. In the first place the schools are nearly always purpose-built. Secondly, they are much smaller, ranging in size from 80 places to 800, the average size being between 250 and 450 pupils. Thirdly, they cover a much smaller age range (13 to 16 or 17) if the primary years are not counted. And finally they cater for the whole ability range with "setting" kept to an absolute minimum — this being possible because of the continuity maintained over nine full years.

Sweden

With a total population of about 8 million, Sweden has one of the lowest population densities in Europe (19 inhabitants per square mile), though it must be remembered that over 90 per cent of that population lives in the south and that estimates for the year 2000 indicate 90 per cent as then living in the towns as opposed to a present 70 per cent.[1] After Russia, France and Spain it is the fourth largest country in Europe, but more than 55 per cent of the total land area is forested and only 7 per cent is arable. Farming, in consequence, if nowadays highly mechanised and efficient, is on a relatively small scale. There are no more than about 150,000 farm owners and more than half the farms have less than 50 acres of land, agricultural workers in total accounting for no more than about 7 per cent

---

[1] It is to be remembered that urban areas can be quite small, often amounting to only a few hundred people grouped around a new and clean modern factory, and with the countryside almost on the doorstep.

of the population.

In the seventeenth century, and during the reign of King Gustavus Adolphus, Sweden reached its peak of imperial power. The eighteenth century witnessed her steady decline as an important European power. She missed her chance of giving a lead to a nascent Scandinavian national movement in the middle years of the nineteenth century (to be pinpointed by her refusal in 1864 to come to the aid of Denmark who thereby lost Schleswig-Holstein to Prussia) and thereafter has remained in a kind of "off-shore" position in European affairs, having fought no wars since 1815 and thereby making neutrality the corner-stone of her foreign policies. On the other hand, from 1850 onwards she rapidly industrialised herself, directed her economy firmly towards exportation of her main products (metalwork and engineering, timber, pulp and paper), and over the last fifty years or so has accompanied shrewd modern planned industrial development with a series of comprehensive measures in the field of social welfare − a major element in the political philosophy of the ruling Social Democratic party which has been in effective power for most of that time. The continued success of the Social Democrats is due in the main to their realistic and practical approach to achieving their aims. Capitalism has not been abandoned because in terms of the modern economy it is seen to work. Over 90 per cent of industry is still privately owned. Largely because of this the old nobility and the bourgeoisie have in turn acquiesced (perhaps more readily than elsewhere in Western Europe) to pressures to create a welfare state based on a more equitable sharing of the national wealth. And the result of this "pact" has been a remarkable absence of industrial strife allied to a high all-round standard of living which carries with it an inevitable high level of taxation coupled with a fairly rigid bureaucratic control. The aim has become that of creating a smooth-working frictionless society.

Obviously education was a key factor in such plans of widespread social engineering, and a committee was appointed as early as 1940 to report. Conscious that Scandinavian education in general had for too long been cast in the traditional German (academic) mode, and reacting strongly against contemporary practice in Germany, the committee began by stating that "the school, its organisation and its work must always be viewed in relation to the society in whose service it works and whose future it will, to no small extent, help to shape". It then went on to affirm that "the final goal of the school should not be the communication of knowledge, but education in the widest and deepest meaning of the word. The school's task is to foster the harmonious development of young people's abilities, not only intellectually, but also physically and morally". Two vital principles which have since guided all reform measures were then carefully enunciated: that the individual should be given the education best suited to his abilities, it being the duty of society and of the school to help him get such an education; that the instruction provided must at all times satisfy the demands of modern society and its labour market. It was further emphasised that (as always) the prime task of the school must be to give pupils good knowledge and skills in the three Rs and languages, to ensure "a good foundation for their general orientation in the arts and natural sciences, and a good grounding in social problems". And the whole plan as it has evolved since 1940 can be seen to be emphasising group work and co-operation whilst retaining careful respect for the individuality of the child who – a peculiarly Swedish phenomenon – is now involved in helping to run his school on a basis of "pupil democracy".

Thus, and despite many practical difficulties which (it is recognised) are far from being solved in the present permissive climate, the Swedish school system as a whole can be seen as a homogenous one, co-ordinated and purposeful but flexible, adapted and adapting to social needs and social change yet respecting the individual and encouraging individuality. As an important element in the Social Democrats policy of social engineering, the school must play its part by helping to produce a society in which all are equal and which is as free as possible from all forms of friction and envy. There is only one type of school for every child (private schools having almost entirely disappeared), and every effort is made to remove handicaps whether they be social, physical or mental. No wonder, then, that the Swedish comprehensive school is at all times under close scrutiny (and taken as a model) by the rest of the Western world. If America first made the comprehensive school a reality, the Swedish experience serves to highlight the dilemma in which all Western European countries find themselves in attempting to make a break with traditional practices and traditional "setting" of pupils.

It is only relatively recently that the Swedes have come to realise the importance to their total plan of comprehensive education of adequate provision of pre-school education. It is now clearly seen, however, that since compulsory education does not start until the age of 7, early efforts must be made to overcome initial handicaps. By limiting the influence of the home and offering children similar environments from a young age, opportunities in education can be made more fair and democratic. All children will (or should) not be in such need, but where there is the need it is the state's duty to meet it. To date, some 250,000 pre-school places have already been provided, taking children only from about the age of 4 (except for day nurseries in large towns). The schools are purpose-built and the social training given there (there is no attempt made to teach the three Rs) is primarily designed to give the children confidence in their ability to make an easy transfer to the nine-year period of compulsory schooling which follows. As is only to be expected, the schools are run along the most modern and progressive lines to be found elsewhere in Western Europe, but, though they are increasingly subsidised, parents usually have to pay up to £160 per annum. Present aims, however, are to extend pre-school education to all 6-year-olds via a country-wide network, and with admission at *all* ages free of charge.

The nine-year compulsory school was finally fully introduced into Sweden in 1966, though for more than ten years previously such schools had been running on an experimental basis in a number of municipalities. It is a municipal organisation and as such comes under the jurisdiction of a local elected education committee on which all interested parties are represented. All municipalities have the lower and middle departments (ages 7 to 13), but out of a total of 900 such municipalities about 500 lack the upper three grades. This means that a number of pupils have to be taken to and from school by public transport each day to attend for the last three years — inevitable given the uneven distribution of population throughout the country. The school day is usually from 8 a.m. to 3 p.m., but there is an excellent school meals service which provides free lunches for all pupils. There are twenty hours of instruction per week in Grade 1, twenty-five hours in Grade 2, thirty hours in Grade 3, and thirty-five hours thereafter. Ideally, no class in the lower departments may exceed twenty-five in number, and classes all move up together to the next grade. One of the characteristic features of the 1962 curriculum was that pupils in the last three grades had to choose between a large number of optional studies over and above their obligatory subjects, the final grade comprising no fewer than nine different theoretical and practical lines. This multiplicity soon gave rise to a number of practical problems, a number of options being entirely ignored. A new curriculum, introduced in the autumn of 1970, has been made far more homogenous in that a larger proportion of the subjects have been made common to all pupils.

For the first three years of their school life in the lower school pupils are usually taught by a fully trained woman teacher. Swedish and mathematics are taught along modern lines. Social topics (history, geography, civics) are grouped as one subject. Art, craftwork and music are properly stressed, with boys and girls jointly being taught needlework, woodwork and metalwork. And English is now introduced as a compulsory subject in the third and last year of the lower stage (i.e. at age 9). Courses in religious instruction (which nowadays means a study of comparative religion and other philosophies, including Marxism) and regular periods of physical training complete the programme. Guidance and remedial work is carried out on both an individual basis and (where numbers demand it) in special remedial classes. It is recognised, however, that in a school designed for everybody it is unrealistic to expect the same performance from all. School work is therefore individualised as far as possible so that each pupil can make the best possible use of his or her capacity and aptitudes. Most studies are expected to be completed in school so that homework becomes optional, and great importance is attached to getting pupils to learn to work together.

As the child moves to the middle school (10 to 13 years of age), which is again of three years' duration, he is taught by either a man or a woman teacher, the only specialists employed being usually for English and craft work. Here no class may exceed thirty in number, and classes are again mixed and unstreamed. Towards the end of the middle school course, children and parents are invited to begin to consider what optional subjects they would like to take from Grade 7 onwards, it being understood that the system is elastic and a variety of permutations possible for the remainder of the child's school career. The most common combinations of options (which in the upper school will usually be allotted five out of the thirty-five periods per week) have tended to be: German/French (five periods per week); German/French (three periods) with Swedish/Mathematics (two periods); German/French (three periods) with commercial studies (two periods); crafts/commercial studies (three periods) with Swedish/Mathematics (two periods); crafts (five periods).

For the last three years of compulsory education in the upper school (ages 13 to 16) specialist subject teachers are employed. The common curriculum in the seventh grade consists of mathematics (five periods), English (five periods), Swedish (three), biology (one), physics (two), religion (two), civics (one), and domestic science, together with a number of periods shared by gymnastics, music, art and handicrafts. There are also two periods a week left free in which a pupil may work on something in which he is particularly interested and which is not included in the ordinary school timetable, this "free work" continuing throughout the remainder of the school course. More time is likewise allotted to such topics as sex education and information, international questions and problems, road traffic, and alcohol, drugs and smoking. From the seventh grade onwards differentiation begins in the teaching of mathematics and modern languages, one course being more theoretical (academic) than the other. Similarly, a child who for some reason did not begin to study a second foreign language in Grade 7 may rectify the omission in Grade 8. Here there are up to twenty-eight periods of common curriculum, usually divided as follows: mathematics (four), music, art and handicraft (four), Swedish (three), gymnastics (three), social subjects, comprising history, geography and civics (three, three and two), physics (two), chemistry (two). The remainder of the time — apart from "free work" — is allotted to various combi-- nations of options. Since the 1970 regrouping (of which we have already spoken), optional subjects on offer in Grade 9 fall under four main heads: theoretical, social–general, commercial, and technical– mechanical. These are usually given seven periods out of the total thirty-five, the common curriculum now consisting of Swedish (five), mathematics (four), biology, physics, chemistry (two each), civics, history, geography (two each), gymnastics (two), religion (one), and music/art/handicrafts (four). A final important feature of Grade 9 is the so-called practical vocational guidance which entails a pupil spending three weeks outside the school trying his hand at a possible occupation of his own choosing. Again, should the pupil by now have shown a definite practical bent, optional subjects can be extended up to twenty-two out of the thirty-five periods, the common curriculum being reduced to Swedish (three), with civics, geography, biology, music/art/handicrafts, and gymnastics having two periods each.

No examinations are set in the nine-year compulsory school, but marks are awarded on a 1 to 5 scale with 5 as the highest award. The cumulative mark record, intended to serve as a continuing guide to both parents and pupils, enables a decision to be made with relative certainty at the end of Grade 9 as to what direction the pupil's further studies will take. Thus, decision-taking is postponed until the last possible moment, and (where ambition comes late or when anxiety is felt over accumulated low grades) it is not unknown for a pupil to stay on a further year in Grade 9 to improve his total mark score. Since 1971, however, when a decision was implemented to have a new comprehensive upper secondary school, all pupils are entitled to admission to it, irrespective of the options chosen in the upper school. Thus, having already achieved the ambition of having *all* children working together for the full nine years of compulsory schooling, the aim is now to extend this well beyond the school-leaving age wherever feasible and possible. It is to be noted, however, that the Swedes are already as worried as the Americans (and some other countries in Western Europe) over the problem of "neighbourhood schools" which do not make for a full mixing of pupils from a variety of different social backgrounds.

6

It is convenient to group together Western Germany (including Berlin), Italy and Switzerland for a number of reasons. In the first place Germany and Italy came to achieve some semblance of national unity much later than other Western European countries. Germany and Switzerland are federal states with considerable autonomy and independence of action reserved for the eleven *Länder* of Germany and the twenty-five *cantons* of Switzerland. All three countries came relatively late to feel the effects of the Industrial Revolution and had to make strenuous efforts to change rapidly from a basic agrarian economy to an industrial one. All have pockets of sparse population together with the poverty and backwardness to be associated with such areas, where pursuits are almost exclusively agricultural, but only Switzerland has escaped the major evils of industrialisation since her use of mountain streams for generating power has meant that industry and commerce are far from being concentrated exclusively in urban areas. Nevertheless, Switzerland along with the other two countries nowadays has its problems of urbanisation with more than one-third of its total population living in the thirty-one principal towns of the country as opposed to only one-twentieth little more than a century ago. Germany and Switzerland have had to find workable solutions to Catholic–Protestant controversies extending over centuries, whereas Italy — predominantly Catholic in outlook — has had to work out a suitable formula for giving the state necessary overall control of education. All the countries have at one time or another come under French influence; the Italians have been influenced in addition by both Germany and Austria; the Swiss in their land-locked position have been influenced by all, and this in the long run has proved to be of great help in making for parity of esteem among the four languages in use of which three (German, French and Italian) are declared as official and of equal importance. Finally, none of the three countries in question has been completely won over to full implementation of the idea of comprehensive education, though Germany has gone furthest. Even here, however, a recent court ruling (June 1975) in *Land Hesse* (the fifth largest state in Western Germany) is bound to have repercussions throughout the country. *Land Hesse* is socialist controlled and has opted for a comprehensive system. The State Supreme Court at Kassel has declared it to be an offence for an education authority to direct a child to a comprehensive school against its parents' wishes. Comprehensive schooling still must be considered under the heading of experimental education, and children must not be turned into guinea-pigs for experimental purposes except on a purely voluntary basis. In other words, parents must retain their freedom of choice and the state must continue to offer them various types of schools, including comprehensive.

West Germany

In 1970 the population of Western Germany was estimated at 61.5 million, of whom some 2.5 million were immigrant workers engaged mainly on menial and unskilled tasks, about 3.5 million (as of 1961) refugees from the German Democratic Republic, and 8.5 million "expellees" — that is to say people who had formerly lived in other areas than the present German Democratic Republic. Most of the inhabitants belong (at least nominally) to either the Roman Catholic or the Evangelical church, with Protestants predominating in the north and Catholics in the south, the ratio between the two denominations being more or less equal. The distribution of population is overwhelmingly urban, with heavy concentration in the main cities and in the Ruhr. It is to be remembered, however, that West Germany is a federal republic comprising eleven separate and highly individualistic *Länder* all of whom jealously guard their autonomy whilst remaining loyal to the Federation (the *BUND*) and being obliged to observe Federal Law. Thus, extremes in *Land* attitudes are constantly to be found ranging from the conservative (and somewhat backward) Catholicism of Bavaria, to progressive industrialisation in the Ruhr and the Rhineland, and to the patent self-sufficiency of mercantile Bremen and Hamburg.

Mainly for historical reasons, education has always remained the special concern of each individual *Land* which has steadfastly maintained its right to develop its own school and university systems according to its own traditions and ideas. Each *Land* has its own Minister for Education and its own inspectorate, and general school policy within the *Land*, curriculum planning, the setting up of examination requirements, the final certification and appointment of teachers, are all handled at ministerial level. There is a certain devolution of power at district and county level within each *Land*, but no deviations from the general policy as laid down by the *Land* ministry may take place without ministerial sanction. Under the short-lived and ill-fated Weimar Republic (1919–33) a slight step towards uniformity in educational practice was taken by agreements freely negotiated between various *Länder* to secure greater conformity over general standards of education, but this was virtually vetoed by the rise of Hitler and his creation of a Reich Ministry of Education to compel adherence everywhere to the Nazi ideal. In the aftermath of the Second World War, and in the confusion that resulted from the total collapse of the Nazi régime, the various Ministers of Education, sensing the urgent need for co-operation between the various *Länder* if the new democratic principles involving a unified Germany were to be realised, formed themselves into a permanent conference with a permanent secretariat in Bonn, and, working quietly and efficiently over the post-war years, have already done much towards achieving a uniform purpose in education for the whole country whilst still scrupulously respecting the German's peculiar allegiance to his *Land* first, and only secondly to the Federal Republic.

The declared aim of both central and *Länder* governments is now

equality of opportunity for all children. Already by 1969 general agreement had been reached on the adoption of grades of equal value; on an
overall formulation to be used on school reports and certificates; on the
introduction of optional foreign language instruction in the primary school;
on the adoption of uniform principles of spelling; on mutual recognition
of certificates of maturity (the *Abitur*) entitling admission to the universities; on the methods of professional preparation of secondary school
teachers; on the standardisation of school holidays. In 1969 provision was
made for a greater degree of Federal involvement in educational affairs,
the Federal Government giving itself the right to participate with the
Länder in "common projects" – notably in the building of new universities, the date being significant in terms of student unrest everywhere
in Western Europe at that time. And in effect this means that the Federal
Government is now committed to meeting 50 per cent of the cost of
establishing any new university anywhere.

By 1957, however, the Federal Government and the *Länder* had already
begun to co-operate more closely in both scientific and university policy,
this leading not only to university expansion but also to an increase in
grants and loans to needy students. In 1965, an agreement between the
Länder and the Federal Government led to the establishment of a German
Education Council to advise on the entire education system with the
exception of the universities. And five years later a joint commission on
educational planning was charged with producing a long-term skeleton
plan for co-ordinated development of the entire educational system
together with financial estimates of the burden to be borne by both the
Federal Government and the *Länder*. Its report – presented during the
summer of 1973, has had a good reception and its main recommendations
were adopted in principle by all the *Länder* in October 1973. It now
remains to be seen how far each individual *Land* will carry out the recommendations, for the constitution of the joint commission is such (eleven
Federal representatives and one for each of the eleven *Länder*) that any
decisions require a three-quarters majority and can only be held as binding
on such *Länder* as have given their approval.

Full-time compulsory education in Western Germany lasts from 6 to 15
years of age with provision of part-time education for the 15- to 18-year-
old age groups, not always easy everywhere to enforce. The present provision of pre-school education only manages to absorb some 34 per cent

of children between the ages of 3 and 6, but the Structural Plan for Education to which we have just referred recognises the urgent need to improve offerings at this level if other developments envisaged are to be smoothly effected. Thus, whilst by 1980 it is hoped to introduce a full compulsory ten-year schooling, dependent on dropping the age of entry to primary school to 5, it is hoped by then to have at least 75 per cent of all 3- to 4-year-olds in some form of pre-school education and to have achieved the target of virtually 100 per cent by 1990.

Present provision of pre-school education depends mainly on *communes*, on the churches, on industry, on various welfare societies, and on private initiative. Parents who can afford to do so are expected to pay a token sum, the rest of the cost being met either by the founding organisation or from grants approved by the Youth Office. The schools are mainly Froebel-inspired, Montessori methods being considered as more suited to the needs of the child of less than average ability. Generally speaking, the aim is not so much to prepare the child for entry to the primary school as to improve his physical, moral and intellectual development, though the intention over the next decades is to re-organise the school so as to form the first real stage in a child's education and so make for natural and easy transition to the primary school proper. At the moment of writing, however, three distinct types of pre-school education can be found. The first is the traditional school which caters particularly for children whose mothers are out at work and which is called upon to function mainly in the social welfare field. Such children spend the whole day at school. They are given a midday meal which is followed by a sleep of two to three hours. Their health is regularly checked, and hygiene (as in France) plays an important part in the curriculum. Another type is the *Schulkindergarten* and is in reality a special section attached to a primary school which accepts only those children who should have begun their full-time education, but who are backward in some way and in need of special care before they can begin on the proper full-time course. Such schools are mainly to be found in large urban areas. They are financed by public funds and are controlled and inspected in the same way as the ordinary primary school. Attendance is voluntary, if encouraged, and the children do not work more than four hours per day. The staff are specially trained and must have spent a minimum of two years working in an ordinary *Kindergarten*. A third type consists of the *Vorklassen* — special classes for children who, though not yet of compulsory school age, have passed beyond what the *Kindergarten* has to offer. Naturally, experimentation and research tends to centre on these classes for the more mature which, incidentally, though small in number (in 1970 there were 7376 children spread among 347 classes) represent an important growth point and are encouraging some *Länder* to plan for 100 per cent attendance of 5- to 6-year-olds there in the near future in preparation for the lowering of the compulsory school age to 5.

The idea of the *Grundschule*, or basic primary school which all children shall attend, is no new one. As early as 1920 the Weimar Republic, in its campaigning for the *Einheitsschule* (one single, common school to cover the whole of compulsory education), decreed that there should be such a school through which every child must pass before being allowed to proceed to any form of post-primary education. And by the same token it discontinued all preparatory schools attached to *Gymnasien*. There has since been considerable divergence of opinion as to whether the *Grundschule* should be of four (as originally intended by the Weimar Republic) or of six years' duration. *Länder* arguing for six years have claimed that 90 per cent of the school population will be passing on to some form of post-primary education which is not academic. Upholders of the principle of a four-year school argue that six years of primary education dangerously shortens, in this age of acute specialisation, the period of secondary education, and also unnecessarily holds back the gifted child. Nowadays the general tendency is towards four years, particularly in view of the fact that the Structural Plan envisages a four-year school from ages 5 to 9 to be followed by an orientation stage of up to two years in which the pupil should come "to recognise his own learning possibilities and fields of interest in order to prepare for the later choice of a suitable main (and specialised) course of instruction".

In any case, it is generally held that the function of the *Grundschule* is to recognise, cultivate and develop a child's natural gifts and to give him thorough instruction in the basic essentials of a good general education. These essentials are variously listed as: confident oral and written use of the mother tongue; assurance with figures; familiarity with the objects and workings of nature; appreciation of poetry (and the arts in general); a sound religious grounding (with a conscience escape-clause for such parents as deliberately seek it); a knowledge of history which gears itself closely to the study of the workings of a democratic society. And all this time the school should be on the watch to distinguish as well as possible at this early stage between what the Hamburg system defines as the practical, the technical and the academic talents of individual pupils. All tuition has been free since the turn of the century, and such few private schools as exist must have a state licence indicating that the curriculum conforms to requirements in state schools, that the staff is fully competent by state standards, and that the wealth of parents is not made a criterion for entry to such schools.

Judged by current practice in America and England (the integrated day, open-plan schools etc.), the *Grundschule* is still far too formal, traditional and bookish in its approach. On the other hand, classes are unstreamed and cautious experimentation is going on all the time with curricular developments (particularly in mathematics, science, social studies, and art and craft) being given high priority. Yet, as the provisions being made in the Structural Plan to cover the whole of the period of compulsory education clearly show, the Germans (like the Belgians, the Dutch and the French) will continue to stress the *suum cuique* rather than the *idem cuique* and to pin their faith in the first instance on a "common" *Grundschule* geared to give a sound, basic and thorough general education.

Italy

In many ways it can be claimed that the whole story of Italy down to the present is that of a people in search of its own identity, it being remembered that it first became a kingdom in its own right as late as 1872. Even today, however, and despite a firm policy of centralisation of administration which as far as the former kingdom of Sardinia is concerned pre-dates the Napoleonic conquest of the Northern Provinces, the Italian people remain strongly aware of their regional origins and of regionalistic differences which command their loyalty much more than does an impersonal state machine. Indeed, to put the state first and the individuals comprising the state second as Fascism once set out to do represents to the average Italian an absolute denial of the principles attaching to a liberal democracy — the goal of all thinking Italians not only since Italy first became a kingdom but in reality ever since the prosperity of the various city-states in the fifteenth century made possible for Western Europe the glories of the Renaissance which in turn led to an Italian concept of humanism carrying its message of enlightened liberal principles, of toleration and of real democracy within a framework both of conscious national endeavour and of the all-embracing Catholic church.

Again, despite the increasingly disruptive tempo of modern urban existence, the family remains an important unit, its importance stemming not only from the church's view that the family must remain the main educative instrument but also from economic and geographic circumstances. Fully 70 per cent of Italy must be listed as mountainous, yet the Italians have managed to put the same amount of land to good agricultural use – mainly by processes of terracing. This, however, has also meant that the family has become and remained an important unit in land cultivation, even with the advent of industrialisation, for the driving of motorways throughout Italy – such again is the configuration of the land – has only served to isolate and even increase pockets of rural life, this to the point of strengthening regional affiliations at a time when one might have looked for some diminution.

On the other hand, Italy's problems today turn on the fact that administrative and social structures have failed to keep pace with rapid industrialisation, for in effect, within the last twenty years or so, Italy has turned herself from a backward agricultural country into a major industrial power. As a result, well over 15 million Italians have changed their place of residence since the end of World War II. Great numbers of poor agricultural workers and their families have flooded to the industrial centres at an ever-increasing rate and have overstrained existing school facilities. Successive governments have tried to cope at all levels. They have recognised the fact that a modern industrial society needs a highly skilled working force. They have tried to extend the age of compulsory education from 11 to 14. They have encouraged parents to keep their children longer at school by creating numerous types of free technical and professional institutions. They have reorganised secondary education generally. But they have signally failed to provide the necessary accommodation, proper tuition and adequate facilities where they are most needed, mainly through a kind of bureaucratic inertia which seems to paralyse every aspect of state activity.[1] To the outside observer, Italy

[1] Consult for example the *Letter to a Teacher* from the scholars of Barbiana, Penguin Books, London, 1970, to see how a rural area can be adversely affected.

at the moment seems to represent a many-voiced and not too stable democracy which, though based largely on egalitarian principles is slow to practice them. There is a latent distrust of all central authority, often turning on selfish regional interests and allied to agitation for recognition, recompense and reward from masses of uprooted workers.

Whilst there can be said to be some truth in the statement that the structure of Italian education has not changed in any significant way since the Casati Law was adopted in 1859, or at any rate since the Coppino Act of 1877, many attempts have in reality been made over the years to improve and up-date educational provision if only to seek some solution to the bedevilling twin problems of poverty and illiteracy. Gentile, Mussolini's first Minister of Public Instruction, was instrumental in reducing the sixty-nine provinces into nineteen regions, each with its own "historical" frontier, and in furthering regional activities the better to have each historical region vary its curricula to suit local bias, local traditions, and possibilities for employment. Alongside this, however, and in furtherance of the Lateran Treaty of 1929 whereby Mussolini became the first Prime Minister since the unification of Italy to reach a *rapprochement* with the Vatican, compulsory religious instruction was introduced in all schools, Gentile arguing that religious studies at the primary level in particular would serve as a basis for the later study of philosophy – in his view the linchpin of any man's education – which children of primary school age were as yet too immature to study. In 1947 the Gonella Plan specifically set out to combat illiteracy and also created the *scuola populare*, a people's school open to all children over the age of 12 and to all adults wishing to learn to read and to write and complete their elementary school studies. In 1958 came the ten-year plan to make education compulsory and free for all for a minimum period of eight years' full schooling, and this was followed five years later (1963) by a new school law principally regulating post-primary education but also stressing the importance of a sound, basic education for all.

The Lateran Treaty of 1929 came to be embodied in the post-war 1948 Constitution, and this, together with the fact that the Catholic movement had emerged with some credit from its role in the Resistance Movement against Mussolini, has led to the Catholic church returning as a force in Italian politics. De Gasperi and other leading Catholic opponents of Fascism were quick to form a Christian Democratic Party which has since gone from strength to strength. It emerged as the party of order which would save Italy from the Communist threat. It has developed as the party of the middle classes and of the rural areas, more especially in the strongly Catholic south and the north-east. It has the support of the Vatican. Indeed, such is its parliamentary representation that it is usually impossible to form a government without its support, and it repeatedly allies itself with the Socialists or Social Democrats to the left or with the Republicans and the Liberals on the right. It has monopolised the post of Minister of Public Instruction since shortly after the last war.

Thus, the Catholic church throughout Italy retains a powerful hold on education even though fully 90 per cent of primary schools are run by the state which also reserves to itself the sole right to grant various diplomas of proficiency. And nowhere is Catholic influence more strongly felt than over the provision of pre-school education. At the moment of writing approximately 1½ million children between the ages of 3 and 6 are catered for in some 20,000 schools, this representing about 50 per cent of the age group with attendance higher among 5-year-olds. Yet only 8 per cent of pre-school education is provided by the state, and this in schools in the main attached to colleges of education. The Italian government fell in June 1964 over a proposed increase in state subsidies for non-state schools. Following up this advantage, efforts were then seriously made by opponents of the Christian Democratic Party, on the perfectly justifiable plea that the church was no longer in a position to provide sufficient *scuole materne*, to introduce a bill to parliament for a much wider extension of state provision in those areas where such schools were most sorely needed, particularly in the south. Care was taken to reassure the church that this would not lead to a reduction in the subsidies they themselves would receive from the state. It was to no avail. The church insisted on its prerogative to care for the very young and also feared that an extension of state influence in this field must lead to breaking the church's monopoly for the training of kindergarten teachers, so far the preserve of its all-female *scuola magistrali*. In January 1966 the government fell yet again over the same issue. By devious means and compromises, however, increasing state provision has been made, notably since 1968.

All nursery schools can be said to fall into two distinct types: those which look after children whilst the mother is out at work; and those which, following the most modern ideas, give an education comparable with the best done elsewhere in Europe. The schools themselves are mainly located in industrial areas and in the larger and more wealthy towns and communes. All schools are inspected by public authorities and, for state recognition, must conform to certain regulations which, whilst leaving the teachers free to use an informal curriculum (which must not include the teaching of reading or writing) indicate areas of learning which must be covered ranging from physical activities to religious instruction. Concern is equally shown to use the nursery school to help the less privileged successfully to tackle a primary school course without having to repeat a grade — the figure of 45 per cent having recently been quoted for such repeats between the ages of 6 and 11. Non-state schools may charge fees, which can vary considerably according to the services provided. And state schools, which attempt to keep the pupil–teacher ratio at about 20 to 1, are gaining in efficiency and consequent popularity in competition with the private sector where the figure can be as high as 35 to 1.

The primary school now extends between the ages of 6 and 11 and is divided into two cycles, the first being from 6 to 8 years of age and the second from 8 to 11. Oral and written examinations must be passed at the end of each cycle, and success at the end of the second cycle leads to the award of the *licenza elementare* which qualifies for entry to post-primary education. Methods of instruction tend to the formal and didactic, though the importance of the individual is stressed, self-expression encouraged, and the children as a whole enjoy school. Along with the study of the usual basic subjects there is emphasis on religion and on civic and moral training. Manual training (*lavoro*) is not interpreted in the narrow sense of manual instruction, or handicrafts, or domestic science, but rather as a form of honourable productive activity. And here there is a certain link with Decroly principles. School furniture will be repaired. Girls will learn the economics of balancing the budget, learn to shop, and learn baby care. Town boys in particular will have their gardens in which to cultivate and produce saleable vegetables. In the present age of automation a stable economy depends on the workman realising that his is an honourable calling. It has to be remembered that Italian labour exports itself the world over; that though half a million children of compulsory school age (under 14) are regularly illegally employed (often for a mere pittance), Italy still has the highest rate for youth unemployment throughout the Common Market countries; and that, in consequence of all these factors,

real basic education at the primary level is of the utmost importance
and must remain a priority target for some time to come.

Switzerland

The emergence of the Swiss Republic as an independent political unit was
an achievement of the late Middle Ages, and its geographical configuration
as well as its land-locked position led to the country becoming a *pays de
passage* as well as one in which a system of decentralisation on a basis of
cantonal autonomy was imperative. And, whilst geographical configuration led to its becoming a confederation of twenty-five autonomous states,
some purely Protestant, some purely Catholic, some mixed, all jealously
safeguarding their autonomy particularly in matters educational, the
Reformation itself proved a powerful impulse towards popular democratic education. Some of these *cantons* (or states) are mainly agricultural,
some mainly industrial, some densely populated, some sparsely populated.
Of the roughly 6 million inhabitants, some 60 per cent would claim
adherence to the Protestant churches, and some 40 per cent would count
themselves as Catholics. There are four distinct linguistic groups, but
though German speakers predominate (72 per cent), amity reigns. The
French-speaking population (21 per cent) are accorded the prestige the
French language holds throughout the world, and the Italian group (5 per
cent), plus those Swiss still speaking the native Romansch (almost 2 per
cent) are in no way disadvantaged. True, only three official languages are
used, but in 1938 Romansch was given status as a language proper.

The harmony which reigns can be said to be due to several important
factors. In the first place, Switzerland originated at a time when the com-
munity-building functions of a language were for all practical purposes
ineffective. Secondly, the predominantly German-speaking *cantons* came
early into contact with French- and Italian-speaking allies, and as Switzerland prepared herself at the end of the eighteenth century to become a
modern state, association among these various linguistic groups was far too
well established for any spread of ideas of nationalism based (as we have
already seen) on a national language and literature to split the community.
Again, long association of the three main linguistic groups with one
another has given each group a special Swiss characteristic which draws
them (even when *culturally* attracted to the nations of their respective

languages) back to a unified feeling for the Swiss homeland. Fourthly, the fact that Switzerland lies at the crossroads of European travel, making of it not only an attractive tourist centre but also an important international centre for banking and insurance, allied to the fact that it must largely live by importing raw materials and exporting the finished product, has meant that language barriers have proved a stimulating and not a disintegrating force, at least for the educated. In a word, the saving principle of Helvetism is that of a continuous dialogue of the various linguistic groups within an identical political will. The Swiss are a nation whose stability depends on a respect for diversity, the basic principle of Swiss democracy being to be communal before *cantonal* and *cantonal* before being federal.

Yet Switzerland, a small country with a justifiably high standard of living and a balanced, stable economy based on wise use of resources to prevent rash expenditure — a country proud of its uniqueness and the neutral position it has been in a position to adopt *vis-à-vis* the greater European powers — today feels proportionately as uncertain about the future and the way ahead as most other European countries. Events of recent years have shown her that her neutrality depends on a balance of power among the other nations, and that when Europe is weighed down by the hegemony of one country alone there can no longer be neutrality as she envisages it. Similarly, just as neutrality is increasingly more difficult to maintain, so is centralism in government — or some form of it — appearing more and more as a necessity if only to ensure economic survival into the next century. Naturally, the communes and *cantons* are resisting various attempts made at centralisation by making increasing use of their legitimate right to demand a referendum, but bit by bit the Federal Council is gaining power.[1] And it is perhaps in the education field that this is most obvious.

If economic circumstances have forced the Swiss to demand a high standard of education from all and for all, historical events have led to a form of democracy which stresses the importance of education as a means of producing the good citizen type who will be a well-informed and progressive member of the community. Each and every Swiss is to be

---

[1] No law passed by the Federal Assembly may come into force until after the passage of ninety days, during which time 30,000 people or more may demand a popular vote to decide for themselves whether the enactment shall become law.

made conscious of his own value to the community, no matter what his employment, and is clearly held responsible for the welfare and prosperity of his country. So far so good. But the immediate post-war upheavals have forced the Swiss — if only for economic survival in an increasingly competitive world market — to scrutinise carefully present educational provision and to begin to invest more than in the past for the development of the Swiss nation as a whole. Since the early 1950s Switzerland has experienced a period of continuous expansion which has led to a rapid change in the distribution of employment. High levels of prosperity have raised standards of living and so increased the demand for knowledge. There are now 25 per cent more children in primary schools and 65 per cent more in secondary education than in 1950. Few are prepared to do unskilled work any more and this has resulted in a vast increase in foreign workers (mainly Italian) who in the late 1960s accounted for at least 11 per cent of the total population and whose children have again increased school numbers. In certain sectors there is overemployment whilst elsewhere there is a serious shortage of qualified personnel — particularly engineers, teachers, doctors and scientific research workers. Middle management in business and industry needs more education than before. And, if the present need for foreign workers (whose influx causes some considerable resentment among the Swiss) is to be reduced, then there must be increased use of automation which in turn calls for equipping semi-skilled workers and those in the lower regions of the salary scale to cope.

In 1958 Professor Rieben urged the necessity to seek out talent wherever it could be found. In 1961 the Socialist Party passed a resolution asserting the right to free education at all levels, not only further to democratise the entire structure of the school system but also to help in finding this talent. In 1963, a new amendment to the Swiss Constitution, authorised by a referendum, called upon the Federal Government to subsidise expenditure within the *cantons* on education, particularly with regard to the granting of scholarships and the improvement of teaching. At the same time two committees of experts were formed to report back, the one on the lack of well-trained people in the medical, scientific and teaching professions and how best to identify the specially talented, the other to estimate the future needs of the universities for financial aid from Federal sources. In September of the same year a new

Federal Vocational Training Law concerned itself with the provision of better general education, the granting of financial support to apprentices, and the creation of adequate extension courses for those seeking promotion.

If we now turn to the provision of basic education (the proper concern of this chapter) and leave further elaboration of the above until later, we have first of all to note that the aim is still less to produce an élite of brilliant students than to give all citizens a sound education in whatever school they may find themselves. It is equally important to remember that education as provided on a *cantonal* basis, giving the country twenty-five different school systems with different ages for starting and ending the period of compulsory schooling, with differing nomenclature and varying curricula, and with transfer to post-primary education occurring at different ages, has made Switzerland so well-endowed with schools that problems of illiteracy do not exist and that the needs of each and every child can be adequately coped with — this becoming increasingly so since the acceptance by the *cantons* of Federal "interference". Nowadays education is the joint concern of the Federal Government, of the *canton*, and of the local community (of which there are about 3000, each having considerable political autonomy and jurisdictional authority). The Federal Government places the responsibility on the *cantons* for seeing to it that education is free, adequate, compulsory and without religious discrimination. No attempt is made to define what is meant by "adequate education". The *canton* must decide that, and should any Swiss in any *canton* feel that education is not adequate he is free to seek redress from the central government. Compulsory education means that the *canton* is responsible for seeing that sufficient instruction is received according to local *cantonal* regulations, but not that children should necessarily attend a state school. All schools, however, whether private or public, must achieve a minimum standard of instruction, and *cantonal* inspectors have supervisory control over the curriculum of both private and public schools. All state primary schools and many of the secondary schools are administered directly by the local communities, and teachers are appointed locally. Local communities likewise maintain their schools and pay teachers' salaries, though the *cantons* lay down compulsory scales of pay and grant subsidies to their local communities. Similarly, the confederation of *cantons* has laid down four general educational principles which are universally applied. These are: that elementary education must be obligatory, free and adequate; that all public schools must be under the direction of the *cantonal* authorities; that freedom of conscience in religious matters must be guaranteed, any parent having the right to have his child opt out of religious instruction; that physical education be compulsory for boys up to the age of 15.

The Federal Government itself subsidises teachers' salaries, building, welfare work and the preparation of teachers for service in the primary schools. It also pays about half the cost of vocational training and supervises this. It finally designates financial assistance to each *canton* according to the number of children of compulsory school age (between 7 and 15) it has in any given financial year on its roll. Supplementary grants are made to the poorest of *cantons* in the mountain areas, and also to *cantons* with bilingual problems. Each *canton*, having received its grant, is free to decide how to spend it and on what basis to distribute it to its various municipalities, whilst the local rate-payers in turn have a voice in deciding how the money shall best be spent.

As might be expected, the Swiss have a well-developed system of preschool education with attendance in some places (e.g. Berne, the Federal capital) reaching as high as 80 per cent. In theory the schools are open to children from the age of 3, but in practice most children flock in between the ages of 5 and 6 or 7. They are a mixture of voluntary institutions (often attached to private schools), municipal schools, schools run by societies or private persons, and in some cases can be subsidised from *cantonal* funds, this usually in markedly industrial areas or in some mountainous and difficult regions. Whilst teaching is mostly modelled on Froebel or Montessori lines, it has to be remembered that the majority of children attend only between the ages of 5 and 7, and in consequence a higher standard of achievement and execution is expected of them than, for example, in a typical English nursery school. More emphasis is laid on acquiring skills than on general social training. Nor are group activities optional. It is held that at this age children must learn to concentrate and should not be allowed to leave a group activity, for which they have volunteered, simply because they have lost interest. Similarly, after the termination of an activity, they are required as a group to clear up the mess they have made.

Usual hours of attendance are between 8 and 11.30 in the morning and from 2 to 4 in the afternoon, the children returning home for a midday meal. The morning and afternoon periods are spent partly in group and partly in individual activities. Organised group activity may last up to an hour, according to the attention and interest of the children *as a group* and the teacher's other plans for the day. When the weather is suitable, activities are interspersed with play in the garden or with walks in the neighbourhood. Regimented though the system appears when described in this way, it has to be acknowledged from personal observation that the children are seldom bored, work hard, and take a keen and lively interest in what they are called upon to do. This undoubtedly stems from the environment created by dedicated and well-trained teachers, an environment in which the children can work and play busily and happily, secure in the knowledge that their teacher is not only a guide and helper but a sympathetic grown-up who treats them as social equals and so establishes excellent personal relationships with every child. Parents' meetings can be held, and are held from time to time, but at no level in Swiss education is there a felt need for close parent–teacher association: the administrative organisation of the school system is such that parents anyway become as deeply involved as they may wish at a local level in *their* school organisation and provision.

The first municipal school to be independent of the church was opened in Geneva as early as 1429, and primary education has been free and compulsory throughout Switzerland since 1874. The age of entry to primary school varies according to *cantonal* law which also governs the duration of the primary school course, fixes the length of school holidays, the size of classes, the content of the curriculum, makes itself responsible for social welfare and the training of teachers, and also decides whether schools shall be co-educational or single-sexed. Children start school at the age of 6 or 7, and the period of compulsory education varies between seven and nine years. The primary school course proper may last for three, four, five or six years, after which pupils pass either to some form of general-purpose education (which can be carried on in the same school buildings) or to the *Gymnasium*. In regions where the primary school is made to cover the whole period of compulsory schooling it is usual for pupils to follow this up by three or four years' vocational training which combines apprenticeship with part-time attendance at a suitable vocational training school which, whilst giving its pupils the necessary basic training in their chosen vocation, insists on a sound general education.

Indeed, the acknowledged aim of all primary education is to educate all children without distinction and by methods carefully adapted to their talents and stage of development to prepare them for the activities of everyday adult life. Thus there is emphasis on education for citizenship, and insistence on character training (which is, however, held to be primarily the responsibility of parents), the school (as in many other European countries) being considered essentially a place for learning. The basic subjects are regarded as the native language (in its pure and non-dialectal form), arithmetic, geography, history, civics and economics. Senior classes include instruction in crafts for boys and domestic science for girls, with the emphasis on vocational training. And, in the bilingual *cantons*, teaching of the appropriate second language begins in the seventh or eighth year of schooling.

It is traditional for the Swiss peasant to be an educated man and to be afforded the fullest opportunities for ensuring the education of his children to the highest possible level required for the job they will take up. It is also the proud and justifiable boast of the Swiss that they owe their political stability and their sense of balance and proportion in all things — as well as their drive — to the sound educational background which, over the centuries, has made every Swiss supremely conscious of his own value to the community no matter what his employment. It is at the level of the primary school that the Swiss insist the problem must first be seriously tackled, and they place special emphasis in this way on the term *Grundschule* (or basic school).

7

England and Wales

It has often been claimed that the Englishman finds his philosophy through action instead of determining his actions by the principles of philosophy, and that formal instruction in the schools has in consequence never been prized as highly as in France or Germany. The discipline of experience, it is argued, has been constantly preferred to the discipline of school. We educate for personality rather than for literary attainment, and in terms of clearly understood (if not actually expressed) social traditions in which the idea is implicit, as Ruskin puts it, that "the character of men depends more on their occupation than on any teaching we can give them or principles we can imbue them with. The employment forms the habits of body and mind, and these are the constituents of man. Employment is the half, and the primal half of education". Or, as Sir Michael Salder more than once observed, just as apprenticeship was the keynote of mediaeval education in England, so does it remain the driving force behind practice today.

This peculiar British form of self-assurance can in turn be exhilarating, irritating or frustrating. Yet it cannot be denied that such an empirical approach (often derided as "muddling through"), always allied to near reverence for what has stood the test of time (compare attitudes towards the independent school system in general and towards the direct grant grammar schools in particular), has nevertheless led to a ready willingness to experiment, to be receptive of new ideas from home and elsewhere, and to a healthily progressive outlook. And nowhere can this be better exemplified than through an examination of the various education acts passed throughout the nineteenth century down to the latest Butler Act of 1944 – still the basic foundation for educational practice throughout England and Wales – and such outstanding later reports as the Newsom Report of 1963 (*Half our Future*), the Robbins Report on Higher Education (1963), the Plowden Report of 1967 (*Children and their Primary Schools*), the 1972 *White Paper on Education: A Framework for Expansion* (which retained the major recommendations of the James Report on *Teacher Education and Training*), and the Bullock Report (1975) on children with reading difficulties.

Pragmatism, of course, has constantly been encouraged by Britain's deep-rooted distrust of planning and centralisation which is allied to a long tradition of government at a local level based on voluntary service. Even when in 1902 the first nationally co-ordinated system of education emerged for England and Wales, it was strongly based on local administration, *in partnership only* with central administration, and the terms of the latest Education Act of 1944 (whilst giving the central authority greater overall control of education) had carefully to respect this partnership. Any education act, indeed, if it is to prove acceptable and workable, must be flexible enough to leave room for local and regional differences, reflect past historical achievements, and make allowances for sensitivities engendered and perpetuated by memories of former conflicts. Thus, whilst it can be maintained that the real vigour of the educational system has resided and continues to reside in a wide diversity of aims and purposes, only made possible through a policy of decentralisation, it has also to be recognised that the present pattern of education (and the difficulties that arise) is an unhappy relic of past conflicts and interests. Examples which come immediately to mind include the position of church schools (of various denominations) *vis à vis* maintained state schools; the future of the independent school system; the peculiar standing of the "direct grant" grammar school; and, of course, the future of comprehensive education throughout the country.

Moves towards securing greater social justice and a desire for a more egalitarian way of life affected the British Isles, of course, as they did the rest of Western Europe, but in England and Wales in particular three important decisions can be pin-pointed as honest and praiseworthy attempts to realise Thomas Jefferson's claim in his draft for the American Declaration of Independence "that all men are created equal, that they are endowed by their Creator with certain inalienable rights, that among these are life, liberty and the pursuit of happiness". The first of these was the creation of the welfare state as a revolt against past inequalities. The second, the implementation of the Education Act of 1944 together with subsequent dependant pieces of legislation. The third, reorganisation of governmental control at a local level which has inevitably affected educational provision. Seen in retrospect, all these measures constitute an attempt to impose more central control over regional activities with a view to securing a homogeneous and overall effort.

Until fairly recently there were no fewer than 315 local education authorities, some very progressive, some extremely backward. By the passing of the Education Act of 1944 these had been reduced to 163. And from April 1974 the number of local authorities has been further reduced to 104 (including eight for Wales) — in the opinion of some critics already proving too large, too impersonal, and unmanageable. The Education Act of 1944 produced "a national policy for providing varied and comprehensive service in every area". A Ministry of Education was created (to replace the former Board of Education) with a Minister of Cabinet rank, and England and Wales were thus brought much closer to general European practice, the Minister having much more positive functions than before. In addition to inspecting and allocating grants (as formerly) he was required to "promote the education of the people of England and Wales and the progressive development of institutions devoted to that purpose, and to secure the effective execution by local authorities, under his control and direction", of governmental policy. As necessary, he can compel local authorities to adopt a definite line of policy; and the Act itself, in order to iron out glaring inconsistencies among authorities, actually commanded these authorities to provide facilities — such as higher education, nursery school accommodation and schools for handicapped children — which had not formerly been readily available, or to give access to them by arrangement with other authorities.

In 1964 the Ministry of Education was renamed the Department of Education and Science and was given a Secretary of State instead of a Minister. The Secretary of State works with a staff of permanent civil servants divided into two groups: those who serve at administrative central headquarters, and those who act as inspectors and who are assigned to areas administered by local authorities. The Department of Education and Science (DES) does not maintain, provide, or directly control any kind of educational institution, but through its inspectorate it none the less exercises considerable influence. The work of the inspectors (who are servants of the Crown and not of the Secretary of State) falls into three clearly defined areas: that of inspecting schools, consulting with local authorities and teachers and giving advice where necessary; that of representing the Secretary of State in their local areas on administrative matters; and that of advising the Secretary of State in matters of educational theory and practice and of being responsible for publications of the DES. Prior to the passing of the Education Act of 1944, only state-aided schools were subject to inspection; under the terms of the Act all schools without exception must be open to inspection and must conform to minimum requirements as laid down by the DES. The function of the local authorities is to provide a full range of educational opportunity at the primary, secondary and tertiary levels, and they are ultimately responsible to the DES for the proper conduct of the schools they establish, each authority having its own chosen chief education officer to implement decisions taken. The DES sets minimum standards for school building, controls teacher education and regulates the supply, administers negotiated salary scales, regulates the recognition of teachers' qualifications, and since 1973 has insisted that all teachers in the public sector must have undergone a period of professional training — though reluctantly and temporarily waiving this requirement for certain categories of teacher in short supply. The local authority is made responsible for providing and maintaining equipment, appointing and paying the salaries of its teaching staff (appointment in practice often devolving on the head of a school), and for the total arrangement of schooling within its area, subject to approval from the Secretary of State. Some large authorities have also instituted their own inspectorate to work side by side with the DES inspectorate but principally to ensure that their teachers are given full support and help in implementing policies agreed at the local level. Decisions about curricula and the detailed running of a given school are entirely at the discretion of the head who, of course, works in consultation with his staff.

One critic has summed up the present approach towards education in England and Wales as being an attempt to secure social equality even though it be at the expense of academic excellence. There is a great deal of truth in this observation, but I would prefer to word it somewhat differently and elaborate more. Successive Socialist governments, in their proselytising zeal for a truly comprehensive form of education, have not only tried to deny parents the right to choose for their children the education *they* wish (this on the argument that wealth can no longer be a factor in determining the quality of education on offer), but have also fallen into the error of confusing equal opportunities with the same opportunities. They have become obsessed with the idea that today the chief function of education must be that of levelling society and so eradicating privileges of wealth and ancestry. And, in their praiseworthy attempts to secure social justice for all, they have placed the needs of the individual in the ascendant and so neglected or overlooked the needs of society as a whole. This is obviously a dangerous course to follow. It is countered by the more conservative elements in government at both national and local levels, who are usually not antagonistic to the introduction of some form of comprehensive education, but who stress the importance of seeking out and nurturing talent (wherever it may be found) in the interests of the nation as a whole. The result, of course, is a patchwork of educational practice varying in some degree from one local authority to another which, based as it still is on regional autonomy and empiricism, and despite increasing central governmental intervention, often defies adequate description and understanding not only on the part of the foreign visitor.

Since 1973 compulsory schooling extends between the ages of 5 and 16, and fully 94 per cent of all children between these ages are in the public educational sectors. It must however be remembered that this figure includes denominational schools (mainly Catholic, and Church of England at the primary level) which were enabled by the Education Act of 1902 to draw all their running expenses from local rates and whose approved teachers (usually appointed by the clergy with or without guidance from the local authority) are likewise paid by the local authority. With the passing of the Education Act of 1944, denominational secondary schools (catering for the age range 11 to 18) have been granted parallel aided status provided they could show they were providing similar education to that offered in a local authority school of the same kind, and that tuition (as in the authorities' own schools) was given free. In addition, such schools as wished to reorganise to fully meet requirements in the Act were awarded building grants to meet up to 75 per cent of the cost involved, the figure being raised to 80 per cent in 1966. On a rough calculation, such denominational schools must account for about one-quarter of the total number of school children listed as attending schools in control of the public sector.

It has long been held that pre-school education for all 2-, 3- and 4-year-olds who need it or whose parents want it should be provided. At the moment of writing, however, provision for such education in England and Wales is lagging far behind that in the rest of Western Europe, though it must be remembered that England and Wales are the only countries at present requiring compulsory education to start as early as 5. Nevertheless, whereas before 1900 half a million children were registered as attending school earlier than 5, this figure had slumped to a mere 23,000 by 1964. Only now is it slowly beginning to rise again with roughly 8 per cent in the 3–5 age group voluntarily in attendance.[1] In the 1972 *White Paper on Education* the government announced a major expansion in such education aiming at providing free places for all who sought them within a decade – this in accordance with the relevant recommendations in the

---

[1] Figures published for 1971–2 showed that 5 per cent of 3-year-olds were at school, and 35 per cent of 4-year-olds. It must be remembered, though, that less than half of these were in attendance in state-maintained schools or classes: the bulk were catered for by private initiative under state encouragement.

Plowden Report. World recession since then has unfortunately slowed down this development, and gloomy figures presented to the House of Commons in 1975 indicated that most local authorities were unable to take up their full grant for providing pre-school places, with at least thirteen unable to make any further provision at all. Meantime, priority is concentrated (as recommended in both the Plowden Report and the White Paper) on attempting to secure full-time (as opposed to part-time) pre-school education for children from socially deprived areas, for children of immigrants, and for children in large cities.

On the other hand, quality at this level of education is constantly stressed. Whilst other countries tend to cram children into pre-school education almost regardless of class size, England and Wales insist on small classes with highly qualified teaching personnel and aides. Nursery and primary school teachers are trained together in the same institutions and receive the same salaries. As new pre-school provision is made, possible lack of co-ordination between pre-school and primary education is reduced by having nursery classes made an integrated part of the whole basic primary structure. There is a wish for increasing parental involvement, parents being encouraged to supervise nursery classes but professional decisions (deciding when a child is ready for further experiences) being left to be taken by a fully qualified teacher. Finally, it is worthwhile noting that the National Union of Teachers (the largest teachers' organisation in the country) recently published its own findings on *The Provision of Pre-School Education in England and Wales* (1973) in which it strongly urged a fully integrated nursery school curriculum concentrating on language development, pre-reading and pre-numeracy skills. Opportunities for gardening, art, craft and music must also be available, and the curriculum could include simple science experiments and practical experiences with weather and seasons. In a word, real schooling and not simply playgroups (usually privately run and financed) is now the aim.

As in France, primary education in England and Wales sees old methods interspersed with the new, though the school is now regarded more as a lively community where the teacher is increasingly becoming a guide and a friend rather than an instructor. Unlike France, however, there is no attempt either by central or local authorities to impose a curriculum, the only firm directive being that concerning religious education which is made compulsory on a non-denominational basis and which is usually given by an ordinary class teacher.[1] Instruction covers the three Rs, history, geography, nature study or some general science, craft, art, music and physical education. Government-sponsored experiments have led to the teaching of French (not always with happy results and now being challenged) in selected schools on the most modern of oral methods to children between the ages of 8 and 11.

Modern methods, whilst in accord with traditional English dependence on slow natural growth and the gradual assimilation of new ideas rather than on sweeping changes, do now realise that a child has his own special and individual needs, and that the timetable must be made as flexible as possible to cope with these needs. The artificial division into separate subjects is increasingly seen as an adult concept not easily acceptable to children, and work in consequence tends nowadays to take the form of projects and centres of interest conducted by groups or by individuals. The common pattern for primary education has usually been that of an introductory two-year infant stage (from 5 to 7 years of age), generally conducted in the same building as the primary school proper but kept separate from it. During this two-year period the child should have learned to read simple books, to write with fair ease, and to do simple sums. In practice, and for a variety of reasons which include shortage of teachers, large classes, and (in most towns of any size) problems associated with immigrant children, as many as a quarter or a third may not meet these simple requirements before passing on to the second state – a four-year period in the junior school (from 7 to 11 years of age). Children usually move up, however, on attaining their seventh birthday and remedial classes then become necessary.

Since the publication of the Plowden Report, many local authorities have already implemented a recommendation therein that the primary school should re-divide itself into a "first" school to about the age of 8, 9 or 10 and then into a "middle" school from the age of 8, 9 or 10 to 12, 13 or 14. There is a wide variety of possibilities, all turning on the provision made by a given local authority for post-primary education up to the compulsory school-leaving age of 16. In the past it has been common to stream classes in the larger primary schools on an intellectual

---

[1] Heated debate recently centred on a decision by the Birmingham local authority to include in a suggested syllabus for religious instruction throughout its schools consideration of Communism as an idealistic form of religion.

basis and with special reference to the basic skills. The necessity to do so vanished, however, once the country as a whole (with some notable exceptions which in principle still stoutly defend such streaming) decided to abolish the notorious eleven-plus examination purporting to indicate for what type of post-primary education a child was best suited. With the creation of various types of "middle" school, debate now turns on the question as to whether 11-plus *is* the right age for transfer to secondary education proper. For the creation of the "middle" school in effect brings education provided at this level in the public sector closer to the pattern followed with conspicuous success over the years in the independent fee-paying sector. There, a child will usually attend a privately run local school from any age up to 8 when he will be transferred (usually as a boarder) to a preparatory school of parental choice charged with giving him the necessary preparation to sit for a common entrance examination at about the age of 13 for transfer to an independent secondary school proper (a *public* school) which again a parent will have chosen in advance. If, however, on the results of the common entrance examination the child does not meet with the requirements of the chosen school, then the preparatory school will endeavour to find some other school willing to take him (or her).

In short, the entire function of the primary school in England and Wales is now under constant review, and pressures to make it more basic and more streamlined to meet and cope with the increasing complexities of modern life have led to all kinds of healthy experimentation. Most of this in recent years has stemmed from the publication of the Plowden Report which contains no fewer than 197 proposals and which may be briefly summarised for our purposes as follows:

(a) The beginning of a new structure for primary education involving a single date for entry. Infant education to be extended to at least three years, the junior school to remain at four, thus prolonging primary education to at least the age of 12.

(b) Schools in deprived areas to be given priority so as to raise schools with low standards to the national average.

(c) Unstreaming in the infant schools in the hope that this will continue upwards to junior school classes.

(d) Maximum size for the primary school class to be reduced, together with flexibility in the length of the school day and in the spacing of the school year.

(e) The abandonment of selection procedures at the end of the primary school course. Where the authorities still feel the need for some selection procedure they should abandon externally imposed batteries of intelligence and attainment tests and seek more appropriate ones in the context of the changing curriculum.

(f) The infliction of physical pain as a method of punishment in the primary school should be forbidden.

(g) Emphasis to be placed on all new approaches to the teaching of mathematics, science and the visual arts — television is with us to stay and children should be taught to use it profitably and to associate it with learning as well as with entertainment.

(h) Trained teachers' *aides* in the ratio of one full-time *aide* to 60—80 children in the infant school, and one *aide* to 120–160 children in the junior school (except in priority areas where the scale must be more generous) to be employed under the supervision of qualified teachers to provide them with help in the classroom. (It should be noted that this recommendation is in close conformity with what has long been the practice in Belgian primary schools.)

(i) Too few teachers are qualified to take courses in mathematics, science and music. There should be a full inquiry into the system of training teachers. The number of courses in which future teachers are trained side by side with entrants to other social service professions should be increased. More graduates are required in primary schools. Every teacher should have a substantial period of in-service training at least every five years. (All these points were further examined in the James Report of 1972.)

We have already noted how some of these recommendations have since been acted upon, and perhaps diversified. How many more will be partially or fully implemented in the near future remains to be seen. It is worth noting in conclusion that the report has clearly advocated a national policy of positive discrimination to favour primary schools in areas where children are most severely handicapped by home conditions, and has urged additional salaries for teachers serving in these priority "black spot" areas. It has also to be remembered that whatever is done cannot be considered as an isolated exercise. The new patterns which are emerging of some form of comprehensive education at the secondary level must affect the primary school, and the primary school (itself influenced by what has gone before in pre-school education) in turn will condition work done at the lower levels in comprehensive schools.

CHAPTER 6

How Comprehensive?

1

Admission to some form of secondary education has become one of the most serious and crucial of educational problems which every country has had to face since 1944. Changing socio-economic conditions have brought about an expanding economy which requires a better educated and better trained personnel for management. Technical and scientific developments have necessitated the formation not of one intellectual élite but of as many élites as possible to cope with the ever-increasing and changing problems in various fields of modern life. And increasing wealth and economic prosperity have made it possible for parents to claim that secondary education should be provided for all children. Successive social reform movements, allied to changing economic conditions and increasing social mobility, have led to the gradual breakdown of social barriers throughout Western Europe — made inevitable, of course, firstly by persistent attempts to introduce a valid system of compulsory free education, secondly by universalising and nationalising education at the basic primary level, and lastly by repeatedly raising the compulsory school leaving age so that everybody beyond the age of 11 or 12 must have undergone some kind of "secondary" schooling, in whatever guise it might be presented.

As long as the traditional practice of a "dual system" was acceptable, providing elementary education for the mass of the people and secondary schooling for privileged-class children, both groups remained satisfied with their own brand of education. Admission to secondary education was neither serious nor important. Since only the children of the well-to-do readily sought admission to such education there were almost everywhere schools enough to take in all candidates. Difficulties began, however, as an increasing number of lower-middle and working-class parents began

164

to consider it more beneficial for their children to continue their studies well beyond the elementary level. And these difficulties sprang mainly from the traditional concept of what secondary education was about. For many centuries the term had become associated with the type of school which offered a traditional classical curriculum and prepared its pupils for entrance to the universities. Attendance at such a school was the only way to gain access to positions of political, economic and social power and influence.

It was not until the nineteenth century that an increasing demand for a still more highly educated person in science, industry and trade focussed attention on the anomalies in the "dual system" and forced the classical secondary school to open its doors more widely to include more and more children from a wider spectrum of the population and to give constantly increasing importance in its curriculum to modern subjects like science, modern languages, history and geography. It led to the creation of new types of schools to rival the old classical secondary school and so called for an entirely new assessment of what was meant by "secondary" education. Tradition dies hard, however, and even today nearly all academic secondary schools in Western Europe remain convinced that they know what education is really about, now and for all time: they possess it, and even though they are prepared to extend its benefits to more people should they prove themselves fitted to profit from it, they are not prepared to vulgarise it. They will have little or nothing to do with training of any kind – except for the mind. They demand a tough intellectual approach, are strongly competitive, often dropping up to 50 per cent of their pupils before the end of the courses offered, and expect to dispatch their successful leavers to the universities (or parallel institutions). They are strictly official about their syllabuses, laying down exactly what and how much shall be taught in a given year. They are exacting in the academic qualifications demanded of their teaching staff who, of course, are in consequence totally different in spirit as well as in career expectations from the staff to be found either at the basic primary level or in technical and commercial institutions, or sometimes indeed in the newer types of secondary schools which have evolved to meet new demands.

Yet something had to give as in every country the transformation of an élite form of secondary education to that of a "mass" form became a reality in response to post-war claims that a fitting and suitable education was the inalienable birthright of every individual. Traditional academic secondary schools might be able to withstand change so long as they still recruited from the same upper-middle and bourgeois classes, but even then — as student revolts and protests of the late 1960s clearly demonstrated — they also were compelled in some measure to conform. *La démocratisation de l'enseignement*, as the French put it, must affect the privileged and the under-privileged alike. And so there gradually emerged clearly recognisable patterns of change in secondary provision aimed at orienting every child, according to his ability and aptitudes, towards his future function in society. Fees in publicly maintained secondary schools were abolished, except for boarders, and many independent institutions came to arrangements whereby they also in certain circumstances could provide free secondary education. All post-primary schools which still had continued to function as a reminder of the old "dual system" were upgraded to secondary level. Examination hurdles formerly used on the completion of a child's primary school course to decide to what type of secondary education (if any) he should proceed were swept away. Everybody was to have the right to some appropriate form of secondary education at least up to the end of his period of compulsory schooling, and everybody would be encouraged and aided to prolong his education as far beyond the compulsory school-leaving age as feasible.

Problems immediately arose. Existing school buildings were often hopelessly inadequate to meet new demands, and there were in any case just not enough buildings to house all pupils now demanding secondary education as a right. Nor was there always enough money to supply new buildings or even properly to adapt the old. Similarly, there were just not enough teachers to cope with swollen numbers, nor enough teachers properly trained or properly orientated to handling the varying needs and demands of the new influx. For with secondary education for all a reality, new goals had to be achieved. It was no longer possible to think only in terms of educating at this level a traditional intellectual élite; at the best, and even when allowing for the fact that varying kinds of élites would now be in demand, it had to be admitted that one could expect no more than between 30–40 per cent of the total intake to be intellectually inclined even in this newer and broader sense. Thus, the "mass" secondary school, in its lowest classes, had to be remedial and make good deficiencies in the basic skills before any secondary course could be of worth. No such problem had previously presented itself, since children who had not properly mastered such skills by the end of the primary school course either never sought secondary education or were held back until the skills had been mastered. Secondly, it had to be remembered that a majority of children would be leaving school as soon as they reached the compulsory age limit; it became necessary, therefore, given the terminal nature of this education, to see that some preparation for work be included in the curriculum whilst retaining the main emphasis on a general education. Lastly, every effort had to be made to encourage as many as proved suitable to prolong their education in a variety of institutions, both academic and non-academic.

For no two countries were the problems exactly the same, and each country responded to the challenges presented in terms of its own peculiar educational and cultural traditions. England and Wales, for example, given its own particular form of decentralisation, evolved four distinct possibilities: either a comprehensive school for the whole age range from 11 to 18; or comprehensive from 11 to 16 supplemented by specialist sixth form colleges (16–18); or the so-called two-tier system (the Leicestershire Plan) having a comprehensive high school from 11 to 14 to be followed by terminal education between 14 and 16 or completed academic education from 14 to 18; or a tripartite division into a first school (ages 5 to 9), a middle school (ages 9 to 13), an upper school (ages 13 to 18). Belgium, having long ago evolved its own middle school for pupils between the ages of 12 and 15 and having elaborated its working procedures in the post-war years to render it more comprehensive in intake, has been content with this until recently when it has begun experimentation with a six-year comprehensive plan envisaging a two-year observation period (12 to 14), a two-year orientation period (14 to 16), and a two-year period of specialisation (16 to 18). France, in elaborating yet another form of secondary education for all (1968), decided that the first year intake at 11-plus must immediately be streamed into possible academic types (some 39 per cent), modern types with possibility for later transfer to the academic group (some 36 per cent), and a general group expected to leave school at 16-plus and go to work (some 25 per cent). Norway and Sweden now have a nine-year compulsory comprehensive school between the ages of 7 and 16. Denmark has a basic school from 7 to 14 (with differentiation taking place between the ages of 12 and

14). Italy has a middle school for all between the ages of 11 and 14. West Germany is following up work in the *Grundschule* with a common-core curriculum between the ages of 10 and 12. Holland has evolved a common-core "bridge year" between the ages of 12 and 13.

And so on. We will consider in detail the provisions made in each separate country later. At the moment it is sufficient to note that everywhere in Western Europe the main purpose is to extend secondary education for all to at least 15 or 16; in so doing to add "dignity" and worth to technical and vocational studies; to postpone choice and specialisation to as late an age as possible; to concentrate more on the needs of each individual child; to replace selection for a particular kind of education (usually by some form of examination) by guidance and counselling; to change the patterns of teacher education and to give in-service training to teachers already on the job; to eliminate as far as is humanly possible all regional and social disparities; to involve parents much more closely in the educative process; so to change and adapt the curriculum as to have the child properly motivated and anxious to learn.

2

Curriculum reform, of course, became imperative with all this restructuring of the educational pattern. Yet even before such change took place the necessity for reform had long been apparent. The growth of new knowledge had so often meant that more and more was being tacked on to the traditional syllabus, and with the teaching body loth to modify its approach or devalue certain subjects in favour of newer and more cogent disciplines, the pupil was being increasingly submitted to strains which, as he sought to acquire the coveted *baccalauréat* or *Abitur*, turned him into a walking encyclopaedia of to him arid and often useless knowledge. The more sophisticated and egalitarian the times became, the more discontented did the student body become with what they increasingly saw as the unreality, the remoteness and the total lack of humanity of the higher educational system (to include not only work in the universities but also that done in other higher reaches of secondary education). And this, of course, sparked off student revolt everywhere, but particularly in Germany, Italy and in France where the May 1968 uprisings almost toppled De Gaulle's government. Participation became the watchword —

participation for the workers meaning a greater share in profits and in decision-making, for the student body (and indeed teachers and parents) a greater share in membership of decision-making bodies as impinging on problems which they saw as intimately their concern.

The chief obstacle to curriculum reform at the secondary level has resided in a deep and sincerely held reluctance on the part of society as a whole to abandon or even seriously modify a system of general education which is rooted way back in a basic humanistic approach. Put briefly, such an education assumed that, in principle at least, the whole of the natural, human and social worlds were suitable for study, and that correct study along approved lines would train the character and develop the personality of those sorted out to be the leaders and governors of society as a whole. The mind would be formed to think correctly and abstractly to arrive at the truth, the only worthwhile knowledge being that which was rationally organised into systems of ideas and theories. Increasingly, a good general education came to be looked upon (in the words of one critic) as "a totality of notions not susceptible to immediate application". It would result from formal intellectual exercises and would grow out of familiarity with great ideas, great books and supporting facts. It would have nothing to do with technical, professional or vocational training.

In practice, teaching was originally centred on a mastery of the classical languages, on mathematics, and (in the higher forms) on philosophy as developing from a study of Latin and Greek. That these languages became increasingly "dead" languages mattered little: because of their highly structured nature, skill in their mastery gave superb training in reasoning and logic complementary to that afforded by mathematics. To this basic core curriculum the French soon added study of the mother tongue — again as an instrument of precision in thought and clarity of expression — and out of the study of acknowledged literary masterpieces made a searching intellectual challenge. When, grudgingly, foreign language teaching had to be included in the curriculum, the approach everywhere was to model the teaching along well-worn lines for teaching the "dead" languages; when provision had to be made for some instruction in the natural sciences, such teaching was again intellectual in content as opposed to being laboratory based. Significantly, perhaps, it needed Germany's late switch from an agrarian to an industrial economy and to becoming a late colonial power, soon to be competing most keenly in world markets with the other powers of Europe, and obliged by sheer necessity in the changed economic order the Industrial Revolution had brought about to establish a place for herself, to shake the complacency of the rest of Europe. In creating its technological universities, Germany brought about the systematic harnessing of science to industry and instanced how the traditional type of secondary curriculum must give way to the new demands now being made by science and industry. She equally demonstrated how colonial exploitation and commercial enterprise depended on an adequate supply of competently trained linguists. In short, the "classical" type of curriculum must be modernised, and laboratory-taught sciences and spoken modern languages must be found their rightful place in that curriculum.

Yet despite all this and despite the urgent call to rethink the curriculum occasioned by post-war decisions to give all pupils secondary education, curriculum change has in no sense produced any far-reaching innovations. With the emphasis still on a sound general education based on traditional humanistic concepts, the principal aim has been to arrange as harmonious a fusion as possible of inheritance with change. And, whilst training in the manual skills must now form an essential part of any kind of general education, such skills should not be dealt with in their strictly vocational aspects, but as representative of the oldest skills known to mankind. Satisfactory spiritual and intellectual experiences must be combined with sensible work experience. We needed not simply *Homo faber* (the skilled craftsman and technologist) but *Homo sapiens et faber* (the well-educated craftsman and technologist). The accent must be placed on all those values which unite human beings. The (supposed) dichotomy between a vocational and a traditional type of education must be resolved. Life and learning must be seen as synonymous and we must in effect begin to think in terms of life-long general education. In addition, teachers need new directives and encouragement to review the emphasis to be placed on specialisation, on traditionally taught school subjects, and on polytechnisation.

Nevertheless, some considerable progress has been made and transformations in the curriculum have been effected much more readily than might at first have been expected. At the upper levels of secondary education the work load has been lightened if only by introducing a wider choice of options made increasingly more relevant to both the needs of society as a whole and the individual's particular bent. Most traditional academic subjects — particularly mathematics and the natural sciences — have been pruned in content and the teaching has often been drastically restructured. Immediately one thinks of the so-called "new" mathematics programmes, and of new science courses which both place the emphasis on topics most related to the present situation and also stress the interrelated nature of all present-day scientific research and experimentation. France, for example, has developed a mathematics curriculum to emphasise the role played by mathematics in both science and technology, and elsewhere in Western Europe integrated science courses of various kinds are becoming as commonplace at the secondary level of academic instruction as they have tended to be in the primary schools.

Recent research has demonstrated the importance of the communication skills in making for successful educational achievement at all levels, and this has influenced curriculum change in the humanities. In teaching the mother tongue the emphasis has tended to shift from literature to language as an important vehicle of communication, whilst instruction in a first foreign language has been increasingly extended to more and more pupils and appropriately revitalised by the use of audio-visual aids of the most sophisticated kind, including of course the language laboratory which possibly best suits the needs of the more mature student or adult and which certainly exacts a special expertise from the teacher if it is properly and profitably to be used. Genuine language practice by study visits to the foreign country is everywhere encouraged, and this is linked with a changed emphasis in the curriculum which now asserts that to truly understand and properly use the language of a people one must not only have as close an acquaintance as possible with their country but also be well-read in their history and institutions, well-versed in their culture. In short, the teaching of a modern foreign language has been given contemporary significance and finally released from the classical mould from which it had been struggling to escape (with varying degrees of success in various countries) for most of the twentieth century. By the same token, the teaching of Latin and Greek is no longer held in exactly the same high esteem as formerly, and those teachers who still stoutly maintain the importance of a good grounding in classical culture have been pressured into placing the emphasis on "culture" to the concomitant neglect of the aridities of grammar and syntax and the niceties of composition, unseen translation and versification.

The general trend towards a greater integration of science courses has been matched in teaching the humanities by what is sometimes awkwardly referred to as "interdisciplinarity" or "pluridisciplinarity". In Western Germany there is a course now compulsory throughout the whole of secondary education which is variously called (in differing *Länder*) either community studies, or social studies, or political education. The emphasis is on the modern world and its problems and the curriculum seeks to instruct along these lines by making a coherent whole of relevant areas of history, geography, civic and social studies, and economics. Sweden and Austria work along not dissimilar lines, and the Danes have a somewhat novel integrated course which combines the teaching of history, geography and biology. The teaching of economics, it should be noted, is becoming of increasing importance in the upper levels of secondary education since it received its accolade of respectability in France by the creation of the *baccalauréat de technicien économique.*

Sweden, needless to say, has become the pace-maker for much modern reform and all eyes have been focussed on the years of experimentation going on there to evolve a form of comprehensive education most suited to the Swedes. It is to Sweden that we must therefore turn in our detailed examination of reform at the secondary level of instruction, for it is from Sweden that we get the urgent message that, if the youngster of today is to be properly prepared to meet the challenges of the year 2000 and onwards, then he must have mastered the communication skills (which involve a thorough grasp of the mother tongue and sound knowledge of one or more foreign languages), be fully equipped to exercise his civic and social rights and responsibilities, and be so attuned to the natural world that he properly appreciates the demands it makes of him as he properly evaluates the consequences of the demands he in turn is constantly making.

3

In the still on-going debate as to the merits or demerits of some kind of comprehensive system, both antagonists and protagonists are ultimately led to some consideration of what I am tempted to call the American reality, the English dilemma, and the Swedish experience. This Swedish experience, extending now over some thirty years and still considered as an on-going process, is both envied and imitated and so repeatedly considered a kind of blueprint for what other countries might achieve that three vital considerations are often ignored. In the first place it is important to remember that, amongst all the nations of Western Europe, it is perhaps only in Sweden that reform of this kind could be possible. Secondly, there is as yet little evidence to prove conclusively that the desired objectives are being achieved. And lastly, it must follow from this that it is somewhat irresponsible to assume that "what Sweden has done we can do", for we neither properly know what Sweden has done nor whether such striving would eventually prove acceptable within the framework of a given national culture.

The conditions leading to a need for reform in Swedish education generally are varied and complex, and turn firstly on her legacy of prolonged isolation in an unchanging rural environment to be upset in the 1920s and 1930s by rapid industrialisation and exceptionally rapid urbanisation which all too soon revealed how under-developed and uneducated were the Swedish people as a whole in comparison with most other Western European countries. Increased provision of schooling became vital, particularly in rural areas but equally so in the growing townships. Again, like all other Western European countries, Sweden felt the effects of the "triple explosion" of population, of knowledge and of aspirations, but also found herself more in an educational void and with no real philosophy of education on which to build: for far too long she had followed the general Germanic trend. The events of 1940 served to shock her into a new self-awareness and into a revulsion against a type of education — particularly the traditional German *Gymnasium* — which had made Hitler possible and was then patently conniving with him.[1] The need for a redefinition of national identity became imperative.

This was made easier, firstly because of the essential pragmatic and materialistic approaches the earlier Swedish life style had engendered, secondly because of the peculiar relationship between church and state which had evolved, and thirdly because the Social Democrats, though never a majority party, have been virtually in office for some forty years. The Reformation in Sweden had been a matter of political expediency

[1] Read Frank Clare's novel *The Cloven Pine*, Secker & Warburg, 1942.

with the king seizing the opportunity to reduce the powers of his nobles by constituting himself head of the Lutheran Church. The simple, unintellectual faith of the rural communities had bolstered the situation, and Sweden in consequence underwent none of the bitter religious controversies which were to affect almost every other Western European power. Church and state worked hand in glove, and as time passed modern Sweden became a highly secularised nation with the church increasingly concerning itself solely with social matters. This again strengthened the position of the Social Democrats by lending support (tacit or otherwise) to the implementation of their programmes; and the Social Democrats, if only because of the unprecedented growth in prosperity of the country under their aegis, were quickly assured the support of other political parties and were able to push through a variety of reforms in line with their own political ideology and ideas of social welfare, which again tapped growing resentment against advantages accruing to what at least appeared to be a narrow privileged élite.

So did the total reform of education throughout Sweden become possible, based (it should be repeated) on a lengthy period of costly experimentation and closely following a traditional pragmatic approach. Comprehensive education in the Swedish style became a reality because of the vast amount of financial expenditure involved, and this was made available because of steady growth in national wealth due to skilful modern exploitation of industrial power, to the industriousness of an ex-rural population, and to lack of involvement in the catastrophic Second World War.

Critics of the whole idea of comprehensive schooling usually point out, indeed, that the major gains and successes made by the Swedes in education are primarily due to the financial expenditure involved and not to "comprehensivisation" as such; that many claims generally made for comprehensive schooling are not supported by the Swedish experience; that factors in reality external to the school situation (delinquency, permissiveness, drug addiction, complacency, pupil—student revolt) are causing the same problems for society as a whole in Sweden as elsewhere; and that the Swedish pattern has so far failed to provide an overwhelming case in favour of "comprehensivisation". With most of these strictures most Swedes would agree. But they would also point out that they are still constantly experimenting, still seeking to improve and build upon what they have so far achieved. Their approach remains dynamic, and they would concede doubts on several important points. In the first place it was originally somewhat naïvely assumed that in the new type of school all children would receive the sort of education formerly available to only a minority, and that notwithstanding the same high academic standards could be maintained. It was held that the highly desirable objectives of a truly democratic way of life, of equality and of freedom and co-operation could be realised only in a unified school with mixed ability groups. It was taken for granted that the Swedish people (parents and teachers) knew what child-centredness was all about and in the long run would come to prefer and truly endorse such an approach rather than still yearn after traditional (Germanic) encyclopaedic instruction.

Criticism, especially from within Sweden, has more recently drawn attention to the fact that "neighbourhood" schools have inescapably developed in large urban areas to cause the same problems as in America or England and Wales, thus disadvantaging the child from the lower in-come groups; that the idealistic attempt to give every child equal oppor-tunities regardless not only of background but also of innate ability has led to a total absence of streaming; that lack of streaming has led to more attention being paid to the below-average child than to the above average, resulting in a general lowering of standards; that this lowering of standards has affected adversely the universities where too many first degree courses have become little more than purely vocational training; that to throw the doors of the university wide open to working-class children is not (as was expected) more closely meeting the demands of the labour market, nor is it leading to increased social equality.

Nor have recent reforms done much to contain criticism. The intro-duction of a new gymnasial school in 1971/2, backed up by the 1973 so-called U68 Report, has further strengthened a growing opposition to the creation of over-large "juggernaut" schools. Teachers' associations, official investigations and research workers have all argued against them, and they have been joined most vociferously by the 30,000-strong secondary school students' union who want to have nothing further to do with "educational factories". Big schools, runs the argument, face great social problems which in turn exact a more elaborate and costly child care service. Anony-mity of staff and pupils causes serious disciplinary problems. A healthy atmosphere and genuine child care are to be preferred to all the audio-visual aids put together. Administration counters these charges by claiming that "talk of schools with 400 to 500 students is romantic nonsense", and claims the last word by showing that the educational budget is already stretched to its limits and arguing that "when deciding school sizes one must take into account the economic realities". The U68 Report, whilst primarily concerning itself with the reorganisation of university and tertiary education, affects the organisation of the upper secondary school in that it argues that "to permit a real choice, on completion of the upper secondary school course, between studies and work, every line of study at the upper secondary school level should in principle prepare pupils both for further studies and for gainful employment to a greater extent than is now the case". Already the universities, concerned with what they consider attempts by politicians to erode their independence and their vital role as setters of academic standards, are complaining that since the introduction of the new gymnasial school standards of new entrants, particularly in science and engineering, have fallen quite seriously.

It is now time to examine in some detail what has been happening at the post-16 levels of instruction since the introduction of the new gymnasial school from the start of the school year 1971/2. The creation of this new type of comprehensive upper secondary school is above all a piece of organisational reform. In essence the new school combines the former traditional *gymnasium* (academic, leading to the university) with the continuation and vocational schools to provide courses of 2, 3 or 4 years duration along 22 separate "lines" of study which can roughly be divided into three groupings: arts/social, economic, and technological. The merger makes it possible for more intensive use to be made of premises and equipment, as well as making it easier for students to change their course of study if they so wish. There is equally a social aspect to the reform in that it is designed to put vocational training on a level with studies of a purely academic nature. It follows that upper secondary education must now be largely vocational in character, but justification for this is found in the simple fact that, since the creation of the new gymnasial school, as many as 90 per cent of 16-year-olds now proceed to either two, or three, or four years of upper secondary education – the corresponding figure for some ten years ago being no higher than 30 per cent.

Enrolments into the gymnasial school are based on guidelines laid down by parliament, and should a course come to be over-subscribed, then admission is based on marks earlier awarded — which leads to some pupils having to embark on courses different from those applied for. The two-year courses are either purely vocational or offer specialisms along social, economic or technical lines of a more theoretical nature designed to lead on to further study. In all two-year courses Swedish, labour-market orientation and gymnastics are compulsory, and at least one optional general study must be chosen from English, French, German, mathematics, psychology, civics, consumer education, religious knowledge, music or art. Three-year courses consist of a "liberal arts" line (the old academic *gymnasium* scene), a social sciences line, an economics or business line, and a natural sciences line (back to the *gymnasium* pattern). The four-year course is purely technical. According to the combination of subjects chosen in any one of these fields, every student must study for a longer or shorter period Swedish, English, another foreign language, mathematics, some branches of science, history, psychology, civics, religious knowledge and gymnastics. It is interesting to note that for the first year's run of the new gymnasial school, 10.6 per cent of pupils chose the natural sciences line, 6.3 per cent the four-year technical line, 5.5 per cent the economics line, 4.4 per cent the social sciences line, and 4.3 per cent the "liberal arts" line.

There is no longer a school-leaving examination or entrance test for entry to some form of higher education, and already some 40 per cent of all "graduates" from the gymnasial school pass on to some further study, the universities accounting for 24 per cent. The leaving examination is replaced by the issue of a certificate (*slutbetyg*) which lists the average mark per subject (out of a maximum of 5) attained by the student. Objective equivalence of marks attained throughout Sweden, however, is difficult to realise and is causing much disquiet and discussion. It is already well known that to follow the natural science line gives the best chance of entry to university — this accounting in part at least for the high percentage figure given above. Similarly, whilst in theory an average mark of just under 2.5 out of 5 will normally gain entrance to a university, it is well known that approaching 5 in natural sciences will be needed to enter a medical faculty, for example. Thus, it is not unknown for students not expecting a high grade mark deliberately to downgrade themselves to be able to repeat a year and so improve their chances.

Yet, despite all these difficulties, the general impression remains that the Swedish school system is a harmonious, well co-ordinated, purposeful yet flexible one, adapted and adapting to social needs and social change but constantly seeking to respect the individual and to encourage individuality. To this end, for example, pupil democracy is deliberately fostered even though it is admitted it can at times get out of hand. Because children will be going out into a democratic society, then the chief concern must be to educate children in the practice of democracy. Along with a progressive educational philosophy, contemporary concerns (international understanding, the environment, the equality of the sexes, problems of economics) pervade the whole of the curriculum. The educational system has with some truth been likened to a factory that has to be kept in constant production but which all the time is being dismantled, reorganised and renovated. It is at any rate a unique system which has introduced progressive reforms well ahead of the rest of Europe and which has sought to keep to an absolute minimum the inevitable time-lag between social and educational change. Thus, for example, many of the newer *gymnasia* have been deliberately designed to serve also as community centres. Apart from the usual workshops and laboratories they can contain well-equipped theatres (doubling as lecture and examination halls), exhibition rooms, and various sports facilities. Adult educational classes are regularly held there in the evenings, and the local public library is often housed in a special wing.

4

Denmark

As far as Denmark is concerned, it will be remembered that basic education for all children is of seven years' duration and is given in the *hovedskole*. With the raising of the school-leaving age to 15 in 1972 an eighth year was added, and from 1974 (when the school-leaving age was raised to 16) the *hovedskole* was empowered either to add a further two years (classes 9 and 10) or to create a *real* section and so prepare its pupils for the *realeksamen*. Pupils who do not enter the *real* section may, if they so wish, sit a state-controlled examination at the end of their ninth or tenth year of study which entitles them to receive a certificate to be presented to a future employer as a guide-line to their particular interests and aptitudes. More precisely still, pupils with marked technical interests can also sit various preliminary and intermediary technical examinations to allow them to graduate naturally to further specialised training. Short periods of work experience are encouraged as appropriate, and vocational guidance and counselling services now have an important part to play.

The *real* section in effect comprises the three lowest forms of what was formerly a traditional type of academic education, and it still exists as such in the *gymnasium*. Transfer to the *real* section usually takes place at the end of the seventh year of study and depends on a report from the *hovedskole* as to suitability. All entrants, however, must show adequate proficiency in mathematics and two foreign languages. Within the *real* section the curriculum comprises Danish (with Swedish and Norwegian), English, German, mathematics, physics, chemistry, history/civics, geography, music and gymnastics. Sex education is compulsory but religious education is not. In the third (and last) year of the course French and Latin are optional subjects and possibilities then exist to strengthen the study of the sciences. The *realeksamen*, taken at the end of the third year, is intended to be a test of understanding rather than of memorising, and consists of oral and written examinations moderated by the Ministry of Education. Success in the written examination not only gives access to higher secondary and technical education but also provides job opportunities in business, banking, municipal administration, etc.

Reforms, however, are still constantly being introduced with the ultimate aim of making the whole of Danish education much more comprehensive and "elective" rather than "selective" as it still tends to be. Thus, it is now possible to take the *realeksamen* after an extra-mural course lasting up to two years. A common-core curriculum of the usual basic subjects is already in force for the first three years of secondary education whether it be given in the extra classes of the *hovedskole*, in a *real* section attached to a *hovedskole*, or in the *real* section which now forms the first three years in a *gymnasium*. There is no streaming allowed in a *real* section, and the intention is gradually to do away with the *realeksamen* and to replace it by an *optional* final school examination which will give no pass mark (and therefore no failure) and for which the pupil may choose the subjects in which he wishes to be examined. Similarly, it was decided as long ago as 1967 to introduce what is called the HF Diploma which permits a student to by-pass the *real* section or the *gymnasium*. Such a student will normally have completed the *hovedskole* to age 17, will add two further years of study and, being successful in the HF diploma examination, will be in exactly the same position as a pupil from the *gymnasium* who has completed his *studentereksamen*.

The three upper classes of the *gymnasium* provide what is now termed higher secondary education, and the vast majority of its pupils are expected to be successful at the *studentereksamen* and to pursue their education still further. Historically, it traces its ancestry to the Latin schools of the Middle Ages, was modernised on German lines during the nineteenth century, and underwent drastic reform in 1958 to provide a broadly-based liberal education of three years' duration leading to some form of tertiary education. Admission to this new-style *gymnasium* (whose traditions and historical background many seek to preserve and are consequently averse to having it merged in a wholesale comprehensive scheme) usually takes place after the *second* year of study in a *real* section or on completion of the ninth grade in the *hovedskole*. It is, however, also possible to enter a year later after successful completion of the *realeksamen* and about one-third of entrants still follow this procedure. A broad curriculum of common-core subjects is followed by all during the first year (Danish, English, French (or Russian), history, geography and mathematics), but in the two subsequent years the common element is reduced to allow students to specialise in one of six "lines": modern languages, classical languages, social sciences, mathematics/physics, science, science with social studies. The *studentereksamen* is pretty searching. On the other hand, since 1971 students have been given advance notice of questions to be set, and they may present themselves for examination with any notes and reference books they feel might be of use. As in the case of the *realeksamen*, it is an able mind as opposed to a well-stocked memory which is sought. It should finally be noted that it is always possible for a student who has the *realeksamen* qualification to attend courses outside the *gymnasium* to qualify himself to sit the *studentereksamen*.

Norway

We have seen how in Norway a comprehensive school compulsory for all between the ages of 7 and 16 has been gradually introduced, legislation coming with a formal School Act of 1969 and full implementation being achieved in 1971. The most academically able pupils, who have been carefully sorted out and given more rigorous academic training, particularly in their last year (the ninth grade), will now pass to the traditional *gymnasium* to follow a three-year course in preparation for the *examen artium*, success in which will gain them admission to university or some parallel form of higher education. Serious attempts are now being made to widen entry to the *gymnasium* which (except in the capital, Oslo, where the entry level is as high as almost 80 per cent of 16-year-olds) caters only for some 30 per cent of school leavers. The majority of *gymnas* are separate institutions which (as in other Scandinavian countries) have a long tradition of academic excellence as former six-year schools of an exclusive nature. In rural areas, however, the *gymnasium* may have to be run alongside the three last years of the basic nine-year school, and staff may be teaching in both schools provided they are university trained. There is also a commercial *gymnasium* offering a course of three or four years duration and which gives entry to higher institutions of learning other than the university. The same commercial *gymnasium* also offers a specialised one-year secretarial course for students already in possession of the *examen artium*.

Present intentions (debated in parliament in 1973) are to combine all existing forms of upper secondary education (*gymnasia*, vocational, commercial, technical) into a new-type school which will retain the name *gymnasium* but become totally comprehensive in character. Towards this end, technical subjects were already tentatively introduced into the traditional *gymnasium* in the autumn of 1969 and were offered as an optional choice for study in the second and third years. For the time being, however, there are five distinct "lines" of specialisation on offer. Almost 96 per cent of students at present follow either the *Engelsk-linje* (specialising in modern languages with English as the main subject) or the *real-linje* (specialising in physics and mathematics). The remaining "lines" are classical languages, Norwegian history and language, and biology with chemistry. Not all schools will necessarily offer all options, and there can be experimental variations introduced on approval from the Ministry. The *examen artium* consists of both written and oral tests, and students must pass in all subjects studied to be successful.

5

To turn next to the Benelux countries and France, it is important to note that, whilst all are in favour of increased social mobility and are anxious to effect reform at the post-primary levels of instruction in the direction of the still further democratisation of education, they are equally firm (to quote Professor Idenburg of Holland) in their refusal "to accept the idea that social mobility should be facilitated by a lowering of educational standards". They hold steadfastly to the idea of *suum cuique*. They all still stoutly maintain those humanist traditions which place emphasis on weeding out the intellectually less able, on polishing and sharpening the mind, and which make them still consider theoretical and abstract studies most worthy of the name of "education". In Belgium the bankers, and in Holland and Luxemburg the big industrialists bolster this belief, and in varying degrees all the countries concerned believe firmly in a way of life which reflects the solid bourgeois values of stability, conformity and industry. Increasingly, however, all the countries have begun to recruit from all walks of life the most able to positions of importance and influence whilst at the same time (through carefully organised technical and commercial education) enhancing the role and prestige of the working class. They exact and get hard work and application from all. And, in effecting reforms they work on the premiss that if you would have your reforms successful then you must start with people as they are and not as ideally you would wish them to be. If France can be said to educate by stressing the absolute human value of each individual and arguing that society owes education to a child more for his own sake (as a future French citizen) than from the advantages he will reap from that education, then we can also submit that the Belgians enhance the worth of the individual through conformity with certain accepted beliefs and attitudes, whilst the Dutch educate for individual autonomy.

Belgium and The Grand Duchy of Luxemburg

In Belgium, secondary education lasts for six years, and as a child completes his primary school course the parents are invited to state what they now want for their child, and they are guided as skilfully as possible to make the right choice in view of school performance and general school reports on the child's proved aptitudes so far. The options are either transfer to the lower levels of technical education, or to the *école moyenne* (middle school) which is either mixed or run separately for boys or girls, or to the *athénée* (boys only) and the *lycée* (girls only). Secondary schools run by religious orders are usually called *collèges* and the sexes are separated.

If a child enters the *école moyenne* he follows a course of study over three years which is so skilfully planned that it can offer both a Greek/Latin and a general section, exactly parallel with the work done in the three lowest forms of the six-year *athénée* or *lycée*, as well as what is termed a pre-professional section in which girls have domestic and home-craft courses (as well as the usual secretarial and commercial work), and boys do general crafts and agricultural and industrial training, with technical streams in wood- and metalwork. Time-tabling is arranged to make it possible within the *école moyenne* for a pupil to change at almost any time during his three years of study from one to another of the three sections. Thus, the final and irrevocable choice of specialised study is postponed until the age of 15, when the work of the *école moyenne* ceases. It is also particularly at the age of 15 that pupils are increasingly seeking and profiting by guidance given by one of the psycho-medical centres which, over the years, have become an important distinctive feature of the Belgian educational scene. There are at present thirteen such main centres in operation, strategically placed throughout the country.

A variety of possibilities is open to pupils satisfactorily completing their studies in the *école moyenne*. Some may enter an *école normale primaire* to begin training as future primary school teachers. Others will transfer to a technical (commercial) school, there joining up with those pupils who, instead of going to an *école moyenne*, either went direct to the technical school where the first three years of study of the cultural subjects parallel the first three years in the *athénée* or *école moyenne*, or came to the technical school at 14-plus after two years extended primary school work. Others will pass to the three upper and specialist classes of the *athénée* or *lycée*. It should finally be noted that a number of *écoles moyennes* have been empowered to offer a full six-year course leading to tertiary education, and thus rank as *athénées* or *lycées* in all but name. These circumstances usually hold when no *athénée* or *lycée* is conveniently placed to cater for the pure academic streams from the *école moyenne*.

As we have seen, the three lowest classes of the *athénée* (*lycée*) have a programme parallel to that of the *école moyenne*, and, in the basic cultural subjects (*not* Latin and Greek), not too dissimilar from that in the 12- to 15-year range of the technical school. Latin and Greek are the core subjects (if not the only important ones) in an *athénée* which seeks to give a sound academic discipline and expects from its pupils a constantly high standard of work and achievement. There is equally a modern (or general) section which includes science and economics and the option of taking a commercial course after the first two years of study. A first foreign language is compulsory from the first year for four periods a week, and this may be either English or the national language not used as a medium of instruction — though in the capital city, Brussels, which is bilingual, the first foreign language chosen has to be that *not* used as a medium of instruction. Modern sections start a second foreign language from the second year (three periods per week), and the classical sections begin a second modern language in their third year (two periods per week). A third foreign language, usually German but occasionally Spanish or Italian, is compulsory for the economics section from the fourth year (the start of the upper secondary level) for three periods per week, but the economics section also delays the introduction of a second foreign language until then and allots it also three periods per week.

Obviously, at the upper secondary level (15–18) pupils will normally continue -their studies as they have been finalised at the lower level, and six lines of specialisation are now on offer. The traditional Greek/Latin section still draws to it some of the ablest pupils in the school, and normally only those who started their secondary school career in the lowest forms of the *athénée* (*lycée*) will opt for this. It is still the traditional form of preparation for entry to university, and despite all attempts (since 1958) to make other sections attractive, and despite all the apparatus for orientation and guidance, it still dominates the whole of upper secondary education. Next in order of popularity comes the economics section, but it is to be remembered that girls' schools have a predilection for this option which will add shorthand and typewriting instruction to the study of a minimum of three foreign languages. Next in popularity comes the scientific A section (based on mathematics and physics); then a Latin/ mathematics section; then a Latin/science section; and finally, the most recent creation, scientific B which is based on a study of the natural sciences.

On the completion of a full six-year course the student presents himself for a passing-out examination which is internally administered by the school but controlled by a special jury to ensure uniformity of standards throughout the country. The examination includes both written and oral tests and must cover all subjects studied in the final year. The successful candidate is then awarded his *certificat d'humanités* which confers on him the right to present himself for an *examen de maturité* in three subjects related to the field of study he wishes to pursue at the university. This examination, however, is not selective but rather diagnostic in an attempt to ensure that the student is properly motivated towards university work, will be able to make good use of his time there, and will not clutter up an already badly overcrowded institution by having to repeat courses. In actual practice, fully 85 per cent of those presenting themselves for this examination are accepted and awarded the *diplôme d'aptitude à accéder à l'enseignement supérieur.*

To say the least, the picture overall is complicated if skilfully put together, and we have so far said nothing about the technical side of instruction at the secondary level. There has been an increasing amount of criticism of this (to some) unnecessary complication, and influential educationists, anxious both to simplify and further democratise secondary and technical education, have finally come up with an entirely new secondary structure which they have labelled *enseignement secondaire rénové.* Put briefly their aim is to have all secondary schools to be clearly divided into three cycles, each of two years' duration, the first cycle to constitute a period of observation, the second a period of orientation, and the last a period of specialisation. The new system was first put into operation in the autumn of 1969 by inviting schools known to be highly favourable towards it to implement it, and by encouraging other schools to follow suit. The response was initially not all that encouraging, but it has to be remembered that the first "guinea-pigs" only completed the full six-year course in the summer of 1975. Catholic *collèges* have cautiously adopted a wait-and-see policy. The *athénée* has been wary. The *lycée* has been the most accommodating. By 1972, however, 137 *state*-maintained schools (out of a total of 281) had embarked on the new scheme, and about 100 Catholic institutions (out of some 700).

The best way to understand the actual working of the new scheme will be to consult the diagram on page 384 which is supplied by courtesy of the *Athénée Royal d'Etterbeek*. It will be immediately noticed that the third cycle of specialisation retains exactly the same options as formerly on offer, and that once a student has embarked on the third cycle there is no possibility of a change of course. The first cycle consists of two main groups — a modern side and a Latin side. During these two years interchange between the two groups is always possible. In the first year of the second cycle (orientation) we have a modern side, a Latin side and a Greek side. After the first year, a wide range of possibilities for transfer exists. What is not indicated on the diagram (because the *athénée* in question remains a traditional classical school) is that in the newer establishments which tie in specifically with the *école moyenne* the orientation cycle provides for technical/commercial studies of two kinds: one will lead to termination of studies at age 16, the other to continuation of such studies to 18 and beyond. It is always possible, however, for a student on the terminal course to be transferred to the longer course. In short, the main aim of *l'enseignement secondaire rénové* (besides simplification) is to cut across class differences which too often and for far too long have meant that the choice of post-primary education has been determined by the socio-cultural milieu into which the child is born. All children must have the same chance of reaching the highest levels of attainment, and, over the first four years of observation and orientation special *cours de rattrapage* (classes for children having difficulties in certain branches of study) are held for between two and four hours per week.

Because of the growing success of *l'enseignement secondaire rénové*, moves are now afoot to alter the general pattern of education to be more in line with what is to be there achieved. It is intended that primary education begin one year earlier at age 5 and continue up to the age of 11. The first year in the primary school will be a transition year to accustom the child to a more rigorous and disciplined approach to school work. This will be followed by first a two-year cycle of studies and then a three-year cycle during which the child's developing aptitudes will be carefully observed. Secondary schooling for all which will then follow will be a transition year. There will then follow three two-year cycles (*enseignement secondaire rénové* proper). It is finally hoped to review the structure of the *maturité* examination which alone gives access to university studies. The overall effect of these changes will be to make the period of compulsory schooling extend from the age of 5 to the age of 15 (as against the present requirement of 6 to 14).

In considering the development of secondary education in The Grand Duchy of Luxemburg it has to be remembered that it is a tiny country of only some 348,000 inhabitants, and that with its prosperous modern economy, based on the manufacture of fine steel, it has existed as a modern state for less than a hundred years. From becoming a province of the Dukes of Burgundy in 1443 it later became absorbed into the Spanish (and Austrian) Netherlands. Annexed as a French *département* during the revolution, it became with Belgium in 1815 part of the Kingdom of the United Netherlands. After the independence of Belgium, the western half (now the Belgian province of Luxemburg) was ceded in 1839 to that country. The eastern part (and the present territory) remained in possession of the Orange family and continued to be garrisoned by the Prussians who had been there since 1815. Only in 1867 did the European powers finally guarantee the independence of the Duchy and the Prussians withdraw.

In consequence, Germanic and Catholic (Jesuit) influence is still a strong force to be reckoned with in the educational field, and until quite recently the Duchy was following the traditional European educational pattern of a dual system: one type of school for a small élite drawn from the middle and upper classes, and another for the working class. Strenuous efforts have been made since the 1950s to modernise and democratise education, and have resulted in the Act of August 1963 reforming pre-primary and primary education; the Act of August 1965 instituting a five-year intermediate school (*école moyenne*) to replace higher primary education; the Act of May 1968 reorganising secondary education; and the Act of June 1969 reorganising post-secondary education. Changes in vocational and technical education are also actively in preparation.

In the past, pupils who had completed six years of primary education but did not wish to transfer to some kind of secondary education course spent the last three years of compulsory education (12—15) either in *classes complémentaires* or in the *école primaire supérieure*. To enter the latter, a pupil had to pass an entrance examination since it gave a more academic course than the former. Both these schools, however, are gradually being closed as the new five-year intermediate school takes shape. The five-year course offered is divided into two cycles, a lower one of three years and an upper one of two years. In the lower cycle the curriculum is the same for all pupils and consists of religious instruction (or a course in ethics), German, French, English (from the second year), mathematics, history/geography, science, civics, commercial practice, art, music, physical education, and (for girls) domestic science. In the upper cycle pupils have to choose one of three specialist branches: the commercial branch, which includes data processing as well as book-keeping and typing; the technical branch (specialising in mathematics, physics and technical drawing); the biological and social science branch (specialising in biology, anatomy and chemistry). Success in an examination held at the end of the course in all subjects studied brings the *certificat de fin d'études moyennes*, and holders of this certificate can normally expect to obtain jobs in junior and middle level positions in the Civil Service or in business and industry. The certificate equally entitles its holder to continue his education at a higher level.

Pupils who elect not to enter the intermediate school at the age of 12 must perforce either embark directly on technical and vocational training (of which more later) or enter the *lycée* whose aim continues to be that of providing a general education for the more academically able to prepare them for university studies (or their equivalent). A *lycée* may be either state-controlled or privately maintained by the church, co-educational or single sex, and the 1968 law made provision to increase the number by empowering *communes* to establish their own. At the moment of writing there are only fourteen *lycées* of which six are church-maintained and for girls only, and of which six only two offer the full secondary school course. The eight state-maintained *lycées*, seven of which are co-educational and one for girls only, have tended of recent years to attract more and more girls to them and recent figures (1973/4) show that out of a total female population of the *lycées* of some 4000, only one-quarter attend church schools. The private schools charge fees whereas state secondary education is free and subsidies and bursaries are available for worthy children from poor families.

The course in the *lycée*, which lasts seven years, is divided into a lower cycle of three years and an upper one of four years. Admission to the *lycée* (as indeed to intermediate and technical schools) is regulated by an entrance examination taken from the primary school at age 12 in German, French and arithmetic. The first year (Class 7) is an orientation year with the curriculum identical for all pupils and equally identical with the first year in the intermediate school and the technical schools – this to make early transfer among the various schools a possibility. In his second year at the *lycée* (Class 6) a pupil must choose between the classical and the modern sides. If he opts for the classical side he adds Latin; if he joins the modern side he begins to study English. A classical pupil will then add English in his third year (Class 5) and as he moves to the first year of the upper cycle (Class 4) he must choose either English or Greek for the rest of the course. From the beginning of the upper cycle specialisation increases for both sides. The classical side splits itself into two sections – a Latin/languages section and a Latin/science section with one option from either science, or mathematics, or economics. The modern side splits similarly into a modern languages section and a modern languages/science section. At the end of the course the student submits himself for the *examen de fin d'études secondaires*. Since most subjects are taught in French in the upper cycle, the language used for the examination is normally French. Pupils who specialise in mathematics or science are required to be examined in only two modern languages. Philosophy is usually included, and to the two (or three) modern languages a student will be bound to add (according to his specialisms) between three and five other subjects from Greek, Latin, history, political economy, a fourth modern language, mathematics, physics, chemistry, biology, and economics. It is a stiff intellectual hurdle. Pupils who fail may re-submit themselves twice more only. Those who pass receive the *diplôme de fin d'études secondaires* which automatically gives access to the university and other forms of higher education both in the Grand Duchy and in other Western European countries.

Holland

The whole of secondary education in Holland has been reshaped by the Secondary Education Act of 1963 (finally implemented in 1968) which was so sweeping in its changes that it has been dubbed, not without reason, the "Mammoth Act". The act insists that, *in so far as it is possible*, every pupil must be allowed access to that type of school which best fits his capabilities and interests, and it virtually regulates all education from primary to university level. On completion of primary education at the age of 12-plus, all children now face a *"brugklas"*, or bridge year, which seeks to make the beginning of post-primary education both less painful and less "chancy". A common-core curriculum is provided at all schools for this bridge year so that, in theory at least, all children can change to a different type of school without having to repeat the year. The year equally makes it possible for teachers, parents and pupils to consult together to decide the exact form of continued education which will best suit the child's needs and potential. In actual practice, as is found in so many other countries, when a switch is made it is rarely to a more academic kind of education, and indeed, present variations in curricula in the *gymnasia* and the lower technical schools make interchange not fully possible. Be that as it may, most people are in agreement over the importance of such a traditional year, and since 1973, taking advantage of the permissive nature of the Mammoth Law, a number of school communities have already in effect extended the transitional period to three years by creating "community" schools to work on a basis of non-streamed classes for all between the ages of 12-plus and 15-plus. This move is strongly supported by the Trade Unions' Social Research Foundation which goes even further and recommends a common four-year school. Comprehensiveness is edging its way in.

The basis of division between types of post-primary schools is founded on the recognition of three different functions: pre-university or preparatory scientific education; continued general education; and vocational education, these last two categories being subdivided into lower, middle and higher provisions. In practice, children are sorted out during their bridge year to be considered in four distinct groups. The first, now known as VWO, comprises the *gymnasium*, the *lyceum* and the *atheneum*, all of which offer a six-year course on traditional grammar school lines leading to university entrance. The second group are termed HAVO schools and they provide a five-year course in general education which gives entry to higher vocational education but not to the university. The third group, MAVO, really replace the former advanced elementary school and offer courses lasting three to four years (the four-year course normally granting entry to higher vocational education, the three-year course to middle vocational education). Lastly there are the LAVO schools which offer technical, commercial, domestic and agricultural courses together with general education (one-third of the time) for two to three years. Their bridge year is different in that only one foreign language (English) is studied instead of two (usually English and German) as in other bridge classes, and a further disadvantage arises in that two-thirds of the time in LAVO schools is devoted to vocational subjects. Actually, these LAVO schools have not proved a success. Their numbers have rapidly diminished, some being absorbed into community schools, others being taken into the lower secondary vocational sector. At the time of writing we can say that, following on the bridge year, some 4 per cent of the 12–16 age group is absorbed by the pre-university schools, some 54 per cent into secondary general, and the remaining 42 per cent into secondary technical/vocational schools.

VWO schools run a six-year course leading to the award of a leaving certificate which exacts passes in seven subjects (which must include Dutch and at least one foreign language) and gives admission to the university. The *gymnasium* teaches Latin and Greek throughout, but divides its pupils into two sections for the last two years of the course. The Alpha section places the emphasis on Latin and Greek, and the Beta section, whilst retaining Latin and Greek, emphasises mathematics and science. There is similar specialisation in the *atheneum*, but for the last three years of the course. Here, the Alpha section stresses languages and economic and social studies whilst the Beta section concentrates on mathematics and science. It is to be noted that nowadays, *officially*, the *gymnasium* and the *atheneum* no longer exist, being combined into the *lyceum* to offer a common first bridge year.

HAVO schools first appeared in 1968, and their purpose is to offer a good general secondary education based on a three-year course common to all followed by two years' specialisation in a choice of subjects. A leaving certificate is awarded after examination in a minimum of six sub-. jects. MAVO schools offer a four-year course which can give admission to the fourth year of a HAVO school, to intermediate technical and vocational schools or (after a preparatory year) to approved types of higher level technical and vocational training. Basically, however, the MAVO

school covers the last four years of compulsory education. Possession of a
LAVO leaving certificate can give admission to a MAVO school though
it usually leads to a lower secondary technical or vocational school.

It all adds up, of course, to an insistence on the doctrine of *suum
cuique* rather than *idem cuique*, to a refusal (so far) to accept the full
comprehensive system, and to a continuing insistence on heeding the
demands of parents and the broad sectional interests of the community.
Amid all this, however, the growth of the Dutch educational system has
been one of the most rapid in Europe since the last war. With limited
natural resources and a high birth rate they must make the best use of
their human resources. As a 1970 OECD report on Holland put it: "A
high and changing technology requires a wide range of occupations – including those where the skill is predominantly manual – a greater ability
from the worker to adjust to growing complexity and mobility; such
adjustment can be facilitated both by increasing the fund of basic knowledge imparted in compulsory education and by modifying the aims and
teaching practice of the schools."

France

No other country in Europe provides over the past thirty years a more
bewildering picture of shifts, stresses and strains leading to first one
reform in education and then another. And all turns on the traditional
major objectives accompanying the concept of *culture générale* – a schooling based on a study of literature and the humanities which will enable the
student to attain that wisdom which is an essential of civilised life, and
which places an emphasis on training in the art of rational, objective thinking (*l'art de bien penser*). Reluctantly over the years the French have had
to recognise that such an education is suitable only for an academic
minority, whilst they have also had to come to terms with the pressing
needs of a modern industrial democracy. It is this dichotomy between the
desire at all costs to retain the benefits of a *culture générale* and the imperative need to invoke the egalitarian principle in education, if only to
flush out all available talent to create necessary new élites (particularly in
the technological fields), which has caused all the strains and led to the
implementation of reform after reform. The latest school plan to be put
realistically into operation was formulated in 1964 and got its blessing

from General de Gaulle who, in a speech at Soissons in the same year, asserted that "we must develop our national education system in a way suitable for the *mass* of young people now growing up happily and in conditions that are adequate for modern times". The distinguished educationist and educational reformer, Jean Capelle, made this more explicit when he formulated an instrumental theory of culture whereby three "communicators" — the mother tongue, mathematics and modern languages — were represented as the indispensable tools of modern learning. For Capelle, these communicators represent the absolute minimum of what should be learned by all who aspire to be "cultured".

The school plan of 1964 became operative in 1968 and represented a real effort at supplying purpose-built lower secondary schools for the 11–15 age range which would in character be comprehensive, heeding Capelle's appeal for adequate instruction in the three "communicators" and yet safeguarding, albeit for a minority, a time-honoured traditional curriculum. In practice, of course, as the new *collège d'enseignement secondaire* (CES) settled down to do its job, it soon proved that it was comprehensive in little but name. By 1974, mounting criticism encouraged the government to consider still further reforms (in essence the so-called Haby Plan), and these were published as proposals to be discussed at length by a variety of interested parties, including representative *lycée* students, two from each *académie*.[1] Never before had the Minister for Education taken so much trouble to stimulate discussion, nor had he consulted on such a wide scale. In its broad outlines, the Haby Plan, if implemented, can with some truth be said to be bringing French education nearer to the systems of other Western European countries whilst carefully preserving (and updating) all that is still viable in the traditional formula for *une culture générale*.

However, before discussing in detail the Haby Plan we must first consider the implementation of the 1964 school plan on which the Haby reforms must inevitably build. Entry to post-primary education is decided on the strength of primary school records and their examination by a commission which includes parental representation. Should the

---

[1] Under the overall control of a Minister of Education, France is divided into major educational regions (*académies*), each with its university and *recteur* who is in charge of all education within his particular *académie* down to primary school level where the *préfet* of each of the ninety-five local administrative *départements* takes over.

record be unsatisfactory, or should the child come from a private institution (which happens rarely), then an examination must be taken. On the findings of this commission a pupil will be directed to one of three streams (*filières*) in the CES. One *filière* is of the traditional academic type and admits children considered to have already shown some aptitude for following a purely academic course, and some 39 per cent of the present intake to a CES is usually to be found there. A second *filière*, absorbing about 36 per cent of the total intake, is more modern in its approach and allows for a more gentle adjustment from the primary to the secondary level. These first two *filières* have a common curriculum for the first two years of study, and built-in possibilities for transfer to one or the other. They have a 27½-hour week on a basis of French (6 hours), mathematics (4), a modern language (4), history and geography (2½), civics (1), biology (2), art and music (3), and physical education (5). The third *filière*, catering for the remainder, is taught by general class teachers (as opposed to university graduates), is considered "remedial" and in consequence does not in practice follow the common-core curriculum. Its bent is strongly practical and it is primarily intended for those who will attend terminal classes until the compulsory leaving age of 16 (established by De Gaulle in 1959). Here, a 27-hour timetable is followed with 15 hours of basic studies (including three hours for a modern language), 4 hours of physical education, courses in biology and various pre-vocational pursuits designed to awaken the child's interest towards the future choice of a job.

For the remaining two years of study (ages 13 to 15) in the CES, the first two *filières* have 29–30 hours of teaching and add compulsorily technology and natural science. Pupils must also opt for *either* the classical stream (adding Latin and/or Greek), *or* a "modern one" stream which adds a second modern language, *or* a "modern two" stream which gives more intensive study to the first modern language and to French. The third *filière*, by a law of 1974, may dismiss three-year students (age 14) to become apprentices in industry and elsewhere. The complete four-year course, however, gains admission to an agricultural school and also, in general terms, devotes the last year to pre-apprenticeship training, this usually provided outside the school in a *centre de formation d'apprentis*. The third year of *filière* 3 also begins special classes designed either to cater for pupils from *filière* 2 who are running into difficulty, or to give a more general and less vocational education to some of its own brighter pupils. It should finally be noted that, where it has not yet proved possible to supply a purpose-built CES, these lower secondary cycle courses have to be held either in former colleges of general education, or in the lower secondary classes of the traditional *lycée*.

As the first cycle of secondary education comes to an end at the age of 15-plus guidance is given to enable a pupil to decide whether he is to take a "long" or a "short" course of further training. Parents may challenge the guidance and opt for a different kind of further education, but in such a case the pupil must sit an examination to prove (or otherwise) his ability to carry on as his parents wish. This examination is final. "Long" education implies that the pupil will stay at least a further three years (for in France a year can always be repeated at least once) to sit one of the various *baccalauréat* examinations which lead to university training. For the first year of this three-year cycle (*classe de seconde*) students are divided into three groups: Humanities, which is predominantly literary and includes philosophy, classical or modern languages, and various options which can lead to later specialisation in economics and the social sciences; Maths/Science which is predominantly scientific with options on the literary side; Technical/Scientific leading to various branches of applied science and technology.

In the second year of study seven clearly defined specialisms are available. If a student goes on the traditional classical side he specialises in Greek and Latin and one modern language (Classical A); he may add some science to this (Classical A[1]); he may do Latin with two modern languages (Classical B); he may do Latin, science, and one modern language (Classical C). Should the student opt for the modern side he may choose between science and two modern languages (Modern M), or science, biology and one modern language (Modern M[1]). A student opting for technical studies may also prepare for the *brevet d'agent technique* and achieve technician level in either industry or commerce. There are two choices open to him: either science, a modern language and fundamental industrial techniques (Technical T), or economics and two modern languages (Technical T[1]). Obviously the classical side is attracting the best brains (as heretofore) and Classical A[1] and Classical C are reputedly the most difficult. The modern side is not so highly esteemed, whilst technical studies leading to a technical *baccalauréat* are considered very difficult.

At the end of the second year a student is moved up to the terminal class (to prepare directly for the *baccalauréat*) on the recommendation of a school council presided over by the headmaster. In this final year the options reduce themselves to five in number: a literary, linguistic and philosophy section; mathematics and physical science; natural sciences and applied mathematics (with specialisation in the agricultural sciences a possibility); applied science and technology; economics and the social sciences, including pure and applied mathematics. It is to be noted, however, that philosophy is a "must" in all options, great stress being laid on the Frenchman's ability to think and reason clearly and cogently. The literary, linguistic and philosophy section, which caters primarily for those who will read "arts" subjects at the university, is none the less careful to insist on almost one-third of the time being spent on science subjects. The mathematics and physical science option tends to attract the best pupils in both mathematics and science but similarly insists on a third of the time being devoted to the "arts" subjects. The natural (or experimental) science option is taken by the perhaps not so gifted scientist who again must devote about one-third of his time to "arts" subjects. The applied science and technology option demands almost half the time to be spent on technical and workshop practice and also includes a minimum of six hours per week literary studies. The economic and social sciences option splits the time roughly between the "arts" and science subjects.

The *baccalauréat* examination is taken in five subjects in which an overall standard of achievement has to be attained, the pass mark being 10 out of 20. Below 8 is a failure. Candidates with marks 8–9 may submit themselves for an oral examination in a further attempt to qualify. And nowadays, if they still do not succeed they are awarded the simple *certificat de fin d'études secondaires*. Possession of the *baccalauréat* at present automatically gives access to the university, though not as previously (because of the wide variety of *baccalauréats* on offer — eighteen in all) for study in *any* department. The *baccalauréat* is an examination notoriously difficult to pass and for long had a failure rate of over 50 per cent with candidates having a second or a third try. New measures introduced, new combinations, and the wider variety of possibilities have now pushed the pass rate up to approaching 70 per cent with consequent overcrowding of the universities — another important factor in causing student disquiet and unrest. It should also be noted that possession of the *baccalauréat* does not give admission to the *Grandes Écoles* which are prestige institutions with a particularly privileged position and which cream off the real academic high-fliers. The most famous of these are: *écoles normales supérieures* (originally intended to provide *lycée* and university teachers by preparing them for the *agrégation* but which have become in the process the forcing ground for the highest learned and political positions in France); the *école polytechnique* (to train engineers but also the proving ground for top administrators and businessmen); the *école nationale d'administration*. There are some 150 of these institutions, of which about thirty, situated in or near Paris, have the highest prestige. Entrance is highly competitive and is based on a special entrance examination which is prepared by highly successful *baccalauréat* candidates in special classes held in a number of old and distinguished *lycées* throughout the country. Thus, these high-fliers are more often than not in residence in a *lycée* offering this training, and will stay there until the age of 20 or 21. It was generally such *lycée* students who were among the prime movers behind the calamitous events of 1968.

But now we must briefly consider those pupils who, on completion of the four-year CES course, take the "short" as opposed to the "long" period of further training. There is a short general course lasting two years which can comprise some practical training with a vocational bias. The successful candidate receives his *brevet d'études professionnelles* (with his speciality noted). There is also a short technical course lasting three years and leading to the award of *brevet de technicien*. The intention has been to house these two courses in the same building in *collèges de second cycle* and have these *collèges* replace the secondary technical schools (formerly *centres d'apprentissage*).

To say the least, the present system in its present state of flux and change is bewildering, and the Haby Plan (which we must now consider) is a serious attempt to bring simplicity and suppleness to the whole of French education right through to the universities and teacher training, and to iron out inequalities such as those which are already seen to condemn a child from a poor background and poor primary record to go into the third *filière* of the CES and stay there. Let us begin by reminding ourselves that the plan envisages the same instruction for all children between the ages of 2 and 16, but advises considerable flexibility regarding the age at which individual children should pass from one level to the next. The primary school course is lengthened by one year (ages 6 to 12), but a child can be admitted between the ages of 5 and 7 according to readiness and so may leave it at any age between 10 and 13 to proceed to secondary education of the lower cycle. This lower cycle, as heretofore, is of four years' duration and thus extends for any individual pupil between the ages of 14 and 17. The basic aim in this lower cycle is to impart that minimum knowledge it is judged all Frenchmen should possess. The three *filières* disappear and all children follow the same course for the first two years, though for French, mathematics and the first foreign language – considered the three basic and essential subjects – pupils will be grouped by subject level of proficiency. This streaming, it is claimed, will allow a pupil to repeat work in perhaps one subject only instead of repeating as heretofore the whole course should he fail one part of it. Such a pupil will be given special help, and all pupils who, at the end of the first cycle, still remain generally below average will be allowed an extra year there to try to pass into the second cycle. For the last two years of the first cycle pupils will split into two main sections whilst still following a common-core curriculum. "A" classes will place the emphasis on academic and technological subjects, whilst the "B" groups will have a distinct practical and pre-vocational bias. Both groups will prepare for entry to the second cycle, but it is expected that the majority in the "B" groups will leave to take up jobs or enter on apprenticeship. Entry to the second cycle will be decided on the results of a given pupil in an examination which confers on a successful candidate a *diplôme de fin d'études du premier cycle*.

The second cycle will now be given in two distinct types of *lycée*, in theory at least to have parity of esteem, and can last between one and three years. Students entering the *lycée polyvalent* will prepare in traditional fashion for either the academic *baccalauréat* or for its technical equivalent, and are expected to stay a full three years. For the first two years of the course, however, two-thirds of the time will be spent on basic subjects (the same as in the first cycle) and one third on specailisation. What is termed a *baccalauréat de base* will be awarded at the end of these two years on a basis of scholastic record and achievement, plus two nationally controlled examinations in different subjects. The *baccalauréat de base* will not give entry to a university but is to be seen as a final secondary leaving certificate which will also allow successful candidates to sit various Civil Service examinations. For entry to university, a student must take a third year beyond the *baccalauréat de base* at the end of which he will be examined in the specialist subjects of his choice, university entrance being dependent on an overall profile, and entry to various departments of the university on the combination of specialist subjects offered for examination. Obviously, preparation for competitive entry to the *grandes écoles* will continue in specialist classes as before. The second type of *lycée*, to be known as the *lycée d'enseignement professionnel*, will normally run one- and two-year courses leading to the award of technical diplomas at various levels, but will also prepare its brightest students for an appropriate *baccalauréat de base* after which they may transfer to the *lycée polyvalent* for a third year.

That at any rate, in broad outline, is the scheme, but as implementation in full cannot possibly begin earlier than 1980 (if then) there is still time to modify and refine plans in the light of experience, consultation, and much criticism already making itself heard, not least from among students and the teaching body generally, including those in higher education. There has been an equally strong (and not surprising) reaction from the public at large who fear that the Haby Plan, sweeping right across the board as it seeks to do, can do much (if unintended) harm by undermining and upsetting traditions so solidly anchored in French society over so many years. The will to educate *ad maiorem Francorum gloriam* is far from being diminished.

6

West Germany

In the immediate post-war years it was an almost instinctive reaction for West Germany to revert in broad outline to the kind of educational provision that had found favour with the Weimar Republic (1919–33). Only West Berlin, under the persuasive influence of the occupying powers, immediately began planning to provide an *Einheitsschule*,[1] and West

---

[1] As early as 1950 this "one-type" school was well under way. In the summer of that year the author was a member of a team invited to West Berlin to advise on the introduction of French as a first foreign language in the *Einheitsschulen*.

Berlin today is in the forefront of experimentation in providing truly comprehensive education, followed closely by the *Länder* of Nordrhein-Westfalen, Hessen and Hamburg — all of them seeking to take fullest advantage of the recommendation of 1969 from the German Education Council (established jointly by the *Länder* and the Federal government) that at least forty integrated experimental comprehensive schools should be established. Today, all *Länder* are experimenting with comprehensive schools, and throughout the whole of Western Germany there must be some 150 such schools in existence. By 1974, Socialist Hessen had already 95 *Gesamtschulen* and was proceeding much more rapidly than other Socialist-controlled *Länder* who see the process as being inevitably a gradual one of educating the public to accept the idea. And Conservative *Länder*, of course, view the whole idea with grave suspicion: though they are willing to experiment they still insist on creaming off their brightest children into the traditional *Gymnasium*.

Thus we have a position not dissimilar from that in England and Wales at the present time in which the advocates of a truly comprehensive system have to contend with entrenched attitudes of those who maintain that a well-proved tripartite system of post-primary education must not be endangered in the interests of experimentation. Naturally, however, impediments to reform in Western Germany are somewhat different. First of all there is the hierarchical structure of the teaching profession with the *Gymnasium* teacher on top and asserting his privileged position in much the same way as does the *agrégé* in a French *lycée*. Next comes the inescapable fact that German society as a whole insists on retaining a marked class structure. Nor must we forget that the family has always been the dominant formative influence in German education, and that family attitudes are, perhaps by their very nature, essentially conservative. Again, and in a way ironically, the decision taken immediately after the war to decentralise the whole of Western Germany by splitting it up into eleven autonomous *Länder* and with each *Land* having complete control of its own educational system has proved to be the most effective brake on reforms. The centralisation of the educational system had been one of the most powerful tools of the Nazis, so that its abolition was seen as a prerequisite to safeguard democracy. Under Nazi rule there had been a marked recession in both educational expansion and standards, and thus the overall aims now became those of undoing the harm brought about by the immediate past, of preventing the re-emergence of the Nazi ideology, and in consequence of effecting a return to the high standards set by the *Gymnasium* under the Weimar Republic. It has finally to be remembered that comparisons with the "other" Germany, the German Democratic Republic, are used both as a justification for the existing form of decentralised government and for maintaining a traditional educational pattern, many West German textbooks still equating the government and administration of the GDR with that of the National Socialists. The main concern, understandably, has been with a return to the pre-Nazi tradition rather than undertaking new reforms, and the 1954 Education Act of Lower Saxony sums up prevailing attitudes when it states that: "Schools have the duty of preparing young people entrusted to them for later life and a vocation of educating them and bringing them up in the traditions of Christianity, of the cultural heritage of the Western World and of German education, and of helping them to become independent-minded and responsible citizens of a democratic, social and constitutionally governed state."

So the traditional pattern for the time being prevails, updated and made increasingly more flexible to give greater equality of opportunity and to cope with social changes brought about by economic expansion and prosperity. The education on offer is thorough, enterprising and forward-looking. It is highly specialised — even the comprehensive schools (of which a sizeable number would be classified as multilateral schools in England) basing their teaching in key subjects on groups differentiated according to ability after a short initial period of non-differentiation — and it constantly seeks to provide an appropriate élite at all levels of public service: academic, commercial and technical. All education is now generally free and compulsory up to the age of 15 with compulsory part-time attendance of 15-year-old leavers up to the age of 18. Methods of selection of pupils from the *Grundschulen* for one or other of the forms of post-primary education vary from *Land* to *Land*, but there is often an orientation stage of one or two years, and also in-built possibilities for transfer from one kind of secondary education to another.

In actual practice, a pupil on satisfactory completion of his *Grundschule* studies will be moved to one of three clearly distinct types of school. He will either enter the *Gymnasium* which offers a nine-year course leading to the award of the *Abitur* which is the passport to the university and parallel tertiary forms of education, or he will go to the *Realschule* (intermediate school) providing six years of study leading to an intermediate examination, or he will attend the *Hauptschule* (secondary modern) giving five years of study to be followed by either full-time or part-time (to 18) technical, commercial or vocational training.

The *Gymnasium*, of course, is the prestige establishment which in 1901 saw the birth of its rivals the *Realgymnasium* (which taught Latin but not Greek) and the *Oberrealschule* which taught neither Latin nor Greek but substituted two modern languages (English and French) and placed the emphasis on the sciences and mathematics. All three are now generically termed *Gymnasien*. Everywhere now, a first foreign language (usually English but occasionally French) is studied from the first year and a second foreign language from the third year. Much thought is given as to how best the *Gymnasium* can fulfil its task of educating the future leading personalities of the intellectual life of the country and yet continue to act as the people's school which will meet the requirements of every type of talent and promote intelligence in every way. It is today felt that whilst the *Gymnasium* must aim at a substantial widening of the intellectual horizons of its students, and at the creation of a mind capable of discriminating judgement, it must also give as full and complete an introduction as possible to the various categories of scientific and scholastic thought prevailing, and that in consequence the traditions of devotion to high academic endeavour must constantly be maintained. The leaving examination (the *Abitur*) is on average taken at the age of 19 or 20, is rigorous and searching, and a recent estimate would indicate that no more than 20 per cent of the intake of a *Gymnasium* proceed so far to be successful, whilst some 40 per cent leave the *Gymnasium* after five years of study to embark on more vocational studies.

The *Realschule* has proved to be one of the most successful ventures of post-war Germany and has proved popular with parents who shied away from the long and academic *Gymnasium* courses. The final intermediate examination can lead to good jobs in industry and administration, though many pupils go on to further vocational training at appropriate institutions. The study of one foreign language is compulsory for all. In contrast, the *Hauptschule* has become very much the "poor relation" and is today in a somewhat parlous and underprivileged position. Like its predecessor, the *Volksschule*, it largely remains the school for the culturally undemanding and for working-class and socially low-placed sections of the population. It is thus inadequately equipped to provide the additional support and education its pupils require, and it highlights the extreme difficulty that exists for a pupil to break out of the vicious circle created by his own and his parents' origins. Nor does the school prepare the pupil for entry into working life or apprenticeship. Most *Länder*, however, offer a sixth year of study at the end of which the equivalent of the *Realschule* leaving certificate can be obtained. Nevertheless, it was estimated in 1975 that, whereas before 1960 around 60 per cent of *Grundschule* pupils were passing on to the *Hauptschule*, the *Gymnasium* and the *Realschule* together now claim that 60 per cent intake.

All this, of course, has much strengthened the hands of reformers who urge comprehensivisation, and has undoubtedly been an important factor in influencing thinking about the Structural Plan of 1970. The plan recommends that after four years in the *Grundschule* all pupils should undergo an orientation phase of ideally two years after which they should pass to the *Sekundarstufe I* which thus will cater for children between the ages of 12 and 16. There should be a common basic curriculum for all through the first two years with streaming and setting as necessary. Specialities should be concentrated upon in the last two years, and a first school certificate (*Abitur I*) could then be obtained after ten full years of schooling at about age 16. The upper secondary stages (*Sekundarstufe II*) would cater for ages 16 to 19 and would now have students specialising according to their proven interests. Some courses would last two years, some three. The most significant departure, however, would be to amalgamate both technical and professional courses and the traditional *Gymnasium* ones, thus forming one genuine upper comprehensive establishment. Successful completion of this schooling would lead to the award of *Abitur II* granting admission either to the university, or to a technical university, or to teacher training. In principle, all *Länder* have adopted these suggestions and it now remains to be seen how over the next few years they will be implemented.

The various experimental comprehensive schools are obviously to be regarded as models for future developments along lines of the Structural Plan, and different organisational types can co-exist in one *Land*, or even within one city. They are generally modelled on the Swedish system of a nucleus of subjects studied without differentiation, the remaining subjects being taught in differentiated groups. The "nucleus" tends to be confined to social studies, music, art, sport and, to a limited extent, German.

The present six comprehensive schools in West Berlin are organised on a basis of (a) *nucleus subjects*, (b) *ability subjects* (mathematics, natural sciences and a compulsory foreign language), (c) *compulsory "electives"* which include a second and/or third modern language, economics, social science, technical, practical and commercial courses, and (d) *optional advanced "electives"*. Differentiation in non-nucleus subjects is at four levels: contact level, basic knowledge, expanded knowledge and advanced level. Optional advanced electives are intended for those students who are not otherwise fully stretched or provided for in an advanced differentiated group – e.g. a pupil might wish to specialise in Classics and ancient history, or to enter the medical or legal professions or some highly specialised branch of technology.

Italy

Undoubtedly, the outstanding achievement of the new school law of 1963 (which became operative in 1966) has been the creation of the new *scuola media* which makes Italy one of the few countries which can boast a single-type middle school which sees the entire school population through to the end of the compulsory schooling period and allows the pupil to postpone his choice of stream until the age of 14. With the creation of the *scuola media* in its present form the elementary school-leaving examination (taken at 11-plus) was abolished, and entry into the *scuola media* now depends on the final report on the pupil from his primary school. The Italian interpretation of the ideal for general culture within the context of the *scuola media* allows of no premature differentiation from either an academic or a vocational viewpoint. The course consists of three years' study of five groups of subjects: (a) historical/literary comprising Italian, English (as the first foreign language), history and geography; (b) mathematical/scientific – that is, mathematics and the natural sciences; (c) artistic, comprising music, art and handicrafts; (d) technical drawing and its application; (e) civics and religion. Music and technical drawing become optional after the first year. In the second year the study of Italian is intended to include some basic knowledge of Latin, and in the third year Latin becomes an optional subject – it being noted that only those pupils who have studied Latin (and passed satisfactorily at the leaving examination) will be permitted to enter the prestigious *liceo classico*. Generally speaking, the optional subjects available in the third and final year are provided to reflect the now growing and evident capabilities and aspirations of the pupils. For pupils who on transfer from the primary school find the going difficult, there are not only special remedial classes but also extra lessons grouped into courses known as *doposcuola* and which are given in the afternoons, the normal school day ending at 1 p.m. Similarly, there is additional work also available in the afternoons (to a maximum of ten periods per week) for additional optional subjects for all.

The expressed aims of the *scuola media* may be summed up as (a) offering a general education without premature differentiation; (b) guiding the pupil, on a basis of a core curriculum and of a set of optional subjects which are believed to be educationally valuable, towards the most sensible choice for the future; (c) adapting itself both to the mental level of its various pupils and to present demands of social and economic life; (d) firmly committing itself to new methods of teaching and learning as suggested by the latest educational research. The problem of training teachers to use new methods, is of course, of crucial importance. Recent classroom observation (1973) suggests that the methods still employed tend to be those of a teacher—pupil dialogue with the teacher the dominant partner, though it must be admitted that a respect for learning along formal lines went hand in glove with warm, friendly and spontaneous teacher—pupil relations.

For those who pass the middle school examination at about the age of 14, various alternatives are open, dependent to a large measure on attainment but also upon social position and ambition. Latest available figures, however, reveal that roughly only 60 per cent obtain the leaving certificate at age 14, and that almost a quarter of the total entry fail to complete the full period of compulsory schooling. Nevertheless, hopes for the future are that roughly only 20 per cent will leave at age 14 to form an unskilled labour force, that some 40 per cent will pursue vocational or middle technical studies, that about 30 per cent will opt for higher technical studies to at least the age of 19, and that some 10 per cent plus will follow the traditional paths to the university.

The real intellectual élite will pass to the *liceo classico* which offers an introductory course of two years followed by three years of preparation for the maturity examination which gives right of entry to the university.

The curriculum comprises: Italian language and literature, Latin, Greek, history, geography, mathematics, natural sciences, one foreign language, philosophy and the history of art. The *liceo scientifico* was created in 1923 for the education of students aspiring to university studies in medicine and science. Originally a four-year course, it was extended to five years after 1945. In its curriculum the study of Greek is replaced by double the time spent on a foreign language, and the syllabuses for mathematics and the natural sciences are considerably widened. Possession of its maturity award admits to all faculties in the university except for Letters and Law. The *istituto tecnico* offers a variety of courses over five years and possession of its diploma grants entry to the relevant university faculty or its equivalent in tertiary education. Finally at this level (also granting university admission) is a four-year course of an academic character in fine arts (*liceo artistico*). The *istituto magistrale* also ranks at the *liceo* level and offers a 3/4 year training course for intending teachers in the primary schools. Highly successful students may then go on to a university to read for a degree and so qualify to teach either in the *scuola media* or a *liceo*. According to Professor King, such students tend to regard the *istituto magistrale* as an "escape hatch" towards the university, do not take it seriously as a teacher-training school, but consider it a poor man's upper-secondary school.

Switzerland

Like the Germans and the Dutch, the Swiss have felt the necessity to prolong education beyond the *Grundschule* proper to at least nine full years of schooling for those children who are not to follow some course of secondary education, and to prepare them more adequately for entry to a society which is becoming increasingly specialised. Pupils who show any ability to profit from some form of secondary education, however, are encouraged to attend a kind of lower secondary establishment (or intermediate school) variously denominated the *Realschule*, or the *Handelschule*, or the *Progymnasium*, or simply the district school. Here, the education is entirely free and admission is either on the basis of a written examination plus a few oral tests or on the primary school's assessment of ability and achievement. The most able and more ambitious pupils will usually proceed directly to the lower forms of the *Gymnasium* for a full nine year course there leading to the award of a Swiss *baccalauréat* known as *maturité fédérale* and which gives automatic access to the university. Fees are payable but they tend often to be nominal and no child of academic ability is denied such an education through poverty. As in Western Germany there are three distinct types of *Gymnasien*: the traditional *Gymnasium* which concentrates on Latin and Greek; the *Realgymnasium* concentrating on Latin and two modern languages; the *Oberrealschule*, without Latin but concentrating on mathematics and the natural sciences. Business school courses are equally on offer.

Courses in the lower secondary establishments (or intermediate schools) will take a pupil up to about the age of 16, and the schools themselves aim at giving a sound general education whilst also preparing the abler pupil to transfer to the *Gymnasium*. The stress is on the teaching of mathematics, science and modern languages, and most pupils, on completion of this school course, enter on some form of apprenticeship or continue their studies at commercial and technical institutions. It should be noted, however, that we have given here a very general overall picture and that considerable variations can appear from *canton* to *canton*. Only the *Gymnasium* remains more or less uniform in its approach, and this is due to the fact that the state lays down exactly what will be tested at the *maturité fédérale* examination and what standards shall be reached. Thus, all schools must conform closely to a "type" curriculum.

Naturally, Switzerland has been much influenced by changes taking place in education among her near neighbours, France and Western Germany, and over the last ten years or so much thought has been given as to how best to reform prevailing patterns. It is recognised that in those *cantons* which still operate on a basis of extended primary education rather than have intermediate schools there must be considerable wastage of potential ability. The intermediate schools too have their wastage problems, but the most telling criticism that can be levelled against the traditional system concerns the process of selection for secondary education: drastic and sometimes final decisions are made at about the age of 11, and a number of pupils of potential academic ability are thereby denied the opportunities of a *Gymnasium* education. It is impossible to cover in detail variations from *canton* to *canton*, but if we take the French-speaking *Canton de Vaud* as an example we shall have a fair picture of what is going on. In Vaud, there has been mounting concern that 1967 statistics revealed only

6–8 per cent of pupils entering a *Gymnasium* continuing to the equivalent of the English upper sixth form, and only 4–5 per cent of a total *Gymnasium* intake proceeding to the university. The first step was to improve the process of selection by standardising examinations for entry to secondary education, by trying to assess a pupil's ability through various aptitude tests, and by instituting a two-year orientation stage to be the same for all pupils, with compulsory German but no Latin (this despite strong traditionalist pressures). This orientation or guidance stage, however, has been limited only to those pupils selected *in advance* for secondary education and the move is now towards extending it to *all* post-primary pupils. In the city of Geneva a further variation holds whereby the orientation stage has three tracks: Latin/scientific for children who hope to go on to the university; a general course for those thinking of entering commercial, technical or vocational schools; a practical course for the less gifted who will undertake relatively unskilled manual work of various kinds. There is no entrance examination to secondary education and pupils (according to proved ability) may switch from one track to another. In Lausanne, each of its four secondary schools has been transformed into a multilateral school incorporating the orientation stage and, as each school has the same curriculum, the choice of school depends solely on the location of the home.

There is, however, still much opposition, even among the teaching profession, to the democratisation of education by creating parity among all secondary school tracks, and some register dismay at seeing so many children, from widely varying social backgrounds, entering secondary and higher education. It is against the traditionalists in the teaching profession, and against those people opposed to Federal intervention in *cantonal* affairs that any educational reformer must fight. There are, indeed, two contradictory tendencies in educational thought which will inevitably slow down the implementation of most progressive ideas. The first sees no reason why all pupils should strive for a university education and boasts (justifiably) of the fine opportunities for the less academic pupil offered elsewhere. They consider that a sound training for a specific job is far more valuable to a child of average or below average intelligence than years wasted pursuing an academic course. And many would not question the logic of this outlook. Yet, with widespread educational reform taking place throughout Western Europe, Switzerland may still be forced to reconsider the administration of its own system. If only to avoid the patent injustice of *cantonal* discrepancies, it may find itself obliged to adopt a centralised system. But as it does so it will inevitably encounter stiff opposition, especially from those linguistic and religious minority groups whose rights Switzerland has always been proud to safeguard.

England and Wales

With the passing of the Butler Act in 1944, secondary provision in England and Wales became mainly of three types to which entry had to be gained by a process of selection based on tests taken between 10 and 11 years of age. The most promising (academically-minded) pupils were drafted to the grammar (or high) schools, the next most able to secondary technical schools, the remainder to the secondary modern school which over the years has fought hard to upgrade itself – sometimes at the expense of the non-academic child it was created in the main to serve. Grammar schools have taken the General Certificate of Education at 16-plus (or even earlier) and an advanced level certificate at 18-plus to gain entrance to universities and colleges of education. Secondary technical schools have tended to follow the same pattern as the grammar schools, with an emphasis on technical and commercial subjects. Secondary modern schools have insisted that they have had pupils (usually late developers) who were academically just as good as many grammar school pupils and have asserted their right to enter such pupils for the same examination. Thus, a bright secondary modern pupil, having gained a satisfactory General Certificate in Education, could easily make the transfer to the sixth form of a grammar school to specialise in two or three chosen subjects and take the advanced level certificate.

In essence, however, the General Certificate of Education was not suited to secondary modern pupils, and as new curricula came to be devised to meet their needs so was a new type of examination called for, one result being the creation in 1965 of the Certificate of Secondary Education available to *all* secondary pupils but being less academically demanding than the General Certificate. The grammar schools would generally have nothing to do with this new certificate, arguing that it was not designed to meet their particular approach and thereby emphasising its second-rate nature. Meantime, as secondary modern schools were more and more urged to use *their* certificate in preference to the General Certificate of Education, a compromise was reached whereby high marks on the Certificate of Secondary Examination in a given subject would be accepted as the equivalent of a pass in that subject on the General Certificate. The situation is both confusing and unsatisfactory and the whole question of secondary qualifying examinations is under full review. In 1976 the Schools Council (established in 1964 to advise the government on curriculum and examinations) proposed replacing both these qualifying examinations in 1980/1 by a single teacher-controlled examination to be sat at 16-plus. This idea has had a mixed reception, one important criticism being that implementation was being unnecessarily rushed: it is too early to make any definite decision about so radical a change without examining further the problems involved.

Side by side with the examination confusion ran increasing dissatisfaction with selection procedures at 11-plus and with the tripartite division of all children at so early an age. Many local authorities soon began experimenting with the creation of a comprehensive school system and gradually several distinct patterns of "going comprehensive" emerged, with total abandonment of any kind of selection for post-primary education. Inevitably the matter became a political issue. In 1965, when it was estimated that already there were almost 240,000 pupils in some 262 comprehensive schools (this representing 8.6 per cent of the total secondary school population), the then Socialist Minister for Education urged comprehensive development on several approved lines on all local authorities and required them to show the progress they had made. A Conservative Minister in 1970 advised local authorities that they were fully free to decide on the kind of school organisation they preferred. By then the total number of comprehensive schools had risen to 1145. By 1975 the number of comprehensive schools had risen to 2593, catering for almost 2½ million pupils, representing 67.9 per cent of the secondary school total. And, with the Socialists back again in power, those local authorities which had so far resisted change began to be forced to go with the tide.

Meantime, and much to the chagrin of committed idealistic Socialists, the private fee-paying sector has continued along its traditional path of pursuing academic excellence for a limited number of pupils and conferring its special social *cachet* on all who attend these schools. Accurate figures are difficult to obtain of percentage attendances, simply because the prestigious public schools are so often lumped together with other establishments, including the so-called direct grant grammar schools which, in return for providing free secondary education for at least a quarter of their intake to the brightest pupils coming from local state primary schools, receive "direct grants" from the Department of Education and Science. The best that can be said is that immediately after the war some 8 per cent of the total secondary school population was catered for in independent schools of all kinds, and that this figure had fallen to about 5 per cent some twenty years later; that the public schools (i.e. those schools whose headmasters have a seat on the Headmasters' Conference of Public Schools — and this includes a large number of direct grant schools) were estimated in the 1960s to be educating about 3 per cent of boys over the age of 13; that 20 per cent of university entrants come from this sector; and that, as more and more local authorities "go comprehensive" and the number of direct grant grammar schools diminishes, so do many affluent and/or self-sacrificing parents opt out of the state system to have their children "independently" educated.

Nor are Socialists any better pleased at the thought that as late as 1972 some 5000 places in independent schools were being taken up and paid for by local authorities for the education of children considered in need of a boarding-school education — such children coming mainly from families serving their country overseas: members of the armed forces, diplomats, EEC officials and various foreign-serving bureaucrats. As early as 1964 the Labour Party had declared its intention of incorporating the public schools in the state system and has still not reneged this decision. Meanwhile, it has attacked the weakest element in the independent system, the direct grant grammar school, and tried to force it within the comprehensive system by witholding grants. The only result has been that, of 173 direct grant schools still in existence at the end of 1975, 109 have been able to secure sufficient financial backing to elect to go independent. To enforce what is undeniably a sincerely held belief in the merits of the comprehensive system as the best way to achieve equality of opportunity, hundreds of academically able working-class children are now to be denied a free academic education in some of the best day-schools in the country. And, by the same token, the parent's right to have his children educated as he wishes is being severely curtailed — unless he be rich!

In a word, extreme positions have been reached where, politically, comprehensive schooling becomes a "must" even though this means in too many cases the arbitrary grouping together of buildings formerly housing schools with separate and distinct functions and having a kind of helter-skelter run of classes (and teachers) from building to building – to say the least uneconomic on time even if we ignore the frustration which must ensue. Undoubtedly, a number of purpose-built comprehensive schools in the right areas and pulling in a wide cross-section of pupils are doing extremely good work and fully meeting all demands made on them. But there are too many "neighbourhood" comprehensive schools, and such a school in a poor or downtown area is disadvantaged all round. That this is so has at last been admitted at a recent meeting (31 March 1976) of 200 head teachers and university dons which has urged universities to use positive discrimination in favour of big comprehensive schools by accepting lower entry qualifications from pupils from such schools than are expected from the independent and grammar school sectors.

From all of this there is one important lesson to be learned. Political involvement in education is inescapable. To that we must all agree. If political involvement, however, so necessary and so often salutary for the greater good of all, should degenerate into political machination, then trouble lies ahead. The various political parties in England and Wales have allowed just that to happen. A new, clean and hard look needs taking at the whole scene. It needs to be remembered that comprehensive schooling is still much in an apprenticeship and trying-out stage. The Department of Education and Science needs above all to remind itself of the well-worn Latin tag: *"Quis custodiet ipsos custodes".*

CHAPTER 7

Technical and Recurrent Education

1

The growth and development of industrial enterprises throughout the nineteenth century heralded a new phase in human existence and relationships which not only altered the character and structure of society but also made it imperative to organise education for the first time for the mass of the people. At the same time, a cool hard look had to be given at the traditional kind of education enjoyed by the privileged few. At first, it was assumed that simple instruction in the three Rs would prove adequate for the masses. When a pupil had a fair grasp of this rudimentary and essential knowledge, then according to the job he was doing and the amount of technical skill required for adequate performance of that job, so would he be encouraged to follow courses in specialised technical training provided for him by some outside and often voluntary body and so gradually improve his wage-earning capacity and his value as an operative to the firm he worked for. Thus, in England, the first attempts made at specific technical and vocational education were not sponsored by the then Board of Education but by the Board of Trade; in France, the Ministry of Agriculture made itself responsible for improving the technical knowledge and resource of the agricultural worker. The mass of workers, however, either through lack of ambition, or opportunity, or adequate preparation, remained as low-paid unskilled operatives.

It seemed a happy and successful arrangement at the time to both England and France, who, first in the field in industrial pursuits, had then no rivals to challenge them. The Paris Exhibition of 1856 proved a catalyst in that it brought home most painfully to both countries that they were beginning to face increasingly strong competition from other European countries whose work forces were already receiving a most thorough and forward-looking training. By 1870, Germany (who had had to make through sheer necessity a determined effort to capture some of the markets) was seen already to be outstripping France in the industrial sphere; and by the turn of the century, chiefly influenced by Kerschensteiner, she had not only reformed her secondary system to include the more modern and technical subjects but was also transforming her higher elementary sector to provide the more highly skilled labour force industry exacted. Smaller countries such as Holland, Belgium, Switzerland and Scandinavia, mainly because of the democratic organisation of education they enjoyed, were able to grasp more acutely the pressing needs of the times and to make for speedy implementation of reforms. And poverty-stricken Italy, whose main export was its willing manpower, was quick to train that manpower competently for the times and to ensure a constantly increasing demand for its craftsmen and technicians. In England, only a very few independent schools were imaginative enough to build engineering workshops or run small farms – Christ's Hospital, Bedford School and Oundle come immediately to mind – but these experiments were largely ignored by the authorities to the point that, after the passing of the 1902 Education Act, the newly created secondary schools "aped" the grammar schools by following a traditional academic pattern, and such schools as had a definite bias towards training for employment in industry or commerce were relegated to the inferior status of higher elementary schools. Only gradually, and often reluctantly, did technical and commercial studies infiltrate the secondary schools curriculum throughout the early decades of the twentieth century. And in France, technical education only became a reality for the mass of the people by the *Loi Astier* of 1919 – that is to say when it became obvious after the First World War that highly trained and highly skilled workers were going to be increasingly needed in industry side by side with skilled technical experts.

In the period between the two wars, Western European countries generally had evolved for themselves patterns in education which gave varied provision (not primarily of an academic nature) for the age range 12 to 15 in what were often called middle schools and which stressed the practical aspects of learning. Some of these middle schools, of course, had been founded many years earlier, and the Belgian *école moyenne*, created by the School Law of 1850, can be seen as an example of how most tended to develop. Children passing through the middle schools in Belgium were originally expected to become "d'hônnetes bourgeois, d'hônnetes artisans, des cultivateurs habiles, satisfaits de leur situation".[1] The programme of studies laid great emphasis on a thorough grounding in the mother tongue, written and oral, on mathematics, and on the teaching of a first foreign language. History and geography were also taught, and the needs of the locality, whether agricultural, commercial or industrial, had to be considered. In 1881, the *école moyenne* was allowed in its own right to provide its own particular form of secondary education, and admission to it was put on a level with admission to the purely academic sectors. In 1887 the school was attacked as tending to "saturate the country with intellectual workers". A more practical instruction geared much more closely to the economic needs of the times was called for. In 1897 a fourth year was added to the course and separate commercial, industrial and agricultural sections were created. By the same token, the curriculum of the academic schools was revised to include two new sections: a scientific section with the emphasis on mathematics, and a commercial section to fit pupils particularly for entry to trade and business. By the 1920s an efficient and highly organised technical and commercial system of schools had been evolved, and the role of the *école moyenne* became the triple one of duplicating the lower cycle of academic secondary education, of handing over its promising technical and commercial pupils to the technical institutions proper for advanced and specialised training, and of recruiting potential primary school teachers to the training colleges.

By now, problems still very much with us in the technical and commercial fields were beginning to emerge. Scientific discovery, leading to increased sophistication and consequent complexity in technical studies if the demands of highly industrialised countries were to be adequately met, quickly revealed that narrow specialisation and the acquisition of a limited number of skills were no longer viable objectives. It became no longer possible to think of teaching a young person the basic principles of a trade or craft to which he would afterwards devote the rest of his life. Similarly, apprenticeship — at least along traditional lines — must be abandoned, or retained solely to prepare for certain specific one-man jobs such as butcher, baker, hairdresser. Flexibility and adaptability had to be developed to as high a degree as possible. It was no longer good enough to teach the future young worker a job and no more — to equip him with

[1] *Annales parlementaires*, 29 May 1850.

the techniques and just so much of the theory lying behind those techniques as to make him efficient; he must in addition be prepared to emerge into the world of work ready to deal in an intelligent way with the changes and complexities he would increasingly find about him. He had, in short, to be prepared to face a life of uncertainty, and education henceforward must be, as Professor Edmund King has cogently put it, "education for uncertainty".

Several problems immediately came to the fore, the most important being that of the relationship between occupational training and a general education. How much general education should the trainee have, and of what kind? To what extent should a general education impinge on technical instruction to humanise the approach? As we shall see, in various countries various solutions have been tried out, but all are agreed, in practice, that industry today needs primarily the communication skills — reading, writing, speech, number; the social skills — co-operation and ability to get on with others; mental qualities of alertness, interest and clear-thinking; and personal qualities of self-discipline which imply a sense of responsibility, self-respect, and willingness to work and tackle problems with an open and inquiring mind.

A second problem, in a sense inseparable from the first, is that of determining how soon shall general education end and specialisation begin. It is increasingly recognised that too early specialisation does not always sort out the right workers for the right jobs, but on the contrary too often restricts potential and the resourcefulness and initiative of the worker. The general aim must be to postpone specialisation until as late as possible. In all technical schools everywhere there is a growing reaction against extremes of specialisation and even where schools are geared to deal specifically with regional needs, and to build their programmes according to these needs, they are now attempting to see that each student has a conspectus of the whole. He must know and appreciate the relevance of the task he has to perform, and its importance, in relation to the total regional economy. The verdict of modern industry is that the individual be given a broad general/technical education with his training in the highly specific skills reserved until he is best able to appreciate them, which is usually "on the job". Actual workshop practice, therefore, looms large in the final stages of a student's training.

A third problem — and in reality a fundamental social problem — is that of persuading the right kind of person to take up technical work, of making such work "respectable" and attractive to those who have traditionally sought a white-collar job (or an academic education), no matter how unsuited in reality they were to perform such jobs. France has perhaps characteristically sought a solution to this problem by showing that technical studies can be made as rigorous a discipline as any other branch of study. Most countries, however, have been at pains not only to include technical and commercial studies as desirable options in their general secondary school courses but also to ensure that there is a basic curriculum for all children up to the school-leaving age of 16 which also enables transfer easily to be made from one branch to another throughout this part of the secondary school course. Only after 16 does any kind of specialisation begin, and many who then leave school are to be found on either short or long courses, and studying either part-time or full-time according to circumstances. Thus, the former practice of recruiting a child immediately after completion of his primary school course into the lower levels of technical/commercial instruction is disappearing, and by the same token increasing use is being made of vocational guidance centres in conjunction with parental consultation to ensure that the right decision is taken at the right time.

Lastly, there is the problem arising from the rapidly changing needs of the world of work and the newer and more complicated techniques to be employed throughout the whole of the economy. Over the last few decades important structural changes have been taking place in the deployment of the total work force. Between 1958 and 1970 the agricultural labour force throughout the whole of the EEC declined by some 40 per cent, and estimates for the 1980s are that then only some 6 per cent of the total active population will be following agricultural/horticultural pursuits. Those redundant in agriculture, or no longer attracted to work on the land, have moved to the manufacturing industries, but this move has been paralleled by transfers from industrial to service occupations. Within the last fifteen years the coal and textile industries have lost around a million jobs, and all the manufacturing industries together must have lost double that figure. The number of white-collar workers in Holland, for example, had risen from 18.5 per cent in 1955 to 27.1 per cent in 1967; and in West Germany there has been a more spectacular rise from 25 per cent in 1959 to 43 per cent in 1968.

The lifelong habits of an entire population are being affected by these changes which also give rise to considerable feelings of insecurity, and the EEC has reiterated on several occasions its belief in the importance of vocational training *of the right kind* with each country taking its own decisions in terms of its own peculiar problems but subscribing to general, overall guidelines. These are, briefly, that the young must be trained to an acceptable level of competence both before *and immediately after* starting on their first job; that the adaptability and competence of those already at work must be retained by in-training and also by increased opportunities for better performance and promotion; that there must be adequate provision in government-sponsored centres for the re-education of the unemployed to avoid their remaining unemployable; that lifelong (or recurrent) education and training must nowadays not only be seen as a necessary corollary to technical education but also as the right of every man and woman: *no* education can nowadays be considered as terminal; that in consequence of all these factors there must be increasingly close collaboration between employers and the educational authorities. In this last respect, Belgium, as we shall see, offers an extremely good example of what can be achieved. The EEC generally, however, has been much influenced in its overall pronouncements by Swedish ideas and the Swedish experience, Sweden being the first Western European nation to recognise the need for publicly sponsored adult training and to come to terms with the dual purpose of all training. It is, therefore, to Sweden in particular and to the Scandinavian countries in general that we must first look.

2

Sweden

We have already discussed in some detail the organisation of the new gymnasial school in Sweden which in effect has led to the absorption of basic education and training for a wide variety of occupations into the secondary school system. The argument is that, since the circumstances in which the training of young people "on the job" could be properly undertaken in industry, commerce or public organisations of one kind or another disappeared immediately after the First World War, the only logical conclusion to a development in technical and vocational education which started over fifty years ago is to bring the systematic acquisition of skills and vocational theory into the secondary system proper. Obviously, the system in operation is most complicated with at least fourteen vocational choices open. According to circumstances, skill training elements of the course taken will be provided either wholly or partially in firms outside the school. Programmes are built up in stages, and near-related categories are merged into blocks with identical basic education for all, greater and greater specialisation following. It is most probably the former two-year vocational school which has most profited by assimilation into the gymnasial school in that this lowest level preparation for the world of work for the first time receives the attention it merits, its status also being enhanced. Most striking, however, is the role of the former *fackskola* (a four-year continuation college). Some of the studies on offer are already beginning to attract students who formerly would have gone on to the university: they see no point in protracting their studies several years more to obtain a formal university qualification when they will be entering a world of employment which repeatedly puts the emphasis on work experience.

It is at the university, of course, that (as usual) the highest technological studies will continue, but there also exist important institutions outside the aegis of the universities which offer their own individual specialisms. The latest creation is a College of Librarianship in Boras. There is the College of Economics and Business Studies in Stockholm which is the only private foundation of its kind left in Sweden. There are also colleges for social work and public administration, agriculture and forestry, veterinary medicine, and journalism.

Amid all this, informal or recurrent education has become an increasing concern of the Swedes. It is first of all recognised that a young person entering industry, commerce or the public service with the kind of basic training we have just described will usually need a period of induction and specific training before becoming really competent. Suitable provision is made by the employer who is estimated as devoting at least 1 per cent of all emoluments to this on-the-job and off-the-job training. The immediate main concern, however, is to cater for the many middle-aged and more elderly citizens who, through no fault of their own, have not been able to benefit from the relatively recent and rapid transformation of the educational pattern. It was discovered in 1970 that out of some 5 million Swedes between the ages of 20 and 69, only 9 per cent had had a secondary education, and only 2.6 per cent had attended a university. Forecast percentages for the 1980s show a possible increase to 15.1 per cent and 6.2 per cent respectively. A variety of programmes have now been instituted (obviously building where possible on already existing provision), and a distinction is generally drawn between three kinds of adult education, though the boundaries between these categories is not always distinct.

First comes what is termed qualifying adult education. Municipal Adult Education was started in 1968 based on the curricula laid down for the last three years of the nine-year compulsory school, the *gymnasium* (academic), the *fackskola*, and the vocational school. The minimum ages for admission are 16 for the nine-year compulsory school courses and 18 for the rest. Instruction is free of charge and is generally provided in ordinary municipal schools which also provide the teachers. Most courses are held in the evenings. Students may read one or two subjects at a time and so, if they wish, gradually accumulate the full leaving qualifications of the branch chosen. Norrköping and Härnösand have *state schools for adults* which provide correspondence courses catering for about 6000 students. Usually (but not necessarily) students visit their school for certain periods (generally three weeks) for supplementary oral instruction. All instruction is free. The most extensive adult education facilities in effect combine both qualifying adult education with the category of leisure-time studies. These are *the popular education movements* attended by some 1½ million students annually grouped into some 150,000 study circles. These study circles are usually held in the evening and are sponsored by twelve study associations approved by the state which are paid grants to help finance their activities. Most of them are connected with popular movements such as the labour movement, various political parties, the free churches and temperance movements. Languages, social studies and aesthetical subjects are their main concern − cf. the English Workers' Educational Association − but they are now taking over some of the courses which would otherwise be sponsored by *Municipal Adult Education*. They are likewise attempting to attract people with poor educational qualifications who have not availed themselves of the adult educational facilities on offer by the municipalities. Similar state grants

(75 per cent of the costs involved to pay instructors and buy textbooks) are likewise paid to study circles run both by trade unions and by the extra-mural departments of the universities. There is finally a special committee for education by radio and TV which provides a number of broadcast courses for adults quite separately from the regular radio and TV broadcasts for schools.

Labour Market Training is the second category, and it stems from the establishment of the Labour Market Board in 1955 to retrain for new occupations for which there is a demand by those unemployed or threatened by unemployment. It now also runs advanced courses to upgrade existing skills, beginners' courses for young people, and re-activation courses for those who wish to return to employment after a prolonged absence away. Most of the training focusses on industrial trades and clerical work and is in tune with the labour market policy. The duration of the training naturally varies from one course to another. The courses are jointly sponsored by the Labour Market Authority and the National Board of Education and are attended by some 100,000 persons a year.

The final category, of which we have briefly spoken, is that of leisure-time studies. And here the folk high school comes into its own, of which there are 115 in Sweden, most of them of more than 100 years' standing. Much has already been written about folk high schools. A Danish creation, they owe their inception to a desire to bring about a spiritual renaissance within Denmark, and to Bishop Grundvig's belief that, since farmers and artisans were being called upon to take an increasingly active part in legislation, then they should be educated for this purpose in special schools for adults. It should also be remembered that though the folk high schools were never intended to give instruction in vocational studies, the real strength of the farmers' co-operative movements is held by Danes in particular to be due to the influence of these schools over succeeding generations. Again, as we are about to see, it cannot seriously be maintained today that these schools do not include vocational studies as part of their curriculum. Most of the folk high schools in Sweden are residential. The aim is to provide an all-round education, but most students today wish to acquire a basis for further education. There is no centrally framed curriculum: each folk high school draws up its own. The minimum age for admission is 18. Courses are free of charge, but students must pay for their own board and lodging. They can attend for one, two or three years and can qualify for higher education on the completion of appropriate folk high school studies. Apart from general courses, many folk high schools have special lines such as music, drama, art, the mass media, and youth leader training. The emphasis is on study groups and on such specific topics as sports, labour problems, religious and temperance questions as well as on social, scientific and practical subjects. They set examinations and award students differing grades on results obtained. For all these reasons they have been more successful in attracting a much larger cross-section of the community than the folk high schools of either Denmark or Norway.

Denmark

The practicality of the Danes is probably best reflected in their system of vocational and technical education. Since the country has few resources and depends heavily on overseas trade, the acquisition of relevant skills has always enjoyed high priority, and links between technical schools and the world of work are close and strong, all such schools being self-governing towards this end, though under the direct supervision of the Ministry of Education. Vocational guidance is highly developed and is sensibly backed up by short periods of work in possible fields of employment. A number of alternative types of training covering a wide range of occupational choices are freely available, and *none* is final: all afford possibilities for continued and recurrent education. Apprenticeship training, which is long and thorough, still supplies the bulk of the skilled labour force; but, since 1956 when the amount of theoretical instruction to be given on apprenticeship courses was significantly increased, its relevance to modern world problems of industrial training has been challenged and the part it should play *vis à vis* the technical school system scrutinised. At the time of writing, a special commission is examining the possibilities of re-structuring the whole system with a view to changing its duration and increasing still further the general education element.

All apprentices must be over 14 years of age and must have completed the ninth year of education. Industrial/handicraft apprentices follow three- to four-year programmes of practical work combined with theoretical studies in special training institutions, and the certificate received at the end also confers upon its holder the right to further technical training. Commercial apprentices embark on a two- to four-year course which combines practical work in an office or shop and attendance at a special training school for the theoretical part of the course. Unskilled workers — i.e. those who have not acquired the necessary qualifications to embark on apprenticeship — must have completed the minimum period of compulsory schooling and be under 18 years of age to be able to follow vocational courses in youth schools. For unskilled workers over 18 there exist courses and re-training courses in special state managed institutions. There are no apprenticeships in agriculture, though training facilities do exist in residential establishments — offshoots of the Folk High School Movement — which are state-supported and which grant no examination qualification.

At a higher level there exist commercial schools of two kinds, further technical training schools, and *teknikums* (for engineers). Applicants for entry to the lower level commercial school must either hold the commercial apprentice's certificate or have passed the *realeksamen*. The school offers two-year day or evening classes in general subjects, languages, accounting or the retail trade leading to the *handelseksamen*. The higher level commercial school offers full-time courses leading to a higher commercial examination, and is open to holders of the *handelseksamen* (for whom the course lasts two years) or to holders of the *studentereksamen* (one year). Further technical training is provided in a wide variety of specialisms, and access to the courses depends on the previous training of the applicant. Normally, a student must either have completed his apprenticeship or passed the *realeksamen* or its equivalent. Courses last one or two years and are both theoretical and practical, except that the practical side is omitted for those with adequate experience. Studies in the *teknikum* take four years and are divided into five specialisms: civil engineering, mechanical engineering, production engineering, and shipbuilding. Applicants must either have completed their apprenticeship training, or passed an intermediate technical examination at the end of compulsory schooling, or passed the *realeksamen*.

Post-school education still occupies a central position in Danish life, the tradition going back for over a century and stemming, of course, from the imaginative creation of the folk high schools in the 1840s. Traditionally for the agricultural labouring class, they have continued over the years to provide full time residential colleges for young adults, the average age of attendance being nowadays about 23. The schools are mainly privately run or owned, but they can be helped directly or indirectly by public funds, and lack of money is never a bar to attendance by a serious student. Classes are usually held during the winter months when the land is impossible or difficult to work, but supplementary classes have been introduced during the summer, often open to women also, whereas winter classes have tended to be the prerogative of men. The Danish folk high school is still characterised by having no fixed syllabus, no examinations, but rather an emphasis on a general education in Danish literature, history, sociology, religion and music, in order to foster a spiritual awakening rather than impart knowledge. In recent times, however, the general drift from the land and increasing urbanisation have led to a decline in enrolments to about 15,000 annually, whereas before the last war it was estimated that easily one-third of the population had at one time or another attended a folk high school. It is now recognised that the democratic, co-operative and nationalistic principles which the movement was designed to foster have long since come about; that as the formal system of education becomes itself more flexible and democratic so does the need for extra-mural organisations of this particular type become less; that the urgent present need is for technical and practical skills rather than cultural awakening. In consequence, many folk high schools have evolved for themselves a specifically vocational curriculum whilst still catering principally for farmers. The Danish language and arithmetic tend to be basic, but the main emphasis is on theoretical aspects of modern agricultural practice — it being remembered that most of the students will already have had up to ten years or more of practical farming.

Outside the folk high schools there still remain a number of institutions of both a general and a vocational kind. Some, naturally, grew from a desire to found non-boarding institutions more suitable for the worker living in urban areas; others have been created in response to particular vocational needs. We have already discussed the youth schools, and those are complemented, as appropriate, by youth boarding schools. Continuation boarding schools (*efterskoler*) provide residential continuation schooling for youngsters aged 14 to 18 in a folk high school atmosphere, and these are still the most important direct educational influence bearing on the rural population. Nor must we omit evening class provision, notably in towns, catering for thousands of students attending various kinds of practical, technical and general courses held at various levels. As to correspondence courses, geographical configuration makes communication so easy that this, allied to the general adequacy of the educational services provided, renders demand relatively negligible. Such private correspondence schools as exist operate under state supervision and cannot be said to cater for more than about 30,000 students.

Norway

We have already seen how from 1969 technical studies have been included as optional offerings in the *gymnasium*, and how the intention is to combine all existing forms of upper secondary education into a new kind of comprehensive school and so closely follow the Swedish trend. Similarly, in the last two years of the nine-year basic school (and particularly since the school-leaving age was raised to 16) an increasing number of possible electives have been provided to meet most likely demands, and these can range from "messing about" with motor-cycles, reindeer husbandry, fishing or seamanship, farming, traffic or consumer studies, to typing, drama and film-making, nature protection, local history, social work, and even company law. The intention is plainly both to make the last years in school worthwhile in the eyes of the pupil of low ability (and who is often chafing to put school behind him) and also to encourage all to pursue their studies further along what is hoped will be increasingly seen as meaningful paths.

Norway tends to lump all kinds of vocational and technical training together under the general heading of trade schools and then to differentiate under headings such as schools for handicrafts and industry (technical schools), commercial schools, agricultural schools, seamen's schools, schools for domestic industry and handicrafts (men and women), and domestic science schools. Each school is usually divided into a lower and a higher school, and the programmes range from evening part-time to full-time courses of up to four years' duration. The most important provision at the lowest level is the workshop school which gives a one year course (which can be extended). Next come the apprenticeship schools and then the technical trade schools. Apprenticeship schools give theoretical training either through part-time day release, or sandwich courses, or evening classes for persons already in employment, and they, together with the workshop schools, can open the doors to specialised study in the technical trade schools. In this connexion, one full year spent at a workshop school can be counted as the equivalent of ten months' practical experience, and there has been increasing pressure of recent years to have workshop schools themselves provide full apprenticeship training. Most recently, it has been recognised that the workshop school is proving the mainstay of the Norwegian vocational system to the extent of catering for fully 25 per cent of the age group concerned in the 1970s. The aim is to strengthen it in every way, and by the same token to have all Norwegian vocational schools fully participating in retraining and, in collaboration with the main federations of labour, organising courses for skilled workers, production leaders, and so on. The technical schools now run a three-year course based on the comprehensive nine-year school course and supplemented by a period of practical work, but applicants from the mathematics/ science line of the *gymnasium* are allowed to follow a shortened course of one and a half to two years.

Technical and vocational training at a still higher level is of two kinds. First there are the specialised institutions which cater for maturer students or for those who have already had some previous professional experience. Into this category fall schools of midwifery, psychiatric nursing, children's nursing, librarianship, schools for nurserymen, and public service training schools. The latter offer both initial training courses and in-service courses for such public bodies as the customs, the post office and the railway system. The second group is in its own right a degree-awarding body and is registered as being of university level, recruiting its students in the same way as the universities. At Oslo is the State Veterinary College (in operation since 1935). The State College of Agriculture, concerned with training in horticulture, agronomy, dairying, forestry and agricultural research was first opened at As in 1859. The State College of Business Administration offers courses in economics, administration and commercial law. It dates back to 1936 and is situated in Bergen. The apex of pure technical studies is what is now the University of Trondheim, originally founded in 1910, and to which has since been added the State Institute of Technology (1936) and the State College for Teachers (1968). Here, courses last for about four and a half years. There is a basic general studies course to be followed by all students (which includes technical physics), and then follows specialist training in architecture, mining, constructional engineering, electrical engineering, mechanical engineering, chemistry and ship-building.

The folk high school was introduced into Norway during the 1860s and has had an important effect on every aspect of rural life. Regulated by the latest Folk High School Act of 1949, it is still independent of all but minimal state control and provides further general education for young-sters over 17 years of age. In the main, folk high schools are now used to give courses parallel to the work done in the continuation schools and also to prepare students for entry to specialised technical institutions. They are chiefly honoured for having provided the impetus for the development of the *folkeuniversiteit* (people's university) and of adult education in general.

As a result, there is a long tradition of adult education throughout Norway which, until 1965, had been left entirely in the hands of voluntary bodies with some supervision from the Ministry of Church and Education. In 1965, however, adult education was given equal status with initial education. A special department of adult education was created within this Ministry and given responsibility for co-ordinating all adult education groups, approving the educational context of courses on offer, and certify-ing examinations taken. In other words, recurrent education (or perma-nent education as the Norwegians prefer to call it) is now accepted as an essential element of the whole educational system.

Such adult education is, in general, given either through correspondence courses or the *folkeuniversiteit*. For those Norwegians whom the geo-graphical nature of their country forces to live in relatively isolated com-munities, correspondence courses are important, and the government in consequence keeps a watchful eye on their activities. All correspondence schools are privately operated, but they are registered and regulated by the Correspondence Schools Act of 1948, and they must receive Ministry approval regarding both the subject matter and the educational content of what they offer. Whilst some cover the whole range of courses offered within the ordinary school system, others specialise in certain fields or subjects — for example, courses for merchant seamen. Norway has the fourth largest merchant navy in the world and the largest merchant fleet per head of population, this making merchant seamen a highly important sector of employed manpower. In port, the Welfare Office for the Merchant Marine provides educational facilities, films and recreational material, but it is in actual fact the seamen's correspondence courses which provide sailors with opportunities for both widening and improving their general and professional qualifications.

The *folkeuniversiteit* (FU) can justifiably claim to be one of Europe's oldest educational institutions specifically concerned with promoting adult education. The first institution was founded in Oslo in 1864, and the present FU was created in 1948 by amalgamating the extra-mural boards controlling adult education then in existence at Oslo, Bergen and Trondheim. The early founders of the movement sought to provide a broad liberal education free of charge for those who had been unable to take advantage of post-primary provision but who could profit from taking courses in their own spare time. Whilst this original conception is still much in evidence, the FU has undergone considerable change over the last century. Though it is still not part of the state educational system, its importance and influence is recognised by the Ministry of Church and Education which gives it strong financial support, the rest of the budget being made up from local communes and students' fees — for, alas, rising costs have killed free education at this level. Today, there are over 270 local branches scattered throughout the country with a total enrolment of close on 100,000 students. Courses vary from one branch to another dependent on local demand and the availability of teachers, but generally they divide themselves into (a) academic courses to prepare students for an external degree or some professional qualification; (b) general courses of a less academic or examination-orientated nature; (c) vocational and practical courses. Of recent years there has been a noticeable increase in enrolment for the more advanced academic courses paralleled with a decline in the number of students wishing to study English — this most obviously being a reflection of improved standards in general education as well as of the efficiency and high quality of English teaching in the schools.

Mention should finally be made of the most recent development in vocational education leading to the creation of non-university higher education colleges. First opened in the late 1960s as regional colleges by the Ministry, they are geared to providing alternative vocational education to that on offer in the universities, and to be completed in a shorter timespan. They are also designed to integrate into major non-university institutions such activities as are now pursued in mono-professional teachers' and technical colleges. By 1974 there were eight colleges with an attendance of some 3000 full-time students and 2000 part-time. New courses are constantly being developed such as tourism, fishery, transportation, oil engineering (for the North Sea field), and communications and the media, though the most popular to date is a course in business economics based on innovative work done in the commerce faculty of the University of Bergen. Most of the courses run for two years and are intended to terminate in employment, and some already link up with teacher-training by providing qualifying courses for teachers in junior classes to upgrade their diplomas to teach in the middle school. Reports suggest that these new colleges have already succeeded in recruiting excellent students who have all obtained jobs without difficulty. There are links between the colleges and the universities for those who, after two years, want to transfer to academic studies, but the aim is to build up alternative institutions to universities and not institutions in series, as it were. In this way it is hoped to prevent the new colleges from being drawn into the university net or to give up their two-year vocational approach in a quest for respectability. It is remembered that short-cycle courses have always been well supported and have recruited high standard entrants, whilst the universities, with open access to all who complete the upper secondary school, have increasingly found themselves taking a less well-qualified entry than the technical universities and, in many cases, even the teachers' colleges. With all this in mind, it is now estimated that by the mid 1980s there will be some 90,000 students in tertiary education with just about half in the non-university sector.

3

Belgium

Technical education in Belgium began first of all through the initiative of private organisations and then through that of the state, the provinces and the municipalities. At the present time there are state schools under direct state management and recognised schools which are subsidised and controlled by the state. Curricula and certificates in both types of school are identical in value and grant access to private employment as well as to public offices. A central administration for technical education co-ordinates the initiative of industrialists and of the schools in order to elaborate the best training methods. This central body is assisted by a higher council of technical education composed of representatives of industry (managers and trade union leaders) and of the administrative and inspectorate divisions of the Ministry of Education. The council in turn is assisted by *conseils de perfectionnement* composed of managers and workers whose task is to see that curricula and methods in each technical school are constantly being adapted to technical progress. These "competence boards" (as we may call them) also arrange "refresher courses" for former students of the schools, either to bring them completely up to date with changing techniques or to give them an opportunity to improve their career prospects. Managers in industry equally study problems related to the training of future technicians and arrange discussion groups in an attempt to see their suggestions implemented. The training of technical teachers also receives careful attention at these levels.

The organisation of technical/commercial education is now so complex that it would require an entire volume to discuss it adequately. It must suffice to note that some 350,000 students are currently enrolled in some form or another of technical/commercial instruction, and that the vast majority of these are in "free" institutions (204,000). In round figures, state schools educate 59,000, provincial schools 30,000, and communal schools 43,000. Non-university institutions for higher education absorb a further 29,000 of which 17,000 are in "free" institutions; the state educates 6000, the provinces 4000 and the communes 2000.

Pupils may enter the technical sector directly from the primary school at about the age of 12, but the general course of instruction they follow is not dissimilar from that now on offer to all children between the ages of 12 and 15. In point of fact, the newer and more flexible structure of secondary education at the lower level is planned to absorb the more ambitious and intellectually more able of those pupils seeking technical instruction. These pupils, on satisfactory completion of the lower secondary school course, enter technical education proper and train for about three years (to age 18) to qualify as technicians. Those pupils who enter technical training direct from the primary school are usually of low calibre and after four years' training emerge as what we can best describe as semi-skilled vocational workers, though about 20 per cent show themselves over the four years to be superior to the rest and capable of continuing to qualify as technicians along with the intake from the lower secondary schools. Of this block of what we may call middle-level technical students again about 20 per cent show enough ability to warrant retaining them for a further three or four years after the age of 18 to become fully skilled non-graduate technologists, and for their advanced training they join forces with pupils who, after completing a full secondary school course, now elect for commensurate technical or commercial training outside the universities. Courses in the various establishments at this level vary in duration from three to five years, and many of them have a standing comparable with that of the university proper. Amongst these should be mentioned: the agricultural and forestry institutes at Gembloux and Ghent, the Military Academy in Brussels, and a veterinary college near Brussels. In addition there are a higher textile institute at Verviers for the study of cloths and fabrics, and three *universités de travail* at Charleroi, Mons and Ghent. These latter institutions can best be described as comprehensive technical institutions in that they take pupils from the age of 12 as full-time day students and carry them up to the highest levels besides running complicated part-time and evening school courses.

Like its full-time counterpart, part-time education includes a vocational and a technical section which are in.turn divided into grades. Certain courses lead to the same titles and qualifications as full-time courses. The curriculum is then extended over a larger number of years: six instead of three, usually. Part-time training also has courses intended to fill in gaps left in earlier training (recurrent education) and courses for those seeking promotion by the acquisition of further skills and diplomas. There is also what is termed "short-term technical education". Schools in this category are designed to meet an urgent and perhaps temporary need of manpower, or to promote an enterprise undertaken by industrialists on an experimental basis.

Outstanding characteristics of the Belgian system of technical and commercial education are: the deep personal interest taken in all aspects of the work by industrialists and trade unions to the point of often large and valuable gifts of both machinery (to have the schools thoroughly up to date) and money; the lack of an apprenticeship system (except in trades such as butcher, baker, plumber, hairdresser, tailor and decorator — mainly businesses that are run as one-man concerns or family affairs) and of any system of day release; the healthy rivalry between province and province in an attempt to secure the best possible training that can exist. close collaboration at all times amongst the various interested parties which, whilst safeguarding the academic and disinterested nature of technical education, maintains a close connexion between it and the economic life and needs of the country; the bias given towards the specialities of the region where the schools are located; the luxurious boarding accommodation provided for both boys and girls in the larger schools in the provincial centres, usually heavily subsidised and therefore well within reach of all who come from a distance and need to live away from home to pursue their studies; the provision of adequate grants-in-aid for needy students, though many schools pride themselves on making all tuition either free or of negligible cost; that women, as they wish, may follow any course on offer (though in actual practice, except for working in biological and chemical laboratories geared to medicine and cosmetics, most women are found on the commercial side); perhaps most important of all, the creation of a carefully articulated system of recurrent and permanent education for commerce and industry well before any other Western European country had even begun to give the matter serious consideration.

Given this already full provision for recurrent or permanent education, it is not really surprising that general adult education is not of particular interest.[1] Nevertheless there are several hundred organisations working in the field in receipt of state subsidies from the Ministries of Culture (French and Flemish), and the Socialist and Social Christian movements are quite active at their own political levels, the Social Christians, for example, running sixteen centres for advanced education where courses are on offer in politics, economics and social science. In April 1973 a novel piece of legislation – *loi sur les crédits d'heures* – marked an important agreement between government, management and the unions, whereby certain categorised workers in industry were granted an amount of extra paid holiday leave equal to the number of hours of approved study they had followed after ordinary working hours. But there is still no day release which, many argue, would respond more fully to workers' needs.

[1] The expressions "recurrent" and "permanent" education are often used as inter-changeable. It is, however, generally accepted that "recurrent" implies the need for periodic retraining, whilst "permanent" indicates that education nowadays must be a lifelong, on-going process with formal schooling reduced to providing only the basic (if essential) elements.

The Grand Duchy of Luxemburg

We have already seen how, in The Grand Duchy of Luxemburg, a pupil entering the new intermediate school at age 12 could specialise there for the last two years of the five-year course in commercial or technical subjects. Those pupils who at age 12 elect neither for the intermediate school nor the *lycée* pass to a technical school which provides a five-year course for those wishing to become skilled workers or technicians. The first two years are devoted to determining and developing general aptitudes and in the last three years the pupil specialises in a chosen branch. Success gives him a *certificat d'aptitude professionnel* (CAP). Since 1970/1 ambitious and promising pupils may stay on a further two years to qualify for a technician's diploma. Commercial subjects exact four years' attendance at an appropriate school followed by one year's practical training, but this course has become less attractive since the creation of the intermediate schools. There are other full-time courses available, most of them starting at about the age of 14 and lasting two to three years (but five years for the paramedical professions) in business management, secretarial training, salesmanship, the hotel trade, agricultural training and the paramedical field. Apprenticeship still exists for various trades and lasts between two and a half to four years. The articled apprentice must, however, attend between eight and sixteen hours of approved study per week. At the end of apprenticeship he obtains either the CAP, or (if he is unable to master the theory) the CCP (*certificat de capacité pratique*).

At the top level there exist the *école technique de Luxemburg* and a recently created school of commerce and management designed to train middle-grade executives. The courses usually last four years and are open without examination to students who have either completed a minimum of five years in a *lycée*, or who hold the leaving certificate from the intermediate school or an appropriate technical school qualification. Holders of the CAP only, however, must take an entrance examination. The first year is preparatory, after which, in the *école technique*, students may specialise in either mechanical engineering, civil engineering or electrotechnology. Those who obtain the mark of "good" at the final examination can be admitted to any university abroad to read for an appropriate engineering degree.

The need for adult or recurrent education has so far not claimed any serious attention, and the first official courses for adults were started as recently as 1965/6. Courses available are at present all vocational, but they have proved very popular. In the main they prepare for the secondary school-leaving certificate, the technical school-leaving certificate and for the qualification of *ingénieur–technicien*. There are, of course, private bodies and enterprising *communes* who have long been running their own courses, but these are mainly in the fields of languages, technical or commercial subjects and art. These courses, if approved, are subsidised by the state. There is in addition a specialist *école supérieure de travail* which caters for the needs of workers in law, economics, politics and social sciences.

Holland

Like the Scandinavians, the Dutch have had to recognise the importance of flexibility and adaptability in catering for a type of technical education to match the country's changing industrial and commercial concerns, but unlike Scandinavia, Holland is (along with Belgium) one of the most densely populated countries in the Western world. It is singularly lacking in coal and mineral resources, but its position at the mouth of three great rivers and its adjacency to the great continental powers have forced it to take a great interest in commerce and the carrying trade, and this (together with intensive farming and agriculture) provides the most important source of its income. In the manufacturing industry, Holland is noted for its ship-building, distilling, making of cigars, chocolate and margarine, and also of late for electrical apparatus (particularly radio valves and accessories). Delft is famous for its pottery and Amsterdam for its diamond cutting. Most of these are high-grade industries requiring a minimum of raw materials and a maximum of skilled labour. Thus, technical education of a really high quality must loom large in educational programmes, and, whilst it is still felt necessary to move some children from the age of 12-plus towards some definite specialisation of a technical nature, it is nowadays emphasised that a broad cultural background is equally necessary if really enlightened workers are to be recruited into industry. Similarly, it is necessary to make the universities and the higher research institutes more readily accessible to the product of the technical schools.

There are in Holland four clearly defined offerings in technical and commercial education, and all have been affected by the implementation of the "Mammoth" School Law. There formerly existed at the lowest level the LTS which was attended by roughly 30 per cent of boys and by somewhat fewer girls. Originally catering for pupils in the lowest to middle ability ranges, it gave a two-year course end on to basic six-year education. All LTS have now in effect become LAVO schools. General subjects have been given more time, and the aim is to "kill" the traditional somewhat narrow basic specialisms and make a bridge for promising pupils to attend higher technical schools. For such pupils, special classes are in existence to help them attain their objective. Under the terms of the Apprenticeship Training Act (1966), a pupil may proceed to apprenticeship, usually at the age of 15–16, on obtaining his lower secondary technical school certificate. His contract gives him practical trade training for one or two years from a specified employer who must release him for one day a week (two days for 15-year-olds since 1974) for complementary general education and technical vocational training in an approved school. Apprentices may also attend evening classes. At the end of the apprenticeship, certificates are awarded to successful candidates, those failing in theory being granted a certificate of proficiency in practical work.

The MTS (a post-1945 development) is a middle-range technical school accepting students in the 16–20 age range. Pupils are accepted from LAVO (or the LTS) but qualification through a bridge year is demanded. Students can also be accepted from the MAVO sector of secondary education, or even from the HAVO sector, these latter gaining certain course exemptions. Graduates from the MTS are expected to occupy low management positions in industry or commerce or to run small businesses for themselves. One year of supervised practice in industry or commerce is exacted before the final certificate is granted.

At the third level comes the higher technical school (HTS) offering a four-year course to students either with appropriate earlier qualifications or experience or who have satisfactorily completed four or five years of a general secondary school course. This means that some 40 per cent will come from the MTS and the remainder from HAVO. The first two years consist of formal study in the college. The third year consists of practice in industry. The final year is a specialised period based on experiences gained in the third year "in the field". Most of these schools have a building section, a hydraulic engineering and road-building section, an engineering section and an electro-technical section. Certain schools have sections for naval engineering and for chemical engineering. There are two textile schools, one mining school, and one for leather and the footwear industry. There are also evening schools for students who follow a trade during the day. Graduates from the HTS come to hold important posts in charge of technical sections in large industrial concerns, or in part charge of small concerns, and they are all much sought after abroad.

Parallel with such technical provision are the arts and crafts schools teaching drawing, painting, modelling, the applied arts, advertising, and also interior decoration – a popular subject with girls. There are also training schools for navigation and for ships' engineers, schools for sea-fishing, and schools for inland navigation. In a farming country like Holland it is equally highly important that the farmer's wife be suitably trained to do the many technical tasks her husband will expect of her. Besides a multiplicity of courses in domestic science generally, therefore, there are special agricultural domestic economy courses. Schools for agriculture, horticulture and dairying have an organisation and a high standard of work parallel to that of the technical schools proper. Entrance to secondary agricultural schools is determined by an entrance examination of about the standard a pupil will have reached after three years in a secondary school. Entry to the dairy schools is also by examination and the minimum age for entry is 19. Courses last for two and a half years. There are also certain winter day schools for agriculture and horticulture, the duration of tuition being two winter periods of six months each.

Summit technological training is given in six schools of university standard: the technological universities of Delft (1905), Eindhoven (1957), and Twents (1961); the School of Agriculture at Wageninen (1917); Schools of Economics at Rotterdam and Tilburg (Catholic). The courses last for five or six years. Entry is usually at the age of 18 or 19, and whilst anyone who has registered may attend courses, only those recognised to have reached an agreed preliminary standard of secondary technical or commerical education may sit the examinations. This peculiarity also holds, incidentally, in the universities. Holders of a diploma from the HTS are in certain circumstances admitted to these technological universities at about the age of 22 to follow a suitably modified course.

Visitors to Holland are often surprised to find that the country has no fewer than seven folk high schools, drawing their inspiration from Bishop

Grundtvig but developing along their own individual lines that make them today resemble more than anything the English residential college of further education. Their importance to Holland lies in the fact that they are able most effectively to surmount the political and sectarian divisions into which the country is split and to become a focal point where people of all religious and political beliefs can meet and examine each other's point of view. The first two schools were founded well before the last war, and one founded during the depression of the 1930s to do something for the unemployed has now set the tone for the rest to follow: some form of practical work must be attempted by all students during each morning session. The standard course is usually of a fortnight's duration and provides the student with an opportunity of understanding more about the world and its problems. Longer courses are held from time to time to give students of technical or domestic subjects the liberal as opposed to the vocational part of their training. And in the summer there are courses of three to four days' duration on subjects like music, puppetry, drama. Students attend from all over Holland and are required to pay one-third of the cost, the rest being made up by state grants and private contributions, often from employers. Many students are willingly released on full pay by their employers who often pay in addition the full cost of tuition.

Correspondence courses, which have existed since 1890, are still popular and meet an increasing demand for refresher training and for the study of new subjects either for leisure or for the improvement of job prospects. An act of 1973 insisted on state recognition and inspection of all institutes providing correspondence courses, thus putting an end to a somewhat haphazard private system of inspection and making for overall competence and efficiency.

Boys and girls who have gone to work early and thus have missed the benefit of an education extended beyond the primary level have long been catered for mainly by the churches on a basis of part-time day and evening classes including classes at work. Present policy is to co-ordinate this better by the provision of a new form of full-time education to be called "participation education" and to consist of both a school and a work component. For adults who have likewise "missed out" there exist twenty-three centres (with ten annexes) for adult vocational training which are designed to give people already in employment the opportunity of training for jobs for which workers are in demand, thus improving their range of skills and prospects for the future.

General adult education is provided either in evening classes run by private institutions or by a municipal *volksuniversiteit*. Classes run by private bodies are extremely popular if only for the fact that they offer a second chance or an alternative route to obtain a variety of state school-leaving certificates, academic, technical and vocational. Such private institutions, however, do not have technical or engineering workshops and therefore concentrate entirely on the theory side. Every town of appreciable size has its own social–cultural centre, the *volksuniversteit*, which is a kind of people's college that offers facilities for non-vocational studies and which (not surprisingly) caters mainly for the middle income groups. It is finally to be noted that, at the time of writing this, the government has under review all forms of recurrent and permanent education, and is studying the links that can be established with multi-media methods of instruction with a view to developing the idea of an open university which, through correspondence courses, radio, television and video recordings will offer education at every level to all who seek it.

France

Concerning initial technical and vocational education in France, little need here be said for (as we have seen in the previous chapter) until the ages of 16 or 18–19 this is made clearly a part of the ordinary secondary school system. Instruction in this field, it will be remembered, is given at three levels. The basic level of instruction, intended to produce unskilled and semi-skilled workers, is concerned with pupils in the third *filière* of the CES. Some will go straight to work on leaving school at 16-plus; others will go to apprenticeship either at 14-plus or at the end of the course; still others will embark on a "short" course of further training (usually given in a *collège d'enseignement technique*) to obtain after one year's further study either the *certificat d'aptitude professionnelle* (CAP) or the *certificat d'études professionnelles* (CEP). The CEP may be either a complete course given in an appropriate institution or a course where part of the training is in school and part in a firm contractually linked with the training establishment. The CEP is also designed to complete the studies of pupils who, though they have completed four years of post-primary studies, have not yet reached the statutory leaving age of 16. Apprentices study to obtain the CAP, and under the terms of three important Industrial Acts passed in 1971 employers of apprentices must (a) prove the adequacy of their training facilities and techniques, (b) prove the technical competence of the trainers, (c) enrol their apprentices in an apprentice training centre for courses of at least 360 hours per year, (d) ensure that their apprentices attend the courses and other activities of the centre, (e) provide in-company training by following a training programme agreed with the apprentice training centre. For those youngsters not following an apprenticeship but taking up employment directly, the new Acts guarantee the right to paid study leave of 100 hours per year. It should be noted that the length of apprenticeship is being reduced generally to two years of full-time studies on an integrated course of education and training, and that the intention is to increase substantially full-time pre-employment courses for all school leavers.

At the middle level of instruction (skilled workers) pupils are drawn from both the second and the third *filières* to follow either a two-year short period of training of a vocational and general nature in a *collège d'enseignement technique*, leading to the award of the *brevet d'études professionnelles* (BEP), given in a variety of specialist subjects, or to embark on long cycle education in the technical/scientific stream. Once in long cycle education the student will have a three-year course leading either to the award of the *brevet de technicien* or to a technical *baccalauréat*, it being hoped that in time the latter will replace the former and so upgrade technical education at this level. Specialisations at the *baccalauréat* level include civil engineering, accounting, business techniques, and computing; in addition the *brevet* has courses in laundry work and hotel management, the clothing industry and radiology. The larger *lycées* can run their own technical department, but elsewhere the courses are given in technical *lycées*.

Top level courses are open only to those who have obtained the appropriate *baccalauréat*. First of all there is the *institut universitaire de technologie* (IUT), first opened in 1966 with the specific aim of providing scientific and technical training adapted to contemporary needs. By definition they offer a more narrowly specialised training than that of the professional (graduate) engineer, but a wider education than that afforded the technician. The courses last two years and lead to the award of the *diplôme universitaire de technologie* (DUT). There are about sixty such institutes covering a range of disciplines such as applied sciences, engineering, public and business administration, commerce, information science, social work, and public relations. It is gradually becoming possible for holders of the *brevet de technicien* to follow courses at IUTs, and for holders of the IUT diploma to begin to read for a university degree.

Next come university studies proper, but we shall deal with these in our next chapter. Finally, at the very top we find the *grandes écoles* with which we must nowadays link a number of other state-recognised institutions. The course at the engineering *grandes écoles* lasts for three years, has a strong theoretical bias, and leads to the award of a *diplôme d'ingénieur*. There is no higher qualification available unless the successful student seeks to read for his doctorate when he is exempt from the first year of study. There are three *instituts nationaux polytechniques* in Grenoble, Nancy and Toulouse, all founded in 1970 and having the same admission requirements as for the *grandes écoles*. They are, however, more closely linked with the university sector and destined (like Compiègne) to become technological universities. There are business schools (*instituts d'administration d'entreprises*) which usually provide one-year postgraduate courses, though business studies may be done either at certain universities or at the *école des hautes études commerciales* (another *grande école* with a three-year course). There are finally three *instituts nationaux de sciences appliquées* in Lyon, Rennes and Toulouse designed to train engineers and to carry out research. They are selective in that entrants coming straight from school must have one of the science or technical *baccalauréats* and must be interviewed for selection. Late entrants are accepted who have completed the first two years of university study. The course lasts for five years, and the *diplôme d'ingénieur* to which it leads ranks with the *diplôme* of the *grandes écoles* in similar disciplines.

It was not until the late 1960s that France began seriously to interest herself in permanent (or recurrent) education. Until then, provision for adult education was usually limited to vocational or retraining schemes held under the auspices of either the Ministry of Labour or Education. Changes came with the *Loi d'Orientation* of 1968 (of which more later) which drew attention to the fact that few universities (Grenoble and Nancy being notable exceptions) had interested themselves in any form of adult education and insisted that in future permanent education must become one of their fundamental concerns, and with the passing of the Industrial Acts of 1971. Continuous vocational training is now very much to the fore. Every firm with more than ten employees must now devote 2 per cent of its salary bill to the training of its employees — this in addition to the 0.5 per cent young trainee tax instituted by the *Loi Astier* in 1919. Training schemes are based on the assumption that the schools' curricula shall remain general, scientific and cultural, and after this *all* citizens shall have the right to continue their education, this making France the first country in Western Europe to have added continuing training to the *rights* of citizens in law. The law again clearly distinguishes among various kinds of continuous training to be on offer. These are (a) *conversion* for unemployed women wishing to return to employment and those wanting to change their job, (b) *prévention* which offers the same training to persons who know they will be made redundant, (c) *adaptation* which implies training either for a first job or a new job — for example, training for an 18-year-old who already has basic general training, (d) *promotion professionnelle* (upgrading) for those who seek promotion, (e) *entretien et perfectionnement des connaissances* (maintaining and improving existing knowledge), given on a basis of *ad hoc* short full-time courses for those in employment to keep abreast of change and innovation.

Study leave is the right of every employee in industry and commerce, and those not released by their employers in the course of the year may request such leave to obtain training of their own choice — this, of course, being carefully checked to avoid abuse. Employers can set up their own in-company off-the-job training courses or they can make arrangements to have the training done for them by approved outside bodies — approved, that is, by both the government and the trade unions. In any case, however, the rapid growth and restructuring of whole industries and the need for greater adaptability to market changes within individual companies has forced many firms willy-nilly to train at least for their own needs. This has called for larger numbers of training specialists with new competencies, and as a result six centres have had to be established to cater for three clearly defined categories of trainers. There is a fourteen- to sixteen-week course concerned with organisation and policy-making; an eight- to nine-week course for those responsible for the design of training programmes and teaching; and a three-week course for supervisors and technicians who will have some responsibility for trainees. In 1973 the *Agence*

Nationale pour le Développement de la Formation Permanente was set up to advise industry and the Ministry of Education on the planning of courses, and by 1974 already thirteen *académies* (out of twenty-five) had their *délégués académiques à la formation continue* to advise their rectors on how best to meet requirements for permanent education in their own particular regions. It is estimated that at least 1½ million workers throughout France received training courses varying from a few days to several months in 1973. The majority of these, it was noted, were white-collar and skilled workers. Immediate intentions are to pull in many more of the unskilled.

4

West Germany

Vocational education in West Germany has a long and distinguished history, and it is perhaps because of this that present labour and unemployment difficulties have brought it under attack, not least from among apprentices themselves who continue to bulk large in all training programmes. When Germany made the switch from an agrarian to an industrial economy in the second half of the nineteenth century, vocational schools, known for more than a century earlier, spread rapidly, and by her Constitution of 1919 the new German Republic became the first country in Western Europe to make attendance at a vocational school compulsory for all young workers and apprentices. So was evolved what has come to be called the "dual system", an avowed amalgam of educational and economic interests whereby any boy or girl choosing to leave school for work at the age of 15 is required to continue his studies in a part-time vocational school for a further three or four years as a minimum on day release from his or her place of employment. A compulsory minimum attendance of eight hours per week is expected, and the part-time vocational school (*Berufsschule*) offers the young worker/apprentice classes in German, mathematics, civics, and other subjects of a general educational nature. The size of the present-day problem can best be judged on the latest figures available (1973) which reveals that about 80 per cent of school leavers were involved: 1,300,000 apprentices and 230,000 unskilled or semi-skilled workers not party to any apprenticeship contract. Of this 1,300,000 apprentices, 700,000 were in industry, 500,000 in commerce or administration, and 100,000 articled to liberal professions. Local chambers of commerce and industry are made responsible for super-vising the whole of the apprenticeship, and it is they who carry out the necessary assessment of the apprentice-trainees and award the final certi-ficate of competence which enjoys official recognition throughout Western Germany. In the country as a whole, about 12 per cent of apprentices fail their examination at the first attempt and about half of these do not succeed at the two subsequent attempts the law allows.

The majority of apprentices are recruited from the *Hauptschule* which, traditionally considered second-rate, is inadequately equipped and staffed to provide the additional support and preparation its pupils can legitimate-ly look forward to before entering on apprenticeship. Too high a propor-tion of them leave school lacking the basic skills. Too many are being trained for jobs for which they find it extremely difficult to obtain em-ployment, for it has to be remembered that, since the dual system relies on the apprentice spending 80 per cent of his training time on the job, the choice open to an apprentice is of necessity determined by the range of firms in his locality unless (which rarely happens) the apprentice is willing to move from home.[1] Again, not all firms by any means take part in the apprentice scheme — the figure is estimated as low as 16 per cent — and many of those who do take part allow abuses of the system to creep in which are not easily checked, simply because the necessary supervision by the *Land* and the Chambers of Industry and Commerce is inadequate by reason of lack of staff: a firm is lucky to be inspected once in every five to ten years. Nor is the *Berufschule*, usually municipal but some-times private, in any position to compensate for any deficiencies in in-firm training. It is the Cinderella of educational establishments and suffers from shortage of space, equipment and teaching staff, and this staff shortage alone causes at least 50 per cent of apprentices to enjoy less than the legal minimum of theoretical education.[2] Classes are often bursting at the

---

[1] It is estimated that in industrial occupations as many as two-thirds of the people trained change their job as soon as training is completed.

[2] There are wide regional disparities in the provision of part-time vocational education. In 1970, only 62 per cent of the vocational schools in Bavaria offered their pupils the minimum of eight hours education per week; in West Berlin the figure was 51 per cent; in Northrhein-Westphalia, a mere 12 per cent.

seams, and apprentices in minority professions often have to join classes not intended for them – this being particularly true in rural areas where there are not enough apprentices to form separate classes for each trade.

It is not surprising, then, that once student unrest generally was unleashed in 1968, apprentices were emboldened to draw attention to their own grievances. Certainly the universities needed reforming, but university students were a privileged and eloquent minority wheras apprentices were the forgotten majority. Learning from the activity and protests of university students, often acting independently but also in co-operation with trade unions, apprentices revealed the conditions under which they were working both in firms and in the *Berufschulen*. They began to organise themselves as never before. Newspapers edited by apprentices began to appear. Throughout 1968 and 1969 they organised demonstrations not only in large cities such as Essen, Hamburg and West Berlin but also in smaller towns like Göttingen and Neustadt an der Weinstrasse.

Publication of the failings of the vocational educational system forced the government into action, and a hastily drafted bill became law on 12 June 1969. It satisfied nobody, however, but the employers. Demonstrations and protests continued, but these now became linked with increasing criticism of the educational system as a whole as fostering inherent social differences. So came in 1970 the Educational Report of the Federal Government containing proposals for a fundamental restructuring of the entire educational system and a scheme for a form of comprehensivisation extending from primary right through to tertiary education. In November 1970 the Federal Government announced its Action Programme for Vocational Education which had two main aims: (a) apprentices would no longer be trained exclusively in one specialist skill but would start from a broad base leading to specialism; in this way it would be possible for them to be more easily retrained in an allied trade as demand for various skills increased or decreased, and (b) the introduction of a foundation year for vocational studies to count as the first year of a three-year apprenticeship and to constitute the last year at school for pupils intent on apprenticeship – though it has not yet been decided whether the foundation year will constitute an additional year of full-time education or merely replace the final year. Meantime, vocational guidance at all levels has been stepped up and improved, and all *Länder* have agreed to make this foundation year practicable by dividing the multitude of vocational trades into eleven major fields: economics and administration, metal, electrotechnics, construction and woodwork, textiles and clothing, chemistry, physics and biology, printing and paper, painting and decorating, health and hygiene, nutrition and domestic science, agriculture.

Employers' organisations have attacked these actual and proposed reforms on several grounds. Firstly they express the concern felt generally throughout all the *Länder* at too much Federal Government interference in any matters considered by the *Länder* to be their own regional concerns. More specifically they resent that apprenticeship should be taken out of their control where it has been from the beginning. They fear that vocational education, no longer the care of the Chambers of Commerce and Industry but (implicit in The Structural Plan for Reform) of the various Ministries of Education, will lose its contact with the practical world of work and become increasingly theoretical. They foresee that the number of pupils trained by the dual system (63.1 per cent in 1970) will easily have declined to less than 50 per cent of the age group by 1985 as a still greater proportion of students will avail themselves of the opportunities for a full-time vocational education. They ask themselves from where their admittedly cheap labour is to come in the future and see themselves employing more and more foreign workers at a higher cost. They see their enforced contributions (at present both employers and employees pay 1.7 per cent of their net income to the Federal Labour Office) towards the support of vocational education being increased. And already, a bold piece of legislation passed in April 1972 has decreed that everyone engaged in training in industry, commerce or trade must have "some knowledge of youth problems, social law and educational methods", and that this knowledge must be tested by appropriate written and oral examinations. Such persons as fail to pass these examinations may no longer employ or train apprentices.

Thus, it is at last understood that vocational education cannot just be evaluated in financial and economic terms. The vocational school will no longer have to be the educational cul-de-sac it has been, especially if upward mobility is to be encouraged so that industry has the increasing numbers of better and better skilled workers it requires. The aim must now be not simply to impart skills and train workers, but also to teach people how to learn throughout life so that they can adapt to changes in their work and in society. As Kerschensteiner put it as early as 1906:

"The most valuable thing that we can hand down to our pupils is not knowledge but a sound method of acquiring knowledge and the habit of acting on their own initiative."

Against this necessary detailed background of the development of vocational education to the present, we can fill in the rest of the story of technical and vocational education quickly. After the *Berufsschulen* come a number of full-time technical schools maintained either by the local community, by a vocational organisation, or by private persons. The schools are usually comprehensive in character and offer courses varying in duration from one to three or four years. It is now increasingly possible for an apprentice of promise to pass from the part-time vocational school to the full-time technical school as it is possible for a *gymnasium* pupil or a pupil from the *Realschule* to do the same. For entrance, satisfactory completion of primary and middle school studies is required. In the past, such schools have been frequented by twice as many girls as boys, this being largely accounted for by the fact that it is here that thorough training in commercial subjects, stenography, secretarial work and domestic subjects and skills is given. This pattern is obviously going to change in the future.

The advanced technical school only admits students who already have sufficient practical experience in a vocation and/or have satisfactorily completed an approved course in a full-time technical school. Courses last up to four years and a successful student receives a specialised diploma which, if it bears an overall "good" mark entitles him to continue his studies in a technological university, of which there are at present nine. Here he will be studying alongside students who have entered directly from the *Gymnasium* after passing the *Abitur*. Like the traditional university, the technological university is divided into faculties – usually civil, mechanical and electrical engineering, and a further faculty to promote education in the humanities (philosophy, political science, and to some extent in languages, literature and the arts). The intention is that there shall be no dichotomy of "the two cultures", and also to ensure that an all-round education is not threatened because higher education is taking place in a technological institution. It should be noted in passing that all higher institutes of learning (including universities) are classified under the generic title of *Hochschulen* and that Germany was well to the fore in establishing such technological universities.

Obviously, since attention has been almost exclusively given to the provision of recurrent and permanent education in the vocational sector, thus enabling those of ability to proceed right up the ladder from apprenticeship to the technological universities — the "second educational path" as it is sometimes called — nothing much has so far been done in the field of adult education to change existing provision. Adults however have been favoured by the passing of a law guaranteeing them financial support for further education, and all children over 16 embarking on this "second educational path" now receive a monthly allowance scaled according to parental income. General adult education is provided by a network of *Volkshochschulen* (people's universities) which, though under centralised control from the federal capital, Bonn, remain autonomous and free to develop courses as they will. In large cities they are to be found housed in large modern buildings and they offer a comprehensive range of subjects for continuing education. These are in turn supported by twenty-two parallel boarding establishments which pick up where night classes ended in the other people's universities and, whilst pushing earlier studies still further, also offer courses in civics, politics and general cultural subjects.

Italy

Technical and vocational education in Italy have enjoyed comparatively favoured treatment at the hands of the various Italian governments. The Casati Law of 1859 provided already for a six-year technical school to follow on the elementary school, divided into lower and higher divisions, each of three years' duration. Theoretical though the teaching in such schools may have been, they proved their worth in securing many foreign jobs for Italians and they provided a sound basis on which to build in the 1890s when a new burst of interest in technical studies captured the attention not only of Italy but of the whole of Europe. Thus, apart from the years of the Fascist régime, policy as regards technical instruction was far in advance of policy for other forms of secondary education. Newer types of technical schools were introduced in the 1930s, but Mussolini made it quite clear that the training for trade and crafts was peculiarly the province of the people rather than that of an academic élite. It has been left to post-war governments to try to iron out this discrepancy.

Possession of the leaving certificate from the *scuola media* is now necessary for entry to all forms of industrial, commercial or agricultural training, though pupils who do not possess this may (on the results of a special examination) gain entry to the *istituto professionale*. Founded in 1950, this school offers courses varying from two to four years dependent on the qualification desired and seeks in particular to meet the needs of local industrial or commercial concerns. There are, however, five broad specialisms: industry and skilled trades (e.g. art for workers in ceramics, and for interior decoration); commerce and agriculture; the catering and tourist trade; seamanship in its various forms. There is in addition a parallel school for girls with offerings in domestic subjects, home management, hygiene and commercial courses. A good diploma at the end of the course has both professional and academic value since it will allow the holder to proceed to the terminal classes in the *istituto tecnico* in his chosen field. Experimentation began in 1969 in extending courses to five years in the *istituto professionale* to give a more integrated form of training, leading to the award of a "mature" diploma enabling its holder either to go directly to some form of tertiary education at the university level or to enter into higher grades of management. It should finally be noted that, whilst day release is not common in Italy, industry looks kindly on the work done both here and in the *istituto tecnico* and provision is made in both establishments for part-time courses which can exact a weekly stint of up to twenty hours of study.

The *istituto tecnico*, of which we have already briefly spoken, traces its ancestry back to 1819, and today some 34 per cent of successful candidates in the *scuola media* leaving examination enrol in one or other of these institutes. The present five-year course was established in 1961. The bulk of students have clearly vocational ambitions at medium-level technical or administrative grades, and quite a number of students return to full-time study after a period in paid employment, whilst others are actually employed for part of the day and arduously pursue their studies for the rest of their time. Thus, though the official age range is given as between 14 and 19, there are many students well into their twenties.

These institutes are highly specialised, and in addition to the usual commercial and economic subjects offer courses in agriculture (horticulture and viniculture), land-surveying, nautical training, purely feminine occupations (domestic subjects, dietetics, child care and welfare), and in industrial specialisms such as mining, metallurgy, mechanical engineering, electro-technical engineering, building, textiles, industrial chemistry and optical instrument work. In addition to the specialised professional training there are compulsory courses in Italian, history, and an appropriate foreign language. Successful completion of the course entitles the graduate to a diploma in his speciality, and this in turn secures him entry to the appropriate university department or equivalent institute of higher learning, except that for university schools of engineering, science and agronomy a supplementary examination is required, mainly in cultural subjects to ensure that the undergraduate has the same basic cultural background as the student passing out from the *licei*.

We have already had occasion to mention the government's preoccupation with the problem of illiteracy, and it is following this up with an equally determined drive in the fields of adult and popular education. The Statute of Italian Workers which recently came into operation gives every worker the right to enjoy paid leave of absence in order both to go on with interrupted education and also to bring himself up to date *culturally*. For, as Professor Limiti has been careful to point out, "if education has as its main aim to give a taste for, and the means to go on learning in or out of school, it is clear that method should have an aesthetic dimension." Workers' representatives have made it known that they want a school which *educates*, which is *qualitatively* competent to do its work. They see permanent education as the ultimate expression of so-called social rights, and it is not by accident that they defend the disinterested aspect of a cultural education. Bearing in mind an experiment in regional cultural education in Tuscany which, through local television programmes, successfully encouraged the workers to participate to the full in recording and evaluating their own regional traditions and achievements and their relative importance for the whole of Italian culture, other countries in Western Europe would do well to keep a close eye on further developments in Italy in this complex field of permanent education.

Switzerland

There is in Switzerland the same close co-ordination between the educational syllabus and technical requirements as in Belgium or Holland; there is the same necessity to produce technicians in a variety of different fields and to secure a maximum of highly skilled labour; there has to be the same emphasis on extensive technical education both in the schools and on a part-time basis; there is insistence on providing a broad basic general education and achieving thereby parity of esteem between secondary technical training and the ordinary secondary school courses; great importance is placed on fundamental studies in mathematics and science in training the technologist, and there is universal postponement of specialisation to as late a stage in the student's career as possible.

The diversity of arrangements which exist from *canton* to *canton* make it impossible to be other than general in a survey short as this must be. Some *cantons* forbid a pupil to enter on a job straight from school without prior vocational training, and the usual practice, indeed, is for a pupil who has completed his period of compulsory schooling (where he has already received the elements of technical training) to pass to some form of apprenticeship which will last for at least one year.[1] During apprenticeship, attendance at a vocational training school is compulsory on one or two half-days per week, the ages of those attending varying between 15 and 19. Those who do not take up an apprenticeship or go to work will attend full-time technical or commercial schools up to about the age of 19, or superior schools of commerce which can award a diploma to promising students granting access to university training. There are equally full-time professional schools run by professional associations (hotel-keeping and management, cheese-making, druggists, etc.) whose recruitment cuts across *cantonal* dispositions but whose programmes and examinations are carefully controlled at federal level. Apart from such *supra-cantonal* establishments, there is always careful adjustment of the schools' programmes to meet regional needs.

Another institution, the *technicum*, only admits young people who have served a three- or four-year apprenticeship in industry. The course lasts three years, and because of the period of apprenticeship and the obligation for military service the average age for entry is 20 or 21 years. There is an entrance examination designed to make sure that the candidates have retained sufficient knowledge of their basic schooling and subsequent education to be able to cope adequately with the work. The great success of the *technicum* is due to the fact that students come

---

[1] It is estimated that about 40 per cent of 16-year-olds take up apprenticeship. Only some 6 per cent go straight to work.

quite voluntarily because they are determined to improve their prospects. Instruction usually starts in the basic subjects – mathematics pure and applied, physics, chemistry, and then proceeds to more technical aspects. In addition, every student must take a language and literature course, and some instruction in works organisation, accountancy and book-keeping. Satisfactory completion of the course leads to the award of a technician's diploma which in turn can bring admission to certain university courses or to the technological university.

This instruction, known as the *école polytechnique fédérale*, again emphasises a broad general training and postpones specialisation until after the first two years of study, or later. Workshop visits bring students into regional contact with industry with the idea of having them get the feel of different occupations before committing themselves to too narrow a specialisation. The *école polytechnique*, situated in Zürich, is the only federal institution of its kind in existence, all other universities being administered by the respective *cantons*. Students are admitted no earlier than 18 on the results of the *maturité* examination or on the recommendation of the *technicum* and parallel advanced schools. The duration of the course is about four years. The school itself comprises twelve departments: architecture, civil engineering, mechanical and electrical engineering, chemistry, pharmacy, forestry, agriculture, rural engineering and surveying, mathematical and physical sciences, military science, and a department of general education.

It will be obvious from all we have had to say on Switzerland that permanent and recurrent education is not really a problem. It is traditional for all Swiss to be at least literate. Economic dependence on skilled engineering has constantly geared education to the development of skills required at all levels. The working class are well off and know that their standard of living must always depend on the quality of their education and their ability to adapt to changing circumstances. The individual *cantons*, jealous of their prestige in divers economic pursuits, make certain that their working force is fully educated and prepared not only to further *cantonal* economy but also to exercise responsibly its civic and political duties. And, at the *communal* level (as we have already seen) there is constant and often direct involvement by all citizens who so desire in the making and shaping of educational programmes. Only in a country the size of Switzerland is this possible – and only then because the complex topography and the ensuing difficulties of communication have from pre-Roman times resulted in the region being split up into a number of separate states represented today by the twenty-five independent *cantons*.

5

England and Wales

It is no exaggeration to claim that in England and Wales the provision of technical and vocational education of the right kind has lagged behind such provision in the rest of Western Europe for far too long. Sporadic attempts have been made by various governments to do something to better the situation but these have tended to fade away in the face of mounting pressure from other priority areas. Before the 1914–18 War technical schools of a kind did exist – some extremely efficient in doing the job they were allowed to do – but no real attempt was made to have compulsory post-school technical education until the passing of the Fisher Education Act in 1918, and no real attempt has yet been made (as elsewhere in Western Europe) to have technical and commercial studies become an integral part of the general secondary school course up to the compulsory leaving age of 16. The Fisher Act tried to remedy the general lack of such training for most school leavers by instituting part-time complusory education and training, but the scheme soon collapsed from lack of funds except in a very few towns of which Rugby remains the outstanding example. The treatment then went on very much as before: the provision of a great deal of part-time and usually poorly co-ordinated instruction for those who sought it over the age of 16.

The 1944 Education Act envisaged technical and vocational education, along with general continued education, as the third main stage in education and gave the combination the title of "further education". And as with the other two stages (primary and secondary education) it made it the duty of each local education authority "to secure the provision for their area of adequate facilities for further education, that is to say: full-time and part-time education for persons over compulsory school age; and leisure-time occupation in such organised cultural training and recreative activities as are suited to their requirements, for any persons over compulsory school age who are able and willing to profit by the facilities provided for that purpose". Thus it created a clear overlap with secondary education in that full-time secondary education includes all who are in secondary schools between the ages of 16 and 19. Similarly, further education overlaps with university education and with colleges of education — though these now rank as higher education even though LEAs are responsible for most of the colleges.

But this intention was not to be fulfilled either, even though there did result some moderately successful "part-time day release" from employment for further educational purposes. The Crowther Report (1959) recommended that the raising of the school-leaving age to 16 should have priority over the introduction of compulsory "county colleges" intended to fulfil the requirements of the act, and the Newsom Report (1963) also assumed that "county colleges" could not have priority. It was not until the Industrial Training Act was implemented in 1964 that a full half century of neglect in the field of technical education in particular was in some measure remedied. The Act sought to induce firms to undertake their own training, if possible, and otherwise to pay for training in local colleges of further education (or technical colleges as they still often tend to be called). Training boards were set up for various industries and these have been granted statutory powers to raise funds by a percentage levy on a firm's payroll. Yet at the time of writing this the impact seems to be fading. By 1972 the proportion of boys entering employment with no training had risen to 36 per cent in contrast to a figure for 34 per cent in 1970; and whilst in 1968 the number of boys entering an apprenticeship on leaving school stood at 43 per cent, this figure had slumped to 39.5 in 1971.

To understand the structure of further education one has to think of it as being divided into three main fields: vocational education, which is directly related to specific occupations such as the release of apprentices; formal adult education such as given in Workers' Education Association classes; and social and recreative activities which can be provided by some sections of technical colleges and colleges of further education, or in evening institutes, or by some voluntary organisations such as the WVS (Women's Voluntary Services). These fields, however, have considerable overlap and the same course can easily be attended by different people for different purposes.

Broadly speaking, we can say that technical and technological education is now organised in the form of a structure of four stories, pyramidal in shape, though many colleges of further education still offer courses at many different levels – an unfortunate legacy of the haphazard growth of the system. At the top of the pyramid come what were formerly colleges of advanced technology (CATs) but which are now fully fledged universities. These devote themselves entirely to advanced studies, as any other university, with specialisations in such fields as science, technology, communications, engineering, and they naturally include higher degree and research work.

On the next level are a larger number of regional colleges of technology. These concern themselves also with higher studies, and since 1966 most degree-level work outside the universities has been done in them – this under the dispensation of the National Council for Academic Awards (NCAA), a body set up in 1964 to grant degrees from B.A. or B.Sc. to Ph.D. level and which now also awards the relatively new degree of B.Ed. Those establishments offering such degree courses are designated as polytechnics, but all the work done at this level brings some of the highest awards available in the technical field. There is a high proportion of full-time students, many recruited on the "sandwich" basis whereby employees spend alternatively fixed periods – usually six months at a time – full-time in their college and full-time in employment. Some institutions have in addition been allowed to undertake teacher training.

On the third level comes the area college, the main local technical college in a large town, and such a college handles work at a middle level. The chief examinations prepared for here are those leading to Ordinary Certificates of various kinds at roughly the technician's level. Students are mostly part-time day students released by their employers. Finally, and at the lowest level, we have the district colleges which cover the more elementary studies.

Technical colleges, at various levels, also prepare students for many external examinations including all levels of the General Certificate of Education (GCE which at its *advanced* level may be considered the rough equivalent of the *Abitur* or *baccalauréat*), and one interesting present-day phenomenon is that increasing numbers of school pupils are leaving school after taking the GCE at ordinary level there, in order to study for the advanced level amid the greater freedom and more adult atmosphere of the technical college. Some colleges prepare students for the award of external degrees of London University. Most prepare for examinations leading to membership of professional associations such as accountants, bankers, bakers, etc. There are courses in art, agriculture and commerce, leading to nationally recognised certificates and diplomas. And there are a variety of non-vocational studies provided by local LEAs through their own colleges or by joint arrangement with other colleges. Classes held by the Workers' Educational Association (which we have already mentioned) can be paralleled and complemented by extra-mural departments of the universities, and today the armed forces provide full adult education coverage for all their members up to and including secondment to read for higher degrees in appropriate non-military establishments including the universities.

Specifically in the field of permanent education mention must be made of a number of adult residential colleges which are, broadly speaking, of two kinds — the long-term and the short-term. Many long-term colleges, such as Ruskin College, Oxford, have existed for some time and have a deservedly high reputation. None is examinational in that it provides a recognised qualification, but it is nevertheless possible for students at Ruskin College, for example, to offer themselves for the economics and politics diploma of Oxford University. Like the universities, these colleges are not state institutions but are governed by their own councils on which, in some cases, representatives of the DES and other bodies closely interested in their work have a seat. They are much akin to the universities in their curricula and teaching, but they admit men and women who may not necessarily have had an academic secondary education and who are already at work in some calling. The period of study is usually one academic year, sometimes two. Some students return to their former jobs on completion of their course, others make their way to university or other parallel establishments with the intention of embarking on new careers.

The short-term college is of more recent origin, dating mainly from the implementation of the 1944 Education Act when LEAs were given powers to establish such centres. They offer short courses of study (sometimes a mere weekend) in a great variety of subjects and recreational pursuits and will rent themselves out (as they have time over from responding to their own local needs) to professional bodies who wish to hold specific courses for their members — e.g. income tax inspectors, courses for aspiring bank managers, or the needs of the LEA (or teachers' unions) for specific courses for teachers. Sixth-form week-ends can be held for students in the local schools who are contemplating going on to university to let them know what it is all about, and French and German *assistants* serving for a year in the schools of the area are often brought together for a few days once or twice during their stay in England to "nurse", encourage and enlighten them about the peculiarities of the English educational system! Almost all these colleges are housed in what were once stately homes and in this sense remain living monuments to the vision in particular of Sir Richard Livingstone who, both true to his classical calling and fired with enthusiasm for the ideas behind the development of the Danish folk high school, maintained that "education is atmosphere as well as instruction; it is not an assemblage of piecemeal acquisitions and accomplishments, but the formation, largely unconscious, of an outlook and attitude".

The most recent and remarkable innovation in British higher education, however, is the creation of the Open University (1969). Like other universities it has an independent charter. It is financed by a direct grant from the DES and by student fees, and with some 40,000 students enrolled for the session of 1973/4 it had already become Britain's largest university. Intended originally for adults over the age of 21 who for a variety of reasons had missed out on higher education, it began in 1974, on an experimental basis, to admit students from the age of 18, about half of whom were expected to have obtained GCE "A" level qualifications which might have allowed them to follow an ordinary university career; the other half were expected to consist of young men and women who had not pursued a school career beyond the school-leaving age of sixteen. Lowering the age limit for acceptance to 18 was expected to attract more students than are at present enrolled from among the working class: the younger such a potential student is, the narrower the gap between leaving and resuming formal tuition and instruction and the greater in consequence the incentive and motivation. The experiment, however, has not proved a success and has now been dropped.

The "open" teaching system employed allows students to work at their own pace, to drop out between courses without jepardising their future prospects, and lets them take virtually any combination of courses. B.A. and B.A. Honours degrees are built up on credits, one of these being awarded at the completion of a one-year course lasting from late January to November on the basis of continuous assessment and a final three-hour written examination. Six credits are required for an Ordinary degree and eight for Honours. Each course credit exacts about ten to fourteen hours' study per week over thirty-two weeks, and many students in consequence will take about six years to complete an Ordinary degree and up to eight years for Honours.

Courses on offer are shaped and presented with skill and imaginative flair, the teaching staff showing real dedication and enthusiasm for their task. Text-books are specially written and published (and increasingly often used by students in other universities and higher education establishments). Audio-visual tuition is available for all on the BBC programmes, and students are given careful guidance, have their work meticulously checked through correspondence courses, are grouped into appropriate study centres, and are required annually to attend short vacation courses which are usually held in an appropriate university setting.

Costs, however, are constantly rising and from January 1977 (when student numbers reached 51,000, with already almost 10,000 graduates) the minimum cost for each credit course rose to £45. The fee for the week's summer vacation course on campus increased from £50 by at least another £10. Since the total outlay for a student to obtain an ordinary degree was then in the neighbourhood of £600, and £900 for an honours degree, and £900 and £1300 respectively for science degrees, such increases are serious and would seem already to have increased the drop-out rate from around 10 per cent to 13 per cent. But there are still more than enough students to keep officials fully occupied, and pressure on space has become such that new premises have had to be acquired near Oxford. Following on the Oxford purchase, and in view of the constant rise in rent and rates for rented property, the Open University has now been allowed by the government to invest further in its own property so that one by one (it is hoped) all thirteen regional offices will be owned rather than rented. Amid all this, and despite many admitted shortcomings and growing pains and difficulties, one thing is clear: Britain's experiment in mass higher education is now more than justifying the faith of its early supporters.

CHAPTER 8

Educating the Teachers

1

Problems of teacher recruitment and of the education of teachers have already been discussed in some detail in Chapter 4, and we can therefore limit ourselves here to a review of the difficulties with which *all* establishments concerned with the preparation of teachers have to contend. It is usual to claim that these difficulties have been mainly created by the expansion, democratisation and modernisation of education, but this is only superficially true. What has really been happening over the last few decades has been the undermining of the main traditions on which a stable society is normally based. And this has come about, ironically, through unprecedented scientific and technological advances which, whilst increasing wealth and aspirations, have strengthened the product–consumer aspect of living, and induced at the same time a kind of mirage of materialistic man capable of all things. We have been educating for success rather than for living. We have so dedicated education towards economic growth that we have come to regard people as instruments of production, and so taught them to think and behave as such, jettisoning in consequence established norms of behaviour, glorying in often "empty" transient values, and contemptuous of anything that smacks of tradition. Indeed, every field of human thought (including that of religious experience) has been affected and challenged by the progress of science from determinism to indeterminacy, and the result is that perhaps as never before present-day society lacks a commonly accepted view of what is an educated person.

In the world as we now know it everything is organised into larger and larger units and the effect is to rob the individual life of significance. Man has become a creature of his environment instead of remaining in control of it, and it is against this intolerable human condition that the most articulate and intelligent members of the younger generation — the student

258

body — have in effect been chiefly in revolt. Like the students, we must take stock of what man has done and is doing to man. We must put man back once again into the centre of things where, despite the tremendous pressures of modern organisation of life and business, he can have significance. He must be brought to realise himself to the full in his present-day environment. He must learn all over again to make meaningful choices. We must use education to give man back his dignity in terms of the present industrial and technological society which we have created and must accept. In this sense, we need a new conception of man and his place in the universe which can only come about through a new kind of education.

In attempting all this, however, we must not be led into the error of assuming that modern technical and scientific progress has in any way changed or impaired the goal of all human existence: to live fully and to know that life is not just compounded of a series of ill-related or unrelated happenings. Whatever man is and whatever meaning is to be attached to life, if the dignity of man is to be upheld we have to recognise and act on the premiss that he exists neither to exploit his abilities nor to have them exploited by others, but rather to expand and develop his whole consciousness, his whole sense of being. We need to educate man to educate himself and to want to go on perfecting himself to become an increasingly more useful (and therefore more happy and contented) member of that social group (or nation) to which, usually by the accident of birth, he belongs. Education for today must be educated for responsibility and the discovery of self in society — whatever that society might be. Seneca once claimed that "God divided *man* into *men* so that they might help one another". Education's prime task today is that of putting these human relationships in perspective and in order.

Thus, the task of those committed to the preparation of teachers is today no easy one, and the more honest among them will readily admit that they are ill-prepared both by background and experience properly to discharge it. Slowly and cautiously they are feeling their way. They have to recognise that in society as now constituted there can no longer be one pre-eminent system of values. They have to recognise that the present pragmatic, materialistic and meritocratic view of society offers far too little opportunity for questions of value to arise, let alone be adequately discussed. They need to grasp the implications of having all the forces of present-day culture directed almost exclusively towards developing producers and consumers and thereby creating an ever-widening gap between present cultural aims and the permanent aims of education. That gap must somehow be closed, and it can only be closed by giving first the teacher, and then through him the pupil, an awareness of things in their proper perspective, a connected view of the human condition. Understanding is paramount, but for true understanding there must be imaginative assimilation of what is being learned, and imaginative assimilation in turn depends on receptivity (open-mindedness and a willingness to consider the full range of known facts) and sensitivity.

Put at a more practical level we can say that the prime requirement for a good education today is a teacher who has not only been intellectually stretched but also made vibrantly aware of the challenge with which he is faced. He must have faith in what he is attempting and faith in himself to carry it through. He has to be a model and a moulder of character. He has to mirror and strive to perpetuate those values which make life worth living. He has to bring into school a moral quality which for its effectiveness will depend on the intensity and seriousness of that school's intellectual life. He has to be alert to change which implies the necessary knowledge of where and how to look for (and anticipate) change. He has to be highly professional, as intellectually mercurial and lively and questioning as are his pupils, and with bread to offer – not stones. He must believe in the power of education to give man back a sense of dignity and purpose and must seize every opportunity which presents itself to help produce the well-adjusted person the times so sorely need. A well-adjusted person has self-confidence, a wide range of intelligent (not necessarily intellectual) interests, a power to appreciate beauty in all its forms (including the machine), a humane feeling for others. He can form relevant and present-day judgements because his sense and knowledge of the past has trained and disciplined him to do that. He is firm but tolerant because of his studies which, centred mainly on the expression of human feelings and also obliging him to express judgements of value, have taught him the infinite variety of life.

The prospect should be seen as a challenging but not a daunting one, and as we now pass in review the attempts today being made to meet the challenge in each of the countries with which we are concerned, we should particularly note how all the mechanics of reform in teacher education are geared towards teaching that infinite variety of life. These include closer links with universities and more university involvement; later admission to courses in teacher preparation which in itself alone exacts higher intellectual performance and greater maturity on the part of the intending teacher; the lengthening of all courses for all teachers, and thus again assuring greater maturity by raising the age for qualification; an all-round vast improvement in the quality of teacher education to include a thorough acquaintance with educational "technology" and the provision of in-service training at all levels. Recent French strictures, for example, that teachers are "out of touch with social reality and entirely lacking in social authority" are being met. The individual teacher is being guided to be less of a "master instructor" and more of a "bridge man"; to take an active lead in closing the cultural gap; to relate more effectively not only with his pupils and their parents but also with his colleagues everywhere and with the greater world outside the narrow confines of the school. In short, he is being brought to believe firmly with Professor Niblett that "the ultimate significance of any man is his creativeness in the lives of others" and to act on that belief.

2

Sweden

Sweden has fifteen schools of education all concerned primarily with providing basic training for intending teachers in the lower and middle departments of the comprehensive school system. There are also fourteen pre-school colleges which offer a two-year training course for women teachers who intend working in the pre-school sectors. Six of the fifteen schools of education are also geared to provide a one-year postgraduate course for such university graduates as opt to become specialist teachers at the upper levels of the comprehensive school, and a further two back up the pre-school colleges by offering parallel courses. Special colleges also exist for the preparation of teachers of vocational subjects, physical education, music, art, handicraft and domestic science, but from 1972 all vocational subject teachers began to be trained in the same institutions as middle school teachers and efforts are continuing to bring all teacher preparation within the framework of a single school of education. Because of the relatively high salaries paid to teachers and the good social standing the profession enjoys there is no lack of recruits, and entrance to colleges of education is highly competitive and has become increasingly so since 1973 when, because of over-production, the intake had to be reduced.

Entry to schools of education has now been raised from the age of 16 to 19 and preparation takes a full three years. Graduates entering the profession will have completed at least four years of study at the university and thus will not qualify earlier than about the age of 24. Basic training for pre-school teachers demands that slightly more than half the time be devoted to the study of practical and academic subjects which, apart from the usual courses in psychology and methodology, place the emphasis on creative activities (including drama, music and movement, handicraft, painting and modelling), on social child welfare, general science, hygiene and medical child welfare, voice and speech training and Swedish. Practical training divides itself into two block periods: one consisting of visiting classes in day care centres, nursery schools and special institutions of various kinds, the other of full-time teaching practice under the supervision of a tutor in either a nursery school or day care centre.

For intending teachers undergoing a three-year period of training in the schools of education there is an introductory course designed to give the background to present school history, and this is coupled with encouraging the student to acquire an open and critical attitude to his future profession and a will to renew (in the light of experience) his teaching methods and approach. Subject studies must be based on and relate to the experiences and knowledge already possessed by him. However, since English is compulsorily taught as a first foreign language from Grade 3 through to Grade 9, all teachers concerned with handling these grades must follow appropriate courses of instruction in that language, and grants are readily available to enable specialist language teachers to study abroad. Compulsory subjects on the basic course for both lower- and middle-level teachers are Swedish, English, mathematics, general subjects, pictorial and design work, and physical education and music — the middle-level teacher being able to choose either physical education or music, but obliged to offer the other as a general subject. Lower-level teachers must in addition choose two subjects for further study, one from each of the following option groups: Option One — Swedish, English, mathematics, general subjects; Option Two — pictorial and design work, music, physical education. Middle-level teachers must take an option course comprising one of the following combinations: Swedish/English, Swedish/religious knowledge, English/history, mathematics/civics, religious knowledge/history, history/civics, civics/ geography, geography/biology, biology/chemistry, chemistry/physics. It is all highly complicated, but it has of course to be so if the requirements of the complicated structure of comprehensive education are to be adequately met. Specialist subject teachers following the one-year postgraduate course must have met final degree requirements in at least two of the subjects taught in schools, and whilst still at the university must also have followed an introductory course in pedagogical training (usually in the first term) backed up by appropriate methodology studies centred on the subjects they hope to teach.

Teaching practice comprises visits to classes, practice lessons and a probationary period. It is jointly planned and conducted by the education staff of the school of education, the teacher's tutor and the head of the school to which the student is assigned. Practice lessons are grouped in periods varying from a single day to a fortnight. The student begins by visiting some of his tutor's classes, then takes over a number of periods, and finally works up to handling a whole class on a full-time basis. The probationary period is of one full semester and is worked in specially selected schools, coming usually towards the end of the full training period. All teaching practice is closely co-ordinated with ongoing theory in the school of education. and it is to be noted that the tutor assigned to a student is a fully serving teacher chosen for his aptitude for the job. One-year postgraduate students spend the first semester basically on theory with some teaching practice. The second semester is wholly devoted to teaching practice combined with seminars and school visits.

In-service training is compulsory for all teachers, who must attend suitably arranged courses for a minimum period of five days each year, during which period the schools are closed. For the purpose of further teaching training, Sweden is divided up into six regions, so that there are six schools of education closely involved. The aim is to cover all immediate needs as well as to look to future development, and some of the schools of education offer specialist courses in the social sciences, in modern languages and for the preparation of future heads and key teaching staff. Arrangements are so diverse that it is possible here to give only a fairly representative picture of what actually happens. A course can take between five and fourteen days of a teacher's time during school holidays and a further fourteen days during term time. This part of the course finished, the teacher returns to his classroom to read, reflect and present a report. Some two months later he returns again to his school of education when reports are read, discussed and in practical terms evaluated.

Norway

Teacher preparation in Norway has also been considerably reorganised in recent years to cope with new comprehensive patterns evolving there and leading (it is hoped by 1980) to twelve years of comprehensive schooling (nine years compulsory and three years optional). Training is still given, however, either in four-year training colleges for those students who have completed the full nine-year basic school course, or in two or three year college courses for entrants from the *gymnasium*, or at university schools of education for university graduates, or at a special state college for teachers if they want to obtain a qualification roughly similar to the English B.Ed. degree. As in Sweden, there are also specialised teacher-training courses, and these can be given either in regional colleges or in appropriate vocational/ technical institutions. The minimum age for entry to the four-year college is 17, but the majority of those accepted for training tend to be between the ages of 18 and 25, many students having worked for several years in agricultural or other practical pursuits before seeking admission and as mature students, being considered as having a valuable contribution to make, unlike but just as important as that of the academically trained graduate.

All colleges — there are eleven in all — are under the centralised control of the Ministry of Ecclesiastical Affairs and Education, and the training given is in consequence of a uniformly high standard. The course itself provides a mixture of general education and specialised training. Instruction in the theory of teaching begins in the second year and practical instruction in the third year. Whilst some of the colleges have their own practice schools, most students go for their practical teaching (usually one morning a week throughout the school year, though there can be many variations from this — e.g. periods of "block" teaching away from the college in a remote country school) to recognised schools where the teachers are solely responsible for them to the point of teaching them methodology and granting their practical teaching mark. Two- and three-year courses will concentrate mainly on the theory and practice of teaching, but will add additional subjects of a practical nature (singing, music, drawing and needlework) to counterbalance the essentially academic nature of the studies in the *gymnasium*, for these students will also be teaching in the primary section of the nine-year school.

Teachers at the lower and upper secondary ranges must be graduates, and preparation for the lower (B.Ed. equivalent) degree lasts from four to five years, and for the higher degree from six to seven years after completion of the *gymnasium* course. Thus, all graduate teachers begin their career at the earliest at about the age of 25. An examination for a teacher's degree covers three or four subjects, for there are still many small schools in small towns and country districts and therefore only a small number of teachers at these schools. On the arts side an intending teacher will normally choose his three subjects from Norwegian, Latin, Greek, English, French, German, history and geography. On the science side he will often take four subjects from mathematics, physics, chemistry, zoology, botany, geography, astronomy and mechanics. On the completion of his course the intending teacher then spends six months (one semester) in the university department of education. His course is very much the same as that of a graduate in an English university department of education. As in the case of the primary school teacher, however, he does his teaching practice under experienced teachers who are also responsible for assessment and the final teaching mark. Once qualified, all teachers have to serve a probationary one- or two-year period, and once their position is confirmed they can only be dismissed for gross incompetence or misconduct.

Chiefly for historical reasons dating back to when the church's educational influence was dominant, principals of schools are generally men, though almost 60 per cent of teachers are women. There is still a teacher shortage, especially in the more remote and country areas, but for all that only about half of those applying to embark on training are admitted. The shortage is mainly accounted for by the extension of compulsory schooling combined with the necessity to train all teachers in new methods and approaches. In-service courses, indeed, are frequent, and like Sweden and Denmark, Norway has a central body specifically charged with the co-ordination of all in-service work. This is done mainly through the creation of seven regional centres of which we have already briefly spoken, and whose continued development should ease the strain on teacher preparation generally. Summer courses on a large scale are run not only by these centres but also by various teachers' organisations. Correspondence courses are also popular, and since 1970 further training has become possible, spread usually over about 16 months, in connection with the *folkeuniversitet*.

Denmark

Denmark has rapidly stepped up its teacher-preparation programmes so that pressing demands for a new kind of teacher can be fully met. In 1972 there were thirty establishments for teacher training, though only eleven of these are run and maintained by the state. The remainder are private institutions but they are generously subsidised by the state (sometimes as high as 85 per cent) and students may receive grants who attend them, tuition being free in the state colleges. All colleges run courses of four years, three years and two and a half years, the last being intended for women wishing to specialise in infant teaching. Intending students who already hold the *studentereksamen* do only three years. The four-year course absorbs the rest and, as in Norway, many mature students join this course and can be required to do an extra preparatory year should they not fully meet admission requirements. Eighteen is the minimum age for embarking on the four-year course, 19 for the three-year course, and 20 for the course in infant teaching. All students on the three- and four-year courses receive the same uniform training which is designed to fit them to teach any of the grades from the age of 7 to 16. There is the usual instruction in the theory of education, etc., and to this is added more general instruction in Danish, religious knowledge and history. In addition, a student must specialise in one or two of the subjects taught generally to equip him to become a specialist teacher to be fitted into an appropriate teaching vacancy in the higher forms of the school(s) in which he will later serve. Much attention is also given to instruction in the use of "educational technology" and also in the choice and wise use of text-books and other didactic material. All colleges must run their own teaching practice schools or have entered into an arrangement with a local authority to "appropriate" some of its schools for practice purposes. The period of teaching practice has been gradually increased so that at least one-third of the total training time is devoted to practice, and this is under the control (as elsewhere in Scandinavia) of the teachers responsible for receiving the students.

Teachers of technical subjects are drawn directly from the ranks of those with proven engineering, technical and trade experience, and they are submitted to a full-time course of fourteen weeks' duration covering methodology, psychology, school organisation, study techniques, and including teaching practice. Short further training courses are also readily available as required. *Gymnasium* teachers must be specialist university graduates, and at the moment that is sufficient to obtain a first teaching post. To become permanent, however, such a teacher must have completed a four-month practical training course leading to the *eksamen paedogogicum*. Needless to say, the *gymnasium* teacher tends to consider himself in a different social category from the rest of the teaching body and to have a much closer *rapport* with his university colleagues. It should be noted that this situation is not peculiar to Denmark and it constitutes one of the greatest problems to be overcome in Western Europe generally in the reform of education.

In-service training of teachers to cope with the new demands made upon them by the new and varied interests of the young who are now staying on much longer at school was first tackled as early as 1963 with the establishment of the Royal Danish College of Educational Studies, an establishment now employing 100 full-time and 900 part-time tutors. Courses can be held either in term time or during the holidays. Term-time courses can vary in length from a few days to a few months, and holiday courses usually last a fortnight. Any re-training activity undertaken by a teacher which lasts at least six months automatically allows him a reduction in teaching hours. Correspondence courses are also available and local authorities are setting up teacher centres which establish close links with the Royal Danish College which in turn is opening its own branches in eight carefully chosen regions to secure the maximum of coverage for the whole country. Even so, there is still a long way to go, present estimates indicating that little more than one-third of the teaching force has so far availed itself of the opportunities open to it.

3

Belgium

Belgium has been particularly fortunate in that modernisation of educational programmes was first mooted in 1936 by the then Minister for Education, Bovesse, and, though they had to wait for implementation until after the last war, these programmes (carefully amended and elaborated) have eased the way to the implementation of reform generally and made for clear-cut directives as to what was to be expected from the teaching force in particular. The Bovesse Plan aimed at bringing harmony, cohesion and simplicity into the entire school system; at ensuring that every child received the kind of education for which he was best suited; at extending the facilities of the already well-developed system of child and vocational guidance; at the establishment of parallel classes of study to make for easy change from one type of education to another; at replacing the workshop apprenticeship system by vocational education which did not neglect the cultural aspects. The plan further argued that, whilst the first and most important task of education must be to furnish the mind and to enable children to acquire the basic techniques so to do, next in importance must come the process of exercising the mind and forming the character by a double action which is both intellectual and moral. To this end, spontaneous interests must be encouraged, a sense of values developed, and the child must learn to look, observe and experiment. Full use should be made of unexpected happenings in the world outside, the field of knowledge being extended beyond concrete reality by every possible means – radio, television, films, carefully organised visits and inter-school exchanges. All teaching should be adapted to the social and regional environment. Each lesson should be, as far as possible, a response to the native interests of the child. Confidence should be placed in the child's instinct for freedom, and an appeal should constantly be made to his own individual efforts.

Obviously, it is all very much Decroly-inspired, and the global method of teaching how to read and write is fundamental to the whole. Moreover, post-war implementation and amendation of the Bovesse Plan has led to the fusion of the general management of state teacher-training colleges with that of the primary schools so that a single line of policy is followed by the school in which the intending teacher is trained, by his lecturers in his college, and by whatever school he later serves as a fully qualified teacher. Furthermore, a director-general of teacher training encourages the establishment of education study circles, open to all practising teachers, and placed under the direction of the inspectorate and the staffs of the training colleges. In non-state colleges the system is perhaps more flexible; but since to ensure uniformity of standards of training *all* colleges are inspected by state inspectors and *all* final examinations proceed under state supervision, a general overall policy is secured, whilst the existence of non-state colleges makes for much healthy experimentation and produces considerable rivalry between colleges which has an overall beneficial result. Of the 140 or so colleges at present in operation only thirty-six are maintained by the state. Eighty-four are Catholic-controlled, and twenty-five are maintained either by local education authorities or by the provinces. Teaching staff must all be university graduates, though exceptionally a brilliant teacher who has the *régent* qualification may be appointed. Entry to college is not, as in France, on a competitive basis except in so far as the number of applicants exceeds the number of places available. The applicant must submit himself to a simple examination and an interview, and recommendations from his teachers together with his school record are also taken into consideration. There are in all three distinct types of college: the *école normale gardienne* which trains girls for nursery school teaching; the *école normale primaire* to prepare boys and girls (usually in separate institutions) to become primary teachers; the *école normale moyenne* which prepares *régents* (or *régentes*) to teach either in the *école moyenne* or the lowest classes of the *athénée* etc. In 1968 the academic content of the teacher-training courses generally was strengthened, and in 1970 came an overhaul of the training curriculum. All students are now required to undertake a simple piece of educational research according to their interests but centred mainly on educational objectives, curricula and learning, creativity in the classroom, and social adjustment. At least half of the second year of professional training must be spent on teaching practice. And theory programmes in the colleges were revised to include the philosophy of science, observation and guidance, classroom techniques and techniques of group leadership.

Girls who train as nursery school teachers enter college at 15-plus and follow an intensive course, much of it on the job in a nursery centre, for four years. The first two years, however, are taken up with completing the upper secondary general education of the student. Primary school teachers take a five-year course from the age of 15-plus, but the first three years are made identical with work done in the last three years of the *athénée*, and a student who successfully passes his maturity examination at the end of his three years may, if he wishes, abandon his teacher training and proceed to the university like any other *athénée* (*lycée, collège*) student. On completion of his two years of professional training a student is awarded his teaching certificate and he can then either begin his teaching career or (if his overall performance both academically and professionally is outstanding) proceed to the *école normale moyenne* where a two-year course will give him the qualification of *régent* and put him on the same level as students who have been admitted directly to the *école normale moyenne* on satisfactory completion of the full *athénée* course at 18-plus. A *régent* (or *régente*) is in effect a non-graduate specialist and his qualifications very roughly compares with that of a student from an English college of education in possession of his B.Ed. degree.

Most training collèges are day institutions and, as the numbers given above indicate, are much smaller and therefore usually more intimate in the handling of students than in most other Western European countries. Colleges in the Flemish areas have particularly in mind the training of boys and girls who must later take an active part in instigating and promoting cultural activities in the rural areas − though all colleges are noteworthy for paying particular attention to the local customs of the area in which their students are later likely to serve. Much attention is also paid to all forms of artistic expression, and students are taught in particular to use a blackboard artistically and with telling visual effect.

Intending teachers for the *athénée*, etc., must be in possession not only of a university degree in the subjects which they wish to teach, but also of the title of *licencié-agrégé*. In theory this implies a further year's study beyond the four years normally required to complete the degree course proper. In practice the law allows intending teachers to run this professional training parallel with the last year's work for the degree. The disadvantages and drawbacks of such an arrangement will be obvious, but it must be said in fairness to those students who have made teaching their vocation that their interest is genuine and they usually work hard to give of their best. It will be noted that there is no competitive examination like the *agrégation* in France. The usual theoretical courses are followed in principles of education, history of education, psychology, methodology; certain practice periods are set aside for teaching in schools; and to qualify at the end of the course a candidate must receive a satisfactory mark on two lessons given by him before an examining board, the lessons to be taught being indicated by the examiners.

There is no highly centralised control and direction of teachers to their appointments as in France. A teacher is appointed by the authority responsible for the school: the state for state schools, the church for Catholic schools, the provinces and the communes for their own schools. In effect, therefore, a teacher is not appointed to a particular school which he may have in mind, but rather to one of a system of schools in

In effect, therefore, a teacher is not appointed to a particular school which he may have in mind, but rather to one of a system of schools in which his diploma entitles him to teach. For these reasons mobility from school to school is greater than in France, though nevertheless restricted. Secondary teachers are on probation during their first year out from university and are placed under the guidance and control of a "mentor" who is a member of the teaching staff of the school where the teacher is employed.

We have already indicated how the inspectorate generally makes itself responsible for providing adequate in-service training, and this is supplemented by voluntary efforts on the part of a number of active teacher organisations. In addition, two new important teaching centres were established in 1966 to draw in teachers throughout the country. The first makes its chief concern the in-service training of teachers in the use of audio-visual materials; the second works in close liaison with the universities and is concerned with training in the teaching of the new mathematics.

As regards technical and commercial teaching, general secondary courses in the 12–16 technical school are given by *régents* whilst university graduates are employed for the same purpose in 15–18 schools. Technical teacher training for girls exists to cover feminine specialities such as domestic science, dress-making, hair-dressing, the decorative arts and business and secretarial studies. For young men, who are almost inevitably recruited from industry or commerce after several years' successful experience, most of the courses are part-time though two full-time state teacher-training sections are in operation at Morlanwelz and Deurne.

The Grand Duchy of Luxemburg

Until 1972, intending nursery school teachers received a three-year training in a number of private institutions which received state support, and to gain admission they were required to have completed a minimum of four years of secondary education. Since 1972, however, these courses have been integrated with courses run for primary school teachers at the *Institut Pédagogique* — the one teacher training establishment Luxemburg possesses. The Institute is co-educational and applicants must now hold the *diplôme de fin d'études secondaires* should they wish to embark on the two-year training course for primary teachers. Entry is highly selective and students are in receipt of a monthly allowance throughout the duration of the course. Such students as wish to specialise in the teaching of handicapped children of various kinds must add a third year.

Teachers for the first three years of the intermediate school must in future have spent two years at a university abroad to be followed by a two-year period of training in Luxemburg, though as a temporary measure teachers from the former *écoles primaires supérieures* are able to transfer without additional training. Former primary school inspectors may also qualify by taking a one year special professional course. Teachers for the last two years are almost invariably university graduates and will have received the same training as *lycée* and technical teachers.

Such teachers must, on satisfactorily completing the full secondary school course, proceed first of all to the recently instituted (1969) *cours universitaires* which in essence provide the first year of a university course proper. The remainder of the degree course (lasting usually three or four years) is then taken at a foreign university – Belgian, French or German, Luxemburg having also in 1969 decided to recognise the French *maîtrise*, the Belgian *licence* and the German *Staatsexamen* as "competent" qualifications. In addition, any student who proposes teaching a foreign language on graduation must have taken his degree in the country where the language concerned is spoken. On his return to Luxemburg the graduate must then follow a two-year course of professional training in what are called *cours complémentaires*, and following this there is a one year probationary period.

In-service training is provided on a voluntary basis for primary teachers by courses held regularly at the *Institut Pédagogique* which annually attract about one-third of the total primary teaching force of about 1600. So far there are no in-service facilities for secondary teachers but many of these are ardent supporters of courses arranged in their specialisms in the countries in which they graduated.

Holland

Teacher preparation throughout Holland has been universally affected by the implementation of the Secondary "Mammoth" Education Act in 1968. Admission to pre-primary training is from the age of 15-plus and applicants must hold either a four-year MAVO certificate or have com-

pleted the first three years of a pre-university or HAVO school. Basic
training takes three years, and those who pass may proceed to a further
year's study to qualify for a head teacher's certificate. Those who hold
both certificates become eligible for primary teacher training.

This is given in a total of ninety-eight teacher training academies of
which forty-four are Catholic controlled, twenty-seven maintained by
the Protestant churches, twenty-four either state or municipally controlled, and three non-aligned. For admission a student must hold either
a HAVO leaving certificate or the leaving certificate of a pre-university
school. A number of academies also admit students for a preliminary
two years to take the fourth and fifth years of the HAVO course before
beginning their training proper. The course extends over three years and
requires a minimum of 240 hours' teaching practice in primary schools.
The curriculum is closely related to that of the primary school and places
the emphasis on Dutch language and literature, Dutch and general history,
geography, arithmetic, natural science, music (including singing and
wherever possible the study of the piano or violin), physical education,
art and handicrafts, and aspects of social and cultural life. The first part
of the course lasts two years. The second part (originally conferring
eligibility for appointment as a head teacher) was optional until 1970
but it has now been made compulsory and there is ónly one final examination to be taken on completion of Part Two. Thus, primary teacher
training has been in effect lengthened by one year. Also in 1970, teaching
practice became much more closely integrated with the newer and specialised instruction provided.

Upon completion of their studies and practical work, students are
examined for their teaching certificate by their own lecturers and tutors
under general supervision of delegates appointed by the Ministry of
Education. It is also still possible — and this is a unique feature for Holland
— for private persons to train for a teacher's certificate whilst carrying
out some other job, their competence being eventually assessed by special
examiners from the Ministry of Education. Similarly, certain colleges run
special sections for those who, already holding the ordinary earlier certificate, wish to improve their qualifications whilst still serving as full-time
teachers. Classes are held in the evenings, usually over a three- to five-year
period, and it has become almost traditional for most ambitious Dutch
teachers to seek to upgrade themselves in this way in their spare time.

Supplementary diplomas are available, for example, to qualify teachers as specialists in modern languages or advanced mathematics, and it is not unknown for a former primary teacher to acquire patiently, over the years, a whole string of extra qualifications so that he may finally be appointed to a secondary school or even to the headmastership of a secondary school.

To deal with the urgent need for a new type of secondary school teacher occasioned by the implementation of the "Mammoth" Act, teacher training institutes have now been opened, and these institutes will, of course, gradually phase out the kind of part-time training to which we have just referred. The first institute was opened in Utrecht in 1970. Others followed in Amsterdam (1970-71), Groningen, Leeuwarden, Tilburg (1971), Nijmegen (1972), Rotterdam and The Hague (1973). The aim eventually is to establish such an institute in every university town, each institute being associated with its university but financed directly by the Ministry of Education.

To date, the institutes are only training teachers for the MAVO and HAVO schools, teachers for VWO schools remaining the responsibility of the universities in which they take the degrees. The minimum qualification exacted for admission to an institute is a HAVO leaving certificate. Two teaching subjects are studied during the course with teaching practice running concurrently. Intending MAVO teachers follow a three-year course with an extra half-year's practical experience. Teachers for HAVO schools follow a four-year course, again with an extra half-year's practical experience, but they can also later qualify to become VWO teachers by spending a further two years at the university to reach the "doctorandus" level – i.e. their four-year course is accepted as the equivalent of the first part of a university degree course proper. By a new regulation which came into force in autumn 1972, all technical teachers must have had a minimum of four years' professional experience before following a basic two-year training course. This is supplemented by varying periods of practical teaching experience, and the newly fledged teacher has to undergo a probationary period of forty lessons before his appointment is confirmed.

Since a very high proportion of university graduates become teachers, the practice has arisen for all undergraduate students to be required to follow specified courses organised by the university department of education in pedagogics, general methodology of the degree subject(s), and psychology of the adolescent. This training usually takes place during the two years prior to sitting for the "doctorandus" degree, and is supplemented by sitting in on sixty lessons (during which time a student may be invited to teach) given in VWO schools. For the present, this is all the training required, and it cannot be claimed that it is taken very seriously. Attempts to improve on the situation are likely to be geared to a proposed reduction in the length of the average degree course: as and when this takes place all professional training will become postgraduate, will last a full year, and will be supplemented by a period of supervised teaching.

France

Amid all the bewildering reforms taking place in secondary education in France the role to be played by the primary school teacher remains virtually the same — that of providing a sure foundation on which others may successfully build. High intellectual qualifications are required of him in proportion relative to those required of the teacher in a *lycée*. Because he is a civil servant and part of an efficient and highly organised and centralised bureaucratic machine, then his entry to the teaching profession must be on an entirely competitive basis as with all other civil service appointments. Because the country as a whole is still firmly wedded to the idea of *instruction du peuple* and *préparation d'une élite* and cannot yet see how the two can properly be mixed, the traditional distinction between the simple *instituteur* and the specialist *professeur* (*agrégé* or not) still persists despite renewed attempts to have implemented the firm recommendation of the Langevin Commission for the post-war reform of education that primary and secondary teachers should all be trained together and educated to university level. All that has really been achieved is to raise the standard of recruitment for entry to teachers' colleges (*écoles normales*), to ease the way for promising students to take university courses (or their equivalent), to oblige the university graduate to take some kind of serious professional training, and to have the *école normale* now train "bivalent" (as opposed to "monovalent") specialists for service in the lowest classes of the CES.

By 1869 France had established efficient training colleges for primary teachers in every *département*. By 1879, it was made compulsory by law for each *département* to maintain one training college for women and one for men, and by the end of the century the general character and constitution of the *école normale* was fixed. Each *département* has its council responsible for the whole of primary education including the recruitment, training and promotion of primary teachers, and, whilst the *département* is held responsible for the provision and maintenance of its *écoles normales*, the Ministry of National Education pays the salaries of staff, prescribes the courses of study and general time-tabling, and supervises the conduct of examinations. All students are resident members of their respective *école normale*, are almost entirely supported by the state, and since 1947 have received a modest salary from the time they begin teaching practice in the schools. The governing body of an *école normale* consists of the *recteur* of the *académie*, the responsible inspector of the *département*, two representatives of the council, and four members (including the principal of the *école normale*) chosen by the *recteur*.

Each year it is the duty of the *départemental* council to decide how many teachers need to be trained for service two years later and so fix the number of places open to public competition. Until 1972 intending primary teachers were admitted at about age 15 but were expected to complete the *baccalauréat* before beginning their professional studies. Since 1972 the *baccalauréat* must be held by the intending teacher before he submits himself (herself) for entry to an *école normale*, and the professional training course now last for two years and includes, during the second year, three periods of one month each of practical teaching in an ordinary school situation. The competitive entrance examination is a searching one designed not only to discover the knowledge already possessed by the candidate and his special abilities, but also to test his mental alertness, sensitivity, and gift for clear and lucid expression. Satisfactory completion of the course requires a student to give proof of his ability to teach any of the classes which fall within the province of the primary teacher as well as the general range of subjects, including physical training and music. The theoretical part of the course leads to the award of the *certificat de fin d'études normales* which is completed after one year's probation as a full-time teacher by the conferment of the *certificat d'aptitude pédagogique*. The newly fledged teacher is now entitled to appointment within the *département* to whatever suitable vacancy exists. He cannot choose his own post, nor can he be moved from the post to which he is appointed unless he asks for it, or unless he incurs disciplinary punishment for some kind of proved incompetence or unprofessional conduct − a rare occurrence. It should also be noted that the intending nursery school teacher follows the same course as the trainee primary teacher (with practical work based on the *école maternelle*) and that she has the same professional status as the primary school teacher. Five special *écoles normales* (three for boys and two for girls) have also been opened to train teachers for service in the *collège d'enseignement technique*.

The total reorganisation of post-primary education has not unexpectedly had its repercussions within the *école normale* which fortunately was in a position to cope in that it was at the same time phasing out its pre-*baccalauréat* classes and ceasing to be a five-year training institution. The most urgent demand made upon it has been that of providing in-service training for former primary trained teachers who now found themselves willy-nilly upgraded to teach in the CES. It has followed this up by devising specialist "bivalent" courses for its own students who, on certification, also hope to teach in the 11−15 age range of the CES. In addition to the usually broadly based education, such students become specialists in the teaching of two or more subjects and qualify with the title of PGCE (*Professeur général de l'Enseignement de Collège*). The function and status of such teachers would seem to be not very dissimilar from that of the *régent* in Belgium. In pursuance of these extended aims, the *école normale* has now (wherever possible) established closer links with the universities and sought to have its courses in mathematics and linguistics in particular taught for it by university lecturers. At the lowest level, however, it is still having to cope with large numbers of primary school teachers who had to be recruited (untrained) straight from passing the *baccalauréat* for service in school (so great has been the shortage of primary teachers) and to provide for them adequate on-the-job training. All this upheaval has occasioned much re-thinking of the teacher's aims and objectives, and important changes in training methods have resulted: not only has the scope of courses on offer been widened but more attention has had to be paid to the personal development of the intending teacher and to extending his general education as far as possible beyond the *baccalauréat*. New teaching techniques have had to be devised to include the latest theories in child development and the learning process; and the trainee-teacher has to be shown not only how to teach his subject(s) to a wide ability range but also how to motivate children who were not previously considered worthy of secondary education − and often still consider themselves as such. In short, the function of the *école normale* is increasingly spilling over to include training teachers for the lower cycle of secondary education and trying to make practical sense within its own walls of Whitehead's notion of education as being "a seamless robe".

Today, then, teachers in post-primary education are very much a hotch-potch mix of former *instituteurs* at the higher primary level who may (or may not) laboriously have later acquired either the PGCE or even the CAPES, or some other suitable training, of craft and technical teachers (trained in the *école normale nationale d'apprentissage* which has recently increased its training period for former workers in industry from one to two years), of holders of either the highly coveted *agrégation* or CAPES, or of *auxiliaires*. These auxiliary teachers are graduates who will be preparing for CAPES or even the coveted *agrégation* (or some other high qualification) in which case there is no guarantee that, having achieved their goal, they will necessarily remain in teaching. At one time the academic *lycée* could boast that its staff was almost entirely composed of *agrégés*. Today, with the vast expansion of university education, there are fewer and fewer *agrégés* in the secondary sector, and auxiliaries must make up some 20 per cent of the total teaching force, even though they have no security of tenure and are re-appointed annually.

The most highly rated teachers throughout the whole of France are still the *agrégés* who are in effect recruited by nation-wide competition for permanent appointment to the highest and best paid positions in what is now the "long" second cycle of post-primary education. They have permanent tenure, teach only fifteen hours per week, and can also transfer to teach in the universities (or some parallel higher institution) as the opportunity occurs. The traditional method of preparing for the *agrégation* is from the *école normale supérieure* (originally two establishments for men, two for women), entry to which is on a competitive basis. Candidates must be between the ages of 18 and 23 and already in possession of the *baccalauréat*. They may not compete for a place more than three times, and their preparation is usually carried out at the *lycée* they have been attending. All students are compelled to reside in the *école normale supérieure* for the full duration of their studies except in very special circumstances. All expenses incurred are covered by the state. The ordinary degree work is done at the Sorbonne, the *écoles normales supérieures* concerning themselves with preparation of their students for the *agrégation*. Until 1966 this involved ensuring the student obtained his *diplôme d'études supérieures*, but since that date all candidates for the competitive *agrégation* examinations must hold instead an appropriate *maîtrise*. Thus, the duration of a course in the *école normale supérieure* is at least five years, the last year being given over entirely to preparation for the *agrégation*. As we have already seen, however, preparation for the *agrégation* regularly goes on elsewhere than in these prestigious *grandes écoles*; at the universities, at special training centres (IPES, of which more later), by correspondence courses, all catering for the needs of the many auxiliary teachers of whom we have spoken. A candidate who fails the *agrégation* may re-sit as often as he wishes, but there is an upper age limit of 30, and examiners are so determined that the standards shall not fall that it is no uncommon thing for them to refuse to fill all the places competed for in a given year on the grounds that the quality of the candidates presenting themselves is not of a sufficiently high standard. Holders of the CAPES may present themselves for the *agrégation* examinations without any further training.

CAPES *(certificat d'aptitude au professorat de l'enseignement public du second degré)* was originally conceived to cope with the demands for a larger and differently trained body of secondary teachers occasioned by earlier reforms in post-primary education offerings. Until the 1970s candidates had to be under 30 years of age and in possession of a university degree. They could take their training either in the *école normale supérieure* (after gaining admission), or in the university, or in the IPES *(institut préparatoire aux enseignements du second degré)* which was first created in 1957 to encourage secondary school teacher recruitment. An IPES will usually recruit its students either after the termination of the post-*baccalauréat* classes preparing for competitive entry to the *grades écoles*, or after one year of university study. On acceptance, each student must sign a ten-year agreement to teach and will then receive a small monthly salary. He will first of all prepare for the appropriate university degree, but will at the same time follow the theoretical part of his training to enable him to sit the theory papers of CAPES. Success here — and like the *agrégation* the examination is on a severely competitive basis demanding proof of real competence in the subjects the candidate wishes to teach — offers two alternatives. The candidate may elect to push on further to submit himself to the ordeal of the *agrégation*, or he may choose to complete the CAPES by taking a year's professional training when he will go to one of the regional education centres (*centre pédagogique régional*) established in each of the twenty-five *académies* into which France is educationally divided. Each student during this practice year is assigned to a *conseiller pédagogique*, usually a teacher of long standing and outstanding ability. At the end of his practical training the student submits himself to a passing-out examination consisting of at least two lessons with different classes given before a special examining body. Possession of CAPES (or of CAPET if the student has taken a technological degree to teach technical subjects) entitles the teacher to a permanent appointment with security of tenure exactly as with the *agrégé*, and he will be able to teach anywhere in the secondary system. He differs in status from the *agrégé*, however, in that he is paid a lower salary and is required to do a minimum of eighteen hours teaching per week.

Obviously, though admittedly at a lower level, the aim was to make CAPES as searching a test as the *agrégation* and the failure rate over the years down to the 1970s has given ample proof of this. As late as 1971, for example, only about one-third of those candidates who sought the qualification to upgrade themselves and better equip themselves to meet the newer demands made on them in the C.E.S. were successful; and of those who followed the preparation I have just been describing the failure rate was well over half. If only because of the growing number of such unqualified teachers in the schools some immediate action became necessary. Proposals were mooted for the reorganisation of CAPES preparation to take effect as from 1973/4, but the Haby Plan for the reform of the whole structure of education caught up with these proposals and in effect engulfed them.

Under the terms of the Haby Plan, if and as it is finally adopted (and of course refined), future *instituteurs* will be recruited as previously on a competitive basis for entry to an *école normale* from amongst students already holding the *baccalauréat*. The training will be basically the same as previously but each student accepted will have the title of *élève-maître* and will in consequence draw a modest salary. In addition, during his probationary year, when he is preparing for the practical part of his certification, he will be compelled to return frequently to his *école normale* for concurrent tuition.

A common basic training programme for all secondary teachers is envisaged to be given in specialist institutions attached to the universities, and success at the final examination will lead to the award of the title of either *professeur breveté* or *professeur certifié*. The *agrégation*, needless to say, remains (at least for the time being) sacrosanct, but it may equally be prepared for in these specialist institutions and will be considered as a test of suitability for promotion. Any *instituteur* who has taught for a minimum period of three years after full certification is eligible to present himself for selection to study for the diploma awarded at the end of the first university cycle of studies. Success automatically makes him a *professeur breveté*, and he will have been given one full year's leave of absence to study towards this end. Students who have just gained the first cycle university diploma may present themselves for selection on a competitive basis to pursue one full year's professional training, after which they will be required to teach for three years before taking a practical teaching examination to have the title of *professeur breveté* conferred upon them.

Future *professeurs certifiés* are again to be competitively recruited from amongst holders of the first cycle university diploma, but they will follow a two-year course of training, partly academic to obtain a higher university qualification, partly professional. On acceptance they immediately assume the title of *élèves-professeurs* and receive a salary. At the end of two years they will submit themselves for the theoretical part of their examinations and then spend a further year in a fully responsible teaching post but obliged also to follow prescribed tutorials at their training institutions. A practical teaching examination at the end of the year will then give them their full title. In addition, any *professeur breveté* who has taught in this capacity for a minimum period of three years (and also certain specified categories in the administrative field) may present himself for selection for upgrading to the level of *certifié*.

So should CAPES gradually be replaced by a more flexible method of training and, more importantly, by a system of selection which chooses the prospective *professeur* before his studies have ended, thus allowing him to relax and fully profit from his further studies since he now knows that the competitive element is well and truly behind him and his future career normally assured? As I write this, full and final details for the implementation of the teacher-training plan have to be worked out, but one thing is certain: if these reforms are implemented along the general lines just outlined then a revolution will have been achieved in French education which, whilst bringing it much closer to practice in other Western European countries, will also carefully safeguard those excellences of which the French are justifiably proud and which can still serve, in the future as in the past, as an inspiration to others. It is again to be noted that *agrégation* still remains the special concern of the *école normale supérieure* (which, incidentally, also trains future lecturers for the *école normale*) though it can be prepared for elsewhere; that it is still open to nationwide competition; and that it is still as severely selective as heretofore. The only change envisaged is that successful *agrégés* must now follow a one-year course of professional training comprising a theoretical element and a successful period of teaching.

4

West Germany

Coming late in comparison with other Western European countries to a switch-over from an agrarian-based to an industrial economy, Germany as a whole had early in the nineteenth century to give much thought to the development of an efficient educational machine and to the thorough preparation of the kind of teacher the times exacted at both the primary and the secondary levels. In 1810 Humboldt raised the profession of the *Gymnasium* teacher to a high level of dignity and efficiency by introducing the measure (still in force today) that all secondary teachers be required to do a minimum two years' probation work in the schools, at the end of which time they must submit themselves to a test both as to competence in the subject(s) professed and as to ability to teach. The primary schools were geared to producing the manpower urgently needed by the newly industrialised state, and so, as training colleges for the preparation of primary teachers grew in numbers and importance, there appeared (as in France) a distinct cleavage between the kind of training on offer for the intending primary teacher and that given in the universities for his secondary counterpart. As early as 1848, however, there came a demand from the German Teachers' (primary) Association − the very first in Western Europe to have such a policy − that all primary teachers should be educated alongside their secondary colleagues in the universities, but nothing came of it. It was the year of the Revolutions! The German state clamped down severely on such unorthodoxies. The training colleges became increasingly dedicated to reconciling the interests of the teachers they turned out with those of the state, whilst the universities were enjoined to encourage their students to pursue knowledge in depth for its own sake and to eschew political matters as not being primarily the concern of the intellectual.

It is true, of course, that the regulations enforced by Prussia on the whole of Germany rigidly to control the work of the training colleges were modified in a more liberal direction in 1872 when the University of Leipzig made it possible for the best students from the training colleges to embark on university courses, and further modifications followed in 1901. Nevertheless, the "two-track" system of education and of the preparation of teachers remained more or less cast in the same rigid Prussian mould until the German Republic, under the Weimar Constitution, sought to liberalise teaching generally and to prepare primary teachers "according to the principles which apply generally to higher education" (Article 143 of the Constitution). Though the attempted reforms were optimistically greeted and though newer progressive methods came in with the introduction of outdoor activities and projects which went with an expanded curriculum, they were finally killed by the gradual rise to power of Hitler; and as far as West Germany is concerned it was left to the new German Federal Republic of the post-1945 period firstly to clear up the educational chaos into which the country had been plunged and then to try to pick up the story all over again from where the Weimar Republic's liberalising movement had failed.

One of the first steps taken was for the whole of the *Länder* to agree in principle at a meeting of the Permanent Conference of Ministers of Education firstly that satisfactory completion of a full secondary school course must be a prerequisite for embarking on any course of teacher preparation, and secondly that all colleges of education should henceforward be designated as *Hochschulen* and so be officially recognised as university-level institutions. Each *Land* has since implemented this agreement along its own individualistic lines. Hamburg, for example, has given the lead by enrolling all primary and secondary teachers-in-training in the University's Faculty of Philosophy to enjoy exactly the same rights and privileges as other university students. Hesse and Bavaria keep their colleges of education autonomous but enrol the students as undergraduates with the same rights and privileges as any other undergraduate. North-Rhine-Westphalia has grouped together its fifteen separate colleges to form one "Pedagogical University". Other *Länder* are currently attempting either to associate their colleges with the nearest university or to incorporate them in a comprehensive university along with other institutions of higher learning. The only category of teacher trainee not being considered in all this is the kindergarten teacher: she is still recruited after satisfactory completion of the *Realschule* programmes to follow a two-year course of training in a professional school (*Fachschule*).

The *Pädagogische Hochschulen*, then, have the task of preparing teachers for service in both the *Grundschule* and *Hauptschule*. Recruitment is usually at about the age of 19 (after the *Abitur*) but about 10 per cent of the entry still has no final secondary qualification and must sit a special examination for admission. The course lasts for six semesters (three full years) and aims at giving an equal balance of subject study and teaching method. In all *Länder* except Bavaria students have to choose a particular teaching field for study in depth, such as English, mathematics or history, and all teachers anyway are expected to be capable of dealing with all subjects taught in every grade up to the final ninth year. There is a solid grounding in educational psychology, philosophy, and sociology linked with pupil observation and periods of teaching practice, though there is now a move to postpone teaching practice until the probationary period. This probationary period follows success at the first state examination, the teacher being appointed to a full teaching post where he works under the supervision and guidance of "mentors" (experienced teachers delegated for that purpose by the Ministry of Education) who runs seminars and generally help the "young teacher" to find his feet and prepare for the second examination which takes place after two or at the most four years. For this second "pedagogical" examination the teacher must submit a dissertation on some educational practice, present a report on his experiences on in-service training, and give two trial lessons, one of which is chosen by the candidate and the other imposed by the examiners. An oral examination follows; thesis, report and trial lessons are discussed and the successful candidate (now at least 24 years of age) is then awarded his certificate of qualification and made eligible for permanent appointment.

The training of *Realschule* teachers varies from *Land* to *Land*. In Hamburg, Bremen and Hesse it is closely linked with training for *Grundschule* and *Hauptschule* teachers. In the other *Länder* there are two possibilities. A fully qualified *Grundschule* teacher can, after sufficient experience, prepare himself by attending special courses. Alternatively, the candidate chooses to undertake at least six semesters of specialised study at a university or *Technische Hochschule*. Bavaria, Baden-Wurtemberg and Lower Saxony have special institutes for training *Realschule* teachers. In any case, the first state examination is taken after three to four years' study in two subjects in certain prescribed combinations. This academic training is followed by a one or two year probationary period in the course of which practical training is given. A second state examination then follows, similar to that for *Grundschule* teachers, and permanent certification is obtained at about the age of about 26 *if* the candidate has embarked on training immediately after obtaining his *Abitur*.

Like the *professeur de lycée* the *Gymnasium* teacher is recognised as an academic and enjoys considerable prestige. All *Gymnasium* teachers have, for more than a hundred years, received their training in the universities and uniform standards are thereby assured throughout the country. There are uniform examination requirements after a minimum of eight semesters' study, although in practice this stretches to up to twelve or even fourteen semesters. Some universities (notably Hamburg) insist on intending teachers spending short periods in schools of different types to make sure they feel fitted for teaching. Until recently a number of *Länder* insisted on a three-subject degree combination but the principle of a two-subject examination is now accepted. Economics, social science, pedagogy and psychology have recently been added to the possibilities, but the hard core of the training is academic specialisation in the subjects actually to be taught in school.

On completing his university studies proper the candidate is then admitted to a two-year period of in-service training in appropriate *Gymnasien* (usually one year in each of two schools) where he has to observe the instruction given by experienced teachers and do some carefully supervised teaching himself. In addition he has to attend weekly seminars where the problems of practical teaching are related to educational theory and at which he must present appropriate papers for discussion. This teaching is shared by appropriate university professors, the head of the school in which the candidate is currently serving and by specially selected teachers. His training terminates with the pedagogical examination which again consists of two trial lessons, the presentation of a dissertation, and an oral concerning his knowledge of educational theory in general and the methods of instruction in his particular subjects, again usually two. The successful candidate is now eligible for appointment on a *provisional* basis (usually at the age of 25 or over) as a *Studienassessor*, and he usually has then to wait several years before the authorities confer upon him the coveted title of *Studienrat* which gives him recognition as a permanent and fully qualified teacher of civil service status.

All primary and secondary teachers have the same official standing once their appointments are confirmed. They are, however, civil servants who owe their allegiance to their *Land* which employs them, pays them and secures for them professional advancement. It is as rare (though now possible) for a teacher to move outside his *Land* as it is for an intending student to seek his training under some other authority. For despite sincere protestations of the necessity for moving towards a really democratic way of life which shall embrace the whole of the German Federal Republic, the various *Länder* jealously guard their autonomy and their age-old responsibility for the welfare of those who comprise the *Land*. In-service training, as we have seen, is an integral part of the preparation of all teachers, but each *Land* has increasingly seen the necessity for providing updated further training for established teachers, particularly in recent developments in psychology and methods. Special institutions are run to achieve this end, but attendance is optional and the institutions have no power to give extra qualifications. Inspectors and various teachers' organisations similarly run appropriate optional courses as the demand or need arises. The training of teachers in technical and vocational subjects takes place in appropriate vocational colleges, but the students must have a minimum of one year's service in industry or commerce before recruitment, and they again, on qualification, must serve a two-year probationary period.

However, with reform much in the air and as schools throughout Western Germany are beginning to be reorganised (as elsewhere) on comprehensive lines, the necessity for training a "comprehensive" teacher is now being emphasised. There is equally a problem of teacher shortage, not particularly due to the population "explosion" into secondary schools but occasioned by the rigid "class" differentiation between teachers, whereby they are paid not according to their qualifications but according to the school in which they teach. In 1970 the Ministers for Education of the various *Länder* met to attempt to cope with these difficulties and reached agreement on proposals for the harmonisation of teacher training and teachers' salaries. In future teachers will no longer be distinguished by the type of school in which they have been trained to serve, but by the age or grade level at which they are recognised as competent to teach. Thus, and much to the annoyance of academic "diehards", the traditional distinguishing terms and formal titles will disappear: there will no longer be a *Volksschullehrer* (primary teacher), a *Realschullehrer*, or a sacrosanct *Studienrat*. Instead, and in keeping with the changing patterns in the schools, there will simply be a *Lehrer für die Primarstufe*, a *Lehrer für die Sekundarstufe I*, and a *Lehrer für die Sekundarstufe II*.

A revision of training arrangements of necessity follows. In future *all* intending teachers will have to take the same basic course in educational studies, this course linked to specialisation in one or two particular subjects. The minimum duration for any course will be three years, but teachers for the upper secondary level must do a minimum of four years. On passing the first state examination *all* teachers must undergo a supervised probationary teaching stage of eighteen months (three semesters).

Italy

Today, Italy still follows the traditional Western European pattern of preparing all primary and most lower secondary school teachers in colleges which properly fall within the secondary and not the tertiary level of instruction. True, there is much talk of implementing reforms to change this but any reform movement has to bear in mind the simple fact that of the 631 teacher-training colleges in Italy, 350 are operated by the church, which tends to see any change in the present system as a threat to its undoubted waning influence on Italian education. And when in 1971 the then Minister of Education tried to extend the training course in the *istituto magistrale* from four to five years he was roundly defeated by an unlikely combination of Communists, the clerical wing of the Christian Democrats and the Neo-Fascists. The general pattern thus remains of recruiting for the *istituto magistrale* from amongst those pupils who have obtained the necessary leaving certificate from the *scuola media*, that is to say at about the age of 14 or 15. Obviously most of the time must be devoted to completing the student's general secondary education, and because of this (as we have earlier instanced) the *istituto magistrale* has despite itself become a kind of poor man's secondary school much favoured by many parents because it awards a coveted paper qualification at the end of four years instead of five or more exacted in other higher learning establishments. Many students passing through the *istituto magistrale* have no intention of teaching. Many remain unemployed. And, even amongst those who do intend to teach, unemployment is high. In 1972, for example, some 40,000 students qualified to fill some 14,000 teaching posts. Needless to say, most of the teaching staff at primary school level are women, and those girls who seek to become kindergarten teachers qualify at about age 18 after only three years of teacher training. It is not a very happy picture and all are agreed that reform is imperative if not in agreement (politically) as to how best achieve it. On the other hand, personal observation has revealed real dedication among primary school teachers in permanent function even though their professional training has been perfunctory and not necessarily up to date.

Secondary school teachers must have a degree or its recognised equivalent. There is no professional training as such, though there are a few university courses which prepare specifically for a career in teaching. Neither the possession of a university degree, however, nor of the teacher's certificate from an *istituto magistrale* entitles the right to teach. Appointment to a permanent post depends on the passing of a publicly advertised competitive examination (open to all between the ages of 18 and 45 who already possess the necessary preliminary qualifications), and that appointment needs ratification from the Ministry of Education in Rome. Meantime, and until present bureaucratic inflexibility and political manoeuvring can be circumvented for the greater good of all, there exists a paradoxical situation whereby, despite a surfeit of qualified teachers, there can occur a teacher shortage in certain places in certain subjects at certain levels. And such is the position at the secondary levels (particularly the upper-secondary levels) that up to 50 per cent of teachers are listed as *non abilitati* (not officially recognised) and therefore employed on a temporary basis. The number of *non abilitati* for the entire teaching strength was given as late as 1973 as at least 70 per cent, and it was at the same time estimated that it was taking a fully qualified primary teacher as many as ten underpaid insecure years to achieve a permanent position in the state teaching system. Fortunately for Italy, the position of teachers in technical and vocational institutions is much more healthy, and they are also regularly being offered refresher courses of six months' duration to bring them up to date on changes in the occupational sectors of industry and commerce corresponding to their activities. These institutions are not directly under state control.

Switzerland

As in Italy, training colleges for primary teachers do not come under the official heading of higher education but under that of secondary education, and students are recruited at about the age of 15 or 16 to follow a four or five year course which (again as in Italy) aims primarily at completing the secondary education of the intake. Bright and ambitious students, however (as in Belgium), can present themselves for the *maturité fédérale* examination and so gain access to the university. Bâle-Ville and Geneva on the other hand insist that an intending student already has his *maturité* and the training course then lasts for only two or three years. One important feature of practical training in certain *cantons* is that part must be spent in schools in rural communities and part in an urban environment. The appointment of a qualified primary teacher is a matter for the local *commune* which has considerable authority also in deciding hours of work, length of holidays and even pay. The mode of election for a primary teacher varies from *commune* to *commune*: it is done either by secret ballot, by decision at a general meeting, by the local council, or by the school's authorities.

All other teachers must hold a university qualification, or (in the case of technical and commercial teachers) its recognised equivalent, or have been specifically trained (after obtaining the *maturité*) in a training college designed to prepare intermediate school teachers over a period of two to three years. The training for a degree usually takes three to four years after *maturité*, though the ambitious will often proceed further and take a doctorate. Certain universities then offer one full year of pedagogical training (Lausanne for example) which grants a successful student a *certificat d'études pédagogiques*. To make for greater uniformity an

Institut Pédagogique was opened in 1960 specifically to train any graduate who wished to teach. The course lasts for one year and consists of training in classroom theory and practice together with lectures and demonstrations in the use of modern teaching aids and audio-visual techniques. In 1969 it was considered necessary to open a Swiss centre for the further training of secondary teachers. A wide range of choice of courses is on offer, varying in length from a few days to a few weeks, but the emphasis is placed on pluri-disciplinary courses, on modern methodology, on the co-ordination of the various disciplines, on educational psychology, and (for head teachers) school management. It should finally be noted that all secondary teachers are employed at a *cantonal* level.

5

England and Wales

In England and Wales training colleges for primary school teachers have been created in an individual and haphazard way, being at first established by voluntary or religious bodies, and much later by local education authorities. Gradually the system settled down to two years' professional preparation after satisfactory completion of a secondary school course, though insistence on this did not become general until well after the passing of the Balfour Act in 1902. Even then, however, the kind of preparation offered from college to college varied enormously both in quality and in standards of performance expected from the students. There was no overall co-ordinating policy, little vital contact between college and college and — what was far worse — a feeling of inferiority engendered in the training college student *vis à vis* his more academically or financially fortunate school-mate who managed to secure for himself a university education on a promise to teach after completing a four-year course (three years to a degree and one year postgraduate training in the university department of education) paid for him by the then Board of Education. There was, of course, no contact of any real value between the training colleges and the universities. It was a dual system of teacher education, a cleavage equally as strong as that holding in France or Belgium (or indeed most of the Western European countries), but in addition lacking the merits of uniformly high standards of preparation that a centralised system could exact.

The first attempt at securing professional training for secondary school teachers came with the foundation of the College of Preceptors in 1846 and its establishment of the first Chair of Education in 1872, which was in existence for only four years. University chairs in education were established in 1876 in Edinburgh and Saint Andrews. In 1878 the Maria Grey Training College for Women was founded. In 1879 a teachers' training syndicate was started in Cambridge, and a Cambridge training college for women was opened in 1885. In 1890 university day training departments were opened, primarily to train future primary school teachers (who could also read for a degree), though they increasingly reacted in favour of training teachers for the new secondary schools that came to be established in increasing numbers after the Balfour Act of 1902. And, as is still the case in Belgium, those who read for a degree in these day training colleges ran their professional training concurrently with their academic work. It was not until 1911 when the present system of one year's professional training to follow on the degree course was introduced, and not until 1951 that the unsatisfactory method of recruiting secondary school teachers by paying for the whole of their university education and exacting a promise to teach at the end of it all came to an end.

With the passing of the Education Act of 1944, a system of teacher preparation that would have more organic unity became a necessity. In 1926 a move had been made in this direction by the Board of Education's decision to delegate the responsibility for the certification of training college students to regional boards on which the universities and the local authorities were represented, and by the association of a group of training colleges for this purpose with a university (or universities). The McNair Report now took the necessary and decisive step forward by recommending the establishment of area training organisations involving the pooling of resources and facilities by the universities, the training colleges, the local education authorities, into a teacher training centre based administratively on a university and to be known as the university's institute of education. Seventeen such institutes were then created, the number later rising to twenty-two. Their functions were variously described as (a) supervising the course of training in their member institutions, including the university department of education, (b) the recommendation of properly qualified students for certification as teachers, (c) to plan the development of all kinds of further training at all levels in the area, (d) to provide an education centre not only for teachers in training but also for serving teachers, (e) to provide opportunities for further study, to encourage research and to organise courses (in consultation with the authorities and teachers' representatives) for serving teachers. Thus the university became (as never before) a focal centre for the training of *all* teachers and a constant source of help and inspiration to schools within its area.

The chief merit of these reforms lay in the fact that not only was a workable decentralised system of teacher training evolved, reducing governmental control to an absolute minimum, but also that general agreement on curricula in training establishments as well as a uniform standardisation were achieved whilst allowing a maximum of freedom for experimentation and pioneer work. On the other hand, it cannot truthfully be claimed that the dichotomy between training colleges and university departments of education did in actual practice disappear. Nor was the country as a whole as yet convinced that a fourth year of professional preparation was really necessary for the graduate who had studied his subject(s) in depth and sought to teach in the academic type of secondary school. Up until 1973 there was still no legal requirement for a university graduate to possess a teaching qualification before taking up a post *in any type of school*, though many authorities had already begun exacting such preparation. From 1973 this did become necessary, but teacher shortages in certain subjects (mainly mathematics, science and modern languages) have since caused the Department of Education and Science to waive the requirement temporarily in these specified subjects.

Meantime, changes were taking place in the training colleges. In 1960 training there was extended from two to three years with the chief aim of giving the student more time to perfect his own education. On the recommendations of the Robbins Report (1963) teacher-training colleges were renamed colleges of education. By the same token schools of education were established in the universities to integrate more closely all teacher training and educational studies and also to make it possible for the more able students in the new-type three-year colleges to stay on a further year and read for an appropriate university degree. Today there must be some 211 institutions devoted to the education of teachers, and since university departments of education have been unable to cope with all postgraduates now obliged to seek professional teaching qualifications, the colleges of education have been encouraged to admit post-graduates (up to a limit of 30 per cent of their total intake) and provide their one-year period of training. This has proved a healthy move on two grounds: firstly it has noticeably further bridged the gap between the colleges and the universities; secondly it has for the first time allowed graduates to be trained for service in a variety of schools (including the primary level) as opposed to service in the academic secondary school only – for it is to be noted that, unlike the rest of Western Europe, a teacher has the right to seek employment in whatever kind of school takes his fancy: only university departments train specifically for service at "academic" levels, and some of these are now beginning to diversify. Gradually the academic "respectability" of the colleges of education improved. They became able to raise the minimum standard require-ments for entry to approximate more closely to those exacted by the universities, and the creation of the B.Ed. degree (awarded by the uni-versity with which a college is associated by virtue of its membership of an institute of education) now allowed them to recruit a more highly qualified staff.

Yet there was still much to criticise. The universities, jealously guarding their autonomy, proved as a body far from helpful over provisions made for the award of the B.Ed. degree. Some universities were frankly opposed, others refused to have a B.Ed. degree with an honours award attached, and still others made near-impossible demands (often at subject level) of students reading for the degree. Even in the most enlightened and helpful universities some of the colleges of education had sometimes to fight hard to get the academic board (or senate) to approve certain subjects they wished to teach, objections being raised against their academic respectability. On the other hand, there were academics who not only welcomed this hybrid degree (one element an academic study and the other the study of education) but who also sought to introduce a new-type general degree in their own universities which would be awarded after only two years' study to be followed by a further two years by those who sought a higher qualification – this obviously closely follow-ing the new pattern in French universities. All these matters, of course, focussed attention on the colleges of education as never before, and they were soon seen to be anachronistic in several ways: they were often far too paternalistic towards their students; students had far too little say in the management of their own affairs – and they contrasted their position with that of their fellow undergraduate students; there were too few innovative courses on offer, and little (if any) student consultation on academic and professional issues which seriously concerned students. All these points were highlighted by student unrest everywhere in the mid-sixties which culminated in the dramatic 1968 confrontations in France in particular. Much more important still, however, was the artificial situation in which the college of education student was placed in contrast with students training either at a university or a polytechnic or even at one of the four colleges specialising in training teachers of technical subjects: he was being trained in total isolation with little if any chance of either sharing the studies or even of mixing with students preparing for a totally different career and future. This was a situation which could not be allowed to continue given the necessity for increasing teacher involvement with the social realities of the times.

Thus teacher training was at last seen to be in need of total reform and Lord James was given the task of instituting an inquiry into teacher training generally and of making recommendations for change. *Teacher Education and Training*, as the James Report was called, was published in 1972, was eagerly and passionately debated, and resulted in swift publication of a government White Paper, *Education: a Framework for Expansion*, which detailed what official policy was now to be. Advantage was first of all taken of the fact that implementation of change should in practice coincide with reorganisation of local authorities into larger units, and area training organisations were correspondingly re-structured to develop in effect into regional committees. No longer would a group of colleges of education depend upon a "parent" university but the university's own function as an institute or school of education would be merged with that of the greater regional committee charged specifically with the task of co-ordinating the education and training of all teachers within its area and being responsible to the Secretary of State, himself guided by an Advisory Committee on the Supply and Training of Teachers. This necessary attenuation of college–university connections patiently forged over the years is already regretted in many quarters.

As for the colleges themselves, they also have undergone an attenuation and a transformation. Certain colleges, usually considered too small to be viable in the new set-up, have been instructed to close. Others have been allowed to merge, as circumstances warranted or permitted, with a college of further education. And the new resultant institutions have been firmly designated as forming part of tertiary education and re-named liberal arts colleges. Admission to these new institutions will be on a par with that to the universities (two or more "A" level qualifications obtained at about age 18) and they are charged with offering a two-year course of academic studies leading to the award of a Diploma of Higher Education. The possessor of this award may then do one of three things: either he may leave and seek employment, or he may convert his diploma into a higher degree or degrees, or he may decide to teach. If he chooses teaching as a career he may add a third year to obtain an *ordinary* B.Ed. degree, and still a fourth year to convert this into an *honours* B.Ed. It is naturally hoped that the universities will also decide to run parallel identical courses.

Like the polytechnics, however, these new institutions will not be allowed to award their own degrees. They may either continue their previous association with a given university to secure the award or they may have their courses validated by the National Council for Academic Awards – a practice begun earlier by some of the former colleges of education. A further possibility is for a college to seek integration proper within a university or even, exceptionally, to become itself the nucleus for a new university.

Just as this new degree structure echoes French reforms in tertiary education, so does the subsequent care of the teacher approximate to what has long been German practice. A newly qualified teacher is now obliged to follow an "induction" year of training on the job under the close supervision of competent tutors. He must be released for not less than one-fifth of that year to follow in-service training and will have his teaching load proportionately lightened. Needless to say, given the present economic climate, the shortage of teachers and the clear lack of suitably qualified mentors for the newly fledged teacher, this requirement is probably not going to be implemented fully for some time to come. The same will also apply, at least in the immediate future, for a final requirement that all teachers shall be released every seven years for one term of further study and training. In-service training, of course, as we have already seen, has for years been most competently provided on a voluntary basis for all teachers who sought it through the various university institutes of education, and local education authorities have been generous in giving teachers time off and paying either their full expenses or at least their immediate out-of-pocket expenses for travel and the like. Similarly, it has to be remembered that teachers constitute about one-third of the total enrolment of students in the Open University. They can obtain the B.Ed. there, and special courses are arranged for them particularly in the fields of educational psychology, curriculum development and school organisation.

CHAPTER 9

Dilemma in the Universities

1

By time-honoured tradition the universities of Western Europe have acquired to themselves common qualities which clearly distinguish them from all other social and educational institutions. They have become places where highly qualified people pursuing disciplines of their own choosing can follow lines of inquiry entirely directed by themselves (either individually or collectively) with no fear of outside interference of any kind on either ideological or practical grounds; and to this they have added the freedom to teach what they will as they will to all seeking to participate in a common concern to be constantly extending the frontiers of knowledge. They have come to regard their role as that of fulfilling four major objectives: that of conserving the great bulk of established and proven knowledge passed on to us from former ages and civilisations; that of interpreting this knowledge and its inherent values in terms of the contemporary world; that of initiating their students into the processes involved in such activities, of disciplining their minds properly to cope, and of recruiting the most able and promising to stay within the fold; that of carrying on the vital task of research into new spheres of knowledge.

In pursuance of this role they have found that their cherished twin freedoms of inquiry and teaching are best secured by faculty self-rule, particularly in matters concerning appointments, curricula, and the maintenance of academic standards, and they have come to consider their student body as a privileged class whose minds are to be stretched and developed to the full by practising those disciplines they themselves have voluntarily chosen for study. It was emphatically not the university's business to train any particular student for a particular job — that was the specific role of other forms of tertiary education — but rather to isolate him for a given period of time from any kind of major involvement with the real world outside, the better to prepare him objectively to seek the kind of involvement he would eventually find most congenial. This intrinsic dualism of function of the university has repeatedly led to certain disconcerting contradictions. By the very nature of its commitments it has had to be both forward-looking and backward-looking. It seeks to inculcate an adherence to and a proper respect for the received traditions of the past, whilst on the other hand it has to be innovative in its furtherance of scientific and social progress. It has tended to be paternalistic in outlook yet emancipatory. It has also had to seek solutions to tensions created by its determination to maintain its own freedom and approach when faced with the demands and increasing expectations of the state and the influences and changing outlook of society as a whole. Receipt of state funds (and in increasing amounts) carries with it an implied allegiance to the state, but to serve it *as best the university thinks fit*, still brooking no direct state interference. Innovation has finally compelled it to become involved with immediate economic and social problems and to undertake specific commitments towards their solution. And it has had to yield to increasing social pressures for more people to be educated to the highest possible levels.

All this was slowly beginning to take shape in the period between the two wars, but up until 1945 it went almost unnoticed and universities everywhere (except, of course, in Nazi Germany and Fascist Italy) were still accepted in terms of their own evaluation and left to get on with their self-imposed tasks of teaching, training and research as they best knew how. Up until 1945 a university education was still regarded as something special, a peculiar reward available only to the brightest or the most wealthy, and students were looked upon as a race apart, an élite group comfortably closeted in an academic playpen at the edge of the real world. The supreme authority of the academic staff was never challenged since those who wanted to get on in life and enjoy the material prosperity and social prestige which would later accrue from possessing a degree need only accept, digest and reproduce under examination all they were told or set to read. The general public still viewed the university with its ivory-tower exclusiveness as a sort of finishing school and the university responded to this image of itself.

2

In the immediate post-1945 period there came a noticeable increase in student numbers at universities mainly due to the process of demobilisation of men and women from the fighting forces who either had earlier intended to go to university or even who had had their university studies interrupted by the war years. In addition, however, many others who would not earlier have done so were now enabled to profit from a university education both by granting them special conditions for entry and by making appropriate financial arrangements for their support whilst studying. Expansion continued slowly from this point onwards, the Continental universities in general responding more slowly than their English counterparts, and the great "boom" came in the 1960s, to culminate (as we have already noticed) in a whole range of student protests (fiercest in France and Western Germany) which, to the consternation of bewildered professors and administrators, often received tacit if not overt support from junior members of the teaching staff. It has been estimated that students nowadays comprise between 10 per cent and 30 per cent of their age group generally, and figures for Great Britain alone show that, whereas in 1960 only 4 per cent of the age group attended university, this figure had risen to between 16 and 20 per cent by 1974.

This significant increase in the number of students seeking a university education was not generally accompanied by a corresponding level of governmental expenditure on education, particularly since the universities themselves were initially confident that they could absorb all who came along. Limits, however, were reached all too soon. The ratio of students to teachers worsened beyond manageable proportions and brought with it physical overcrowding of students in university and college buildings which in turn led to a general worsening of the material conditions of student existence. German universities were soon forced to introduce a *numerus clausus* to limit the number of students attending a particular university — a move bitterly attacked as an infringement of the liberty and rights of any holder of the *Abitur* to attend a university if he so wished — and West Germany along with Great Britain sought to ease the situation both by upgrading other higher education institutions to university status as well as by building many new universities. Other countries found themselves having to adopt similar measures, but France "dragged her feet" until 1960 and did not even then seem fully to grasp the immensity of the problem which confronted her.

The continued rise in student numbers, of course, stemmed from rapidly changing post-war conditions and the tremendous advances since made in science and technology which have obliged all industrial nations to change from being "cosy" simple bureaucratic democracies into high-powered and highly efficient technocratic ones. Inescapably the primary role of higher education became that of training the mass of technicians and manipulators required by such an advanced technocratic society for its continued development and prosperity. Industry, government and education had together somehow to meet the demand for highly trained and intellectually skilled manpower and management, and for the first time in its history Western Europe began experiencing the need for a mass *intellectual* labour force. Science-based industry was leading to a science-based society, and this was not lost on the mass of the people who, beginning to realise the need for new skills and new opportunities both for themselves and for their children, brought pressure to bear on their respective governments to provide more and better education. The consequent reforms in secondary education led to a greater demand for higher education which, previously seen and accepted as the privilege of a select few, was now insisted upon as a right for the many who might profit. And this gradual transition from an élite to a "mass" higher education was also seen as a further and logical step towards realising the ideal of equality of opportunity, students being now conditioned to think of a university education as mandatory before going out into the world of work. Higher education was no longer to be regarded as a privilege but as the natural right of all young persons.

Never before in their long history had the universities been looked upon as devices for establishing equality of status and least of all as career-orientated institutions, and their dilemma was not eased by having to cope with an impossibly large increase in student numbers housed in by now inadequate buildings. Recruitment of adequately trained additional staff was another problem. Initially this situation was coped with by recruitment of outstanding teachers from the secondary schools, but this move simply weakened the quality of education given in the specialist upper forms of secondary schools (particularly in the fields of science and mathematics) and led to the need for some kind of remedial teaching once the student was in the university, or at the very least to some lowering of standards for admission to university for such science students. Not surprisingly the number of potential science students began to diminish and increasing numbers of undergraduates opted instead for courses which led to manipulative and managerial positions and began to demand as a right that appropriate courses be devised for them. This in turn led to further recruitment of teaching staff to supply the courses, and it was this staff (usually a younger element itself schooled and conditioned along lines not dissimilar from those followed by the students they were to teach), who, to the consternation of their elders and the more traditional members of the teaching corpus, rallied to the support of students who clamoured for administrative and teaching reform.

It had to be recognised that an increasing number of students had no strong intellectual interests in the traditional sense and that the transition from élite to mass higher education brought with it a demand that the universities become less remote, less idealistic, and more practical in their approach. Relevant training was what counted, training for administrative, professional and quasi-professional occupations, but also training in the social sciences which would encourage and lead the student to understand and participate in the apparatus of social control and government at various levels, and not least in his own immediate environment at the university level. Work and study must be brought together and the university must abandon its ivory-tower approach and reach out into the world of real life and real-life situations. Purely technological institutions have, by their very nature and by the inception of sandwich courses of various kinds, in some measure already achieved this, and steps taken by West Germany to institute a comprehensive university are seen as a move in the right direction.

It should finally be noted that the continued process of expansion of the universities has inescapably brought not only more and more investment of government funds but also closer links with industry and important business concerns who, along with the state, have an increasing vested interest in university development where a great deal of research vital to industry and commerce must take place. Higher education has thus become the "knowledge industry" accounting for a high proportion of the country's gross national product. And so wide have the universities' commitments grown that they are beginning to merit the title of "multi-universities", an appellation already in principle conceded to a growing number. In short, the university, once regarded as an Elysian field devoted to the production of the "whole man" of humane learning has become the knowledge factory indispensable to the national economy.

Never before has so much been demanded of the universities and never before have they been under such scrutiny nor, largely due to the tensions created between faculty and students, had so much often unfavourable publicity. Perhaps in the long run this will prove to have been beneficial for all concerned. Perhaps the high prestige of university teachers, the Olympian aloofness of the professoriat, their supreme confidence in themselves, in their intellectual ability and in their professed subjects needed challenging, and there was certainly no body better placed and better qualified to do this than the student body. Their whole training consists of challenging received assumptions and exposing fallacies. In various ways and guises they have done this throughout the centuries. The turbulent and precocious Peter Abelard awoke the mediaeval university from *its* slumbers. The more cautious and timorous Erasmus had his effect through his writings. The firebrand Shelley made his own particular and (for him) valid point. What is new today is that it is a highly articulate mass student movement (sometimes inescapably going to extremes to make its point) urging the increased responsibility the universities must show towards society, insisting that the only way to preserve our much-cherished democracy in the present world situation is first to establish that democracy in our own lives or at least to attempt to run our society on free democratic principles. The argument further runs that the new democratic university of the future must surrender its treasured academic freedom to make way for greater participation in the construction of society as a whole. It will have to face up to the real difficulties of involvement in the progress of mankind in this day and age. It must keep alive the democratic spirit of the young who may one day manage to save society from the extreme depersonalisation of advanced capitalism and finally create a real society of vitally minded and self-organising individuals. It is a noble ideal, but in proportion as at least some aspects of it come to be realised it will be important to ensure that the "new" universities vigilantly safeguard their reputation for honesty and disinterestedness and retain and strengthen their traditional academic concerns. Ultimately they must constitute the essential stabilising element.

3

Scandinavian countries in general still represent an almost pure example of the continential European tradition in higher education, the universities basing their organisation on early nineteenth-century German ideas (stemming from Humboldt) that they should be primarily concerned with the unhampered pursuit of pure knowledge, that teaching and research should be closely co-ordinated, that they should be academically self-governing, and that they should hold apart from other tertiary forms of education giving strictly professional instruction. Throughout the nineteenth and well into the twentieth century they were able to remain as calm havens of scholarship and research, but the aftermath of the Second World War has brought them innumerable problems all hinging on an unprecedented rise in student numbers. Thus, whilst Denmark little less than a century ago had about 1000 students, this number had risen to 21,000 in the 1960s; corresponding figures for Norway are 500 and 18,700 (of whom some 3500 were studying abroad); and Sweden, rising from barely 2000 undergraduates to 45,000, had already multiplied its intake twenty-two times! Each of the countries has in turn had to appoint various commissions to consider problems posed, Sweden being first off the mark in 1955 and following this up with further recommendations in 1959, 1963 and 1973. Norway reported in 1961 and 1964. Denmark followed a preliminary series of recommendations in 1962 with a new law on university government in 1970 and a new act in 1973.

Today, Denmark has well over 55,000 students enrolled in institutions of higher education (almost 13 per cent of the age group) of whom 39,000 are in attendance at the three existing universities of Copenhagen (1479), Aarhus(1929) and Odense (1964). The remainder are catered for in thirteen "colleges" specialising in engineering, pharmacy, dentistry, architecture, verterinary studies, business administration and so on, which, though not having the status of universities as such, are in effect more selective in their student intake than the universities. The universities are self-governing (though falling under the direction of the Ministry of Education) and "free" in that anyone holding the *studentereksamen* or its recognised equivalent has the right to attend and is left free to decide what, how, and for how long he will study; lectures are open to all, there are no structured courses, no regular assessment, no advice on progress, and drop-out rates are accordingly high averaging around 60 per cent. In practice courses can last from five to eight years and are controlled by an intermediate and a final examination, written and oral, and both taken when the student himself feels he is ready. Successful students in the arts and science faculties receive the title of *magister* and those in law, medicine and theology that of "candidate". Postgraduate doctoral awards are rare, highly esteemed, and are granted on successful public defence of a thesis which can take up to fifteen years to complete.

Colleges on the other hand, besides being more rigorous in their entry requirements, have structured courses to be completed in three or four years, make many of these courses compulsory, and in consequence have a much lower rate of drop-out. Like the universities they have strong research interests, but unlike them they limit their intake each year to the most promising students for their various specialities usually basing their selection on a close study of a student's performance in relevant subjects at the *studentereksamen*. They are not free to develop as they will but come under the control of an appropriate government department. The unprecedented demand which came for higher education in the 1960s, mainly occasioned by growing all-round economic prosperity and the opportunities for increasing governmental aid to students, affected both colleges and universities alike, which, to avoid impossible overcrowding, had to open new establishments. A new engineering college opened in Copenhagen in 1957 and a further one in Aalborg in 1965; Aarhus acquired a new dental college in 1958 and an architectural one in 1965; and an entirely new university, opened in Odense in 1966 for a limited number of students, had passed the 3000 mark some seven years later. Indeed, in the decade 1960–70 the numbers of university students rose from 9100 to more than 35,000, the colleges doubling their intake from 5000; and whereas only 4 per cent of 19-year-olds were entering university in 1960 and 2 per cent the colleges, these figures had risen to 11 per cent and 3 per cent respectively ten years later, the significantly higher figure for the universities being due to students, frustrated at being unable to enter a college of their choice, exerting their right to attend the university as a second best.

The government came to the rescue of the universities in 1970 by authorising the creation of a new type of institution, a "university centre", which has sought to placate mounting dissatisfaction with the defects of the traditional university system and also to combine the kind of education traditionally given in colleges *and* universities. The prerogatives of the universities, however, are still strictly safeguarded in that none of these centres will offer all the traditional university programmes (e.g. *not* medicine). A first centre was opened in Roskilde in 1972. A second followed in Aalberg in 1974, and a third is to open in Esbjerg-Ribe. Student intake is democratised by accepting a variety of qualifications. The old inflexible division between subjects is broken down by offering a two-year general basic course to be followed by three years of specialisation.

As the universities grew in size unrest increased among the non-professorial staff who by the 1960s found themselves in a ratio of 4 to 1 as regards chair holders yet having less say in the direction of university affairs than did the student body through its students' council. An impossible situation in Copenhagen, where 1500 students were trying to read psychology (Copenhagen being the only university where this could properly be done) under the direction of only three professors and a handful of teachers, led to a sit-in in April 1968; students and junior staff together pressed for an end to the monopolistic and dictatorial control of all matters by the professorial staff; some ugly scenes and bitter acrimony followed; and finally the government had to pass legislation in 1970 and again in 1973. Briefly, the present situation is that the kind of "integration" the non-professorial staff sought has been achieved. All teaching staff are regarded as equal and the top posts of president and vice-president can be filled up by any full-time teacher. Members of the senate are to be elected by all teaching staff, by technical and administrative personnel, and by students, and teaching representation shall amount to no more than two-thirds. All university committees must be made up of between one-third and one-half of student delegates, the remainder representing the staff, again regardless of rank. Full-time teaching staff must devote 45 per cent of their time to teaching, 40 per cent of time only to research (it was formerly 45 per cent), and the rest to administration.

Finally, as part of the structural change a Directorate for Higher Education (DVU) is established which now brings all the colleges within these general regulations since all budgeting for all higher education will be its responsibility, and it will be generally responsible for all matters pertaining to discipline, will oversee the organisation of major subject areas through appointed advisory boards, and will act as a general watch-dog to see that all runs as smoothly as possible. It is all very heady and exciting, but in reality, though this reform goes much further than in most other countries, it still satisfies neither conservative academic opinion nor radical student thinking. Increased teaching loads have already had their effect on research, and the complicated new organisational structure compels scholars to spend much more than the allotted time on administration (15 per cent). It is also held that student participation in study boards has led to too much freedom in curriculum planning with a consequent deterioration in quality of work achieved. Examining also has suffered in that the traditional methods have been replaced by unsupervised "work-at-home" examinations in self-chosen subjects and with the added possibility of submitting jointly prepared exercises. Student and technical–administrative staff representation on boards responsible for recruiting new teaching staff is equally considered not necessarily to be in the best interests of the universities or colleges as a whole.

Norway

Until 1948 when the University of Bergen was opened, Norway had made do with one university, that of Oslo which was founded in 1811. In the immediate post-war years enrolment at the tertiary levels generally was slow, and even between 1950 and 1960 student numbers only increased from 7500 to 9200. But then over the next nine years there came a dramatic rise to around 47,000! Fortunately, a very comprehensive *Report on the Expansion of the Universities and University Institutions* had been published in 1961 and the findings in this document were followed up by another team in 1964 which began by immediately recommending that the State Institute of Technology and the State College for Teachers, both at Trondheim, should merge to form the University of Trondheim, which officially came into existence in 1968. Later planning has led to the creation of the University of Tromsø, opened in 1972 with 300 students but hoping to increase within the decade to some 3000 students and specifically designed to encourage both academics and students to stay in the north and take an interest in that part of their country. To these four universities must be added seven state colleges for athletics, agriculture, business administration, architecture, fisheries, music and veterinary culture, business administration, architecture, fisheries, music and veterinary studies, and also the independent theological college in Oslo. No instruction fees are charged. Ninety-nine per cent of the financing comes directly from the state, the remaining 1 per cent being collected from examination and laboratory fees. Some 30,000 of the 47,000 students already noted as being in higher education are in the universities.

For obvious historical reasons the overall running of the university in Norway is not dissimilar from that in Denmark, and we need here only note that each university is maintained on a faculty basis, Oslo having seven faculties, Bergen five, Trondheim ten (because of its technological sides), and Trømso aiming at six. Each university is governed by its own senate and enjoys considerable autonomy. The senate is composed of deans elected by their respective faculties, an elected representative of the non-professorial staff and one from the student body. It is presided over by a rector and vice-rector chosen at a full meeting of all professors, and all seats on senate are renewable every three years. Each faculty has its own faculty board presided over by its elected dean and composed of all titular professors and senior lecturers, representatives of junior staff and also of the student body. Entrance to either a university or state college is based on the *examen artium* (or its equivalent in a commercial *gymnasium*) but is *not* automatic: certain faculties insist on a prospective student having followed certain specified courses with outstanding success in preparing for his *examen artium*; others impose a *numerus clausus*. The result is that competition for places is intense, but even then the drop-out rate can be as high as 50 per cent. As in Denmark, many start their studies, then leave perhaps to go to work, then return, and finally present themselves for examination when they feel they are ready.

Degree awards in all faculties are generally speaking at two levels: that of *candidatus* and that of *magister*, and the minimum period required for study is usually five or six years — and up to eight years for medicine. Standards throughout remain high. Research facilities are excellent, many of the teaching staff enjoying a world-wide reputation, and (again as in Denmark) preparation for a doctorate is a long and gruelling exercise. There have (to date) been no marked student disturbances but dissatisfaction with overcrowding in often cramped and occasionally impossible conditions is rife.

Sweden

All higher education in Sweden now comes under the aegis of the Office of the Chancellor of Swedish Universities – a governing body of ten members appointed by the Crown which in effect sees to it that university education is centralised in the same way as school education and that degree courses are largely uniform throughout the country. There are now six universities, of which the two most ancient, Uppsala (1477) and Lund (1668) which are sited in provincial cities, long enjoyed a reputation in their own country parallel to that of Oxford or Cambridge. The universities of Stockholm and Gothenburg were originally private establishments called "higher schools" and were so founded in 1878 and 1891. The state decided in 1949 first to finance them and finally to take them over and then turn them into universities – Gothenburg in 1954 and Stockholm in 1960. A new university was opened at Umeå in 1964 to cater for students in the northern half of the country, and Linköping has only just received university status and in consequence has the smallest population of just over 3000. In addition there are three small branch universities at Örebro, Växjö and Karlstad which are affiliated respectively to Uppsala, Lund and Gothenburg, which concentrate on the humanities and the social sciences, and which teach only up to first degree level. They average about 1500 students each. Finally, the Caroline Institute of Technology in Stockholm and the Chalmers Technical Institute in Gothenburg (specialising in engineering and technology) have been accorded full university status and between them account for some 12,000 students. Total student numbers for 1973 amounted to some 116,000 with a teaching staff of just over 8000.

The imposition of a *numerus clausus* restricts entry to certain faculties (notably medicine, dentistry, pharmacy, engineering and technology), but elsewhere entry is generally unrestricted. Unrestricted faculties also admit mature students of any age provided they can produce evidence of having had a secondary education, of possessing adequate competence in Swedish and English, and of having had a minimum of five years' certified job experience. These facilities have of recent years produced a tendency for the number of full-time students in the 18–24 age range to decrease with a corresponding increase in the age range 25–47. At the new University of Linköping fully 80 per cent of the annual intake consists at present of part-time students.

A first degree will, in normal conditions, take three years and is now built up on a credit-point system at a uniform rate of 40 points per annum. It is not uncommon, however, for a student to earn so many points, go out to work and then return (at intervals if he so wishes) to increase his points total. For the award of a doctorate a candidate usually pursues up to four years of postgraduate studies allied to practical research experience and he can qualify for a special research stipend from the appropriate national research council, usually amounting to over £1000 per annum, to maintain himself over this period. Two degrees, intermediate between a first degree and a doctorate, have now been abolished. They were the *filosofie licentiat* (roughly corresponding to an English master's degree) and the *filosofie magister* which, until 1970, was taken mostly but not exclusively by students seeking to become graduate teachers in the upper forms of the school system. Two more specialised degrees at these levels in political science and economics and in political science and law have also disappeared. It should also be noted that all basic research programmes are carried out in the universities or in partnership with them.

It can with some truth be claimed that the decline of university autonomy in relation to government authorities as well as to students has proceeded more rapidly in Sweden than elsewhere, and there are several important causes for this. Firstly, Sweden has developed into a welfare state based on syndicalism; all employees belong to an appropriate trade union and the student body itself is no exception. Students have an important role to play at every level of university life and for years have taken their role seriously and responsibly. They have constantly made suggestions for the organisation and improvement of teaching. They have equally had a real concern for the social well-being of the student body, and it is this side perhaps which has attracted most attention from abroad in terms of the excellent student halls of residence which have been built and subsidised by the state but maintained directly by the student associations who also take it upon themselves to man them and turn them into hotels to catch the summer holiday trade.

A second cause stems from the investigations of a university committee in 1955 which inquired into the reasons why so many students were failing to satisfactorily complete their courses — as many as 30 per cent in the natural sciences, and 40 per cent in the humanities. Their recommendations included making university studies free of cost from 1958 (apart from a compulsory students' union subscription— and also led to the much-advertised loan scheme (first started in 1950) being first modified in 1961 and then finally abandoned to give each student a basic "salary". And this, in effect has brought increased state concern with intimate university matters which (as we have already noted) culminated in the creation of a centralised governing body for all universities. Such total financial dependence on governmental authorities in the long run stifles individual initiative, kills positive identification of former students with their own individual university, and breeds a kind of grey uniformity of outlook. It should further be noted that the general public has never considered its "ivory-tower" institutions as capable of contributing in themselves to help the country keep abreast of international progress, and as a result too few professors have ever been drawn into decision-making of any importance concerning Sweden's general welfare. Indeed, when they have gone into politics at all it has usually been in association with right-wing and liberal groups who for decades have been in permanent opposition.

As we have already observed, Swedish universities remained very small establishments until well into the 1950s. As elsewhere in Scandinavia there was only one professor per department and a department could consist of as little as three or four teaching staff. When in the late 1950s the government upheld the tradition of unrestricted faculties, departments in such faculties were swamped. The professor was left to take care of graduate students only — and to cope with an increasing burden of administration — and extra staff was recruited at the lecturer level to deal with basic undergraduate courses, given a teaching load too heavy to allow of any time for research, and compelled to give courses so broad that any real treatment in depth became well-nigh impossible. The quality of teaching suffered severely. Staff and students were highly discontented. Mutual lack of confidence increased between staff and government. And when it became clear that, thanks to earlier government policy of seeking political advantage by swelling numbers in unrestricted faculties at no really prohibitive cost (which would not have been the case had they done the same for medicine, the sciences and engineering), increasing numbers of graduates were going to find it virtually impossible to secure a suitable job, thoughts of insurrection were already being aired.

The government reacted in what (seen now in retrospect) was an ill-advised way. Realising that something must be wrong when still so many students were dropping out before completing their studies, they introduced a tightening-up measure which aimed at both cutting down the time to be allowed for completing a first degree course and also at expelling students whose work was proving consistently unsatisfactory. This not only interfered with the quality of work which could be expected to be achieved, thus alienating faculty members, but it also was seen as a blow at student freedoms, and particularly so when the proposed reform tried to limit possibilities to combine courses in favour of pre-determined lines of study designed to make university courses on offer more occupationally relevant. Faculty protestation was immediately reinforced by determined student opposition, the more militant amongst whom denounced their own representatives on university governing boards as a band of self-seekers and self-promoters only too anxious to collaborate with government bureaucracy. May 1968 saw the student body triumphant in that the plans had to be so watered down as to become in practice meaningless.

In the spring of 1969 a new system was introduced broadly in line with student demands. An arrangement dating from 1964 whereby the departmental head would in future not necessarily be the titular professor but a carefully chosen "prefect" who must consult with a departmental council comprising *all* teachers and two student representatives was scrapped. Departmental councils must in future consist of four or five representatives freely elected by the teaching staff and a similar number elected by the student body, the prefect's role being reduced to that of ensuring that his council's recommendations were fully carried out. It was a policy of expediency to give the government time to plan a more comprehensive reform, but by and large, though with misgivings on all sides, it has been made to work.

Meantime, in the spring of 1973 a commission appointed to recommend on the total restructuring of post-secondary education presented its long-awaited report now referred to as U68. Its main proposal aims at bringing the universities into a common administrative system with all post-secondary establishments. To this end Sweden is now to be divided into nineteen "higher education areas" each run by a board of higher education appointed by the government. A majority of these board members must be "representatives of public interests" (i.e. politicians, and representatives of trade unions and business concerns), and whilst the faculties of a university in a given educational area will still retain their research and research training interests these will be subject to general board approval. Programme committees will also advise the universities to ensure that the education generally offered has relevance, and these programme committees will again consist in part of "persons taken from occupational life". The six existing universities will not be allowed to expand their student numbers from their present size, thus allowing for available resources to be channelled to higher education in a number of designated cities some of which are least already have university branches for undergraduate education.

Of course, all now needs working out in detail. A number of contradictory statements have to be reconciled, loopholes plugged, and ambiguities clarified. What is clear is that this is a sincere attempt fully to democratise higher education in line with education at the lower levels. It seeks to overcome the irrational differences in prestige value of the various kinds of higher education even if it involves dissolving the traditional independence of the universities. Why should a university, totally financed by taxpayers, exist as a kind of separate republic to be run by professors in quasi-total isolation from society at large? So runs the argument. What about academic freedom which has for so long played so vital a part in keeping democracy alive and in constantly furthering the interests of democracy, runs the counter-argument. What is certain is that the Swedish experience in education at all levels will continue to be closely scrutinised from outside for some time to come as various other Western European nations grapple with their own not dissimilar problems whilst seeking to maintain and extend what they consider to be basic to a prolongation of their own democratic way of life into the next century.

4

Belgium

Whilst some ten years ago Belgium had only four universities — the two state universities at Ghent (for Dutch-speakers) and at Liège (French), and the two "free" universities (the Catholic University of Louvain and the Free University of Brussels) — there are now eight. An extra university has been created at Antwerp (based on the former Colonial University) for

Dutch speakers, and this has been paralleled by turning former higher institutions in Mons into a French-speaking university there. Both of these are state institutions. The Linguistic rift in the country which reached a peak of intensity and student insurrection in 1967/8 led to the "creation" of two further free universities in that Louvain has now split into the *Katholicke Universiteit te Leuven* (which remains in Louvain) and the *Université Catholique de Louvain* which has been obliged to build for itself an entirely new complex called Louvain-la-Neuve at Ottignies in the French-speaking part of Belgium; similarly the University of Brussels, which until this date continued amicably to give parallel courses in Dutch and French, had to separate itself into the *Université Libre de Bruxelles* (ULB) and the *Vrije Universiteit Brussel* (VUB). There are in addition a number of university centres situated at Brussels, Gembloux and Namur which could later develop into full-scale universities, and also a special centre for postgraduate studies in Hasselt. The University of Louvain is the most prestigious if only for its worldwide reputation for theological studies, and it was founded by Papal Bull as early as 1425, brutally suppressed by a French administrative decree in 1797, and then re-opened after the gaining of Belgian independence in 1834. The same year saw the creation of the Free University of Brussels as a challenge to the Catholic pretensions of Louvain, and the state universities of Ghent and Liège were opened one year later. Louvain has always restricted entry (except for foreign students) to practising Catholics. Brussels has always worked on the principle of "free" admission and has increasingly attracted to itself, particularly in the last decades, Catholic students who sought the kind of training it had to offer. The two state universities (now four) have always had a fair mixture of Catholics and non-Catholics of both students and teaching staff.

In the case of the "free" universities, admission requirements and the drawing up of syllabuses etc. are entirely their responsibility; all state universities are controlled in these matters by government regulations. Besides differing in their administrative organisation, the "free" universities also differed in the amount of funds they received from the state, but by a law of July 1971 each university now receives the same amount per capita — and this again exacerbates the linguistic problem in that Flemings outnumber the Walloons on a 56/44 ratio and do all they can from their present position of political and economic strength to try to have funds available allocated in the same proportion. University education is not free, and the same law raised registration fees in all universities from 2000 to 5000 Belgian francs per annum (plus an extra 1000 francs for examination fees) except, of course, for students on scholarship grants who today number over one-third of the total student population. This move has caused widespread protest but so far the government has stood firm.

In 1939 student numbers only reached some 10,000, but by 1960 this number had been raised to 30,000 to go on to more than double itself over the next decade to its present level of over 75,000. A sizable proportion of these are, however, foreign students whose numbers have risen dramatically from a mere 3000 in 1962 to 10,000 for the academic year 1972/3. This spectacular rise is in the main due to the fact that no *numerus clausus* exists, except in applied sciences, in any Belgian university, and Belgium thus becomes a haven for students from neighbouring countries (especially German medical students) who have been affected by the application of a *numerus clausus* in their own universities. Fully two-thirds of the total student body is at present in attendance at one or other of the "free" universities which have acquired for themselves a greater prestige than their state counterparts. Indeed, students at state universities will normally not be fervent Catholics nor will they be attracted by the humanistic climate of Brussels; very generally speaking they can be classified as relatively poor students who see no point in incurring unnecessary expense involved in having to live in lodgings or university accommodation away from home when they have a perfectly satisfactory university on the doorstep. They are, however, and as is only to be expected, fervently French or Flemish in their aspirations and can get suitably politically heated as occasion warrants.

Though there are, of course, two main national student organisations – one for Flemings and one for Walloons – the real life of students tends to centre on the faculty to which they belong. Each faculty in each university has its own descriptive and highly coloured headgear and students proudly wear these caps as they go about their general everyday life. Faculty traditions and loyalties are strong, and members of the teaching staff associate themselves with the students of their faculties in several ways, social and academic. Old students' associations are equally strong and they rally round their particular university and particular faculty to see that traditions are maintained, that the professional interests of present students are safeguarded, that they secure employment which is their due, and that no student suffers for any reason unnecessary pecuniary hardship. In a variety of ways, therefore, students are called upon to share in the actual organisation of their university and in the application of social and cultural measures which affect them, and this is carried down to faculty level where pure academic matters are discussed with the staff concerned. On a more mundane level, students' organisations collaborate with university authorities to run students' restaurants and social clubs, whilst halls of residence, though provided by the university, work in close liaison with students to keep costs at a minimum. The total approach is "bourgeois" in the best sense of the word, the universities being geared to fit in with the bourgeois aspirations of the Belgians as a whole — aspirations which encourage all with proven ability to join the bourgeoisie. Thus, Belgium has at least 23 per cent of working-class students following some form of higher education (though only 11 per cent in the universities proper) and so ties with Norway to take second place to the USA and the United Kingdom who each average about 27 per cent. The relatively low proportion of working-class students in universities is primarily due to the excellent provision of technical and commercial education which we have discussed in an earlier chapter, there being currently some 28,000 such students enrolled in various kinds of non-university higher education as opposed to a mere 8000 for the year 1954/5.

For admission to a university a student must have passed the *examen de maturité*, and admission to a particular faculty will then turn on the combination of subjects he studied at school. The Greek/Latin option is necessary for students entering the Faculty of Law or that of Philosophy and Letters; students in medicine, pharmacy or dentistry will have taken either the Latin/Greek, the Latin/mathematics, or the Latin/science option; the Latin/mathematics or scientific A or B options admit to courses in mathematics or pure science; a student wishing to read applied sciences may have prepared himself in any of these options (usually not Latin/Greek) but, as we have already noted, a *numerus clausus* operates here and an intending student must prepare for and submit himself for a special entrance examination.

In most cases the lowest qualification, the *candidature* (which carries no weight outside the university) is obtained after two to three years' study and lays the foundation for the first degree, the *licence*. This requires a further two to three years' study of a specialised nature built on the foundation course and entails the submission of a thesis. The course in medicine consists of two years' *candidature*, three further years to the *licence*, and a minimum of a further two years to the *doctorat*. The *licence* in pharmacy or the applied sciences is obtained after a minimum of five years' study. In all subjects but medicine the *doctorat* (by thesis) may be taken one full year after completion of the *licence*. Students who intend to take up university teaching (or its recognised equivalent) must hold the *doctorat* and spend at least a further two years working for the higher *agrégation*. This consists of the submission of a thesis which must make a definite contribution to the advancement of knowledge in the student's specialist field, and proven ability (via teaching exercises and a tested lecture) to be able to communicate with students.

The academic year divides itself into two semesters: October to February, and February to May. Attendance at lectures, seminars and practical work is necessary to obtain the permit to sit examinations which are held annually. A second round of examinations is held for those who fail at the first attempt, a student being allowed only one re-sit (or two if he has changed courses). Examinations are both written and oral, the amount of emphasis given to either being dependent on the subjects studied. Because of the high number of school leavers who are successful at the *maturité* examination (over 90 per cent) first-year courses at all universities are often hopelessly overcrowded, but by the same token there is then a disquieting high drop-out rate of around 60 per cent. Comparatively few students who survive the *candidature* fail to obtain a *licence*, success figures being as high as 85 per cent in arts subjects and over 90 per cent in various science courses. Should a student be supported at the university by state grants or scholarships then failure at any of the annual examinations automatically leads to suspension of the award.

The only really violent student protests have centred (as we have seen) on the linguistic question and led to the splitting of the two "free" universities in 1969. This does not mean, however, that there are no reasons for disquiet manifesting itself amongst staff and students. Flemish–Walloon controversies still smoulder on and to these can be added genuine anxiety firstly about the rapid and unprecedented increase in student population which has been estimated to reach 125,000 in the 1980s.

With this bulge goes the total inadequacy of present university buildings to cope and inadequacy of government grants to make for real expansion — though 35 milliard francs have already been allocated for expansion in the 1970s. Students are particularly anxious about staff—student ratios (at present 11.3) and can see them worsening to approach the catastrophic level of France (23). University administrators are themselves worried on two counts: first of all there has been a disproportionate rise in numbers opting for courses in the social and economic sciences, due in the main to the relatively recent creation of an economics section in the upper secondary school and attracting large numbers of girls besides a far from negligible group of "undesirables" who consider such subjects soft options to enable them to use the university as a kind of "finishing" school; secondly and more importantly, that too few students in both pure and applied sciences are willing to do research (jobs come too easily) and so provide the universities with all the extra teaching staff they need to cope with the expanding numbers. Nor is this situation helped by the fact that a student (who has had his period of conscription to the armed forces deferred until the end of his studies) may opt out of conscription entirely by taking a post on a three-year contract overseas where Belgian interests (particularly in the applied sciences) are widespread and Belgian skilled personnel in great demand.

A second present cause of anxiety turns on what is now considered to be a disproportionate number of both female and foreign students. In 1939 female students counted for little more than one-tenth of the total; today they number easily a quarter. That the emancipation of women should lead them to embrace the liberal professions, medicine and pharmacy is fine — but what about the large numbers flocking to take courses in the commercial and social sciences (4000 in 1970 as against 2000 reading science and 4000 in the Faculty of Philosophy and Letters)? It is felt that many of these women would find greater satisfaction in attending appropriate courses in one or other of the higher technical and commercial institutions, and present recruitment of women to the *Université du Travail* of Charleroi tends to bear out this contention. Not surprisingly, the greatest number of foreign students comes from the former Belgian Congo and its dependencies, but the USA follows a close second, and after these come in order Holland, Italy, Luxemburg and France, and with quite a sizable representation from most other Western European countries.

Statistics again reveal, however, that most students from abroad (excluding the former Belgian Congo) are reading the political, economic and social sciences, and considerable doubts are expressed as to the wisdom of allowing this to continue. Medicine and pharmacy are the next most popular courses, to be followed by theology (at Louvain), applied sciences, pure science and law. The government has recently decided that in the interests of everybody it must impose its own *numerus clausus* on foreign students from industrialised Western nations so that in future they form no more than 5 per cent of the total student population.

A final and less definable cause for anxiety is the undoubted suspicion still felt by students as a whole of the working of university machinery in which they have been called upon to play an increasing part. New laws promulgated in 1970/1 provided for greater student participation at every level and reviewed both examinations and teaching methods. They also (most importantly) sought adjustment in the awards of various degrees and diplomas to make them the equivalent of those in other European countries and so comply with the requirements of the Treaty of Rome. Students, however, are still reluctant fully to co-operate, and new attempts to ensure student participation in the running of the universities by making voting for student representatives on the various governing bodies compulsory (this being logically in line with requirements at ordinary governmental elections) have not bettered relations. Students with whom I have spoken from Louvain complain that, whilst organisational changes are being made, the content of instruction remains the same if only because the older and more traditionalist teachers will not adapt themselves to new conditions. Belgium may be thinking about education in the broadest sense and in the context of societies which will no longer be either hierarchical or self-contained as they were in the past, but there is a certain disenchantment among the younger generation with the continued drive for economic and technological growth. There is no real understanding of the needs of the young. And as one articulate medical student put it to me: "the time is long past for sorting out the causes of the present lack of understanding between students and university authorities; measures must be taken *now* to re-establish confidence amongst *all* corporate members of the university so that the university may regain its former prestige and influence."

The Grand Duchy of Luxemburg

For obvious reasons there has never been any real demand for an independent national university in the Grand Duchy, students preferring to
study in the universities of neighbouring countries. It was, however,
necessary for the government to exercise control in some measure over
the various kinds of qualifications obtained abroad before making appointments to the legal, medical and teaching professions, and also to the civil
service, and this was done by insisting that all holders of foreign degrees
seeking such appointments must submit themselves to a supplementary
examination held by nationally appointed examining bodies. With the
passage of time and with more and more students taking foreign degrees
in increasingly more sophisticated subjects, this machinery began to appear
outmoded if not unfair on the graduate, since it inevitably led to increasing
lack of co-ordination between the subjects studied by him and the kind of
examination he was forced to take. Thus in 1969 a new law was introduced to solve this and other problems in the field of higher education.
The three main provisions of the new law were: (a) that foreign degrees
should automatically be recognised subject to ratification by the Minister
of Education on the advice of appropriate *ad hoc* committees; (b) that
the national examinations in competency should be abolished as from
1974, students in the meantime being allowed to opt for either system;
(c) that a University Centre (*Centre Universitaire de Luxemburg*) should
be created which would offer two types of university courses to be named
cours universitaires and *cours complémentaires*.

The University Centre is governed by an administrative council whose
members are elected for a period of four years, the council designating a
president from amongst its members. Members of the teaching staff are
appointed on the joint recommendation of the council and the department concerned by the Minister of Education, and many of them (at this
present juncture) are serving part-time only, being recruited from some of
the nearest foreign universities — in particular from Liège, Nancy, Strasbourg and Saarbrucken.

The *cours universitaires* are intended to provide the first year of a university course and are open to all holders of the secondary school leaving
certificate. There are departments of law and economics which provide
two different courses to suit the requirements of students who intend

studying later in France or in Belgium. Other courses are provided in philosophy and psychology, classics, French, Italian, German, English, geography, history, mathematics, chemistry, physics and biology – the science groupings also providing for the requirements of students who will later specialise in medicine or pharmacy. As is common elsewhere on the continent of Europe, the year is divided into two semesters, but unlike the rest of Europe examinations are taken (both written and oral) at the end of each semester. On a basis of these examinations, and taking the candidate's work over the full year into consideration, a successful student is then awarded his *certificat d'études* in the appropriate subject(s). In practice students may now attend any foreign university of their own choice, though they mainly opt for Belgium, France, Germany and Switzerland, with a few in Austria, the USA and Great Britain. All these universities (with the exception of Great Britain) accept these certificated students into the second year of the appropriate course. It is, of course, still the prerogative of any student who so wishes not to attend the *cours universitaires* but to go straight into the first year at a foreign university. The *cours complémentaires* provide postgraduate courses to give further training, as necessary, to graduates entering one or other of the professions. One further institution of higher education, *l'Université Internationale de Sciences Comparées*, is in process of being reorganised and should now logically become part of the *Centre Universitaire*. It was founded on private initiative in 1957, receives state support and financial backing, and runs postgraduate courses in comparative law and economics with specific reference to the European communities.

Within one year of implementation of the new law, the *cours universitaires* had already attracted 157 students; and the numbers of students attending foreign universities rose from 975 in 1961 to 1835 some twelve years later. Latest available statistics (for 1973) reveal that the large majority of these go first to France (542), then Belgium (533), and then West Germany (482).

Holland

Holland has twelve institutions of university standard, six of them meeting the requirement of having seven or eight faculties to classify as full universities. These are Leiden (1575), Groningen (1614), Utrecht (1636), Amsterdam (founded in 1632 but achieving full status only in 1876), the Free University of Amsterdam (1880), and the Catholic University of Nijmegen (1923). Tilburg (a Catholic foundation) and the Erasmus University of Rotterdam have only three faculties. The remainder have departments rather than faculties and include the Agricultural University of Wageningen (1917), and the Technological Universities of Delft (1905), Eindhoven (1957), Twente (1961), of which the oldest, Delft, has the most comprehensive range of technical and technological courses. A further university to include another medical school is planned for Maastricht. All are state universities with the exception of the Free University of Amsterdam (Protestant) and the two Catholic universities of Nijmegen and Tilburg, but all three "free" universities are in receipt of state grants (as in Belgium) to cover almost all their total expenditure.

Friesland once had its own university, but this was closed by Napoleon and since that date students from Friesland have had to go to the University of Groningen as being the nearest. The provincial capital of Friesland, Leeuwarden, already has a college of adult education; it has shared a teacher-training institution with Groningen since 1971, and a social science department was opened in Leeuwarden in 1972; there is now a distinct possibility that this nucleus will be turned into a new Friesland university. A further possible development affects the universities of Tilburg and Eindhoven which are only some 19 miles apart, which each offer a limited range of subjects, and yet which jointly have a student population of around 10,000 students. If a full arts faculty were added this would relieve considerably the pressures on Nijmegen, the two could federate to become the University of Brabant, and the Province of Brabant would greatly benefit in that at present, whilst it supplies 12 per cent of all Dutch university students, it only has facilities to cater itself for around 7 per cent. These proposals have added importance when it is remembered that Dutch students traditionally prefer to live at or near home, and that only the most recent creation, Twente, has evolved as a largely residential campus-style institution.

Admission to a university is open to anyone who has obtained a secondary school leaving certificate based on an examination in seven subjects including Dutch and one foreign language, but (as we have already noted in Chapter 7) the real selection takes place after the end of the primary school course when the most promising academic pupils are drafted into

VWO schools. As in all other Western European countries, numbers qualifying for and seeking university education have grown beyond proper manageable proportions, and this is naturally one of the main causes of student unrest. Immediately before the last war the total student population was a mere 12,628. In the immediate post-war years these figures rose to 22,000, had reached 40,000 by 1960, and for the session 1971/2 totalled 112,873! In 1972 it became necessary to impose admission limits to medicine, dentistry, biology, veterinary studies, social geography and history, and this was done on a lottery basis devised by the Central Office for Admissions. A student unlucky in the draw might be offered a place to study, say, chemistry instead of biology. On the other hand, bad luck in the lottery could lead to automatic admission the following year. Needless to say, students have been further incensed by this curious administrative ploy which restricts traditional freedom of study.

The university course lasts between five and seven years, and until recently students could delay or re-sit examinations at will. The first examination, *kandidaats*, is usually taken after two or three years and the final examination *doctoraal*, three years later. The main hurdle is the *kandidaats* examination, and not surprisingly many drop out here or are advised to discontinue their course earlier. In the popular social science courses almost half fail to qualify at the *doctoraal* level, and in the technological universities, though a few may repeat part of their course, there is an overall failure rate of about 30 per cent at the end of the first year. Several measures have now been taken to cope with the failure problem. Firstly, there is closer scrutiny of results on the secondary school leaving certificate, and for certain disciplines only those who have what is considered the right combination of subjects together with good grading are accepted. Secondly, all universities have now laid down the maximum time which may be taken over completing a degree and so are warding off the "perpetual" student as well as those clearly unfitted to continue. With the exception of the Faculty of Law (which only allows two and a half years to complete the *kandidaats* examination) the upper time limit is now four years to *kandidaats*. The *total* time span allowed from beginning to obtaining the *doctoraal* examination is six years for law and the social sciences; seven years for arts, politics and social science, economics, and psychology and pedagogy; seven and a half years for science subjects; eight years for dentistry; nine years for pharmacy and medicine, plus an extra two years internship in medicine. Thirdly, serious thinking now turns on both shortening university courses and on the need to relate university education to parallel fields of higher professional and vocational training. A four-year university course to the degree of *doctorandus* is proposed,[1] the first year of which will be an introductory or orientation year with an examination at the end. Students who fail will be allowed a second introductory year in another field of studies. Students who fail their final examination may extend their course by a further year to re-sit.

The non-university sector of higher education is not giving any kind of encouragement to such proposals, and in point of fact fears that any *rapprochement* with the universities is going inevitably to lead to university dominance. On the other hand, the higher technical colleges already claim that their four-year engineering course is of university degree standard anyway and claim that their more selective admission procedure often yields students of greater ability than those who enter the technological universities. The technological universities in turn are opposed to the idea of a four-year degree course, arguing that this shorter period of study could never be accepted as the equivalent of the present title of *ingenieur*. The debate still continues. What is certain is that in the present economic situation and with an increasing number of students seeking some form of tertiary education *that is relevant* (the constant student plea throughout Western Europe), relative shortage of funds alone will force some move towards greater collaboration between the universities and the higher technical colleges and a much wider use of shared facilities (such as computers); that greater interchange of students unsuitable for one system to the other will occur; and that the universities will have to make more provision for properly orientated industrial training for their *ingenieur* students. There is lastly a possibility of introducing a one-year postgraduate research diploma course for those preparing for the usual arduous doctorate examinations which demand the presentation and public defence of a published thesis, and which can take a student several years of substantial research. But here again, because of the increased number of students, rising costs and the complexity of equipment (other than in the arts faculty), the government is taking a long look at the real value of scientific research within the universities with a view to bringing

---

[1] Or the grade of *meester* in law, or *ingenieur* in technology.

about a transfer to research institutes and industry or at least much more inter-university co-operation, and, for really highly expensive research, greater co-operation amongst members of the EEC.

To get back to the students, however, we note that in Holland as elsewhere the university remains essentially a bourgeois institution with 37 per cent of students coming from the higher socio-economic group, 50 per cent from the middle group, and only 14 per cent from the lower group which is comprised mainly of industrial and agricultural workers. As in Belgium though, it has to be remembered that working-class students are well catered for in an excellent system of technical institutes of all kinds and that many are well content to seek this kind of more practically relevant training. Grants are available on a means test for needy students and are annually adjusted to the cost of living index. Only 60 per cent of the total sum awarded is a straightforward grant, the remaining 40 per cent being considered as an interest-free loan. Gifted students are awarded full scholarships. Medical students only receive loans because of their earning potential. Postgraduate students may receive a loan if they are engaged on a piece of approved research.

Student unrest reached its first peak of intensity in 1968, the most vocal students significantly coming from departments with the highest failure rates — political science and sociology. Extremist Marxist factions were much to the fore to fan the discontent as in other countries, and discontent (as elsewhere) centred on the hierarchical structure, the autocratic attitude of professors, their remoteness, overcrowding, the lecture system (it being not infrequent for a professor to be addressing 400 students at a time), irrelevance of studies, the lack of adequate student representation on various boards and committees. The government quickly responded to the challenge and passed in 1970 a highly complicated University Government Reorganisation Act. In brief, this has now reconstituted the governing body to consist of one-third academic staff, one-third students, and one-third technical and administrative staff. Responsibility for actual teaching and research devolves on separate bodies, each for a particular discipline, and these bodies bring together *all* teaching staff and representatives of the students affected plus a proportion of non-academic staff — the number of student and non-academic staff representation varying from university to university and from discipline to discipline. Needless to say, in Holland as elsewhere, attendance of student members (once the principle they fought for had been gained) has not been particularly satisfactory.

The next crisis succeeded in 1972 in overthrowing the government. It was then, as a desperate economic measure, that the government began fixing its own form of *numerus clausus* for certain faculties and also raised university fees (which had remained fixed since 1930) from 200 florins to 1000 florins (from about £40 to £200). Other anti-inflationary measures to be considered included a threatened cut of 40 per cent in the education budget. A new government insisted on introducing the new fee for the session 1973/4. There were more sit-ins and demonstrations, but in the end most students paid up. Meanwhile the new government, having asserted its authority, agreed to lower the fee to 500 florins, but the students' union advised new entrants for 1974 not to pay even this, and the universities themselves now seem to be intervening in the dispute, the University of Groningen for one announcing its intention of charging only 250 florins. At the time of writing the situation is still far from clear and the government seems indecisive as to what its next steps should be.

France

As we have already had occasion to point out, the organisation of the French educational system is unusually complex by normal Western European standards, and the structuring of education at the university level proves to be no exception. Until reforms first began to be implemented in 1966, to be followed up by the *Loi d'Orientation* of 1968, universities (despite vast increases in numbers) had changed little for well over a century. They have now undergone a complete overhaul of their structure, whilst alongside them new types of institution have been created. Only the *grandes écoles* have remained untouched, and the *Loi d'Orientation*, indeed, sanctioned their monopoly on higher education, thereby conceding that their annual intake of about only 10 per cent of the total student body was still in the right proportion; that their function must still continue to be that of providing a direct route to top-level employment in the professions, in commerce, and in public life. This creaming-off process which results in the "failures" going on to ordinary university courses makes the French universities in effect much more closely involved in the school system than in most other Western European countries, for (since key posts other than in teaching will tend to be filled by graduates from the *grandes écoles*) the one main and important civil service job left wide open to the ordinary university graduate is secondary school teaching.

The whole of higher education is, however, characterised by certain common features. By the law of 1880 only the state has the right to confer degrees (or diplomas from the various *grandes écoles*), and this right has been re-affirmed in the *Loi d'Orientation*. Higher education is not free, students having to pay usually nominal amounts for enrolment, examinations, library and laboratory facilities. They are also responsible for their own medical, insurance and social security contributions. They may however receive grants or scholarships from various sources, though the number of students receiving such grants is as low as about one-fifth of the total. Students in certain *grandes écoles* actually receive a token salary. And for everybody there are subsidised restaurants and lodgings. Finally, any student who passes the *baccalauréat* is entitled to go to a university, though in practice certain faculties (particularly in science and medicine) do operate a selection system by demanding good performance in specified subjects at the *baccalauréat* level — this being a cause of much contention since most Frenchmen regard any attempt to restrict university entrance to those legally qualified as undemocratic. A zoning system has also been introduced (primarily to relieve the pressure on Paris) whereby a student is obliged to attend the university of his own region, but students are already quite adept at getting around this restriction.

It was not until 1960 that the immensity of the problem facing the universities as regards growth in student numbers was fully grasped and it was by then a question of doing too little too late. A massive recruitment of teaching personnel was ordered; four new universities were opened at Rouen, Amiens, Rheims and Orleans as a counter-attraction to Paris; specialist institutes were opened in 1965 at Rouen (chemistry), Paris (civil engineering and electronics), Toulouse (mechanical construction), and Nancy (applied geology); in Paris itself the former *Halle aux Cuirs* became the overspill for the Faculty of Letters, whilst a new science faculty being built at the *Halle aux Vins* had on completion to hold far more students than it had been designed to accommodate; and outside the centre of Paris, in the post-war suburban belt (the *Banlieu*), planners conceived two residential campuses, one at Orsay and the other at ill-starred Nanterre. But still student numbers grew. Between 1964 and 1966 almost 92 per cent of qualified students asserted their right to go to the university, the influx being aggravated by decisions taken at about the same time to raise the percentage of passes at the *baccalauréat* level. In the ten years between 1962 and 1972 the number of students in letters faculties rose from 93,000 to 245,000; in science faculties from 92,000 to 116,000 – an increase of less than 50 per cent to be compared with a more than 300 per cent increase in letters. In 1962 the total student population had been 285,000, and 33,000 in the *grandes écoles*. By 1966 the figures had risen to 460,000 and 50,000 respectively. By 1972 they stood at approximately 650,000 and 60,000. Needless to say, drop-out figures, particularly at the end of the first year of a university course, are high – estimated by some to be as high as at least 40 per cent – but an accurate figure is hard to come by if only because many students are in practice part-timers.

By 1966 professors and teachers at meetings held at Caen and Amiens were already demanding a fundamental overhaul of both the schools and the university systems. In June of the same year the degree structure in the arts and sciences faculties was reformed, and with the exception of a change in the first cycle made in 1973 has remained unaltered since. Put briefly, progress through the university turns on three cycles of instruction each of two years' duration. The first two years originally led to a diploma award on either the literary or science side and was appropriately called DUEL or DUES. For the session 1973/4 this was scrapped in favour of one multi-disciplinary award called DEUG (*diplôme d'études universitaires générales*). It has not met with universal favour. Students suspected they were being sidetracked from meaningful specialist studies and employers could not see the relevance of such a broadly based qualification. Criticisms have since been met to some extent by developing seven different varieties of DEUG which in a certain measure respond to the demand for specialisation whilst still attempting to give a broad and multi-disciplinary education. The intention is that many holders of this diploma will prefer to go out into the world of work rather than attempt to pursue their university studies further and so cut down the high failure rate in these first years. There is also an interesting comparison to be made between this diploma award and the envisaged Higher Diploma in Education to be offered in England and Wales in the new liberal arts colleges.

The second cycle of two years comprises one year of preparation for the *licence* and a further year to the *maîtrise* which is intended primarily for students aspiring either to do research or to have a university career. It is expected that most students will stop at the *licence* (roughly the equivalent of a B.A. degree), and many students intending to teach in the secondary schools will certainly stop off there to begin preparation for CAPES. The third cycle consists of highly specialised study and research in preparation for the *doctorat* which will take a minimum of two years. Above this university doctorate comes the more prestigious *doctorat d'état* awarded to candidates who have defended a published thesis (or a principal and a subsidiary thesis), or who have presented a corpus of original work of high quality. A period of five years must normally elapse between registration for the *doctorat d'état* and presentation and public defence. Whilst the *doctorat d'état* is awarded in any discipline, the lower degree structure varies for other disciplines than in arts and science. Pharmacy has a five-year course leading to the award of a diploma. In medicine the second cycle lasts five years and leads to the *doctorat de médicine*. In law and in economics the second and third cycles last two years and one year and lead respectively to a *licence* and a *diplôme d'études supérieures* (DES).

The IUT (institut universitaire de technologie) was also a 1966 creation, and we have already discussed its function in some detail in Chapter 7. These institutes have expanded to their present total of around sixty from the experimental ones first opened in 1965 in Rouen, Paris, Toulouse and Nancy, and with the passing of the 1968 *Loi d'Orientation* they have become UERs in their own right.

The *Loi d'Orientation* of November 1968 was a recognition of the need for more thorough revision that had been highlighted by the events of May 1968. Implicitly it condemned the remoteness, the unreality and the lack of humanity inherent in the old system of French higher education as well as at the upper levels of secondary education. Basically, it substituted for the Napoleonic *Université* and the small number of traditional universities created mainly in the 1890s, with their constituent faculties, a much larger number of "public, scientific and cultural establishments having legal status and financial autonomy". In effect this led to giving seventy-three institutions university status, and each of these universities is sub-divided into a number of UERs (*unités d'enseignement et de recherche*) of which there are at present some 700. For the Paris area alone there are now thirteen separate universities, and three each in such cities as Lille, Grenoble and Montpellier. A new university was opened at Compiégne in 1973, but it tends at the moment to stand apart from the others in that it is a purely technological university and it also imposes a *numerus clausus* on the admission of first year students.

The watchwords for the 1968 law were "autonomy", "participation", and "multi-disciplinary", and whilst many would argue that these aims are still far from being realised, much progress has nevertheless been made. Universities may now determine their own teaching activities, research programmes, teaching methods and (within limits) their procedures for evaluating their students' knowledge and aptitudes. True, degrees are still national but common regulations are limited to such matters as entrance requirements, length of course and minimum content, qualifications of the teaching staff, and (where relevant) the balance to be held between theory and practice. A global sum is allocated to each university in accord with its own estimates and needs, and the university then shares this out to its constituent UERs. Article 13 of the law makes for shared responsibility in running a university by *all* the teaching staff as well as representatives of research and of administrative staff and students. Students can claim, however, and with some justification, that in actual practice they are still not adequately represented. On the other hand, a politically active minority refuse on principle to vote to perpetuate a "still capitalistic structure", and the apathetic majority (as in many other countries) cannot be bothered. Multi-disciplinarity has come off worst. There has been a breakdown of barriers between some of the more traditional subjects, especially in the sciences, there has been a creation of departments on new lines and a growth of new disciplines, but too many of the UERs are still organised on traditional faculty lines and narrow specialisation still widely exists.

The events leading up to the "night of the barricades" in May 1968 are by now so well documented that it will not be necessary here to refer to them except in the briefest terms. They really began when, at the end of 1967, "mature" students from eight Parisian *lycées* joined in demonstrations on behalf of workers who were holding one of their recurrent strikes. The demonstrators were punished by the Ministry of Education and one student was dismissed. In January 1968, 500 students massed before the offending *Lycée Condorcet* and secured his reinstatement. From then on *lycée* students became increasingly politically involved, declared their right to political action and the right to go on strike, and inextricably became caught up in more ominous student protests from the university to denounce the entire university system. These student protests were spear-headed by revolutionary bourgeois students from that planner's dream, the new Nanterre campus, and the flames were soon fanned throughout Paris and into the provinces — and indeed acted as an inspiration to other students in other universities (and some schools) in other Western European countries who likewise had deep feelings of frustration at apparent irrelevance in their studies, at hopeless overcrowding, at the hierarchical and archaic structure of the university as such which allowed them to take no positive decisions in matters that should be their immediate concern.

Nanterre was a bold new venture. Big names left the Sorbonne to teach there. Money was poured into it. But the charmless environment which was created there only succeeded in creating a revolution. French students demonstrated firmly that they did not want to live isolated from the society around them. They wanted to participate in the changes and developments of contemporary life. They wanted to live in a community and not a barracks where virtually nothing was done to give social coherence to a student population of over 15,000. The more they considered their position the more Kafka-esque it appeared to be. The privileged intelligentsia, and bourgeoisie — for if a student from a working-class home manages to obtain a university place (and only about 5 per cent of the student population do so) the total pressures on him condition him to a bourgeois-type existence — were being required to study amid the most squalid surroundings it was possible to find: *bidonville* on the one side, the shabby façades of state-subsidised workers' flats on the other, the day-and-night noise of trucks constantly being shunted in the SNCF marshalling yards close by. They were offered an olympic-sized swimming pool before even a library was completed. Common rooms, coffee bars and other cultural amenities had been totally neglected. They were being asked amid all this to take the rational nature of the capitalist system for granted. The Nanterre sociologists would have none of it and they soon were to become the mouthpiece of the entire French student body in their condemnation of a society based, as they saw it, on rigid class-stratification and social injustice. On 22 March 1968, at Nanterre, politics were first introduced onto a French university campus. Demonstrators occupied the administrative offices of the tower block to provide the first active resistance to the authoritarianism of the university mandarins who had refused to allow both teachers and students to have any say in the running of affairs which concerned them intimately.

From then onwards the situation steadily worsened to culminate in large-scale fighting and the "night of the barricades". The protest spread outside the universities, and in no time industrial workers from the Renault car factory and elsewhere, and then white-collared and professional workers, had joined in to create what amounted to a general strike with the avowed aim of toppling the government. They were joined by no fewer than 10,000 *lycée* students. A total of at least 8 million became involved and the government was forced to resign. Only the strength of de Gaulle's personal prestige and his authority saved France from utter catastrophe. In the ensuing elections Frenchmen rallied *en masse* to his support, fearful of what might be the consequences of any other action, and his party carried the day with a huge majority. Yet never again would things be exactly the same either in the country generally or in the universities in particular. The following year President de Gaulle resigned after a resounding defeat in a referendum on which he had staked his future. The *Loi d'Orientation* became fully operative. The crisis receded, but rumblings have continued unabated ever since.

In 1973 came a demonstration in Paris organised by pupil and student committees and actively supported by all the left-wing political parties and two major federations of trade unions (including teachers) against the Debré Law which replaced DUEL or DUES by DEUG and also required all young men in future to do their military service between the ages of 18 and 21. This has meant in effect that young men going on to university must now choose between doing their twelve months' service immediately after school and then go to university, or get DEUG first, then do a year's service and afterwards return to university to get a full degree. DEUG, it was claimed, was deliberately designed to discourage or prevent young people from going to university, thereby relieving pressure on university facilities and reducing the extremely high drop-out rate. The largest federation of parents' associations also took part in the demonstration, parents at one *lycée* marching with their children, and the total turn-out was estimated at some 100,000.

In the spring of 1976 came the most violent protests and riots since May 1968, now specifically directed against government proposals to adapt higher education to the needs of the labour market and so cope with increasing unemployment amongst graduates. In 1976 there were an estimated 700,000 students in the universities – more than in Great Britain and West Germany combined – and it was expected that a high proportion of these would either drop out or fail their degree. It was also foreseen that some 370,000 students taking the traditional academic subjects would afterwards find little outlet for their talents. Under the new government plans subjects such as history, philosophy and the "dead" languages were to be phased out in favour of studies more directly related to the needs of industry and commerce. Teacher training would be transferred to special training colleges, and only a few of the seventy-five universities would be allowed to supply a full range of courses up to postgraduate level. *Lycée* students joined in and used the occasion to attack the Haby proposed reforms in primary and secondary education. Student representations gathered in Amiens and on 10 April called for a nation-wide closure of universities. "We refuse to prepare for an economic system that we reject", claimed their most militant Leftist leaders. The government, wisely, stood firm whilst offering to enter into discussions and also pointing out that if the proposed nation-wide strike took effect degree awards that summer would be in jeopardy. It equally pointed out that the proposed reform was the only way to reduce unemployment amongst the young, and especially for teachers whose numbers were already estimated as being eight times as many as could be employed. Meantime a meeting of rectors of French universities was called in Paris and they were effective in taking some of the heat out of the arguments by themselves voting strongly against the reforms as they stood and calling for a complete re-examination of the problems. And when, finally, the workers themselves, on whose support militant students had been relying, came to the decision that this time the quarrel could in no way be interpreted as their concern, the rebellion (if not over) had lost its momentum. Everyone now anxiously awaits the outcome of the talks and deliberations that have been initiated among all interested parties.

5

West Germany

German universities have their origin in the European intellectual movement of the late Middle Ages when free corporations of masters and scholars established themselves in Europe for the purpose of conducting a *studium generale*. The first such German establishments appeared in Heidelberg in 1385, in Cologne in 1388, in Erfurt in 1392 and in Leipzig in 1409. The number continued to increase, and with the growing importance of mathematics and science the mere passing on of traditional knowledge was replaced by the search for truth and new knowledge typified by the creation of the University of Göttingen in 1737. After the defeat of Prussia by Napoleon in 1806 a new era in the German university was ushered in with the foundation of the University of Berlin in 1810 by Wilhelm von Humboldt. The helplessness of Germany was then answered by the Hegelian philosophy of the unified state as the embodiment of reason, and within the ideally unified state Hegel and his successors saw the university as offering an unhampered opportunity for the complete development of the individual. Berlin thus became a deliberate break with the academic traditions of the past. Its aim was primarily to develop knowledge and secondarily to train the professional and official classes. Humboldt saw the salvation of the Germans as coming from the combination of teaching and free research, and he left after him the tradition of academic freedom in which the universities had the right to independent government and to the election of their own teaching staff. This conception of the university soon spread to the others that had survived the upheavals of the Napoleonic wars, and the German university has held on to these ideals which (except for the years of Hitler's dictatorship) have been respected and safeguarded by the state.

By the middle of the nineteenth century the two elements of which the German university was most proud were its academic freedom and its devotion to research, and it was these aspects which were imitated by universities in England and America. *Lehrfreiheit* meant that the German university teacher was perfectly free in the topics he chose to research and teach and in his presentation of them; he had the dignity of a man who, holding an intellectual post, was under orders to nobody. *Lernfreiheit* meant that the student was equally free and was treated as an adult from the day he matriculated; he could choose what courses he pleased and organise his studies as he best thought fit, the only check on his work being the final examination for which he submitted himself when he thought fit. In addition, it was perfectly possible for him to migrate from one university to another, seeking out places where his subject was most vigorously pursued (or, of course, the university which provided the softest option). A further aspect of academic freedom was that of academic self-government which was intended to put an end to censorship by the *Land* in which the university happened to be situated and on which it largely depended for its finances. Organisation, however, was on an oligarchic basis with each faculty managing its own affairs under an elected dean — chosen by full professors only from amongst themselves. Full professors were chosen by the *Land* usually from a list of three submitted by the faculty concerned — but the *Land* could if it so wished reject all three proposals and submit a candidate of its own. The affairs of the university as a whole were managed by the senate, thus carrying self-government above the level of the faculties, but in practice it was largely made up of representatives from the latter — and therefore full professors.

This Humboldtian university was based on the strongly class-conscious structure of German society of the early nineteenth century and on the educational needs of a small number of students both at teaching and research levels. And as Germany moved away from the traumas of the Hitlerian régime it became increasingly clear that such a university was ill-adapted to cope with all the problems besetting the new German Federal Republic, not least amongst which was the steady growth in student numbers which, having reached a total of 204,000 in 1960, soared by an increase of over 50 per cent to 330,000 ten years later. True, and as in most other Western European countries, there is every indication that the increase is easing off, but even so plans are already in hand to cope with a further possible increase throughout the whole of tertiary education of about 25 per cent in the 1980s. This steep rise in demand for university places dates from the 1950s when a post-war generation sought eagerly to exercise its full democratic rights and 90 per cent of those who succeeded in passing the *Abitur* claimed a university place.

Further complications followed. *Lehrfreiheit* was soon criticised as leading to courses which were regarded by the modern student as obsolete and/or irrelevant. *Lernfreiheit* was becoming increasingly impossible with the huge student numbers involved, and limited resources alone demanded that some limit should be placed upon the time a student took to complete his degree course. Something also needed to be done about the high wastage rate — especially in the arts and social sciences — which accom-

panied increased enrolment. An inquiry terminated in 1965 on a group of
students who had entered university eight years earlier revealed drop-out
rates of 38 per cent in arts, 24 per cent in economics and the social sciences,
17 per cent each in law and science, and 16 per cent in medicine, whilst
a further 25 per cent had still not taken their final examinations.

Measures taken to meet the demand for places have included the foundation between 1960 and the early 1970s of thirteen new universities
(a few based on existing institutions), some of which succeeded in making
a novel break with the past, and a doubling of the number of university
teachers. The universities of Constans (1964) and Ulm (1969) have attempted to shorten the length of study, especially in the sciences, by the
introduction of a definite curriculum, by student counselling, and by intermediate examinations after the first two years of study to determine
whether the undergraduate should continue his course. Bielefeld (1967)
has what is considered a favourable teacher—student ratio of 1 : 30 and
also insists on the introduction of fixed syllabuses and curricula. Its most
exciting innovation, however, have been (a) the creation of a centre for
inter-disciplinary research which is intended to invite professors from at
home and abroad to work in teams of thirty or forty on a one-year research project covering several disciplines; (b) an experimental comprehensive school attached to the university to serve as the education
department's laboratory, and with the possibility of grouping the last
two years of this laboratory school and the first year of the university
together; (c) professors to teach for one year and then take a year's
sabbatical to devote to research — this in an attempt to modernise the
German academic tradition of Humboldt whereby the teacher passes on
the results of his latest research directly to his students. Instead of a
rector elected by his fellow professors for a period of one or at most two
years — a rector who could be hopelessly lacking in administrative ability
— Bielefeld's rector is intended to serve for four years and to be supported
by a team of six other professors, and so ensure both greater administrative ability and continuity of effort. Constanz and Ulm go further by
electing their rectors for an indefinite period, whilst Dortmund (1968)
elects its rector for a ten-year period.

Having successfully launched Bielefeld, the Prime Minister of North-
Rhine-Westphalia then announced his intention of opening by 1975 eight
further universities, seven of which would be devoted primarily but not

exclusively to the training of teachers, the eighth having a bias towards medicine and the natural sciences. Having further announced the creation of thirteen new "specialist" universities (*Fachhochschulen*) he promised that all forms of tertiary education in the *Land* would gradually be re-grouped together to form eight "comprehensive" universities (*Gesamthoch-schulen*), thus putting himself and his *Land* one move ahead of the central government in Bonn which had already made this idea an integral part of its future plans for university reform. The main idea of the "comprehen-sive" university is to group (where possible on one campus) all existing institutions of higher education so that doctors, teachers, engineers and so forth may all be trained in the same centre, and all formerly separate in-stitutions have the same standing. Already by 1974 there were five of the eight new-type universities working in North-Rhine-Westphalia, and a few others in embryo at least in *Land* Hessen. Including these newer creations, West Germany now has a total of forty-five institutions of full university status, nine of them being technological universities.

Undoubtedly the most interesting of all recent projects, however, has been the opening of Germany's own Open University in October 1975, the *Fernuniversität* of Hagen. Like its English counterpart with its modest headquarters at Milton Keynes, the *"Fernuni"* is being run on a com-parative shoe-string, but unlike the Open, the *Fernuni* is intended as an addition to the conventional universities. It was the only way to obtain the necessary funds. Students are normally required to hold the *Abitur*, and they fall roughly into three categories: those who do not have to work for a living and will follow courses full time; those who will study part time; and those who have no qualifications at all and will laboriously have to make up the leeway. It is these students (ironically) who will have to pay fees (about £40 per annum) since the holder of the *Abitur* can of right claim university admission. From around 1300 students, numbers rose steeply to around 10,000 by 1978. The work assignment (by English standards) is heavy, students being expected to put in between 20 and 40 hours per week depending on whether they are full time or part time. Students are recruited from all the eleven *Länder* and study centres are in process of being opened throughout the country. All problems are dealt with efficiently and speedily by the on-the-spot professors at Hagen, and students are encouraged to telephone their queries up to 10 p.m. during one day of the week. Just as in England, working-class students have been slow in coming forward. The largest number of applications has come from qualified engineers and scientists (28 per cent) with white-collar workers (25 per cent) close behind. Bank, insurance and commercial employees form 15 per cent of the applications while less than 1 per cent of the demand for places has come from "artisans". Teachers account for only 9 per cent of admissions, but it is to be remembered that once qualified they have full civil service status and additional qualifications make little, if any, difference to them.

The organisation of the universities generally is such that three types of degree are on offer. Scientists will receive their *Diplom* after a prescribed *minimum* number of semesters, but a preliminary examination must be taken about three years before the final one. For the arts and humanities there was until recently no degree before the doctorate, unless of course a student intended teaching (when he sits the *Staatsexamen*). The prescribed period of study is long, and for those who manage to stay the course very few achieve doctorate status within the limitations set. In German, history and modern languages, for example, the prescribed minimum number of semesters is 11−12, but a good and hard-working modern language student of my acquaintance at Frankfurt recently took sixteen. A doctorate may also be awarded in those disciplines which terminate with the award of a *Diplom*, though here it is a pure research degree consisting of a dissertation and a searching oral examination and it usually demands between two and four years of further study after the *Diplom*. Mounting criticism of the length of time it took to reach the doctorate in the humanities generally, and concern with the high drop-out rate in consequence, led some universities in the 1960s to provide a shorter course (to be equivalent to the *Diplom*) for students of the humanities who wished neither to teach nor to proceed to a doctorate. This course is dignified with the title of *Magister Artium*, but traditional attitudes die hard, even among students when their intellectual potential might seem to be called in question, and it has not yet proved to be a popular choice.

As in France, the German students' revolt of 1968 led to significant reforms in the university sector, and many would argue that it was in Western Germany that the term "student revolt" first originated; that the seeds of revolt were sown there to grow to fruition and then wither from lack of sustenance in France. We need not go into any detail concerning the main events. The uprisings, as in France, were led by political activists of the extreme left who were able to take advantage of genuine student grievances, and in West Berlin where troubles first originated it was estimated that during the events of Easter 1968 (when an abortive attempt to assassinate the militant student leader, Rudi Dutschke, was made) as many as 57 per cent of males between the ages of 16 and 30 were fully in sympathy with students in their protests and demands. Briefly they sought to break down the traditional concept of the university, seeking to define its social function anew and to make of it a forum where democracy would really be practised and discussed. They called for teachers and students to work together to make a new structure, to change individual learning into collective learning, and they argued persuasively that they sought participation, not dictatorship, in all aspects of university life, and no decisions to be taken against the wishes of either the student body or the professors. Put in more realistic terms their four major complaints were that they (the students) were denied any kind of participation in university government; that there was no real contact of any kind between students and the teaching staff and that there must be a better ratio of teachers to taught; that courses for degrees and diplomas were excessively long and that much of the content of such courses was irrelevant; that student grants were inadequate. Middle and junior grades of university teachers rallied to the support of the students in their pro-testations against the effect of the predominance of senior professors; there was much unvoiced sympathy with the less radical claims of the students; but the students as a body failed to win any solidarity of support from the working classes and their trade unions.

Nevertheless, a first comprehensive attempt at reform was initiated in 1969 but the Federal government failed to overcome opposition to most of its proposals and a new plan was introduced in 1973 by a new Federal Minister for Education. It recommended that junior teaching staff and students must be involved in faculty government in equal proportion to professors (a 3/3/3 system), but that university *teachers* (it is not made clear whether this should be full professors only), whilst they might be overruled on administrative questions, must continue to control "academic" decisions. It proposes a reduction of time taken over a first degree to 3–4 years in most disciplines, with exceptions only in special circumstances. It calls for a general reform of courses on offer and asks for study commissions to be set up consisting of professors, teachers, students, and representatives of each *Land* to submit detailed proposals for such reform. It asks for control of entrance to universities in certain disciplines, and in this connection a Central Office for the Allocation of Study Places (cf. UCCA in England and Wales) has been set up by agreement amongst all the *Länder* to ensure controlled entry into seven disciplines in which a *numerus clausus* has been universally imposed. Via this central office 60 per cent of places in such disciplines are to be awarded on the basis of school performance; the allocation of the remainder will depend largely on the length of time a student has been waiting for admission. The question of student grants had already been solved in 1972 by the introduction of a new scheme which entirely wiped out prevailing loan systems and tied the awards to fixed periods of study, thus helping to reduce the length of courses, urging students to greater activity so as not unnecessarily to prolong their studies, and to some extent at least reducing overcrowding. All these proposals have in principle been accepted by the various *Länder* if only because they seem to be inevitable, and the next few years will show how in detail they are being implemented.

Italy

The situation within the Italian university system is still so complex and confused, the economy of the country so weak and the political structure so uncertain and vacillating, that it is almost impossible to give a fair or even highly simplified account of trends and changes. We should note that with very few exceptions all Italian universities (of which there are to date about thirty) are state universities, closely regulated by law and having a highly centralised system dependent on the Ministry of Instruction in Rome. Administratively they adhere to the usual continental European pattern and are divided into ten or twelve faculties (each an organic teaching unit) with a tenured titular holder of one chair for each subject taught. All faculty affairs are entrusted to a faculty council which until 1968 was composed solely of full professors. Methods of instruction and preparation for degrees come closest to the German system we have just described in its pre-reform period. And, like all other Western European countries, Italian universities have found the task of coping with a rapidly increasing student population well nigh impossible.

Between 1911 and 1936 student figures rose from 33,000 to 82,000 and were not then by pre-war standards unmanageable. Immediate post-war years were relatively stable, but from 1960 to 1970 an alarming 9 per cent compound average rate of increase occurred, this bringing the total for 1972 to around 800,000. Fortunately, from 1973 onwards the rate of growth has been markedly reduced but almost insuperable problems still exist if only because of the geographical distribution of the universities. Tuscany, for example, is extremely well served by its three universities at Florence, Pisa and Sienna; but until recently there was no university provision at all south of Naples except for Sicily which again boasts three universities — Palermo, Catania and Messina; and the University of Rome, with maximum capacity for about 25,000 students, has an enrolment of around 100,000. Fortunately, many students register who never put in an appearance at lectures and almost half fail to complete their courses. On the other hand, well over half are still graduating in arts, physics and science subjects and their sole job prospects lie in teaching — an over-saturated profession.

A minimum of four years is usually required to obtain the first degree, the *laurea*; chemistry, engineering and archaeology require five years based on a two-year general preparatory course followed by three years of more specialised studies; medicine exacts six years divided into three two-year periods, success at the lower levels being necessary before proceeding. A peculiarity of the degree system is that on obtaining his *laurea* a graduate automatically receives the title of *dottore*, but this has no real significance outside the academic limits of the university: for entry to most professions (including teaching) a graduate must submit himself to the rigours of an appropriate state examination.

It was not until 1968 that politicans at last realised that there was a university problem of such magnitude as to be creating a dangerously explosive situation among the student body, and when far-reaching reform projects were hastily drafted — to be swept on one side. Instead, the left-wing Socialist senator, Codignola, managed in November 1969 to push through a short bill — the "liberalisation" bill — which succeeded only in swelling student numbers to even more unmanageable proportions. It granted open access to all faculties from whatever secondary school a student came, and (subject to faculty approval) allowed free choice of curriculum by each student. In effect, free choice meant the abolition of a distinction drawn between major (compulsory) subjects and minor (optional) ones, and it merely succeeded in further exacerbating student militancy and causing increasing disquiet amongst underpaid and untenured assistants to professors. Students, when baulked by faculty from opting for an easy way to get a degree by choosing only the former "optional" subject, accused faculty of dictatorship and were soon demanding collective (group) examinations or even the abolition of any form of testing. Junior untenured teaching staff, who are traditionally given the optional subjects to teach whilst tenured professors reserve for themselves the major subjects, found their already impossible work-load even greater. Made-to-measure degrees, with cross-faculty fertilisation, however progressive and desirable in theory, were in terms of the realities of the situation merely confounding chaos.

Two further measures of the "liberalisation" bill did, however, have some beneficial effect. Funds were allocated to award a kind of pre-salary to needy students, the amount of the award being based on a sliding scale according to qualifications already held: the higher the qualification the greater the award. Finally, all further appointments to professorship were frozen pending the working out of a new system. This, of course, considerably worsened the staff–student ratios but it also made it clear to faculty that the days of the autocratic academic "feudal baron" were numbered, that one chair could no longer be held to embrace or be the equivalent of one discipline, that faculty must make itself much more democratic in structure, and that exploitation of university status for private professional benefit must cease – today still, for example, almost 10 per cent of the Italian Parliament is made up of university professors, and the "outside" interests of professors in the Faculties of Medicine and Architecture are notorious.

By 1972 student protestation in the universities was ending (to be replaced by equally strong agitation in the secondary schools against a marked deterioration in the quality both of the teaching staff and the teaching), non-professorial members of staff were being heard in faculty deliberations, and a redressment of the proportions between tenured and non-tenured academic positions was promised. Political confusion, however, continued unabated and it was not until the end of 1974 that the Malfatti Bill eventually produced a further measure of reform. Briefly, the bill ensures the creation of 7500 new tenured teaching places in the universities to be spread over a period of three years – a tripling of numbers which, whilst considerably easing the burden placed on the teaching staff as a whole and making for more efficient staff–student ratios, must (in the opinion of most impartial critics) lead to a drastic lowering of standards for recruitment and also further worsen the academic "bite" in the secondary schools, since most new recruits to university teaching must be drawn therefrom. It equally aims at democratising university government by allowing for student representation on the flexible basis of allotting seats in proportion to the number of voters available by department. Clerical staff and junior faculty members must also be similarly elected. There is still, however, no breakdown of the traditional faculty concept, no immediately obvious move to get away from the idea of the faculty as the organic teaching unit in favour of autonomous departmental structures.

Switzerland

The universities of Switzerland are in the main ancient and venerable institutions, are cantonally based, and have a reputation for having up to 25 per cent of their intake from abroad. A high peak of 36 per cent of foreign students was reached in 1962, and, with increasing numbers of Swiss seeking a university education, efforts have since been made to keep the proportion down to a desired 25 per cent quota. The percentage of female students has also sharply risen from 13 per cent in 1949 to 16 per cent ten years later and to 24 per cent in 1971. Total student numbers in 1949 were around 17,000. By 1959 the figure had risen to 20,000, by 1965 to 33,000, and present numbers are around 45,000 with a teaching staff of some 4500 to give a staff–student ratio of 1:10. The situation appears both balanced and happy and calls for no particular comment.

The University of Basle is by far the oldest in the country, opening its doors in 1460 in a humble building on the Rhine which served as its headquarters for almost 500 years. Since the last war it has enjoyed a new lease of life and has faculties of theology, law, medicine (with dentistry), philosophy (including economics), and philosophy with a mathematics/natural science section. The University of Berne is also a legacy of the Renaissance, but came to be fully recognised as a university only in 1834. It has both a Catholic and a Protestant theology faculty, faculties of law (with commercial, traffic and administrative sections), medicine (including dentistry), veterinary medicine and two philosophy faculties.

Secondary school teachers for the canton of Berne have traditionally received their training in an education department within one of these philosophy faculties. These two ancient institutions, together with the University of Zurich and the Commercial University of St. Gallen, are German-speaking.

The three French-speaking universities are Geneva, Lausanne and Neuchatel. The story of Geneva is unique in that, though it only became a university officially in 1873, it can really be said to date back to the Reformation when in 1559 Jean Calvin founded a seminary there for instruction in both theology and pedagogy. Chairs in law and philosophy were added a few years later. During the Napoleonic wars Geneva lost for a time her independence and was annexed by the French Republic, the academy then becoming a part of the Napoleonic Imperial University and having faculties of science added to it. With the restoration of independence in 1814 these new departments remained and continued to expand, and in 1873 the "academy" was finally freed from church authority to become a fully fledged independent university. A faculty of medicine was added in 1876 to the already existing faculties of theology, letters, science and law. In 1915 the faculty of economics and sociology was established and it now tends to be the most heavily attended branch of the university. Many special departments and institutes for the teaching of languages, commercial science, international studies, dentistry, pharmacy and biology have since been added, and the university (through these new additions) has perfected a network of complementary studies which have proved to be one of the chief factors in attracting so many foreign students. A School of Interpreters was added in 1941 which now provides courses in at least twenty-six languages and continues to flourish and attract increasing numbers of students. Equally popular are the Graduate Institute of International Studies and the Institute of Educational Sciences. The former mainly directs its attention to the study of political problems, whilst the latter, as well as being the psychological laboratory of the university, is also the centre for the training of both primary and secondary teachers (and for vocational guidance) for the *canton* of Geneva.

The University of Lausanne (1890) has faculties of Protestant theology, medicine and law, the latter including a college of social and political science, a commerce section, and an institute for scientific police work. Its philological faculty has a special section for modern French and holiday courses for foreigners. Sections for mathematics, physics and natural history make up its natural science faculty, and a technical college (annexed) caters for several branches of engineering and surveying. Founded in 1909, the University of Neuchâtel is the youngest of all. It has four faculties: theology, law, letters and science together with several departments such as a special school for teachers of French and a zoological institute. In addition, its close connection with the Cantonal Observatory (which sets the time for all Switzerland) and the Swiss Laboratory for Research in Watchmaking gives a special character to many of the studies Neuchâtel has on offer.

The University of Fribourg (1889), which is the only wholly Roman Catholic university in Switzerland, serves the other Catholic *cantons* as well as that of Fribourg. In consequence, lectures are given in German, French, Italian and Latin. Its theology faculty attracts most students, but the faculties of law (with political and commercial sections), philosophy, mathematics/natural science, and an attached college of geometrics are well attended. The University of Zurich (which we have already briefly mentioned) was opened in 1833 by a popular vote of the people of the *canton*, and *"By the Will of the People"* has ever since been its motto. It has faculties of law, theology, political science, medicine, veterinary science and philosophy, but it is perhaps for its work in the medical sciences, coupled with developments in the fields of bacteriology and hygiene, that it has become most famous. Though by no means the oldest, it is the largest of the Swiss universities and attracts a fair proportion of students from the United States and England. It has always been characterised for the liberal views of its teachers and teaching, and it rightly claims to be the first European university to open its doors freely to women.

Although each *canton* is entirely free to organise its university as it pleases, they all show wide agreement in fundamentals of organisation and closely follow traditional European patterns. Academically, each university enjoys the greatest freedom, individual faculties being responsible for drawing up their own regulations, particularly those dealing with appointments and examinations, to which the *cantonal* authorities (on which the university is ultimately both financially and administratively dependent) give a purely formal approval. Students enrol for whatever lectures they choose and attend them at their own discretion. True, the length of study required to obtain the first degree (the *licence*) varies from university to university, as from subject to subject, but in general a minimum of six full semesters of attendance is required before a student may present himself to sit his examination. The postgraduate doctorate degree (as elsewhere in Europe) demands a minimum of a further eight semesters' attendance to be followed by the publication and defence of a thesis which embodies the findings of a piece of original research.

6

Great Britain

In the United Kingdom as a whole there are today a total of forty-five universities headed by Oxford and Cambridge which are essentially collegiate institutions with their roots deep in the corporate life of the Middle Ages and in consequence brooking of no outside interference in the administration of their affairs at any level. These are in a sense paralleled by the four ancient Scottish universities of St. Andrews, Glasgow, Aberdeen and Edinburgh, all founded in the fifteenth and sixteenth centuries but with most of their traditions more akin to those of the Continental universities and in particular housing very few of their students on a collegiate or halls of residence basis. Until the beginning of the nineteenth century these institutions, together with Trinity College, Dublin (1591), were able to cope adequately with all the demands placed upon them; but then, once the University of London had been constituted by charter in 1836 to act until the end of the century largely as an examining and degree-awarding body, so taking under its wing a number of important and separate schools of higher education finally to weld them together into one large constituent body, so did the way lie open for further expansion outside the Greater London area.

In this way the so-called "civic" universities came into existence, originally intended to serve local needs but quickly developing into national institutions to draw their students from all over the country as well as from abroad. The largest of these is still Manchester (1880), and there then followed in rapid succession Birmingham (1900), Liverpool and Leeds (1903), Sheffield (1905) and Bristol (1909). The University of Durham was founded as early as 1832 primarily as a centre in the north for the training of Church of England clergy. Armstrong College in Newcastle upon Tyne (1852) soon became associated, and in 1963 became a university in its own right. University provision for Wales came first in 1872 with a college in Aberystwyth. Other colleges followed at Cardiff (1883), Bangor (1884), and the University of Wales was finally formed out of a federation of the three colleges in 1893, Swansea being added in the period between the wars.

Meanwhile, university colleges had been created in other key civic centres and they, whilst they hoped one day to become full universities, were tied down to preparing their students for the award of various external degrees on offer from the University of London. Unlike the older civic university institutions they aimed at providing residential accommodation for a high proportion of their students and their example, in effect, was later to push their seniors in the same direction. The only one of these university colleges to achieve university status before World War II was Reading (1926). The urgent demand for university places immediately after that war, however, soon changed matters. Nottingham achieved university status in 1948, Southampton in 1952, Hull in 1954, Exeter in 1955 and Leicester in 1957. The University of Keele was created immediately after the war as a purely residential and experimental (as regards degree structure) institution on the initiative of the then Master of Balliol College, Oxford, and enjoyed the privilege of teaching for its own degrees under the sponsorship of three other universities until being granted its charter of complete independence in 1962.

It soon became evident, however, that despite all the expansion in university provision so far, more universities were going to be needed, and in 1958 the government of the day, on the advice of the University Grants Committee, approved the establishment of the University of Sussex (1961), The University of East Anglia (1963), the University of York (1963), the University of Lancaster (1964), the University of Essex (1964), the University of Warwick (1965), and the University of Kent at Canterbury (1965). Unlike the earlier university colleges, all these new institutions were immediately granted full degree-giving powers and were encouraged to experiment in a variety of ways (not always with happy results) in offering new degree courses, new subject combinations, and in devising new approaches to secure a more satisfactory framework for the social life of the students and closer and more informal relations between students and their teachers. It is significant that when student troubles manifested themselves in the United Kingdom these newest creations (after the London School of Economics, a constituent college of the University of London, and the North London Polytechnic) witnessed some of the most disturbing and at times incomprehensible upheavals.

Besides creating these new universities, and in effect allowing them to run before they had really learned to walk, the government also appointed by a Treasury Minute of 8 February 1961 a committee of inquiry "to review the pattern of full-time higher education in Great Britain and in the light of national needs and resources to advise Her Majesty's Government on what principles its long-term development should be based. In particular, to advise, in the light of these principles, whether there should be any change in that pattern, whether any new types of institution are desirable and whether any modifications should be made in the present arrangements for planning and co-ordinating the development of the various types of institution". The committee was chaired by Lord Robbins and duly reported in October 1963. No fewer than 178 specific recommendations were made to cover the whole of higher education (including teacher training), and these may be broadly summarised as advocating that more university courses should involve the study of more than one main subject; that there should be a greater measure of uniformity in standards and nomenclature of degrees; that the proportion of graduates proceeding to postgraduate work should be increased, that there should be opportunity for such graduates to study at a university other than the one at which they took their first degree, and that there should be an element of systematic teaching in all postgraduate courses and better arrangements for supervision generally; that the majority of new universities created should be in or near large centres of population; that provision could be made for a growth in the proportion of students taking science, and particularly technology, without reducing the proportion taking arts subjects; that more teaching be undertaken in smaller classes and that every student be assigned a personal tutor and should receive regular personal guidance; that adequate residential student accommodation be provided; that non-professorial staff should be enabled to play a full part in internal self-government.

The Robbins Report repeatedly stresses the fact that it considers the universities as suppliers of social needs and it urges the universities to be more conscious of their social function and therefore to give more attention than previously to pragmatically directed studies. In this connection it turned its attention specifically to the existing colleges of advanced technology (CAT) and recommended that they should, in general, be designated as technological universities with power to award both first and higher degrees. At the time of compiling the report there were ten such colleges which, sorted out in 1956 as technical colleges of high standing, had then been given the label of CAT and empowered to concentrate exclusively on advanced technological studies. They came to enjoy a wide measure of autonomy, received direct grants from the Ministry of Education instead of being dependent on local resources, and they awarded a Diploma in Technology which was recognised as of degree standard and enabled a successful student to proceed to postgraduate studies in a university proper should he so wish. The award of a Diploma in Technology had been controlled by a National Council for Technological Awards. Robbins now urged that this council should be replaced by a Council for National Academic Awards empowered to award both honours and pass *degrees* to students in a variety of non-university establishments following carefully approved lines of study not only in technological and science subjects but over a much broader spectrum. The new council became operative in 1964, and (as we have already seen) soon began awarding B.Ed. degrees to students in colleges of education which preferred not to be associated with their "neighbourhood" university for this purpose; it equally offers degrees at the B.A., B.Sc., and Ph.D. levels to students in institutions which prefer this association rather than continue preparing (as heretofore) for an external London degree. The Robbins recommendation that at least six further universities were still required, coupled with its recommendation on CATS, led in 1966 to the opening of the Loughborough University of Technology, the University of Aston in Birmingham, The City University (London), Brunel University (Uxbridge, Middlesex), Bath University of Technology, the University of Bradford, the University of Surrey, and in 1967 the University of Salford. Scotland responded with the opening of Strathclyde (Glasgow) in 1964, Herriot-Watt University (Edinburgh) in 1966, and the Universities of Dundee and Stirling in 1967. Northern Ireland got its new University of Ulster in Londonderry (where Magee University

College had formerly existed) in 1965.

Central to all discussion in the Robbins Report, of course, was the question of student numbers, forecasts based on an actual attendance of around 130,000 for the whole of Great Britain in 1962-3 suggesting that ten years later the numbers would have risen to some 219,000 and that probably 350,000 places would be needed in the early 1980s, this out of a grand total of about 560,000 in the whole of higher education (which was taken to include both colleges of education and colleges of further education). In the event, the Robbins estimate was already exceeded in 1971/2 when 236,000 alone were actually registered as attending university; and a government White Paper published in 1972 budgeted for a *total* of 750,000 for the early 1980s, of whom roughly half would be in the universities. Put succinctly, the present situation is that whereas in 1960 only a mere 4 per cent of the age group were in attendance at universities the figure has now risen to close on 20 per cent. Since 1972 there has been a tendency for numbers to level out as the birth rate bulge decreases, as a certain disenchantment with some university courses attracts potential students elsewhere, and as financial stringencies consequent on the present economic climate make themselves felt.[1] What, however, is particularly worrying is that too few students are still coming forward to read for degrees in pure science, and that too many of those who are accepted are not qualified adequately to cope. And there are nowadays a number of critics of the Robbins Report and subsequent developments who would argue with Lord Alexander that we have become heavily over-invested in university education and under-invested in the education and training of youngsters aged 16 to 19. "We have under-estimated the importance of those who design and sell," argued Lord Alexander in August 1976, "of those who produce the wealth, and have over-invested in academic values which, important as they are, may not be so directly relevant to the present economic needs of the nation as a whole. We need a new structure (and a new Education Act) to give effect to these priorities."

The universities of England and Wales in particular differ in many significant ways from their counterparts in Western Europe. In the first place they are much smaller institutions, more compact, more sociable and more intimate in all relationships, the University of London, large

[1] Student numbers for 1976/7 were around 280,000 — some 8 per cent short of the target set in 1972.

though it is, dividing itself up into a number of manageable constituent colleges. Secondly, all universities have in the last few decades markedly improved their provision of controlled student accommodation, experimenting constantly in providing various types of halls of residence ranging from those of the traditional Oxbridge college pattern to mixed halls and to do-it-yourself (or self-catering) establishments which include flats for young married couples and special provision for more mature postgraduate students. Thirdly (and heeding an important recommendation in the Robbins Report) they have increasingly made use of small tutorial groups and seminars to bring staff and students into closer contact both at an academic and at a personal level. They have worked through increasingly closer relationships with the students' unions to supply better recreational and sporting facilities and cultural activities in all of which teaching staff quite often participate.

Main differences, however, turn on organisation and administration. Once a university has received its charter it becomes a completely independent institution — independent of all other universities and free from any kind of governmental restraint at either a local or national level. It offers whatever degrees it wishes and devises its own courses and syllabuses, thus making it necessary for any prospective university student to inquire closely into what is on offer from university to university before finally committing himself. Similarly, each university has varying entrance requirements, though generally speaking a prospective student must have good marks in at least two subjects taken at advanced level in the General Certificate of Education. Once a candidate has gained admission to a university — and admission is obtained through a central clearing house (UCCA) situated in London — he informs his local education authority which then decides on a basis of a means test how much towards tuition fees, cost of books and maintenance a parent may be expected to pay; the LEA provides the rest, and in the case of a poor student, of course, total expenses are covered. Oxford and Cambridge in particular have their own private scholarships and the most promising of sixth-form pupils will regularly be competing by special examination for these. A certain number of schools which are well endowed also offer scholarships to outstanding sixth-form pupils to attend either at the university of their choice or at one or other of the Oxford and Cambridge colleges with which they have a "close" scholarship arrangement.

Little more than about 10 per cent of a university's income, however, is obtained from students' fees; the rest has to be made up partly from the university's own private endowments (if it has any) and mainly (at least 70 per cent) from grants from the Treasury – in other words, taxpayers' money. This very necessary financial support is filtered through to each individual university by the University Grants Committee (UGC), a body consisting of university representatives and highly responsible laymen which, until quite recently, acted solely on behalf of the universities to extract from the Treasury the amount it considered a given university needed to tide it over a quinquennial period. Now, the UGC has been made primarily responsible to the DES and misgivings are felt in certain quarters that this is a governmental (Socialist) ploy to bring universities more under state influence and control.

Outside Oxford and Cambridge, where colleges are autonomous and self-governing and together form an abstraction, the "university", the major administrative and governing bodies of a given university are the court, the council and the senate. The court comprises not only the professors, and nowadays elected representatives of non-professorial staff, graduates and undergraduates, but also persons nominated from local authorities, schools, and various other walks of life who can claim some real interest in the general running of their "own" university. Council is, in effect, the court's executive body. It is usually restricted to about thirty to fifty members, with university interests at all levels fully represented, and its main function is to administer university finances. The senate, which is normally supported by a system of faculty boards, is mainly composed of professorial heads of departments together with elected non-professorial and undergraduate members. This is the chief academic body which is called upon to ratify curriculum and syllabus decisions taken at faculty board level, to make recommendations for appointments to academic posts (including that of the university's chief administrative officer, the vice-chancellor), and to exercise general disciplinary authority over students. The office of chancellor of a university is usually titular and some important public figure is normally chosen who can represent the university's interests at the highest levels if and as occasion warrants. Some chancellors inevitably take their duties more seriously than others, and most make a point of officiating at the annual conferment of degrees.

Courses leading to a first degree – the bachelor's degree – last for three and sometimes four years and students can opt to take either a general (ordinary) degree which involves the study of a number of subjects to the same level or an honours degree in which one or two subjects are studied in much greater depth. At the "master" level there is often a bewildering choice of possibilities varying from university to university and leading to a further award either after a one year's taught course or after a minimum of two years spent on research, the results of which have to be presented in the form of an examinable thesis. The doctorate degree (Ph.D.) is awarded solely on the satisfactory completion of a piece of approved original research and takes a minimum of three years to complete. At the top comes the award of a D.Lit., D.Sc., or LL.D. which is awarded solely on proven outstanding merit supported by substantial publications. First degrees in medicine take a minimum of six years. Postgraduate students working for research degrees are supported either by the university, or by the DES, or by research councils, or by some outside business or industrial enterprise with vested interest in the kind of research contemplated.

Whilst it would be wrong to claim that there had been no significant student unrest in the late 1960s (and even afterwards), it would be equally wrong to assume that it achieved the same intensity generally or aroused the same violent passions as elsewhere. The same kind of revolutionary students (Maoist, Stalinist, anarchist, Trotskyist and so forth) achieved for a time a position of legitimacy among the general student body as they queried the very bases of a complacent bourgeois society and of a university subservient to these "effete" bourgeois attitudes. They found some support also among the younger members of the teaching staff. But their activities centred mainly on London and among the discontented undergraduates in the new-style universities which had mushroomed (sometimes remotely) in the provinces. Indeed, most disquiet among the general body of students stemmed from implementation of those recommendations in the Robbins Report which, stressing that the universities should grow more conscious of their social function, inevitably conditioned students to see themselves as a kind of separate and privileged estate who were graciously allowed university places (and a near-adequate grant) in return for the contribution they would later be called upon to make to the economic and social well-being of society as presently constituted.

The question of student grants and allowances, and their adequacy, is still provoking disquiet, and today's students are beginning to receive sympathetic (if passive) support in their claims from university administrators. The students still hold that since their calling dedicates them to the discovery and transmission of truth they cannot be tied down to perpetuate a social system in which they may no longer believe. The most important development of all, however, is that the National Union of Students (NUS), from being essentially welfare-oriented in the 1950s, has now developed into an important politicised body which, despite its many (and understandable) extravagant gestures, will need to be taken seriously in all future developments in the field of higher education.

We must finally briefly record an interesting experimental move on the part of a number of like-minded dons who increasingly have come to feel that the traditional freedoms of university life were being quietly and even insidiously eroded by government action designed to bring all universities under closer state supervision − to make them more accountable than they are at present. They felt the time had arrived to open at least one independent university. Appeals they made for the large sums of money necessary for such a venture were quite generously answered for them to make a beginning, and in February 1976 the Independent University College of Buckingham opened its doors to its first students. It was innovative in that it maintained that a first degree course need only take two years. It sought (as it had to do) to have its degrees validated by the Council for National Academic Awards. The CNAA rejected the application mainly on the grounds that a first degree course, such as envisaged, could not adequately be covered in two years. The Independent University, now inured to the displeasure its creation had aroused in governmental circles, remained unabashed. Nobody could stop it from awarding its own diplomas; and it knew that the reputation of its teaching staff (most carefully recruited) stood high in the academic world; it was confident that its diplomas would come to be accepted as being of degree standard. The opening ceremony in February 1976 was simple and dignified and marked by total lack of government representation of any kind. Accommodation provided for students can only be described as austere, but they obviously do not mind that. They chose to go to Buckingham and to pay the fees which, by 1978, were estimated to reach the £2000 per year mark. In other words, all students are well motivated, and as one of them put it to me: "We don't mind the Spartan atmosphere. We are here to work and the atmosphere is conducive to that. We are equally conscious that we can cover here in two years, by carefully planned work schedules, what other places need three or even four years to cover." Nor do they mind being snubbed by the government. And why should they? Already nine LEAs have agreed to meet the expenses of students from their areas who are accepted at Buckingham.

CHAPTER 10

Towards a Policy of Harmonisation

1

With the expansion of the EEC, the opening of a European parliament in 1979, an increasing free movement of labour, a proliferation of multi-national and international organisations, and with the possibility of the creation of a common currency and Central Bank for Western Europe, it is clear that the European experiment which began in 1950 with the announcement of the Schuman Plan is moving steadily towards its ulti-mate goal of making of Western Europe the meaningful entity it once was. Obviously, there are still many difficulties to be overcome, much prejudice to be circumvented, and many set-backs and disappointments still to manifest themselves and be dealt with. It has to be recognised that meaningful union cannot be brought about by diplomats and poli-ticians but by the expressed wishes of the peoples of Western Europe. They, the peoples, have to want integration and to understand what exactly the word means and how by integration their own individual life-styles are going to be affected. They have to develop a sense of belong-ing to the same "community"; they have to come to understand that, whilst this does not mean abandonment of self-identification as a French-man, an Englishman, or a German, it *does* mean that, for the ultimate well-being of each and every nation, self-identification as a European must in certain circumstances take precedence over being a Frenchman, an Englishman or a German. It does not mean the elimination of traditional national cultures and institutions, but it does require the building up of a new set of institutions, parallel to the old, and which will allow for a new cross-national culture to develop. "Habits, more than reason, we find to be, in everything, the governing principle of mankind", said the Scots philosopher, David Hume, in his popular *History of England* published just over 200 years ago; and he went on to point out that, as different

355

people have had different pasts, so do those differences both determine what they are and limit what they may become.

Thus, for a policy of integration for Western Europe to be successful it must take careful note of national aspirations and national differences, and it must also seek via the educative process to free men's mind from inhibitions generated by unintelligent and uncritical adherence to well-worn (even well-proven) behaviour patterns. Fortunately, and as should have become increasingly apparent throughout this present study, economic and social conditions in the years following the last world war have been such as to force every country to review its educational provision and effect reforms necessary to its own well-being and survival. The new technological age has brought in its train greater social responsibilities; increasingly dependent on a greater sharing of knowledge and experience, it has exacted that the quality of life for the whole community be improved so that not only may all profit but also that each member of the community may make his own contribution commensurate with his own abilities which, through restructuring of education and the modernisation of curricula, are afforded every opportunity for development.

This massive expansion of education at all levels has helped and is helping more than anything else to change the whole outlook of the younger generation, to make it more critical (even iconoclastic), more receptive to new ideas (and more permissive), more concerned about widening its horizons and interests. Perhaps never since the days of Peter Abelard has there been such a ferment of ideas amongst student bodies, and the students are once again wandering abroad — wandering the world this time — in their desire to come to grips with problems which transcend not only national but even European aspirations. It is from amongst this student body that the future administrators of the various nations will emerge; they are already sensing their responsibilities — various forms of student protest are in a sense one manifestation of this; and fortunately present planners throughout Western Europe are providing the framework for their activities either through the creation and development of various organisations of an international kind, or through the establishment of specialist institutions, or by virtue of specific educational change. What is being sought is first a harmonisation of the total Western European community, and secondly positive involvement of that unified community with the wider world outside, and particularly with the so-called Third World whose traumas, difficulties and triumphs have inescapably become the concern of all. Indeed, the major problems of modern civilisation can only effectively be dealt with on a global scale. No nation-state can ever again be self-sufficient. The emergent African nations are already painfully discovering that for themselves. And we in Western Europe, using the EEC as a foundation on which to base all further developments, must in concert seek not only to preserve what is best in our heritage and democratic way of life but also to adapt ourselves to cope with what lies ahead.

Thus, harmonisation is a prerequisite, and the most potent way to secure that harmonisation is through educational change. In preceding chapters we have covered in as great detail as possible most of the major changes and discussed the consequences of such changes. We have again shown, indirectly perhaps, how already the several nation-states of Western Europe have recognised the necessity for a harmonious solution to problems common to all even though they have differed (of necessity) in ways of implementation. In this concluding chapter we must complete the picture by a brief review of specific and deliberately conscious efforts being made internationally towards securing harmonisation or integration of educational policies.

2

The two most important organisations within Western Europe to concern themselves specifically with approaching the ideal of unity in Western European education are the Council of Europe (mainly through its creation in 1962 of the Council for Cultural Co-operation), and the Organisation for Economic Co-operation and Development (OECD). In 1963 the Council of Europe itself organised what was to become a bi-annual conference of Western European Ministers of Education which was given as its main task that of reviewing the best ways of implementing in all member countries the latest research findings in educational techniques. As the conference became more assured in its deliberations and increasingly forward-looking in its approach so did it gain in prestige. The conference theme for 1969 was *Education for all*, and the conference was attended by official representatives from twenty countries as well as by observers from both UNESCO and the OECD. The 1973 conference, held in Switzerland, dealt with the important and highly topical theme of *The needs of the 16 to 19 age group both in full- and part-time education* and attracted similar attention. And now, since all the four large inter-governmental organisations (UNESCO, the Council of Europe, EEC and OECD) have programmes in the field of co-operation in education in Europe, they each report on their work to the Permanent Committee of European Ministers of Education whose senior officials (besides preparing the conferences) keep in close contact with these other bodies, evaluate work already done, and interest themselves particularly in the fields of further and higher education with a view to ensuring mobility and liberal exchange of manpower.

The Council for Cultural Co-operation (CCC) has representatives from all member governments of the Council of Europe and is managed by three permanent committees, one dealing with higher education and research, one with general and technical education, and one for out-of-school education and cultural development. Its aim is "to help create conditions in which the right educational opportunities are available to young Europeans whatever their background or level of academic accomplishment, and to facilitate their adjustment to changing political and social conditions". Its particular responsibility is to increase the dissemination of new ideas and techniques, and to this end it pays attention to all influences bearing on the acquisition of knowledge, sponsors research, encourages the free movement of academic personnel, grants scholarships for students to visit other countries, runs summer institutes and programmes — and, most important of all, publishes and distributes reports compiled for it by appropriate experts. Since 1963 it has been publishing, in English and French, a series of works under the general title of *Education in Europe*, and has since started supplementing these works of general interest by a series of companion volumes of a more specialised nature. It also publishes a detailed guide to the school systems of Europe and keeps this up to date by the frequent issue of revised editions.

The OECD is a consultative and co-ordinating organisation and, as its name implies, is primarily concerned with matters of education in relation to economic development. It encourages member countries to study educational policy and planning and it gives financial support to approved research programmes. In 1961 it sponsored an important conference held in Washington, D.C., on economic growth and investment in education, and the second of the five volumes of reports finally issued dealt specifically with *Targets for Education in Europe in 1970*. It was urged that there should be an immediate generalisation of secondary education to secure the entrance of more young people to the upper levels of secondary education and so provide more highly qualified manpower for the job market. The structure of the school system was discussed, and the rival merits of comprehensive or multilateral approaches were weighed one against the other. Particular attention was paid to possible ways of increasing the educational chances of all young people of ability, irrespective of their origins, and, in practical furtherance of this ideal, conference delegates sought to persuade those involved with European education to extend the time devoted to general education to at least nine years so that specialisation should not begin earlier than the age of 15 or 16. Planning to secure all these objectives was finally urged, and the report carefully discussed types of planning for educational development and economic growth actually possible in the various countries.

A further important piece of educational planning in which the OECD became the sponsor was the Mediterranean Regional Project of 1960 which sought to bring together the poor countries of Europe (Greece, Italy, Portugal, Spain, Turkey and Yugoslavia) who were desperately seeking to relate education to economic growth and social advancement. It is to be noted that this project is the first to seek co-operation between Western and Eastern Europe, and that much more has been accomplished through the agency of the OECD than could possibly have been done at a strictly political level. The countries work through national planning teams in collaboration with OECD and base their work on the assumption that it is possible broadly to ascertain the investment in education required to achieve specified economic objectives. A target date was fixed for 1975, but it is still too early to know what impact MRP has had, or how successful it has been.

3

Languages, of course, have a most important part to play in any programme of harmonisation — and lack of ability to speak other than the mother tongue can create all kinds of problems and difficulties at all levels whenever supra-national decisions have to be taken. In the fields of industry and commerce alone, for example, there are three immediate and urgent needs: firstly, those of immigrant workers to acquire the language of their new country of residence, and whose children will normally be taught and use this language as their first language; secondly, the need for a high degree of competence in one or more foreign languages by both administrators and secretaries; thirdly, the need to be able to converse freely on general everyday topics, to be able to understand what is said between foreigners at conferences, and to be able to mix socially with foreign businessmen and their wives. If the third need is considered to be possibly the most important, the needs of immigrant workers are certainly the most acute and vexatious since the whole problem of an immigrant group retaining its cultural identity, peculiar customs and traditions, and yet being fully integrated, is far from being solved any- where — and it is at its most difficult with peoples from the Far East whose religious and moral outlook can be so widely at variance with that of the so-called Christian West.

It is not therefore surprising that the Western European Ministers of Education were soon deliberating as to how best give increased support for modern language teaching, and their deliberations were followed up by the publication by the CCC in 1967 of an important document, *Modern Languages and the World of Today*. Besides giving a comprehensive survey of present trends and possibilities, the document also made a number of important recommendations for implementation at all levels of language teaching. It argued that more research was needed into the vocabulary and structures of European languages, into factors affecting language learning and teaching for all ages and categories of learners, into techniques of testing and evaluating learning, and into the development of the most suitable materials and methods for language teaching.

In institutes of higher education and other forms of post-secondary schooling, it recommended the modernisation of courses to match the needs in the professional life of many categories of Europeans, that greater attention should be paid to the *contemporary* period (language, cultural background and civilisation, literature), and suggested that the creation of *Inter-Faculty Language Centres* could make possible inter- disciplinary contacts which are most urgently required. Regular visits to foreign countries were considered to be essential for all modern linguists at all stages of their development, and particularly for teachers in function to enable them to keep abreast of modern developments. Teachers in training should in addition have residence abroad compulsorily built into their training programmes; service as *assistants* in foreign schools for periods of six to twelve months should be widely extended; interchanges of students in training colleges, such as already in operation following discussions held at Sèvres in 1963, should be more fully developed. The publication finally urged that the teaching of one widely spoken foreign language should be begun at the earliest possible moment — certainly no later than about the age of 10 — and that greater opportunities should be afforded for a second foreign language to be introduced for all in the secondary school programmes generally.

In 1969 the Council of Western European Ministers of Education enthusiastically adopted an *Intensified Programme of Modern Language Teaching for Europe* which had been prepared for it by the CCC — a programme so vast (and based on the earlier report) that a number of years still will be required to complete it. It is, however, possible to gain some idea of the progress made first of all from W. D. Halls's *Foreign Languages and Education in Western Europe* (London, 1970) and secondly from *Les Langues Vivantes à l'École* (CCC, 1973). Among countries which are near to the proposed target of having a widely spoken foreign language taught to all from about the age of 10 are Denmark, France, West Germany, Italy and the Netherlands. England and Wales have still a long way to go, and Great Britain, indeed, is the only member of the CCC which does not yet make the learning of at least one foreign language compulsory for all pupils at the secondary level. It is again the only country which allows advanced students in other disciplines to "drop" the study of a foreign language at the age of 16. Sweden managed to lower the starting age for learning English to 10 years in 1962, to 9 years in 1972, and is already giving consideration to an even earlier start. Other Scandinavian countries are generally following the same trend, and they are all most obviously aided by the reorganisation of their respective school systems. Even earlier starts are being made in France where by 1971 over 180 *écoles maternelles* were learning a second language (mainly English), and in West Germany where teaching of a similar kind (largely confined to French) is provided in around one hundred kindergartens. What is also clearly emerging is that English is bidding fair to become the most popular of languages to be taught and thus could easily emerge as the *lingua franca* of Western Europe. As regards second languages, however, many countries are tending towards greater diversification than in the past. Within the last decade France has added to its secondary curriculum Arabic and Modern Hebrew *as well as Barque and Breton*; Western Germany has likewise added Arabic, Modern Hebrew, Modern Greek and Hungarian; Switzerland and Italy have introduced Russian for the first time; Norway has introduced Italian and is giving both Spanish and Russian more attention than previously.

Though there is no room for complacency, and though much still remains to be accomplished, the picture is none the less an encouraging one for the year 2000 and onwards. Nor are adults whose formal education ended anything from ten to thirty years ago being neglected. Increasing facilities are being provided for them to learn efficiently a language or languages of their choice and to travel abroad, not exactly as tourists but rather with some definite objective in view. To this end, and also to bring in those whose past educational achievement has (for various reasons) been minimal — the mass of the people in fact — an ingenious arrangement of town-twinning has been encouraged. Thus, the small fishing port and holiday resort of Deal, in Kent (England), is nowadays "twinned" with Vlissigen in Holland and Saint-Omer in France. Each town develops close links with its "twin". There are mayoral visits and civic receptions. There are sporting events, dances, and band concerts and parades, each town in turn taking upon itself the task of entertaining visitors from its "twin", receiving them into their private homes as members of the family and thus cementing strong bonds of sympathy and understanding.

4

Naturally, the teaching of other subjects than modern languages has come in for equally close scrutiny and the CCC began to give an important lead to this process by launching in 1968 a series of *European Curriculum Studies*. The first of these studies was perhaps significantly devoted to mathematics, for by now the so-called "new" mathematics was firmly taking hold throughout Western Europe and a considerable number of Europeans were becoming critical of the kind of curricular homogeneity the CCC sponsored: they feared that such homogeneity could only lead to an inevitable lowering of academic standards. By first of all dealing with mathematics teaching along new approved lines, the CCC sought to dispel these fears and show that, on the contrary, even if mathematics were being now taught uniformly to arrive at "a new conception of the unity of the subject", they were entailing a great deal of syllabus revision and so actually freeing individual countries to develop their own immediate interests. The year 1968 also saw the completion of a survey of university teaching of physics and the publication of *The Teaching of Physics at University Level* to match other and earlier CCC studies such as *Engineering Education* (1964), *The Teaching of Chemistry at University Level* (1966), and *How to Qualify as a 'Biologist' in the Universities of Europe* (1967).

The Ministers of Education have also shown concern for the "Europeanising" of textbooks (and teacher attitudes) particularly for the teaching of geography, history and civics, but also to ensure that the presentation of literature should be altered to emphasise "European styles" in writing. They have remarked that "in view of the growing economic, politcal and social interdependence of the European family of nations and of the tragic results of national isolationism in the recent past, it is essential that future generations should be helped to see their country as part of a civilisation which has long been a cultural whole and which is now striving to achieve greater unity as a society". In 1966 the *Centre International d'Études Pédagogiques de Sèvres* held a conference devoted to the teaching of literature in the higher forms of European secondary schools and stressed that there was equally a European style in painting and in music which deserved to be explored.

Geography textbooks have been found to be chiefly at fault in patterning by national rather than geographical regional boundaries and in a failure to reveal the common problems, opportunities and resources of the EEC. The EEC appealed to the College of Europe at Bruges for help, and the result was the publication of IBF Kormoss's *The European Community in Maps* of which more than a quarter million sets had been sold to European schools by 1967. The CCC complemented Kormoss's work in 1968 by publishing E. C. Marchant's *Geography Teaching and the Revision of Geography Textbooks and Atlases* which, after reviewing the kind of maps needed for the most effective study of *European* geography, proceeded to point out how in too many cases commonly used textbooks and atlases were taking a narrowly national view of resources and the uses to be made of them. A major breakthrough towards the revision of history textbooks came in 1960 with the CCC-sponsored publication of Bruley and Dance's *A History of Europe* which most effectively demonstrated how the idea of Europe can be made central in any history text without either belittling any one nation (and so undermining patriotism) or indeed denigrating the rest of the world. The teaching of civics became the concern of the CCC in 1963 when it both issued its own *Civics and European Education at the Primary and Secondary Level* and a work commissioned by them from Denis de Rougemont entitled *Civics and European Education in Primary and Secondary Instruction*.[1] It is urged that today civics is an essential part of education for all, and that in the teaching of civics it is the imperative duty of secondary schools to implant an understanding of European facts and problems and to do everything within their power to ensure that all disciplines concerned – history, geography, literature and modern languages – contribute to the creation of a European consciousness. Every schoolchild should be made aware of being a member of a larger unit than his own country and of the duties and responsibilities of necessity devolving from this.

The call for revision of history and geography textbooks had, however, begun long before this, mainly on the initiative of teachers themselves, and in Germany Georg Eckert resumed in 1949 an international textbook review which had been interrupted with Hitler's rise to power. In 1951 an Anglo-German history teachers' conference was held in Brunswick and ended with the creation of an Institute for International Textbook Revision. Two years later the Ministry of Culture for Lower Saxony took over responsibility for the Institute which has since developed into a national centre for all attempts at textbook revision, particularly history books, in West Germany. This initiative was followed up twelve years later by the CCC when in 1965 it adopted a resolution calling for the creation of national information and documentation centres in all countries for the improvement of history and geography textbooks. It also expressed the hope that these centres be co-ordinated and argued that the

---

[1] Denis de Rougemont was a member of a university group which even before the end of World War I favoured European integration of a federalist kind. He published from his native Switzerland in 1948 a further pioneering work, *Europe at Stake*. He later established in Geneva a *Service d'Information de la Campagne d'Education Civique Européenne*.

Institute of Brunswick, "which has had long experience and is unanimously appreciated, is particularly well placed to act as the co-ordinating body". The role of each national institute was carefully defined to make it responsible for: (a) the propagation of knowledge of its country through the dissemination of brochures, carefully selected anthologies, or other material illustrative of national life and history; (b) dissemination in its country of information on all other countries; (c) propagation of teaching materials and aids of all kinds; (d) facilitating the organisation of "refresher courses" for teachers of history and geography; (e) supplying, on request, opinions on the accuracy of information on a given country to be found in textbooks. It will obviously still take a long time for such an international body to be fully operative, but already a number of national centres have been opened and are doing valuable work.

To the teachers, then, goes the credit for taking the initiative in this matter, and an enthusiastic and dedicated band of teachers decided in 1956 that it was high time a European Association of Teachers (EAT) was created. General aims and objectives were hammered out at a first meeting in Paris and further refined at a second meeting called in Luxemburg in 1961 which was attended by national sections from Austria, Belgium, France, Italy, Luxemburg, Holland, West Germany and Switzerland; and immediately after the Luxemburg meeting further national sections were formed in Eire, Greece and the United Kingdom. Each section produces its own national journal, and the English journal (*The European Teacher*) summarises the aims of EAT as being for European unity, for international educational advance, and for teacher co-operation in subject and curriculum reform. EAT more specifically spells out its basic aims as being those of creating among teachers an awareness of European problems and disseminating information which has a bearing on the realisation of European federation; of working by all available means towards a deeper understanding of those essential qualities which are characteristic of European civilisation and ensuring their preservation; of developing similar understanding among pupils and in all other fields where the teacher may be expected to exert an influence; of supporting all activity directed towards this end and collaborating with other organisations which have similar international objectives.

5

If we now turn to various institutions which have arisen in furtherance of the ideal of European integration, pride of place must go to the *Collège d'Europe* which first opened its doors in Bruges in 1949 under the direc-tion of a leading Europeanist, Henri Brugmans. Like the Council of Europe, it is a birth-child of the conference called at The Hague in May 1948 to discuss the possibilities of some sort of unification of Western Europe, and the two personalities behind the idea were the distinguished Spanish philosopher, Salvador de Madariaga, and Denis de Rougemont. The latter eventually opted to open his own *Centre Européenne de la Culture* in Switzerland in 1950 which, though remaining independent of the *Collège d'Europe*, has constantly worked with it in support of the ideal of Euro-peanisation. The former, who had occupied the chair of Spanish studies at Oxford, was a great admirer of the English collegiate system and wished the *Collège* to be organised on similar lines. He won the day; and when a Belgian priest, Antoine Verleye, who was a member of the Belgian delega-tion to the Congress of Europe at The Hague, proposed Bruges as the ideal site and secured the backing of his own government and of the Communal Council of Bruges, the other governments of Western Europe agreed to provide the necessary funds and credits.

Put briefly, the aim of the *Collège* has always been "former des Euro-peens", and it offers one-year postgraduate courses leading to the award of a diploma to students drawn from all over Europe (excluding the USSR which to date has put forward no candidates) and the USA. Students are housed on a collegiate basis in a former eighteenth-century hotel which is tucked away in a courtyard in the centre of Bruges and which has the added distinction of having on previous occasions lodged Napoleon and the American poet, Longfellow. Residence "in college" was until quite recently compulsory and numbers were restricted to a maximum of seventy. Administrative personnel and classrooms are located in the former art museum devoted to the work of Brangwyn. There are few permanent teaching staff, the *Collège* relying mainly on visiting lecturers from uni-versities and research institutes all over Europe. Instruction is given in French and English and begins with a compulsory introductory course dealing with the concept of Europe as an entity, contemporary European history, the development of the idea of European unity and European organisations. A compulsory textbook on this course is the classic work of the rector (Henri Brugmans), *L'Idée Européenne, 1918-1965*.

Beyond this introduction to European studies, the work of the *College* is carried on in three specialist areas — economic, legal and political. The economics section deals with specific problems of economic integration and the effects of integration on international trade and economic growth, and each year special problems of integration become the subject of special studies. The legal section has courses on the law of the European Communities, on the relationship between Community law and national law, on the jurisprudence of the Court of Justice, on the legal personality of the European Communities in international law, and on the external relations of the Community. Particular emphasis is also given to problems of competition in the Common Market and the European Coal and Steel Community. The political section covers the present state and future possibilities of European political integration, problems of Atlantic co-operation, the attitudes of major political parties towards European integration, the role of pressure groups at the European level, and particular questions concerning the European organisations. There are also complementary courses in political sociology and political theory, and a special course on nationalism.

At the end of the year students are awarded either a Certificate of Advanced European Studies or (if they have submitted a thesis) a diploma. But that is not all. There is already a flourishing *Association des Anciens Étudiants*, many of whom already hold responsible posts in international organisations, and any competent student who seeks to avail himself of the help of the *Association* will find a suitable posting. Many slip into niches in their own national diplomatic services and in international organisations. Others continue with research and teaching. Still others are attracted into journalism, publishing, and television and radio broadcasting. The *Collège* is undoubtedly a breeding ground for future Eurocrats and its reputation carries weight particularly in Belgium, Holland and West Germany.

Down to 1972, however, it had remained firmly in the control of its first rector, Brugmans, who, though he gave it an unchallenged position as the one place where recent graduates could obtain a sound general grounding in the culture and institutions of contemporary Europe, remained perhaps too inflexible and too committed to basic aims and principles to allow necessary change easily to take place. His last year in office was unfortunately marred by the graduating students' refusal to attend the ceremony for the presentation of their certificates and diplomas as a protest against *his* refusal to call a meeting of the staff and student body to discuss a carefully drafted statement of student complaints. The students argued that, whilst it was commonly agreed that the shared experience of a small residential international college was most valuable, this could be greatly enhanced by a reform of the programme of studies. They had a low opinion of some members of the teaching staff which they thought might profitably be recruited on five-year renewable contracts. They maintained that there was too much teaching and that many of the courses were at too low a level, the college being neither specialised enough for the specialists nor yet able effectively to develop interdisciplinary approaches. They considered that too much importance was attached to bringing in "star" speakers, often elderly father-figures who would prattle on about their personal experiences and old friends rather than give an outline of European events on an analytical and historical basis. Big names, whilst they might be needed to bolster the prestige of the college, were often incapable of getting down to study in depth of current and future issues such as the development of European representative political institutions.

With the appointment of a new rector for the autumn of 1972 reform became not only possible but necessary. As early as 1961, EEC heads of state at a meeting in The Hague had decreed that the time was ripe for the founding of a University of Europe to be sited most probably in Florence. For almost ten years nothing had been done but talk about the project, but now the European Parliament began pressing for a common educational policy, the drafting of common curricula and syllabuses so that the (then) six countries of the EEC could recognise each other's degrees and diplomas, the creation of European chairs in various university centres — and the founding of a University of Europe, first in Florence and afterwards in Luxemburg. Plans for the proposed university to be situated in Florence were quickly drawn up and it is now just beginning to be operative. Obviously, Florence will soon be fulfilling many of the functions monopolised until now by the *Collège d'Europe*, and on a larger scale. Potential students will undoubtedly be attracted to Florence, and ultimately the centre of influence could shift to the larger institution.

Thus, though it was quite rightly held that the *Collège d'Europe*, if only because of its long-established reputation, its excellent library, and its many friends in high places, was in no real danger, it was equally thought that it must prepare itself to meet the challenge. There is still a strong feeling that the character of the *Collège d'Europe* must be maintained at all costs, though everyone knows that life will never be the same again in Bruges once Florence is fully established. A limited amount of expansion was agreed on in 1973. A second "college" has with some reluctance been acquired (though a common dining room remains) and the intake is rising to 100 with the later possibility of further expansion to 400 which would have the advantage of permitting the recruitment of a larger body of permanent staff. There has been a reappraisal of the diploma course in the light of what will be offered at Florence. A more fully integrated course will be on offer, and there will be the possibility of a second research year for the more academically inclined leading to a higher qualification. And the *Collège d'Europe* finally looks to fulfilling a wider "service" role which would include special short courses for EEC personnel.

6

What have come to be called the "European Schools" have already played an important part in the policy of harmonisation and will continue to do so as their sphere of influence extends and since they cater for probably the most important of all age groups (4 to 18 or 19) — generations of youngsters who must be relied upon as the year 2000 approaches to provide the necessary guidance and impetus to make an even more practical reality of the idea of Western European union. There are at present seven such schools originally carefully sited to meet the needs of parents working in connection with one or other of the several EEC concerns. The mother-school is at Luxemburg which is the seat of the High Authority of the European Steel and Coal Community; Brussels has two schools since it houses the headquarters of the EEC; a school at Varese-Ispra (Northern Italy) was opened for children of technicians, officials and research workers of Euratom; there is a further school in Belgium at Mol, near the Dutch frontier, which is the seat of the Belgian Nuclear Research Atomic Centre; the Dutch have their school at Bergen which is the seat of the Dutch Euratom Centre, and the Germans similarly have theirs in Karlsruhe. Though originally intended for children of EEC employees only, the schools are now open under certain conditions to all children without distinction of language, race, religion or social class whenever spare places can be made available. The schools are free for children of EEC employees. Non-entitled parents pay fees, but these are very low and range from about £10 per annum in the nursery sections to roughly £40 per annum at secondary levels. All are day schools, and all are co-educational.

The very first school was officially opened in Luxemburg in 1957 on parental initiative. Prior to this a parents' association consisting of fathers and mothers *from six different nationalities* fought for and obtained a kindergarten for children between the ages of 4 and 6 which was opened at Easter, 1953. The following October a five-year primary school was added, and encouraged by their success so far the parents now asked the High Authority to extend the experiment to the secondary school level. The High Authority, in full sympathy, put their case to the education departments of the member governments, each being asked to contribute something of its own culture and to supply a number of its own teachers. The governments agreed, and in October 1954 the first two classes of the secondary school started. Two more followed in 1955, the school then growing at the rate of one class each year so that by 1958 the full total of seven was reached. From modest beginnings with 140 pupils only in 1954, school numbers rose to 950 eight years later with 200 kindergarten pupils, 200 in the primary school, and 550 in the secondary school, and by this time (so successful had the experiment proved) six other schools had been opened elsewhere in the EEC. Today, the seven schools together are educating more than 10,000 young Europeans between the ages of 4 and 19; the teaching staff are drawn from all of the nine countries of the EEC; and the school at Mol has recently appointed an English headmaster.

It should be stressed that the European schools are not only international schools, but also have legal and educational features which make them something quite new in the history of scholastic institutions. They are controlled by a single Board of Governors (*Conseil Supérieur*) which is assisted on educational matters by two Boards of Inspectors (primary and secondary), and on administrative and financial matters by an Administrative and Finance Committee. Each school has its own administrative board which includes representatives of the teaching staff and of the Parents' Association. The curriculum is planned centrally and has not unnaturally a specifically European character since the syllabuses were originally devised to represent a kind of synthesis of those in force amongst the original six members of the EEC. But the unique feature of the schools is due firstly to the fact that they are today the only examples of "inter-state" schools in the sense that they are recognised, controlled and administered on an inter-state basis, and secondly to the schools' teaching approach which has attracted the attention of educationalists the world over.

Each school has a nursery department catering for children between the ages of 4 and 6, a primary department for pupils from age 6 to 11, and a secondary department from 11 to 18-plus. At the end of their secondary studies, pupils take the schools' own leaving examination, the *European Baccalauréat*, which enjoys equal status with national school-leaving examinations in member states and thus enables successful candidates as of right to enter any university of their choice in any of the member states. This new-type *baccalauréat* is now also accepted by some of the most important universities in the USA, and also in Austria and Switzerland. Teachers for the schools are recruited and paid their *national* salaries by the member states, these salaries being made up, as necessary, by the schools to a common agreed level. Numbers required from each state are determined by the Board of Governors, but the teachers themselves are employed by the schools, appointments normally being for a probationary year to be followed by a four-year renewable contract.

There are now six official languages – English, Danish, Dutch, German, French and Italian – in use in the EEC, and as a pupil enters the primary school at the age of six he has to choose his "mother tongue" from among these. It is in this mother tongue that he will receive his basic education: at the primary level the three Rs, and at the secondary level grammar, literature, Latin, Greek, philosophy and mathematics. In addition, from the primary stage onwards, the children must learn a second language (French or German) by the use of methods best suited to their age. This second language is intended to serve as the *langue véhiculaire* – the working language which, at the primary level will be used in the "European lessons" (six periods per week) during which the pupils are not grouped by nationalities but by age or by sex to be taught singing, drawing, manual work and gymnastics. At the secondary level the working language is used for the teaching of history, geography, biology, physics, chemistry and the history of art. Thus, a considerable part of the syllabus is taught to groups of pupils of different nationalities and languages — in history teaching, for example, no English pupil has his history lessons with an English teacher in English, but rather, say, with Dutch and Italian children in French and with a French teacher.

From the secondary year of secondary school onwards all pupils study Latin for five hours a week at the lower secondary level, and for four, five or six hours per week at the upper secondary levels according to the specialist stream chosen. It is in the fourth year in the secondary school that specialisation begins and pupils must now opt for one of four streams. These are Classics (with Greek being taught five hours per week throughout the rest of the course); Latin, mathematics and science; modern languages, mathematics and science; modern languages and economics. It should be noted that the first three years of the secondary school course form an intermediate or diagnostic stage during which a pupil's aptitude for later specialisation can be assessed; that even those who are weak in mathematics and science have as good a chance as anyone of obtaining the *European Baccalauréat*; that it is quite possible for a pupil, by the time he leaves school, to be fluent in four or even five languages — many children in the primary school becoming already proficient in two or three. This is due in part to the fact that when a child opts for his "mother tongue" as he starts primary school that mother tongue need not be his native language.

It cannot be denied that the "European Schools" and the way in which they came into existence, now work and are developing, afford a striking example of committed movement towards the attainment of that unified community which the EEC is striving to make possible. In creating the system and encouraging its development, the EEC has realised that it is necessary to build a Europe of the hearts and minds of men alongside a Europe of treaties; that since men are to a great extent what their schooling has made of them, then teaching along correct lines must have a crucial part to play in the total enterprise. As the words inscribed on the parchment that is enclosed in the foundation stones of each school eloquently puts it: "Each pupil will be able, whilst following with teachers from his own country the study of the mother tongue and his national literature and history, to acquire from infancy the use of other languages and benefit from the joint contribution of the different cultures which together make up European civilisation. Sharing in the same games, grouped in common classes, boys and girls of various languages and nationalities will learn to know and value each other and to live together. Being brought up in contact with each other and freed from an early age from the prejudices which divide, initiated into the beauties and values of the various cultures, they will as they grow up become conscious of their solidarity. While retaining love for and pride in their own country, they will become in spirit Europeans well prepared to complete and consolidate the work undertaken by their fathers to establish a prosperous and united Europe."

7

There are, of course, critics of the European Schools who would claim that as a model for the future they have not yet begun to live fully up to expectations; that they are not the centres for a cross-cultural, multilingual experiment that they might have been in that they are isolated, élitist, and too rigid and formalised (along traditional European patterns) in curricula and teaching approaches; that there are still no special schools for the children of migrant workers who must now number at least 1½ million, all of school age, and who are condemned to lead bleak, second-rate lives having to make do with whatever state educational provision is available for all in the areas in which they are forced to live. There are also parents working outside their own native countries and within the EEC who prefer not to send their children to the European schools for a variety of reasons but to have them educated along less rigid Continental lines, following an education which will allow them easily to slot back into their studies. And there is finally an English answer to the European schools.

In September 1973 a converted secondary modern school in Ingatestone, Essex, was opened as a secondary day school in a new form to become, as its headmaster puts it, "not a pale imitation of the European Schools, but a real centre for European studies". The scheme has still fully to develop but the Chief Education Officer for Essex calls it an Anglo European school which should not only concentrate strongly on modern languages, but would teach other subjects, particularly history, geography and social and environmental studies (as in the European schools) from the wider viewpoint. Unlike the European Schools, however, which are geared towards a highly academic education, Ingatestone is designed to cater for a wide ability range. Up to the end of the third year there is French for all pupils and German for some. From then onwards there is a common-core curriculum of English, mathematics, French and European studies which account for about half of a pupil's time. The other half is taken up by options to include scientific and technical subjects, a classical language, third and fourth modern languages, and European commercial and business studies — all of which can be taken in various combinations to allow pupils to sit for the *International Baccalauréat* or various corresponding English examinations. It is also hoped to receive exchange students from other European countries who must, via the options on offer, have facilities to continue to some extent preparing for their own country's official school-leaving certificate(s).

The school is naturally open to all children in the immediate catchment area who wish to attend and these make up about half the total capacity. Remaining places are on offer to children from outside the immediate area who choose the school because of its special bias — one or both parents being of Continental origin, family links with the Continent (to include parents whose business interests are abroad within the compass of the EEC), future career intentions of the pupils, and just simply educational interest in and sympathy with the European idea. Exchange visits are to be developed throughout the entire school course ranging from group visits of short duration to prolonged exchanges of one term either *en famille* or in boarding accommodation (though Ingatestone can not as yet provide the latter), and regular staff exchanges are expected to be developed. It is, in short, a bold and far-sighted venture on which the local authority is to be congratulated, and one which could easily lead to the establishment of further Anglo-European schools geared to cater in the main for the average pupil who will need to take just as much interest in the Europe of the future as his more academic-minded peer.

The *International Baccalauréat* (not to be confused with its European counterpart which is taken only by the European Schools) was set up in 1970 to meet the needs of pupils in the many (usually privately run) international schools now scattered throughout Western Europe and to whose existence we have earlier briefly referred. In 1969 there were at least 150 such schools with some kind of international associations and numbers are steadily rising, a fair proportion being schools for the education of American children whose parents are working in Western Europe but which attract children of other nationalities. There is also a fairly recent British School established in Brussels alongside its American counterpart and which also admits other than British children. The *International Baccalauréat* is administered through the International Baccalauréat Office (IBO) which is established in Geneva as a private foundation. It has, however, a governing council consisting of well-known educators from a number of European countries and has been supported by financial grants from West Germany, Holland and the United Kingdom. Five full years were spent in determining the form the examination should take, and when finally launched in 1970 it was put on a five-year trial period. Besides being designed to allow for easy movement of pupils between international schools and from national systems into international schools, it is firmly opposed to too narrow specialisation (as in various English "advanced level" examinations which it implicitly condemns) at too early an age, and it is equally condemnatory of the German *Abitur* or the French *baccalauréat* for putting too great a strain on candidates by examining in too many subjects at too great a depth. Examinations, it claims, should be based on a broad curriculum whilst allowing some specialisation in subjects of the pupil's choice, and it has worked on the assumption that a candidate, to be successful, must have passes in six subjects – three taken at "higher" level and three at "subsidiary" level. Mathematics, science, one foreign language, and the study of man must be taken by everybody at one or other level; candidates can choose to be examined in either French or English; and the syllabuses are re-assessed every three years by an international panel of experts.

Interest in the examination is growing everywhere and it is already being offered as an option in a number of colleges of further education in England and Wales. One of the first of the international schools to adopt the *International Baccalauréat* was the United World College of the Atlantic (situated on the Welsh coast) and which itself was the first of a chain of United World Colleges which now exist in Vancouver (Canada), Singapore, and Trieste (Italy), and with the possibility of a further one in West Germany. These colleges, which have been founded to promote *international* understanding and not in response to the needs of a mobile international community, draw their students (as their name implies) from all over the world, and they have already secured grants-in-aid from European governments and the secondment of teachers. They also differ from most other international schools in that they are entirely boarding establishments and take only boys and girls between the ages of 16 and 19 who are selected by their own respective governments as being capable of profiting from the type of education offered, in general sympathy with the ideals embodied in this education, and most likely (as they move on to some form of tertiary education and into the world outside school) to continue to work towards international understanding. A weekend spent in Atlantic College as a guest lecturer contributing to a conference on "Present Obstacles to International Understanding" — a conference arranged and entirely managed by the students — proved to be most rewarding. It was immediately obvious how well motivated were the students, how hard academically they were working, and how hard they were with equal enjoyment playing — for afternoons must be devoted to some form of outdoor activity ranging from the usual games to rock-climbing, sailing and navigating, sea and mountain rescue work, and (for those with no real athletic aptitudes) social service work of an active and meaningful kind. One was welcomed without fuss or reserve into their own living quarters and private dens to talk endlessly, to listen to "pop" or classical music, to share in the amiable "ragging" as it spontaneously arose. Individual fee-paying pupils can be admitted if and as there is a vacancy, but fees are obviously very high.

United World Colleges, particularly as their numbers increase, will take Europeans "outside" themselves in a way that the European Schools cannot attempt to do; they will make both staff and students increasingly conscious of Europe's responsibilities to the wider world communities; and they should in the process, however indirectly, help Europeans to co-operate more fully among themselves and to harmonise their various aspirations in order to identify more clearly those areas where positive action on the part of the Western European communities in concert will ultimately be of mutual benefit to all. If it is true, as Professor Trevor Roper claims, that "the history of the world for the last five centuries, in so far as it has significance, has been European history", then Europe, having shaken the non-European world out of its past, will at its own peril turn aside from the consequences.

Appendix 1

Constructs to illustrate some of the factors at work in determining patterns of education in selected representative countries.

        1. Belgium
        2. England and Wales
        3. France
        4. Germany
        5. Italy
        6. Sweden

Fig. *A1.1. Belgium*

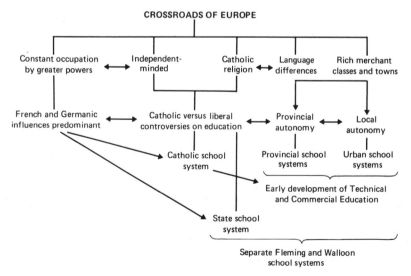

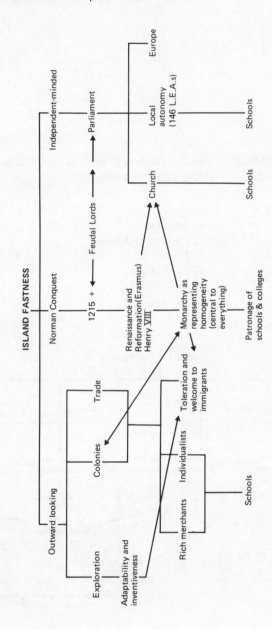

Fig. A1.2. *England and Wales*

Fig. A1.3. France

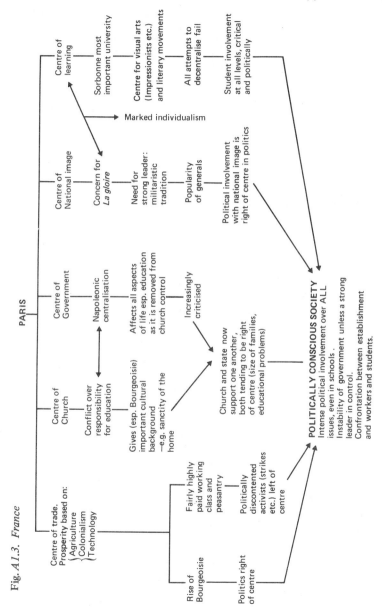

Fig. A1.4. *Germany*

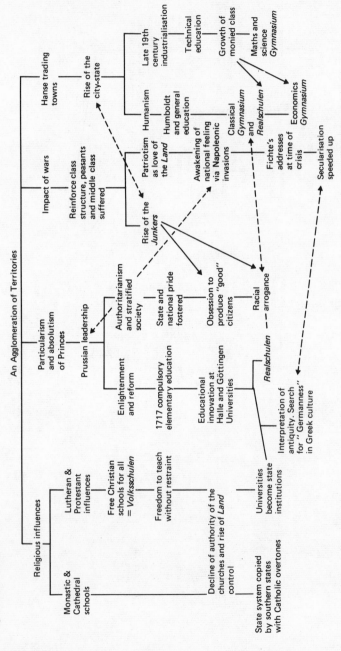

Fig. *A1.5 Italy*

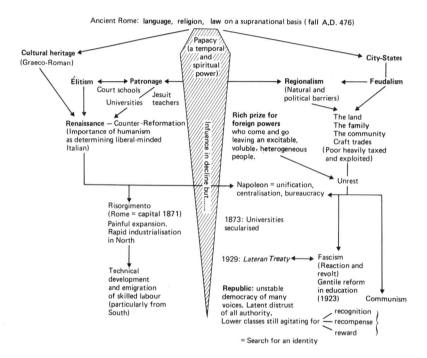

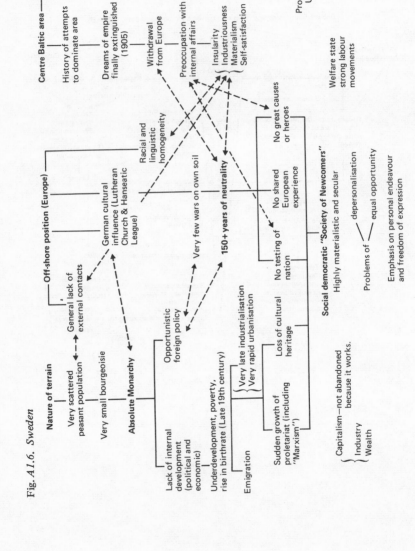

Fig. A1.6. Sweden

Appendix 2

Diagrammatic Representations of Education

Fig. *A2.1a.* *Education in Belgium*

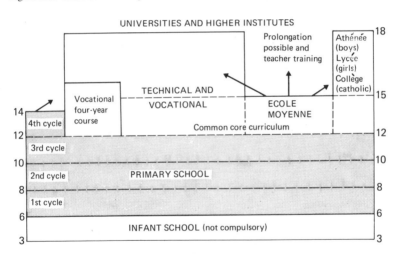

Fig. *A2.1b.*

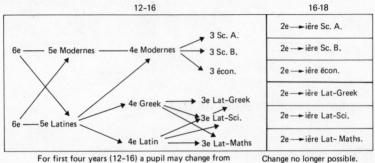

| | 12-16 | 16-18 |

For first four years (12-16) a pupil may change from section to section, as illustrated above.

Change no longer possible. Any section leads to university or technical (commercial) further education, but the university exacts from all a *maturité* examination.

Enseignement Secondaire Rénové – Athéneé Royal, Etterbeek

Fig. *A2.2. Education in Denmark*

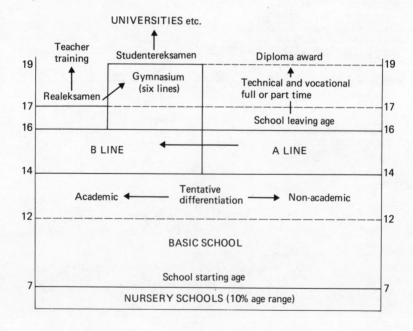

Fig. *A2.3. Education in England and Wales (present trends)*

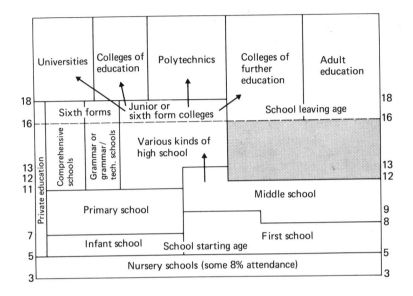

Fig. A2.4. *Education in France*

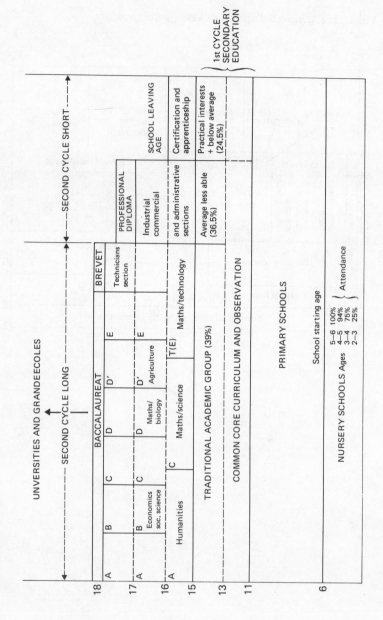

Fig. *A2.5.   Education in West Germany (until recent reforms)*

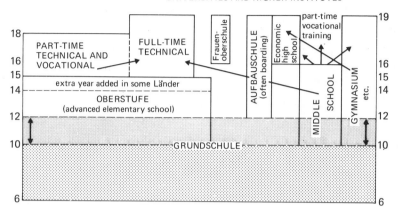

Fig. *A2.6.   Education in West Germany (as developing)*

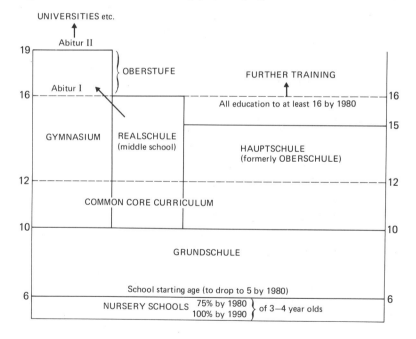

Fig. *A2.7. Education in Holland*

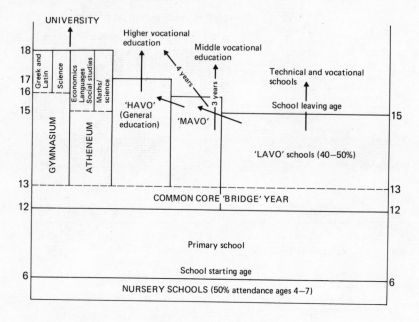

Fig. *A2.8. Education in Italy*

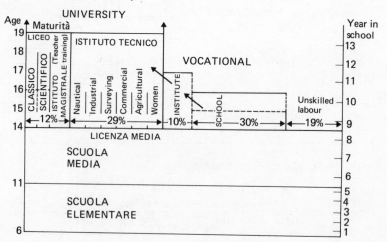

Fig. *A2.9. Education in Norway*

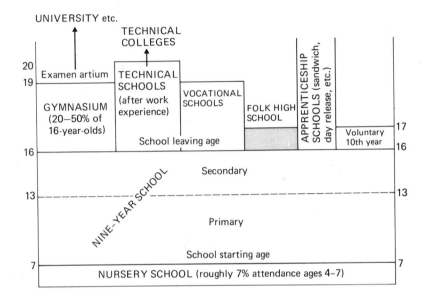

Fig. *A2.10. Education in Sweden*

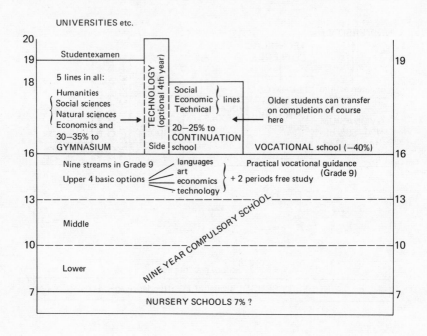

Fig. A2.11 *Education in Switzerland (VAUD)*

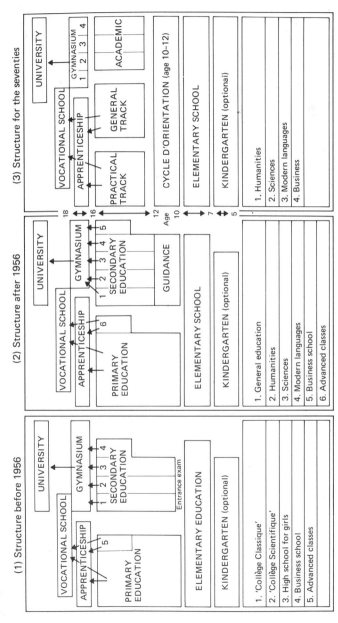

(1) Structure before 1956

(2) Structure after 1956

(3) Structure for the seventies

Selected Bibliography

A. General

Château, J., *Les Grands Pédagogues*, Paris, 1965.
Cobban, A., *The Nation State and National Self-Determination*, Fontana, London, 1969.
Compayré, G., *The History of Pedagogy*, London, 1900.
Hans, N., *Comparative Education*, London, 1958.
Hearnden, A., *Paths to University*, London, 1973.
King, E. J., *Education and Development in Western Europe*, Reading (Mass.), 1969; *The Education of Teachers*, London, 1970; *Other Schools and Ours* (4th edn.), London, 1973.
Mallinson, V., *An Introduction to the Study of Comparative Education* (4th edn.), London, 1975.
Reguzzoni, M., *La Réforme de l'Enseignement*, Paris, 1966.

B. Belgium and Luxemburg

Ludovicy, E., *L'Enseignement au Grand-Duche de Luxembourg*, Luxemburg, 1971.
Mallinson, V., *Power and Politics in Belgian Education*, London, 1963; *Belgium*, London, 1969.

C. France

Alain, *Propos sur l'Éducation*, Paris, 1948.
Capelle, J., *L'École de Demain Reste à Faire*, Paris, 1966.
Durkheim, E., *L'Évolution Pédagogique en France*, Paris, 1938–41.
Fraser, W. R., *Education and Society in Modern France*, London, 1963; *Reforms and Restraints in Modern French Education*, London, 1971.
Halls, W. D., *Society, Schools and Progress in France*, Oxford, 1965.

D. Germany

Becker, H., *German Youth, Bond or Free*, London, 1948.
Kerschensteiner, G., *The Schools and the Nation*, London, 1914; *Education for Citizenship*, London, 1915.
Spangenberg/Mende, *Schule und Hochschule in Deutschland*, Frankfurt, 1973.

393

E. Great Britain

Barnard, H. C., *A History of English Education*, London, 1961.
Baron, G., *Society, Schools and Progress in England*, Oxford, 1966.
Lester Smith, W. O., *Government of Education*, London, 1965.

F. Italy

Borghi, L., *Educazione E Autorità Nell' Italia Moderna*, Florence, 1950.
Gabelli, A., *L'Istruzione E L'Educazione in Italia*, Florence, 1950.
School of Barbiana, *Letter to a Teacher*, London, 1970.

G. Scandinavia

Dixon, W., *Education in Denmark*, London, 1959; *Society, Schools and Progress in Scandinavia*, Oxford, 1965.
Huus, H., *The Education of Children and Youth in Norway*, Pittsburgh, 1960.
Oakley, S., *The Story of Sweden*, London, 1966.
Orring, J., *School in Sweden*, Stockholm, 1967 (English Edn. 1969).
Stenholm, B., *Education in Sweden*, Swedish Institute, 1970.

Index